REVOLUTION AND REACTION

REVOLUTION AND REACTION

1848 and the Second French Republic

EDITED BY

ROGER PRICE

CROOM HELM LONDON

BARNES & NOBLE BOOKS NEW YORK
(a division of Harper & Row Publishers, Inc.)

First published 1975

© 1975 by Roger Price

Croom Helm Ltd
2-10 St John's Road, London SW 11

ISBN   0—85664—204—5

Published in the USA 1975 by
Harper & Row Publishers, Inc.
Barnes & Noble Import Division

ISBN   0—06—495720—9

Printed and bound in Great Britain
by Redwood Burn Ltd, Trowbridge and Esher

CONTENTS

PREFACE

The Second French Republic has attracted growing interest in recent years. It therefore seemed a good idea to gather together a number of articles representing a variety of different approaches to the political history of the period. The basic unifying themes of the volume are protest and its repression. The contributions provide case studies of the manner in which popular discontent is mobilised and becomes political protest, and of the operation of the machinery of government in a crisis situation. It is hoped that they will contribute something to the development of ideas about the methodology of historical studies as well as to knowledge of the 1848 Revolution and its consequences.

Of the various ways in which I might have introduced the essays which compose the bulk of this volume I decided on an interpretative essay as both personally more congenial and hopefully more useful in that it summarises previous research, provides a bibliographical guide to what I feel to be the most useful secondary literature in the field, and of greatest importance a general view of the second republic within which the findings of the more specialised essays might be accommodated.

I would like to express my appreciation of the interest in this project shown by the contributors, and by David Croom, its publisher. I owe a particular debt of gratitude to Ted Margadant for allowing me to read the manuscript of his excellent study of 'The Insurrection of 1851' which I hope will soon be published. This together with works by Maurice Agulhon and A. J. Tudesq substantially influenced the approach taken in my introductory essay. I would also like to thank Alan Hunt for his criticisms of my first draft.

Marianne Bhavsar and Sally Redgrave did most of the typing. In addition I owe a great deal to Robert and Jane Frugère, and especially to Heather, Richard and Siân Price.

INTRODUCTION

In February 1848 a revolutionary movement in Paris led to the replacement of a constitutional monarchy by a republic. In the succeeding weeks and months the major problem facing the republican government was to control the course of events as some men sought major social as well as political reforms and others resisted the pressure for change. The history of the second republic is that of the development of an alliance between governments wishing to govern, and conservative social groups desiring a restoration of the social status and authority they had previously possessed. These aims led them inevitably into conflict with the proponents of reform. The combined power and influence of the state and the traditional ruling elite proved to be adequate to meet the challenge. This is a history of revolution, of reaction, and of restoration. The interest of the period is that the political struggles occurred in a society in the early stages of economic and social modernisation. These struggles exemplify both continuity and change in the patterns of social organisation and behaviour. They illustrate the way in which human beings in developing societies are subjected to a complex of pressures both old and new and the way in which change is mediated by an effort to integrate it into established cultural and organisational forms. However successful this may be, the process necessarily involves a modification of social structure and of human behaviour. This essay seeks to examine the roots of revolution in the social and political structure of the July Monarchy, and then to follow the process by which the republic became conservative and was eventually succeeded by a second empire.

I

During the July Monarchy contemporaries used the term 'notables' to describe a ruling group which seems in fact to have been composed of aristocrats, pseudo-nobles and members of the 'grande bourgeoisie'. The reign of Louis-Philippe was also frequently described as that of the bourgeoisie, and in a certain sense it was. The 1830 revolution represented the failure of the nobility to restore itself to the place of eminence within society to which it aspired. It was followed by the withdrawal of many nobles from active political life. A new political elite appeared to have taken its place.

Economic development and growing wealth and prestige, combined

1

with the political revolution gave a greater self-confidence to the 'grande bourgeoisie'. Ennoblement was no longer necessary to round off a successful career. A new aristocracy came into existence, distinguished not only by its wealth, but as in the case of the old, by birth and the assumption of social responsibility. Its members included financiers, bankers, industrialists and merchants, landowners, the most successful members of the liberal professions, senior administrators and army officers. These were all men distinguished by wealth and the style of life which wealth permitted. They composed an oligarchy whose power depended on the combination of economic, social and political power. Membership depended upon wealth, in whatever form it was held, as increasingly those who possessed wealth sought opportunities for profit in whichever sector of the economy held promise. More than ever before bankers, landowners and industrialists joined to form a single, unified elite interested primarily in the politics of order, stability and peace. Whatever their varying ideological commitments aristocratic legitimists and bourgeois Orléanists could normally agree on these aims and particularly on the need to preserve their shared domination over the masses.[1]

Although these grand notables tended to be attracted to Paris by the concentration of power there, in most cases this was so as to more effectively represent regional economic and political interests. For one essential aspect of their life style and the search for social status was the ownership of land. The ruling elite was distinguished in consequence by dual residence — a town house in Paris, or some other city, together with a chateau and estates. Whatever their other professions, in great majority this elite was orientated, by birth, residence, economic interest, by ideology and sympathy, towards rural France.

Amongst the privileges conveyed by wealth such as freedom from material want, access to secondary and higher education, and the possibility of avoiding conscription into the army by hiring a substitute, was the right to vote. Wealth in this oligarchical system was seen as a guarantee of the political independence of the voter, and of his personal commitment to the existing social system. The electoral law of 19 April 1831, in order to secure a more accurate representation of those with a real stake in the nation had reduced the direct tax qualification for enfranchisement from 300 to 200 f. per annum. Initially the electorate had been doubled, to about 200,000 voters, rising to around 250,000 by the mid 1840s. To be eligible for election one needed subsequently to pay only 500 f. instead of 1000 f. with the consequence that some 56,000 were eligible in the 1840s. Most of the wealth upon which taxation fell was still held in the form of land. The system of assessment for taxation reinforced this tendency for both electorate and candidates to be drawn primarily from the ranks of men who owned land.[2]

2

As well as dominating the legislative, such men controlled the administrative organs of the state. Only wealth could purchase the necessary education, and permit one to establish the style of life and relations in proper society which made admittance to the upper levels of the bureaucracy possible. It was this combincation of legislative and executive power in the hands of the wealthy, which was the chief characteristic of the July Monarchy.

Another fundamental characteristic was the local source of power, usually due to ownership of land within a rural community, and to the prestige and reputation of one's family. It was because of this that many of the legitimist opponents of the regime were able to retain considerable local influence even when they had been deprived of political power. Obviously one should not attempt to directly correlate wealth with social prestige and influence, but it was a necessary prerequisite for both. The notable was someone with a name, and often a title. He possessed power as a landowner over tenants and labourers, as a dispenser of charity over the poor. His status was frequently reinforced by the possession of local administrative authority, particularly as magistrate, and also by activity related to national politics. A major role of the notable was intermediary activity, representing local and regional interests in regional and national centres of administration. This preponderance of notables corresponded to a world of rural communities and small market towns in which they were known personally, or at least by reputation; to a world in which the knowledge every individual possessed of kinship links, of clientele relationships, and of social hierarchy, permitted them to recognise the social status of other individuals.

A. J. Tudesq, to whom the preceding analysis owes a great deal, identifies the link between this oligarchical political structure and the predominantly rural character of French society, and additionally the relative weakness of central power which alone permitted a decentralised politics.

Already in economically and socially more advanced areas — in the north, northwest and Lyon regions — the social power of the traditional elites was being reduced as new groups acceded to wealth and to political ambitions. Moreover, it is always likely, where a heterogeneous social elite holds power, and where some of the groups which compose it assume, or appear to assume more power than others, that internal tensions will be created. This becomes especially likely if it comes to be believed that those who have the major share in political power are failing to exercise this in an efficient or proper manner.[3]

One clear weakness of the July Monarchy was the continued refusal of supporters of the regime overthrown in 1830 to recognise its legitimacy. Although the opposition of these advocates of yet another

3

restoration of the elder line of Bourbon was generally muted in recognition of the shared interest of all men of property in social order, its continuation nevertheless served to weaken potential support for the government of the day when political crisis occurred. If, in economically advanced regions the major problem concerning administrators was already the possibility of conflict between bourgeoisie and proletariat, in more backward regions where historical traditions survived more completely, the hostility of aristocrats and bourgeoisie, enflamed during the Revolution, survived. In Languedoc in particular ideological oppositions still competed with those based upon economic interest, and aristocrats, bourgeois and the masses shared in a complex of variously motivated conflicts.

Actual fusion between notables and grande bourgeoisie was little advanced in most departments. Even in Paris where they mixed in society, intermarriage was rare and when it occurred, normally took place between the well endowed daughters of the wealthiest bourgeoisie and impoverished nobles. When resident in their town houses in Paris or particularly in provincial centres like Orléans nobles maintained a certain exclusiveness, forming a closed society resistant to change.

In most places the basis of the social and political influence of the nobility was ownership of land and the links of association, dependence and obligation this created with tenants, sharecroppers, debtors, and labourers. Their potential social power would not everywhere be capable of realisation. In many places the traditional acceptance by the masses of noble predominance created a psychological climate of subservience based as much on interpersonal relationships as economic dominance. This was the case in much of Brittany – in Finistère, Côtes-du-Nord and Morbihan. Elsewhere the absence of a climate of confidence between nobles and peasants limited their social influence. This was the case in Seine-et-Marne, or in a zone to the east of Lyon, areas where large noble owned estates were common. There is no simple correlation between economic power and social and political influence.

In the west Legitimists were able to base themselves on relatively stable rural societies, whose structures and the mentality of whose populations changed only very slowly due to isolation. They benefited additionally from old traditions of opposition to the central power. The other main regions of Legitimist strength were in the south, where often it was an urban phenomenon in contrast to its bases in the west. In Toulouse, Aix, Nîmes, Montpellier, Montauban, Avignon and Marseille, Legitimist notables (both nobles and bourgeois) were able to appeal to a popular tradition of support for the Legitimate monarch and the Catholic Church against liberals, Protestants and the central government. At Toulouse for example Legitimist supporters included most of the landowners with town houses in the city, many of the members of the liberal professions and of the merchantile classes who

4

depended on the purchases of the first two groups, and also of the clergy whose moral authority and charity they all supported. This alliance with the clergy was particularly important, providing a link with the masses, whose low literacy rates permitted the survival of a popular culture dominated by a militant Catholicism.

Thus a wealthy aristocracy gathered mass support by means of Catholic charity. Through membership of municipal councils, local agricultural and learned societies, and social intercourse in its salons it dictated the shape of social relations for the notables in general. Even the officers of the government it despised had no choice but to avoid offending these opponents if they were not to risk social ostracism.

In rural areas of the South also — in Ariège, Tarn, Tarn-et-Garonne, the *arrondissements* of Toulouse and Villefranche in Haute-Garonne, of Lambez in Gers, or Arles in Bouches-du-Rhône the dominance of rich noble landowners seemed assured. In other regions of France — in mountainous areas of Haute-Loire, Cantal, Corrèze, Lozère, in towns like Lyon, Bordeaux, Moulins, Riom and Limoges, in town and countryside in Flanders and Picardy, influential Legitimists exerted varying degrees of influence, although not on a scale comparable with the main centres of influence in west and south. Every region with the exception of Alsace had its Legitimist notables, whose activity usually centred on a town with a royal lawcourt, where the old traditions of the *parlements* survived, or else on an ecclesiastical centre. The significance of noble political opposition really reflected their ability to attract the support of other social groups. This nobles gained not only through economic activities, and the gratitude of those to whom they dispensed aid, through the prestige conveyed by name, reputation, wealth and dignity, but also due to their habitual pose as the defenders of social order and especially of religion and morality.

The noble generally observed his religious duties down to the finest detail. He was inspired by a relatively simple and coherent ideology, negative in its essentials, denouncing the progressive moral decline of mankind, which only a return to hierarchy in society and submissiveness on the part of those to whom God had allocated an inferior place, might arrest. This truly theological outlook, a totalitarian view of social relationships, gave a certain unity to nobles based on a conception of life, of the correct organisation of society and of their own responsibilities within it. This moral outlook obviates to a large extent the problem of determining who were genuine and who pseudo-nobles. A group existed composed of men who shared a life style and opinions — who in practice conformed to the unwritten rules for good behaviour which determined social acceptability.

One consequence of their social ideology was to confirm to nobles their duty of providing leadership, both in the community and the

nation. Their chosen careers tended in consequence to be landownership or else positions as senior government officials or army officers.
The early years of the July Monarchy in particular temporarily altered
this pattern. On principle, rather than serve the usurper Louis-Philippe,
many Legitimists resigned their offices and commissions, others refused
to participate in politics rather than give implicit recognition to the new
regime. However, the longer a restoration was postponed the more difficult it became to preserve such purism. Isolation and idleness gradually
led to a return to office and politics. The evident conservatism of the
regime helped save uneasy consciences, whilst their reintegration into
public life confirmed this conservatism. It remained the case however
that many members of a very influential group lacked any sort of firm
commitment to the July Monarchy.

Although apparently victorious in 1830, the grande bourgeoisie remained prisoners of two fears, on the one hand of reaction, of the
Legitimists, and on the other of social revolution by the masses. Especially in the provinces liberals resented the survival of the aristocratic
will to dominate, still felt the need to affirm their egalitarian hostility
towards aristocratic hankerings after privilege, their faith in progress,
their anticlericalism, their somewhat shaky confidence in modern
society.[4]

In contrast with the moral conception of society presented by the
Legitimists, with its paternalistic ethos, liberals stressed individual
responsibility. An editorial in the *Journal des Débats* in 1847 expressed
their typical belief that 'the bourgeoisie is not a class, it is a position;
one acquires that position and one loses it. Work, thrift and ability
confer it; vice, dissipation and idleness mean it is lost.'[5] Those who had
succeeded in acquiring or maintaining superior status in society ascribed
their success to their superior abilities. Conversely those who had been
unable to raise themselves out of poverty were morally inadequate. This
pathological explanation of poverty was one increasingly shared by all
notables. Such an explanation of the existence of poverty obviated the
necessity to ask whether the real cause might not be in the basic structure of a society in which to a large extent private property was the
cause and a result of gross inequality at birth. If one accepted that inequality was God ordained, or resulted from unequal ability, then it
tended logically to follow that criticism of the *status quo*, and especially of the social division of property was either blasphemy or perver-
sity.

The notable assumed that he had a right to dominate other, weaker
people. He recognised as superiors on earth only those whose wealth
and reputation were greater. The ruling class was given a certain coherence by the secondary education it shared — classical in its funda-
mentals — based on Latin, law and rhetoric, preparing individuals for

6

polite conversation and public debate. One member of the elite could thus easily recognise another by his manners and the class culture they both possessed. The political system was structured to maintain such distinctions, supported by the belief that political power must belong to an elite, identified by its stake in society and its worldly success.[6]

However the voting qualification established in 1830 at 200 f. in direct taxes did not result in a very uniform electorate. At the lower level it enfranchised much of what is often described as the middle bourgeoisie of members of the liberal professions, merchants, manufacturers, officials and in the larger towns even elements of the petty-bourgeoisie — typically master artisans and shopkeepers owning their workshops, commercial stock and the houses in which they lived. The size of electorates varied. In the department of the Nord in 1837 there was one voter per 152 inhabitants, but the proportion was much higher in the towns than in rural areas — in Lille for example, there was one voter for every fifty-one inhabitants.

In 1846 of 454 deputies whose election results are known, 152 were elected with less than 200 votes, 10 with less than 100, 233 with between 200 and 400 votes. Thus 84 per cent of deputies were elected with less than 400 votes. In most of these constituencies direct influence on individual voters was thus possible; and even where elections were contested, individual relationships and influence were at least as important to a candidate as his political programme. Only in the larger, urban constituencies could a genuine political debate be expected. This situation was reinforced by another modification of the electoral system introduced in 1830 — namely to hold elections at *arrondissement* rather than departmental level. This increased the weight of local influence and personal appeals. The typical candidate was then the notable, a man of mature age and known reputation, judged by his political sympathies and also by his ability to do something for his constituents in Paris. He usually required the support of some of his peers, and their combined clienteles. Where elections were contested this was normally because of rivalry between two individuals or groups of notables, or perhaps between the prefectoral administration supporting one candidate and a local notable.[7]

It is not an easy matter to judge the political complexion of the Chamber of Deputies produced by such elections. There were no real parties, only the extremes — republicans and Legitimists — had a modicum of organisation. In 1840, Tudesq estimates that there were 15 mainly moderate republicans, 104 members of the dynastic left, 43 of the centre left, 22 of the *tiers parti*, 253 conservatives, and 22 Legitimists.[8] Save for the extremes there was little at least in the shape of principle to differentiate these groups. They had no consistent programme or voting behaviour. Many were simply playing the game of 'ins' and 'outs', favouring liberalisation of the political system only when in opposition. The groups were differentiated by personal differences, private interest, or association with an influential individual like Guizot, Thiers or Dupin. Many felt that they had a responsibility to support the ministry in office.[9]

Professionally, few deputies or peers were businessmen, but many who were landowners, members of the liberal professions, or officials developed personally profitable links with financiers. Socially, save part of the extreme left they were 'grands notables' or represented their interests. As such they shared considerable interests in common. The character of debate in the chamber is proof of this. Political debate proper was comparatively rare, and tended to have a strongly personal character, as part of the infighting between the various Orléanist factions, criticism of ministers or else of the king's role in government. The major concern of deputies was the defence of local interests, particularly in relation to the policy of the central authorities on matters of public works, taxation or tariffs. Deputies tended to act as intermediaries between their constituencies and the government, whilst ministers, to gain support, sought to satisfy them. In consequence, the political system at all levels was based on patronage and clientage facilitated by the small number of people involved and the easy maintenance of personal contact.

The free play of local influences was basic to the political system and reflected the relative underdevelopment of the economy, and in particular the isolation imposed by poor communications. Conflict between the representatives of diverging regional interest groups restrained the centralising tendencies of the administration, and hindered the rationalisation of policy decisions based on functional rather than personalised relationships between individuals. Nevertheless, the achievement of the July Monarchy, especially in the fields of education and public works essential to the modernisation of the economy, were substantial.[10]

The 1846 elections coming after some six years of economic prosperity reinforced the ministerial majority in the Chamber. The result reemphasised the dominance of the notables. But even in 1846 a majority of votes in the major cities went to diverse opposition candidates — this was the case in Paris, Lille, Marseille, Nantes, Bordeaux. Even amongst those privileged to vote there was thus a groundswell of opposition, representing a more widespread feeling that the existing political system did not provide an adequate representation of the interests of considerable sections of the community.

In the early years of the July Monarchy the threat of revolution had imposed a significant degree of unity on diverse interests within the middle classes, but as fear declined so particular interests came to the fore once again. In Paris in particular a feeling seems to have grown amongst both enfranchised and unenfranchised members of the middle classes that in order to safeguard their interests they should have a greater share in decision making, through a larger number of representatives of their own choice.

This movement for reform attracted growing support. Although it appealed to some workers, it remained essentially a middle class movement, in favour of varying degrees of reform, and most certainly not wanting revolution. Following the 1846 election, criticism of the regime grew more intense, strengthened in particular by the support of opposition notables hoping to use the question of reform as a weapon against the government, and to reinforce their own position before the next election. Liberal critics, men associated with the centre left in particular, like Rémusat and Dauvergier de Hauranne maintained that the electoral system resulted in a false representation of interests which could be corrected by the elimination from the chamber of civil servants, who invariably supported the government. If this could be achieved then an extension of the electorate would be unnecessary. In contrast, some of the dynastic left, Tocqueville for example, believed that the existing electorate was too small to prevent local and personal rivalries determining in large part the character of representation. Although divided on the question of how large an increase in the electorate would be necessary, there was general agreement that it should be very small. Most proponents of reform rejected universal suffrage which seemed to promise anarchy, and shared a belief that political rights should be given only to those who could give guarantees of capacity in the form of wealth or perhaps higher education.

The use of influence by private individuals and civil servants and the political interventions of the monarch helped to bring the system into disrepute. Bribery or pressure tended to be used by everyone, but more successfully by the government supporters who enjoyed access to official patronage. Corruption in consequence tended to be associated with the government. The publicity accorded to cases of corruption, and scandals in high places from 1846 especially, all tended to reduce the prestige of the regime.[11]

In this situation the notables of the dynastic opposition took the initiative and began a campaign in favour of reform which took the form of banquets at which political speeches were made. These were normally moderate in tone and intent, and made to respectable audiences of lawyers, merchants and landowners. The republican Ledru-Rollin however, engaged in a separate series of banquets attracting a more democratic audience and demanding universal male suffrage.[12]

There were relatively few republicans amongst those with the right to vote. The republic still conjured up remote memories of the Terror. It is difficult to estimate how sympathetic workers and peasants might be, what memories and images they might have retained. Undoubtedly Bonapartism had greater appeal. Often republican and Bonapartist sentiments were confused. This was clearly the case amongst middle class republicans to whom equality and fraternity seem to have held out far greater appeal than liberty. In most small towns there seem to have been middle or lower middle class republicans meeting informally on occasion to discuss politics amongst other things, often disguising their real feelings under the label 'liberals'.

Republican ideology was in practice confused and incoherent. It was expressed most forcefully in two newspapers, whose political importance both before and after the February revolution reveals the potential significance of even a small circulation newspaper, its staff and associates, in a situation in which political parties and meetings are almost impossible. They provided, besides publicity, a minimum of cohesion, and following the revolution, would furnish most of the members of the Provisional Government. These newspapers Le National and La Réforme were not only the main arms of the Republican challenge, but also represented Republican divisions. The National, and people associated with it like Garnier-Pagès, Armand Marrast, Crémieux, Bastide, and Carnot were sympathetic towards the desire to improve conditions for the poor, but only if the measures taken were compatible with the interests of other social groups. They wanted political reform above all, and chided socialists for their materialistic concern with economic reform. In essence, and in spite of their political ideals, they were opportunists, close in their demands to the dynastic opposition. They did not want revolution at any price. Alphonse de Lamartine, more independent, a republican from Christian charity similarly eschewed violence, and was afraid of drastic change. His lack of a coherent doctrine would lead him too, to respond to events rather than attempt more positive initiatives.

With the Réforme were associated men who might be labelled 'democratic republicans' — Louis Blanc, Lamennais, Schoelcher, Etienne Arago, Pascal Duprat, Flocon, Ledru-Rollin, etc. The newspaper was very concerned with social problems. Articles written by Blanc and others often evinced clearly socialist solutions. Besides universal suffrage it demanded that government be responsible and revocable, that all public officials be paid so as to extend office holding to the lower classes, a free press, free education, obligatory military service for all, that the state should assume responsibility for reform of the economic structure, providing credit for workers to establish producers cooperatives. The title of the newspaper was indicative of the pacific means by which they hoped to change society.

The most influential advocates of revolutionary violence, Blanqui and Barbès, remained in prison until after the Revolution. In their place more moderate men like Caussidière, Sobrier and Raspail assumed control of what underground groups survived repression. These can not have been very numerous.

The very diversity of socialist ideas being discussed is indicative of their lack of contact with and appeal to mass movements.[13] Only a small minority of workers through their contacts with lower middle class elements and intellectuals had any awareness of the intellectual critics of the existing society.

Amongst workers there were signs of a slow evolution of mentality, of a new combativeness in some of the strikes of the 1840s and of a wider awareness of the contribution organisation and preparation might make to the success of a strike. This was effectively limited to the artisanal trades with traditions of organisation. Factory workers, mainly unskilled, badly paid, insecure, often recent immigrants from the countryside, lacked the experience, energy and money for strike funds. They might strike briefly and violently in protest against reductions in wages but would not sustain the movement. However, even if political movements did not exist there was inevitably some awareness of political realities, if for no other reason than that legislation directed against workers' associations led to conflict with the bureaucratic and military organs of the state. A rich associational life thrived in most urban centres. In Paris most artisanal trades had mutual aid societies which collected funds to help sick, out of work and aged members, and which were tolerated by the government provided they avoided the support of strikers. These and other forms of voluntary association such as choral societies, or the habitual meetings of neighbours and workers in the same trade in cafés and bars, meant that large numbers of workers met regularly and must have discussed matters of mutual concern, including politics. It meant also that grass roots and informal leadership emerged in the shape of those who stood out in a group because of their personalities and abilities — the literate or articulate who might convey an awareness of events to the others. In this way the popular culture, in a diffuse but nonetheless real manner, was politicised. This kept alive the revival of Jacobin ideas which had been stimulated by the 1830 Revolution and the short period of liberalisation which had followed it. That revolution indeed served as a memory of what the masses might achieve against the monarch by taking to the streets.[14]

II

The prosperous period of the July monarchy came decisively to an end in 1846 with an economic crisis due to a combination of factors, the most significant of which were a poor harvest causing substantial rises in food prices and a resulting decline in the demand for industrial goods; a crisis of overproduction, which might have occurred anyway, in industry; and a financial crisis due to speculation, the sudden withdrawal of English capital invested especially in railway companies, and growing balance of payments difficulties due in large part to the increased cost of food imports.

Small farmers, agricultural labourers and urban workers, with few exceptions, faced high food prices at a time of declining employment. The better off, even those with stocks of foodstuffs sufficient to permit them to make substantial speculative profits from popular hunger, all shared in a growing climate of insecurity. Whereas formerly the regime had claimed credit for prosperity, now opinion tended to blame it for crisis. In many 'informed' circles the speculative activities of financiers closely associated in the public mind with the regime were attacked. The volume of criticism of the regime and the size of the audience for it multiplied, but every economic crisis does not result in revolution. Other factors are evidently necessary. Social discontent must be politicised. The previous stability of the regime must be shaken by a waning of support for it characterised especially by divisions amongst or a loss of confidence on the part of normal government supporters.[15]

The regime was being criticised for its immobility by supporters of constitutional reform. Legitimists and republicans were invariably hostile. Scandals in high places had further reduced confidence in it. Now the myth of prosperity was shattered and a wave of pessimism swept the bourgeoisie, a crisis of confidence which deepened and extended the economic crisis. Even before the revolution, serious and widespread social disorder due in large part to high food prices created a fear of social revolt amongst the possessing classes which throughout the 1840s had become increasingly aware of the existence of a social problem, of countless masses of appallingly poor people.[16]

The occurence of revolution might in large part be ascribed to a process of 'political decay' as the ability of the existing political organisation to adapt to new social and political circumstances declined. It became identified with 'intransigence, corruptability, and inefficiency'.[17] The notion of a contract which had played an important part in the ideology of partisans of the regime, which had legitimised the authority of a regime itself the product of revolution, now tended to act against it as it failed to provide stability and prosperity. When revolution came, its success in large part was due to the resignation of the upper classes and, paradoxically, to the initial overconfidence of the monarch and his closest advisers. Fed with optimistic reports on the situation by officials anxious to provide a favourable image of their own activities and faced with only muted criticism from an unrepresentative parliament, Louis Philippe would be paralysed by shock once he had been made aware of the seriousness of the situation.[18]

The immediate cause of revolution was government resistance to electoral reform and in particular to a reformist demonstration on the streets of Paris. Clashes between military units and demonstrating crowds rapidly grew out of hand and a situation of full scale insurrection developed on 22-23 February. The Paris National Guard which had during the early 1830s supported so firmly the maintenance of order, now refused to repress the insurrection. The army was used indecisively symptomatic of the loss of confidence of the King and his ministers. Louis Philippe simply despaired and abdicated.

In the provinces the revolution was generally unexpected, but as in the past the lead given by Paris was accepted with resignation or enthusiasm depending upon one's outlook. In respect of resignation, the deposed monarch had in fact given the lead. Of special significance for the future was the fact that in most places the revolution did not displace the ruling elite from its position of economic and social power. The bases for the expression of its political influence survived.

The revolution was to be an incident in a continuing conflict. Subsequently, the lower middle classes and urban artisans (and in some areas the peasants) were to challenge the predominance of this elite, on the basis not of new revolutionary ideologies but of older ones, and to demand again the rights of man and fraternity. Even in the early, relatively optimistic period of the Republic, demands for social reform were to be responded to by a government and administration which although different in composition and ideology from those of the monarchy were nonetheless largely composed of members of the same social elite. Conflict within the group of notables would at crucial moments be replaced by unity imposed by a shared awareness of the threat to their social pre-eminence from other social groups.[19]

III

The men who took up the reins of government so unexpectedly dropped by the royal administration owed their new position to their reputation as journalists. They were the best known republicans of their day and were acclaimed by the revolutionary crowd as the obvious successors to the defunct monarchy. They were a heterogeneous group separated by personal differences and by different views of what the duties of this Provisional Government were. The majority of moderates — Lamartine, Marie, Crémieux, Arago, Garnier-Pagès and Marrast — saw its role as being primarily to maintain order and administrative continuity, whilst keeping its acts to a minimum until the election of a Constituent Assembly to declare upon the future institutions of government. The minority, of more radical republicans — Blanc, the worker Albert, Flocon and most notably Ledru-Rollin — believed that it had a duty to transform institutions, and ultimately seek ratification of its acts by universal suffrage once the country had been educated to democracy.

Neither group had a very coherent picture of what it should aim to do, and so the government would react to events rather than make them. It had initially a certain unity of spirit, a genuine, almost religious idealism, believing that a new age was about to begin and possessing a profound sense of mission, but rapidly as decisions were required divisions were evident. Each faction began to look for allies outside the government to support it in the pursuance of what it saw to be the only legitimate objectives. At first the radicals appeared to be in the stronger position supported as they were by the workers of Paris, who had made the Revolution in the streets and who were determined not to risk a repetition of 1830 when they had won a victory and gained nothing.[20]

In the provinces the changes brought about by the Revolution usually took the form of a municipal revolution. Without opposition republicans and liberals installed themselves in the *préfectures, sous-préfectures* and townhalls replacing or adding themselves to the existing municipal administration. This was a middle class revolution in most places, occurring throughout France as merchants and entrepreneurs and members of the liberal professions hostile to the July Monarchy and especially to the grands notables who had dominated society, took advantage of the new situation. The republic imposed itself on France by assuming control of most administrative centres and from there of the surrounding countryside.

Where radical republicans were supported or subject to the pressure of already organised workers, a more complete exclusion of the former municipal elites occurred. Thus at Lyon where initially liberal middle class elements assumed control, workers led by leaders of the secret societies which had survived even the repression which had followed the 1834 insurrection, now insisted on the inclusion of a majority of radicals including workers and small workshop owners in the new municipal council. At Limoges too workers forced the creation of a council dominated by the more democratic bourgeois. These were exceptions. Worker pressure counted for much in Paris, Rouen and Lille and although not achieving the same pre-eminence as at Lyon and Limoges, gave a certain dynamism to the revolution for some months. In most of France the traditional notables continued to dominate.

The municipal revolution occurred only where lower middle class elements were sufficiently numerous and independent to be able to maintain themselves, normally with the support of the commissaires appointed by the government to replace the prefects. In the Paris region this was in the administrative centres of departments, and more rarely in those of *arrondissements*. Elsewhere in most small towns little or nothing changed. If the notables effaced themselves this was only temporarily while they assessed their position and influence in the Republic. Even in relatively large towns like Blois, Toulouse or Chartres they continued to participate in municipal affairs. Where notables resigned or were purged, more often than not they were replaced by liberals drawn from the same social group. In the more isolated and backward areas there were few people with the leisure and education necessary to carry the burdens of local administration. In the west and southwest in particular, where their social dominance was rarely challenged, notables felt little inclined to step down. In most towns, even if municipal revolution had occurred, the National Guards of the July Monarchy with membership restricted to property owners remained in existence and resisted democratisation, anxious to preserve social order and usually constituting the only armed organisation besides the army.[21]

The major problem faced by government at both municipal and national level was to restore normality. In a post-revolutionary situation a large number of people expected, and were prepared to demand, a variety of improvements in their situations, which often ran counter to basic governmental activities, such as tax collection. Violent protest now spread from its initial locus in Paris throughout the country.

One consequence of this situation was to worsen an economic crisis which had shown clear signs of improvement. Lack of business confidence ensured that industrial unemployment reached new heights and constituted a major problem for a republican administration apparently committed, and certainly expected, to do something for the poor. Inability to cope adequately with this situation increased discontent amongst workers, whilst efforts to help the unemployed soon alienated businessmen and peasants, all of whom felt they were having to pay the cost in increased taxation of pampering the industrial worker. More than anything else continued economic crisis and social unrest was to lead to the reconstruction of a conservative and increasingly reactionary alliance determined to introduce effective, and repressive, government.

Outside a few major cities the social consequences of the Revolution were most obvious in the countryside, where more serious and longer lasting protest movements developed. The Paris Revolution was the occasion not the cause of these. It led to the establishment of a government whose authority was at first weak, and whose coercive power was doubtful, of a Republican government moreover, of whose character many of the discontented possessed a positive if vague and confused appreciation. It was thought to be good and just and favourable to the poor. Protest, especially in such difficult times, was an ordered response to a changed situation, and not simply inchoate violence.

In many areas the protest movements of 1848 meant simply the re-awakening of long existing conflicts. Although the demands made were somtimes influenced by new socialist ideas spread by seasonal migrants, or in some cases workers employed in constructing railways, they normally took a much older form, differing in character according to the particular problems the various areas faced: in Brittany, the ending of market tolls; in areas as diverse as the north, northeast, *landes* of Gascony and Brittany, the Morvan, and Mediterranean region for preservation of traditional rights on common land; in Champagne and Vendée for the re-establishment of collective rights to pasture on fallow land; in Alsace for an end to usury; in mountain areas of the centre, east, Alps and Pyrénées, for the restoration of traditional rights of usage in the forests; in the Paris region for the abandonment of agricultural machines and for higher wages for agricultural labourers; and throughout vine growing regions, for the abolition of the tax on consumption of alcohol.

Most of these movements represented an effort by agricultural communities engaged primarily but not exclusively in subsistence farming to protect some of the diverse ways in which they made a living from encroachment by wealthier individuals who sought to improve farming techniques by means of enclosure and the abandonment of collective practices, agents of the government who sought to protect forests from degradation, or private forest owners who sought similarly to protect the trees which constituted their capital. This individualism and state interference was especially resented in regions in which population pressure on resources had grown to such an extent that for the mass of poor only a diverse range of activities and resources permitted subsistence. Other incidents were obviously a continuation of age-old resistance to the tax gathering activities of the state. The scale of the problem can perhaps be judged from the fact that due to the unreliability of National Guards and the inadequate number of gendarmerie, 42,900 regular infantry and 5,250 cavalry, and probably in practice many more were committed in a police role to repress disorders.

The forest troubles evince more clearly than any other the pressure of economic circumstances on the rural poor. In the Paris region, where often large grain farms existed in proximity to forests, and in which bread remained expensive and unemployment high, rural labourers combined with artisans and woodcutters to express their discontent. Forest troubles were worst in the east and Pyrénées where woods and common land occupied a large proportion of the soil – in the Pyrenean region for example from between 17 per cent in the Ariège to 43 per cent in Hautes-Pyrénées. Often not only the poor but large landowners who had enclosed their own pasture, united to oppose implementation of the legislation on rights of usage thus preserving communal unity against the administration. Although not a political movement this kind of conflict tended to heighten the political consciousness of the rural populations.

Protests concerning forests were obviously localised in character. More widespread and therefore politically more significant was the expression of protest against the tax gathering activities of the state. Such protest occurred essentially in two kinds of area — those in which wine production was important, and others which were simply economically backward. The tax on wine consumption reduced sales and was resented by consumers for whom it increased prices. Moreover the inquisitorial methods of the officials involved awakened considerable resentment. In consequence this was a tax which aroused general opposition — at Toul in June troops were helpless when 1,500 peasants invaded the town to protest and were supported by its inhabitants. Such incidents were in 1848 especially likely to occur throughout the south.

Protest against other forms of taxation was less likely in the northeast than in other regions particularly the west and Massif Central. When resistance to the 45 per cent increase in the land tax introduced by the Provisional Government on 16 March as part of an effort to produce a balanced budget occurred, it was typical in the sense that it took place in areas which in comparison with the north had backward communication networks and a lower degree of involvement in an exchange economy. They were areas of polyculture and sharecropping in which movement of money was limited and the accumulation of cash to pay taxes always a problem. Relative overpopulation meant that the surplus out of which taxes could be taken was reduced. Now economic crisis intensified the problem.

Within the general areas of backwardness it has been shown that the most serious resistance to the collection of this tax would occur not in those villages most isolated from market influences, where protest too was isolated but in wine growing areas suffering from cash shortage because of crop failures or declining prices. In such areas a number of villages linked by a shared central marketing centre might band together to offer resistance, with the aim of intimidating the authorities by their number. To this the habitual response was a display of military power intended similarly to overawe without actual resort to violence. Protest was a matter for serious concern where one type of production — for example of wine, or forestry — or the predominance of a particular form of exploitation such as sharecropping established a community of interest in the population. The severity of the situation was multiplied where contacts between villages were sufficiently close and frequent to

17

allow for an awareness of their shared interests and the mobilisation of population on a multi-village basis — that of the 'standard market area'.[22] Measures which might have alleviated some of the problems faced by the rural population — more extensive rights in forests, reduction of the burden of taxation and indebtedness — could have won them over to the Republic, but instead they received vague promises and were subjected to new taxes, and repression.

In the towns more diverse forms of agitation occurred which were more likely to have an immediate political impact. Most obviously the very character of the streets was transformed in the centre of major cities as newspaper sellers appeared, and demonstrations — in favour of this or against that — combined with idle sightseers to give an impression of ferment. The legal requirement on newspapers to deposit caution money in case of transgression of the repressive press laws, and the stamp duty which newspapers had paid, simply disappeared, making newspapers cheap to produce and to buy. As many as 300 new newspapers appeared in Paris and many others in provincial towns between February and June, often ephemeral, many with names like *Ami du Peuple, Père Duchesne, Robespierre*, inspired by the first great Revolution, others more representative of the spirit of the age with in their titles words like *Peuple, République, Démocratique*. Most of these new newspapers represented the republican cause — whether moderate, radical or socialist. They all contributed to the political education of the population but it is necessary to note that most of the newcomers had few readers. Their influence was nowhere as great as that of the established and more conservative press.

Another phenomenon of the post-revolutionary period was the appearance of a large number of political clubs. Peter Amann estimates that in Paris in April there was a minimum of 203 clubs with at least 50-70,000 members. They saw their mission as being the education of the population, discussion of the problems of the day and propaganda and preparation for the general elections due in April. Members believed also that they had the responsibility for the surveillance of the government, of ensuring that it, unlike the regime established in 1830 would not betray those who had fought to bring down the monarchy. The Provisional Government was thus to be under constant pressure to act to introduce radical reforms. It was essentially in the clubs that such manifestations of discontent as the popular demonstrations of 17 March, 16 April and 15 May were mooted and prepared.

The largest and best known of these clubs were the *Club de la Révolution* dominated by Barbès and the *Société républicaine centrale* of Blanqui. Whatever their image in the conservative press, speeches made in the former at least were not violent. Social reform was demanded and expected but initially at least it was hoped that further violence would not be necessary. The spokesmen of the *Société républicaine centrale* were more violent, from the start more suspicious of and hostile to the government. Significantly, neither of these were involved in organising the demonstrations of 17 March and 16 April and both were swept along by events rather than organising them on 15 May. As revolutionary bases they were ineffective but as means of maintaining popular agitation and of frightening the upper classes they were successful. Efforts to coordinate the activities of the numerous clubs had little success. Paradoxically, most clubs were too concerned with the details of voter registration and electoral procedures, with the scrutiny and nomination of candidates for both the election of National Guard officers and the parliamentary elections to arouse popular excitement and stimulate a mass movement. Thus their actions belied their often revolutionary phraseology.

Many club members had migrated to Paris from the provinces and there was a general awareness of the political backwardness of much of the country. One mission which the Club of Clubs, established to co-ordinate activity, did partially accomplish was the despatch of agents into the provinces to stimulate revolutionary zeal and political organisation, primarily with the elections in mind. Due to their activity and more especially to local initiatives every provincial town had its club or clubs, conservative as well as radical. The effort was not too successful. Where a single club existed this was often divided between moderate and radical republicans, and where there was more than one club they were often bitter rivals. More often than not clubs were considerably more moderate than their names would imply. In the Haute-Vienne for example, only those at St Léonard and St Yrieux, affiliated to the Société Populaire of Limoges, and containing like it a large proportion of discontented porcelain workers, were really radical. Most clubs quickly declined. Debate degenerated into conflicts between personalities. Members tired of listening to interminable speeches. Few peasants ever attended, most knew of clubs only by rumour which was generally unfavourable in its references to idlers, talkers and communists. In the majority of clubs members of the lower middle classes assumed a dominating role due to their greater eloquence, even if the majority of members might be workers.

However, for the first time since 1830-1 men were freely able to write and to hold meetings. The club movement reached its apogee in April and then declined once the *raison d'être* for most of them – the elections – had occurred. Events such as the demonstration in Paris on 15 May and subsequent repression further reduced their numbers so that by June only around fifty survived in the capital.

Besides the clubs the first months of the republic were significant for the development of a range of both formal and informal associations amongst workers. In Paris this was stimulated by the need of the various trades to elect 730 delegates to the commission, established to enquire into social reform by the government, which met at the Luxembourg Palace. Even in the 1840s militant workers in the clothing, printing and building industries in particular had formed associations to organise demands for improved conditions. The tendency was accelerated after the revolution. The worker delegates to the Luxembourg Commission in March established a *Comité Central des Ouvriers du Département de la Seine* to encourage and coordinate this movement. These worker militants evinced a clear fascination for ideas of producers' associations, a means of reducing competition, spreading more widely the ownership of property and reducing the insecurity of employment which workers habitually faced.

The process of organisation amongst Parisian workers after February appears to have been especially successful amongst engineering and metal workers, including men employed in the railway workshops, in the leather and building trades — significantly groups which were to be heavily committed to the June insurrection. Workers in most trades tended however to meet frequently to discuss the political and economic situation — on an informal if not a formal basis — which contributed to the continuing agitation, and growing solidarity and desire for social reform.

The picture was not always the same in provincial towns. Lyon and Limoges shared the agitation of Paris but organisational activity did not achieve even the limited degree of success attained in Paris. The agitation merely frightened conservatives and many moderates without achieving anything durable. At Limoges demands for a forced loan from the rich which might be used to finance producer cooperatives created especial alarm. In numerous places agitation directed against the employment of foreign workers, the use of machinery and price competition from prison and convent labour, demands for higher wages and a shorter working day occurred, and then declined of its own accord. Workers expected much from the Republic but when it was not immediately forthcoming became discouraged. In a period of economic crisis their main concern was to find work. Few, especially away from the centre of political events at Paris, were able to sustain an interest in politics.

The political effectiveness of workers depended on their previous experience of organisation and awareness of mutual interest within professional groups, and this in turn depended on their entire life style — their work, its rewards and the patterns of sociability this permitted. In an economy undergoing the initial stages of industrialisation, the organisation of production, working conditions and standards of living were very diverse. Paris itself exemplifies this. Tilly and Lees in their article describe five main groups of workers — an elite of well paid highly skilled men in such trades as engineering, fine metal work, printing, and some trades producing *articles de Paris*; artisans in the sweated trades — especially furniture and clothing and sections of other industries, where work was put out and wages were lower; other trades where both the level of skills and working conditions varied; factory workers; and unskilled labourers. Although the small workshop and artisanal techniques predominated a significant concentration of the organisation and financing of production had already occurred. The marketing of the products, the supply of raw materials and often of tools was controlled by large scale wholesale merchants who imposed a certain division of labour on the separate workshops. Workshop owners, and the artisans they employed were often more conscious of their hostility towards these merchants, than of the interests which separated them. Indeed, working together, having common skills, not separated by any great gulf in wealth or living standards, meant that close personal ties might easily develop. This would be seen during the June insurrection in the reluctance of many *patrons* to join their National Guard units and possibly fight against their workers. Similar diversity of structure existed in most industrial centres, even the most modern, whilst in smaller towns workers were isolated and orientated towards the rural interests of their neighbours, and thus totally devoid of any sense of class interest.

Organisation then was a characteristic primarily of the skilled, working together in small groups, with numerous contacts with each other both at and after work. Their negotiating position with their employers was stronger; because of their skills they were more difficult to replace than unskilled workers. They were able therefore to defend their economic position more successfully. They moved less often in search of work, because of their qualifications and immobility achieving a reputation within their trades and towns. The skilled artisan had status and a pride in this status and in his skills. He was better educated and better informed than his unskilled brethren.

William Sewell has in studies of Marseille refined this kind of analysis by making a distinction between skilled workers able to control entry into their trade, i.e. the supply of labour, and to maintain relatively high wages and greater security — a genuine aristocracy of labour — and others, also skilled but unable to control entry, and who more frequently had to struggle with their employers to safeguard their interests, but who still possessed the craft traditions and experience of organisation to effectively do so. In the particular context of Marseille, Sewell suggests it was these more combative groups rather than the less dissatisfied 'aristocrats' who became politically militant. Due to the freedom of entry into them, and the variety of experience of their members, often migrants to Marseille, these 'open' trades were less isolated culturally and socially than the 'closed', which were socially as well as professionally more exclusive. Sewell further suggests that in Paris and Lyon, trades able to establish similar controls over recruitment, because of their established radical traditions, were likely to transmit a radical rather than a traditional culture.

In large scale industry, particularly in textiles — the major employer of factory (as well as of rural) labour — although there existed permanent tensions between employers and workers due to the miserable conditions of the latter, the ease with which they could be replaced, and the lack of professional traditions and solidarity, protest was generally limited to spontaneous outbursts. Not only were working conditions unfavourable to politicisation but frequently home life was dislocated due to low wages and the desperate need for women and children to find employment. Exhausted by the unending struggle to earn a living such workers had little physical or moral energy to deploy in organisational activity. Only the better off workers engaged in organised labour and political protest: the more deprived workers might be present in crowds, but continued militancy was unusual.

Factory workers should not be considered as a uniform group, however, for there were significant exceptions within the ranks of factory labour. In many respects work in some large scale industries, engineering and metallurgy for example, retained artisanal characteristics including high levels of skill, of wages, a sense of pride and the rapid development of professional organisation. Many workers had been recruited from small workshops. In the wave of strikes in Paris after February and during the June insurrection such groups, especially employees of the railway workshops, played an important part.

A shared profession was obviously not the only source of solidarity amongst workers. Historians have too frequently stressed the disorganising effects of rapid urbanisation. In unfamiliar surroundings, frequently unemployed, removed from the pressure for conformity and the mutual support of the small community, migrants were believed to morally disintegrate, mental illness to become frequent, and crime and the propensity to protest increase. The 'constant stream' character of much migration should encourage suspicion of this attitude. It is likely that many people were led to bitterly regret their move to the city, but even there neighbourhood relationships developed and networks based on this, on common origin and the re-establishment of kinship ties soon provided a structure within which people could live out their lives. A network of formal and informal ties was established based on employment as in the case of mutual aid societies many of which became the basis for social clubs meeting in the backrooms of cafés, and similar to the *chambrées* described in the villages of Provence, or else simply on an habitual presence in the same café. Informal and formal relationships both served as bases for organisation and as means for the diffusion of political ideas.[23]

Under considerable pressure and from a desire to help the poor the Provisional Government made its concessions to social reform. On 25 February it proclaimed the right to work which was to be implemented through the establishment of National Workshops. This was to be of major significance to the future development of the Republic. Security of employment was one of the main demands made by workers. Militants in Paris seem to have expected the National Workshops to be a permanent organisation providing employment in their own trades to the unemployed. In fact the government was implementing the most obvious means of aid to the unemployed — the charity workshop already created in 1846-7 in many areas which provided unskilled labour on public works projects. Moderates amongst government members and middle and upper class opinion more generally, whether republican or not, found the prospect of permanent state intervention in production most unacceptable. The National Workshops were to become a symbol of hope for workers, and of the dreadful prospect of social revolution for the others.

In the short run some kind of relief for the unemployed was essential, if only to keep masses of workers off the streets. In the months after the Revolution unemployment in Paris reached 56 per cent of the total number of employed workers, varying between 20 and 75 per cent according to the industry. It was smallest in the food industries, much higher in industries producing non-essentials — in furniture, building and metal working for example, industries which were to supply large contingents of insurgents when the threat to close the National Workshops led to insurrection in June. By this time there were just over 100,000 workers employed being paid 8 f. a week, a sum inadequate for the maintenance of a family, and employed at hard physical labour, exhausting and degrading for many skilled artisans. Even then they were better off than the 40-50,000 unemployed who were not taken on.[24]

To reduce continued unrest on 28 February the Provisional Government made the further concession of a commission to sit at the Luxembourg Palace to consider and advise the government on means of solving the social problem. It included 231 delegates of employers and 699 workers, but had no executive powers and after the first euphoric days the government tended to ignore its advice. The idealistic criticisms of the existing economic structure voiced there tended to provide a salutary warning to the bourgeoisie of the dangers of socialism.

The most pressing of worker demands — for the abolition of *marchandage* (a system of labour contracting which tended to force wages down), and for a reduction in the length of the working day — were decreed by the government on 2 March. Petitions poured into the Luxembourg Commission making these and other demands but with little further effect. They contained few signs of socialism. Besides practical demands from particular trades the petitions and worker delegates to Luxembourg seem to have desired recognition of the right to work as a fundamental human right.[25]

The combined effects of the concessions made by the government were to stimulate the diffusion of socialist ideas, to encourage worker solidarity and organisation in Paris, and to facilitate the exertion of pressure on individual employers by workers able to find employment in the National Workshops during strikes. In short these concessions stimulated the pressure for more, and once made would not easily be reversed. The Revolution had in a variety of ways led to unrest and protest which a government anxious to preserve its authority and social order must eventually be led to combat. In so doing it would enjoy the support of all those for whom the Revolution only offered the prospect of unwanted change.

IV

Revolution had been a profound shock for the socially dominant groups. Initially they tended to conceal their indignation and favour conciliation with the new Republican authorities in order both to moderate the course of the Revolution and avoid disorder. Fear of what might happen paralysed the will to oppose the establishment of a republican administration in the provinces. Fear of communism, particularly in the Midi, west and centre, combined with an obsessive memory of 1793.

It is possible to contrast two situations in the provinces. In towns like Lyon, Limoges, Rouen and Lille, as well as Paris, the presence and activities of frequently armed workers effectively paralysed the notables for some months. Elsewhere notables usually retained control of the local situation. The new administration came from the same social groups as the old. They clearly desired to act in a moderate and legal manner, and in response to this terror subsided, and was succeeded — in many areas from early in March — by a growing will to re-assume control of the situation, to prevent the social revolution which news of agitation in Paris and of disorders elsewhere made evident might still occur. The failure of the government to restore order and prosperity rapidly reduced its prestige. Its financial and taxation measures alienated potential supporters. It might be tolerated as a bulwark against further revolution but more drastic measures were increasingly demanded from it, and each day of disorder in Paris reinforced conservative doubts about its ability to act effectively. Increasingly it was going to be asked to prove its moderation by closing the National Workshops and thus making a practical disavowal of socialist tendencies.

In the meantime traditional conservative leadership in the nation was restored in defence of property. In much of the Midi and west the Legitimists were already organised. Their position had not been sufficiently threatened to force them to efface themselves. In the east and in Picardy former representatives of the dynastic opposition made use of meetings of chambers of commerce and agricultural societies to stimulate resistance. In the Paris basin in particular, where the threat was so close, influential notables assumed leadership over an alliance of social groups, at least outside industrial towns like Reims or Troyes. An intense desire for a return to normality came into being.[26]

In such a situation government officials could normally look for the cooperation of responsible and respectable notables throughout the provinces in their effort to maintain political control. The Provisional Government had however inevitably added some disorder to the situation by means of the purges of the administration it conducted. All prefects and sous-prefects were replaced — as were almost all of the procureur-généraux, the state prosecutors. Their successors — commissaires and sous-commissaires — took over their functions and began to purge the administration at lower levels. Already popular pressure had forced the resignation of many mayors, especially in the larger towns. Ledru-Rollin at the Interior Ministry in a circular of 8 March advised caution on the part of the commissaires, advocating replacement of local officials only when this was absolutely necessary, in order to avoid provoking local unrest. The results tended to vary with the personality and views of the commissaire, the degree of hostility on the part of mayors to the republic and the possibility of finding replacements to those in office. In Ille-et-Vilaine where hostility was evident, few replacements could be found with the necessary education and willingness to risk public hostility. Only 25 of 346 mayors were revoked. In Vaucluse by contrast only 40 of 145 mayors were retained after a systematic enquiry by the new prefect Laboissière. It is not possible to generalise about the extent of changes. They did however occur everywhere and even mayors who survived the purge must for some time have felt at risk.

At prefectoral level most of the replacements were initially found amongst local notables and were often former members of the Orléanist dynastic left, but following further changes in April at least eighty· departments had as commissaires individuals who had been republicans during the July Monarchy, and many were of lower social status than had previously been the case, especially in some of the larger towns.

The re-organisation of the judicial tribunals was also of considerable importance given the role of the state prosecutors in a situation of unrest. Here the problem of finding replacements was compounded by the need for legal qualifications. Below the level of procureur-général the purge was extremely limited, and even for these senior positions giving authority in three or more departments, the replacements had of necessity often to be former sympathisers with the dynastic opposition. The magistrature remained an obviously conservative body.

These changes imposed by Paris often awoke resentment. Six commissaires — at Bordeaux, Amiens, Valence, Montauban, Beauvais and Troyes — were forced to flee due to the hostility of local notables with a mass following. Commissaires of local origin were particularly resented where their humble social background or a reputation as old conspirators as in the case of Delescluse in the Nord made them suspect. Some saw themselves repeating the roles of the representatives on mission of 1793 and aroused opposition with their verbal violence. Others by their moderation were able to secure election to the Constituent Assembly from the areas they administered. The mission of local representatives of the government was to republicanise the provinces. As the elections drew close, and conservatives began to re-assert themselves, the circulars from the Minister of the Interior grew more aggressive. They were encouraged to act radically. To achieve their ends the traditional means of control, of patronage and the establishment of a devoted clientele could be used. It was vital to gain the support of subordinates in the communes especially the mayors and justices of the peace in order to influence the mass of the population which remained fundamentally apolitical. They could not however assume that such cooperation would be forthcoming.

The justices were usually moderately well off rentiers, former notaries, retired officers, lawyers or law officials or especially landowners. In the towns the functions of mayor or deputy mayor took up too much time to be held other than by individuals able to afford a considerable amount of leisure. In the countryside the problem was rather to find people with sufficient education, competence and a reputation for probity. In all these positions were likely to be found individuals hostile to substantial social changes, concerned to preserve the *status quo*. In poorer regions especially notables sought such administrative posts to increase their prestige. Relationships within such a structure were as likely to be determined by questions of personality as by defined responsibilities. The commissaire and sous-commissaire needed cooperation to implement administrative decisions but could equally well meet with passive obstruction from mayors and councils. To an important degree the commissaire depended on the good will of local notables. But at the communal level many of these were engaged in struggles for local power. The revolution with its purges inflamed these localised conflicts and intensified the efforts of various groups to strengthen their positions. If the commissaire was able to satisfy one group he was likely to alienate another. His position was sensitive in the extreme. With the advent of universal suffrage it was more than ever necessary to secure support or at least compliance from influential persons.27

The elections, which had been postponed from the 9 to 23 April under pressure from Parisian crowds demanding longer for the left to organise its propaganda, were preceded by a confused campaign in which large numbers of committees put forward large numbers of candidates, on lists which often included representatives of diverse shades of opinion. The statements made by candidates were normally extremely vague, emphasising such factors as the past patriotism of the candidate, particularly if he had served in the army, the defence of liberties, the need to do something for the poor. The government was rarely criticised directly although conservative attacks on the centralisation of political decision making at Paris were common, and represented a barely veiled attack on the revolution. The habitual predominance of local personalities and issues in election debate was reduced in this election when the revolution was so close. Attitudes to Paris and events there, particularly the possible radicalising of the revolution were of pressing concern especially in regions in close proximity to the capital. Even so the main determining factors remained local. This first election with universal male suffrage indicated that in spite of the exhortations of delegates from the Paris clubs the reign of the notables was not over. The results would depend primarily on the behaviour of the administration and of the notables, on local political conditions and historical traditions, and the type of conflict which had previously existed in localities.

There was great diversity in the activity of notables. In general, unsure as to the consequences of the extension of the suffrage those previously involved in politics tended to efface themselves, being replaced as candidates by less prominent members of the 'middle' rather than the 'grande' bourgeoisie. In Paris and Lyon, in the east, most of the Paris basin and Alpine region members of the liberal professions came to the fore. In other areas this self-effacement was not as evident — in areas with large industrial centres like the Nord or Seine-Inférieure, the urban middle classes and large landowners tended to ally against the threat of social revolution. The same was true in agricultural areas close to major cities, like Seine-et-Oise. In southern departments like Haute-Garonne, Gers, Gard, Bouche-du-Rhône, and especially Tarn and Tarn-et-Garonne Legitimists supplied the lead in resisting Paris inspired change. There were yet other areas in which this effacement behind the 'middle' bourgeoisie hardly occurred at all —

in Meuse, Haute-Saône, Doubs and above all in the west. In Normandy, Anjou, Touraine and Poitou former representatives of the dynastic opposition retained their influence. In Brittany Legitimist nobles supported by the clergy re-asserted themselves to such a degree that at Nantes and Rennes bourgeois notables allied with republicans to resist them. Elsewhere a Legitimist lead was frequently accepted in the interests of conservative unity.

Even where effacement occurred notables by means of economic power, social influence and their frequent membership of electoral committees exercised considerable influence on the choice of candidates and their potential for success, especially in the countryside through their influence on voters. Everywhere in the last week before the poll, the representatives of the old parties became increasingly assertive. Only in the large towns and in areas where the agents of the Provisional Government, particularly its commissaires, exerted their influence with a success which indicated the ingrained habit of supporting government candidates in hope of reward — 67 of the 110 commissaires named were elected — was the political monopoly of the former ruling elite effectively challenged.

The challenge was organised primarily by dissatisfied members of the middle classes. These groups were mainly conservative but their education, greater articulateness, possession of financial resources, experience of organisation and politics, permitted the minority of radicals to dominate movements whose rank and file membership was composed mainly of politically inexperienced workers. This was especially the case of members of the liberal professions. Their various political options are indicative of the great diversity within the middle classes. If many of the less prosperous members of the lower middle classes shared the general attitude of condescension or contempt for the poor, they were themselves insecure particularly in a period of economic crisis. Thus within the bourgeoisie many individuals would support the political challenge to the ruling notables.

In the voting process itself, various influences were exerted. In many places local notables and priests led their flocks to vote. Intimidation could be and was used but was generally unnecessary, given the widespread survival of traditional attitudes of deference. Pressures were also applied in the opposite direction. At Limoges peasants arriving to vote were intimidated by groups of workers on the outskirts of the city and at polling stations.

One might, but only in very general terms affirm that support for republicans came from towns and from rural areas where large proportions of the population through access to land possessed some social independence. Most of rural France re-affirmed traditional loyalties and hostility to change.[28] The result was a Constituent Assembly not too dissimilar in its social composition from those of the July Monarchy in which the bourgeois professions predominated. This was seen as a triumph for the moderate republic and eased the fears of those afraid of a socialist or democratic victory. In fact it has been calculated that of the 851 deputies who took their seats after the election only 285 were known or reputed to have been republicans before the revolution. Of these only about 55 were radical or socialists, the rest moderate republicans — 231 might be identified as former sympathisers with the Orléanist centre left or dynastic opposition, only 19 as former firm supporters of Guizot. There were fifty-six obvious Legitimists. Amongst the 122 difficult to classify politically was a large majority of magistrates, officers and landowners most of whom were socially conservative. In short this was an Assembly which would oppose significant social reform.[29]

The result encouraged a conservative resurgence. In most departments outside large towns, their influence was restored. In many places the departure of leading republicans to Paris after the election disorganised republican cadres. Events subsequent to the election — riots at Rouen and Limoges by workers disappointed at their inability to elect deputies who might genuinely represent their interests, the invasion of the Constituent Assembly by Parisian demonstraters on 15 May, as well as frequent minor disorders — all seemed to call for strong government. This, together with the disappointment of the popular desire that the Assembly and its elected, moderate republican dominated executive commission would solve the economic crisis, served to restore the leadership of conservative notables in the provinces. To an impatient public, even at this early date, the Republic seemed to have failed. To radicals, the clearly conservative character of the Assembly and of the Executive Commission it elected composed of Arago, Garnier-Pagès, Marie, Lamartine and Ledru-Rollin, the replacement of commissaires and sous-commissaires by more moderate men seemed to signify that the revolution was betrayed.

V

This appeared to be confirmed when the forthcoming closure of the National Workshops was announced on 21 June, following a period when both inside and outside the Constituent Assembly, conservatives demanded the restoration of social order and the government of the Republic struggled to assert its authority and restore normal conditions. Its efforts confirmed the suspicions of radicals about its lack of revolutionary ideals, whilst not satisfying conservative demands. To avoid political isolation the Executive Commission was forced into growing dependence upon conservatives both moderate republicans and former monarchists. The 15 May demonstration at the National Assembly calling for support of the Polish insurrection against Prussia, which degenerated into an attempted revolutionary 'putsch' was especially important in determining the conservative orientation of the Government. Moreover, this could be seen as an assault on the authority and dignity of the nation's representatives elected by universal suffrage and was bitterly opposed by undoubted democrats like Ledru-Rollin. Its failure strengthened the desire for repression. The ease with which order had been restored on 15 May led to a dangerous underestimation of the capacity for resistance to reactionary measures which existed in Paris. Thus the decision to close the National Workshops was taken in almost light-hearted fashion, but because this threatened unemployment and the National Workshops were the symbolic representation of the Revolution, of hope for a better future, it led to massive insurrection.[30]

Both sides in the ensuing conflict were heterogeneous in composition. Amongst the insurgents could be found representatives of most social groups, but the great majority were workers. Estimates of the total number involved vary between 15,000 and 50,000. Some participated more fully than others. Most workers sat at home or went to work — the National Workshops continued to offer a day's wage which family men desperately needed. Conservative opinion identified protest with moral degeneracy, and often stressed the participation of the *classes dangereuses*, the most desperately poor elements of the population — the vagabonds, porters, ragpickers, knifegrinders, etc. who were a common feature of the Paris streets. Undoubtedly, attracted by the prospect of loot, excitement, and no doubt wanting to protest about their condition, many of these people fought. Many relatively unpoliticised workers, not previously organised, perhaps illiterate but vaguely aware of the new political slogans were ready to express their desire for a better world by fighting. Thus large numbers of unskilled labourers were involved. Predominant however were workers in the skilled trades, those who would normally be involved in workers' organisations, who might participate in strikes. They demanded the fulfillment of the promise of February. Rather than the elite artisans of the luxury trades, the typical insurgents were from trades with mixed levels of skill and varying rewards, like furniture, building, the metal working industries, with large proportions of unemployed in June and combative traditions because they had both possessed organisation and been especially liable to wage cuts and unemployment. Additionally there were significant numbers of small employers and merchants involved — men who worked and lived amongst the poor and shared their chronic insecurity. This was far from being a revolt solely of workers. Significantly, however, the students and middle class intellectuals who habitually gave a political lead seem to have been absent. This was then a revolt of the poor in all its diversity demanding a more equitable sharing of society's wealth, and at the very least provision for the poor in time of exceptional difficulty.

The revolt was essentially spontaneous in character. It took the form of a series of localised struggles in the poorer quarters of Paris, in which neighbour fought alongside neighbour and leaders emerged who had proved themselves in the past or during the struggle. The existing neighbourhood organisation of the National Guard facilitated this. Subsequently arrests removed much of this grass roots worker leadership including many former delegates to the Luxembourg Commission and the more militant of the Paris workers turned to producers' cooperatives as a means of escape from exploitation and insecurity. Although by early 1850 more than half of these arrested had been amnestied, June represented the high point of politicisation amongst workers in Paris during the Second Republic. The crushing of the insurrection turned them back to apathy or into the dead end of association. The focus for revolutionary change would move into the provinces.31

There too in June insurrection was crushed at Marseille; at Lyon, exploiting the discouragement caused by news from Paris, the army was able to regain control of the city and begin the disarmament of the organised workers — the *voraces* — who had dominated the city since February.32

The social polarisation which had occurred in Paris prior to the revolution is clearly indicated by the composition of the forces of repression. These were divided into three groups — National Guard, Mobile Guard and regular army. In all around 25,000 regular, 12,000 Mobile Guards and perhaps 18,000 National Guards were available.

Five main social groups have been identified serving amongst the National Guards — proprietors, shopkeepers, clerks, intellectuals and members of the liberal professions, and workers. Significantly, with the exception of units with large liberal-profession participation most National Guard elements could not be relied on to serve outside their own streets or quarters. Worker Guardsmen either saw the rising as a threat to the Republic perhaps inspired by reactionary plots or joined their units once failure of the insurrection seemed inevitable. The reluctance of small shopkeepers, merchants and workshop proprietors to do anything other than protect their own premises which were often in insurgent areas was common. The reinforcement of the Paris National Guard by guardsmen from fifty-three departments was generally too late to have any practical effect but reveals something of the generalised hostility to the Parisian lower classes in the provinces.

The mobile guard had been raised by a decree of 25-26 February, designed both to create a police force to fill the vacuum caused by the exclusion of the army from Paris after the revolution and the discrediting of existing police; and also to remove from the streets and discipline large numbers of unemployed young men, many of whom had been insurgents in February. Twenty-four battalions of 1,058 men each were to be raised. Most of their officers were to be elected and it is revealing of the speed with which these new recruits developed an *esprit de corps* and respect for military professionalism that they generally elected NCOs and officers detached from the regular army to direct their training, so that by June thirteen of the twenty-four battalion commanders belonged to the regular army. Although their reliability was often doubted by contemporaries, they proved themselves by their zeal in combatting the insurrection. Marx subsequently characterised them as *lumpenproletarians* — *déclassés* and degenerates — but Caspard has recently shown that they were mainly workers — an estimated 74 per cent of them — recruited primarily from the skilled trades as were the insurgents, but in comparison usually younger and unmarried and because of this more liable to dismissal, less well integrated into the society, organisation and ideals of older workers. They had welcomed the comradeship and security of the Mobile Guard. About one in twenty of those engaged would become casualties.

Prior to the insurrection the army had been reinforced and had begun to make serious preparation for combat. It was the most important element of the repressive forces. The Minister of War, the moderate republican General Cavaignac directed the action and with the resignation of the Executive Commission on 24 June in recognition of its political failure he became effective head of Government, in which role he was confirmed by a grateful Constituent Assembly once revolt had ended. At times of social crisis conservatives inevitably looked towards the army to defend them.

Its failure in February had shaken the confidence of the army in its leaders. The revolution had led to a crisis of morale, to a wave of indiscipline including demands for the removal of unpopular officers and demonstrations in favour of the Republic. Officers had found their authority challenged as they sought to avoid compromising themselves and perhaps gain some personal advantage from the change of government. When the Provisional Government began to assert its own authority so discipline was restored in the army. Soldiers were again isolated from the civil population by frequent changes of garrison. Long periods of service and poor communications prevented them from maintaining close links with their families. The normal unity of this closed group was gradually restored. The army was deployed in a police role throughout France to contain the waves of protest. These and its own disorder convinced many officers, conservative by social origin and military instinct, that the Republic was a synonym for anarchy. They would passively obey the new Government, just as they had accepted the overthrow of the old, but would be far more sympathetic towards a strong government willing to repress the more extreme manifestations of democracy.

The suppression of the June insurrection, in which the army was the main factor is indicative of the political importance of control of the military, and of a willingness to use it ruthlessly. For many conservatives the army now became the heroic defender of civilization. The insurrection and its crushing hastened the restoration of conservative unity, political leadership in the nation and reaction to reverse the February revolution. This event and the simultaneous uprising in Marseille, and more generalised disorders contributed moreover to the maintenance of social fear and to the desire for further repression.33

VI

Cavaignac's administration remained anxious to conciliate conservatives but they increasingly felt that his was an insufficiently strong government. In the Assembly, opposition mounted to all projects of reform and especially to vague projects in favour of progressive taxation, and a proposed article of the new constitution recognising the right to work. Pressure from Paris had influenced debate before June, now the mainly conservative representatives of the provinces had a relatively free hand. Conservative resurgence also marked the municipal elections at the end of July. Only in the south and southeast did a significant change in personnel occur, with new councillors still usually drawn from the same social group of local notables, replacing many of the old. The 'outs' replaced the 'ins', stimulating local rivalries. In most large towns conservative notables were dominant but mayors appointed by the Government were usually Republicans and this was to be a source of dissension. In spite of the suppression or disappearance of many political clubs and newspapers of the radical left, elections continually strengthened the habit of voting, and made the abolition of universal suffrage less and less likely.34

In the general election in April and in supplementary elections in June, one of the successful candidates had been Louis-Napoleon Bonaparte, nephew of the Emperor, known best for his two clumsy attempts at a *coup d'état*. By means of these and his electoral successes he established his claim to be heir to his uncle, and gained massive sentimental support throughout France. He was able to take advantage of a glorious legend created by the memoirs of the Emperor and his subordinates, by the novels of men like Stendhal and Balzac, by a mass of engravings and popular songs such as those of Beranger, and above all of a popular tradition uniting military glory to material prosperity. A long period of peace had permitted men to forget the sufferings of war. The legend awoke differing reactions between individuals, generations, social classes and regions. For some, Napoleon represented the Revolution, for others social order.

Conservative parliamentarians who had since the end of May met regularly in rooms in the rue de Poitiers now in the Autumn needed to select a candidate to represent them in presidential elections due on 10 December. Their problem was to find a candidate agreeable to both Legitimists and Orléanists. However, it became increasingly evident as support for the candidature of Louis-Napoleon grew in the country, that between him and Cavaignac a third candidate would have little chance of success and might even let in Cavaignac. Molé, Berryer and especially Thiers, the most influential members of this group consequently recommended that there should be no separate conservative candidate, but that Cavaignac should be opposed, and in practice therefore, Bonaparte supported. They appear to have been convinced that his personal nullity would allow them to control him. From hostility the conservative press switched to lukewarm support matched by a growing hostility to Cavaignac and the moderate republic suspected of favouring reform. Security seemed to lie in the destruction of the republic.

The results of the election made clear the limits to the support enjoyed by Cavaignac. Some conservatives believed he had already sufficiently proved his determination to defend social order, whilst Bonaparte was an unknown, even suspected of socialist sympathies. Some Legitimists affirmed their hostility to the imperial tradition. Businessmen, especially in ports with bad memories of the Empire, also supported the General. He gained a higher proportion of the votes cast in the larger towns than in market towns or in the countryside — those of the lower middle class voters in situations in which they were not subject to the influence of the notables. The efforts the republican government had made to collect the 45 centime tax contributed significantly to the alienation of the rural population. With 1,400,000 votes Cavaignac came a very poor second to Louis-Napoléon, with over 5,400,000 — 74.2 per cent of the votes. Even in Paris where the latter gained only 58 per cent this was a far higher proportion than expected, and was much higher in the poorer quarters of the city representing the failure of the democratic and socialist press to win support for their candidates Ledru-Rollin and Raspail. Here the worker vote for Louis-Napoléon expressed the disappointment they felt with a Republic seemingly incapable of ameliorating their lives and responsible for the brutal repression of June. The dictatorship of a Great Individual was perhaps more acceptable than that of another class.

The influence of press and parties was minimised by the emotional popular wave of support for Bonaparte. In some regions — in the Alpine area, south of the Paris basin, mountain departments of the centre like Creuse and Puy-de-Dôme, and in Paris — the masses voted for Louis-Napoleon in spite of the notables. Elsewhere notables either led or followed the popular impulsion. In Brittany, Provence and lower Languedoc where Legitimists had conserved their greatest influence the result was a low vote for Louis-Napoleon. In most departments his election appeared as a manifestation of unanimity under the leadership of the notables.

Although some conservatives were frightened by the independence which such a great victory might give to the President as elect of the people, more generally the result was viewed as an affirmation of the desire for order and a disavowal of February. Universal suffrage in April and again in December had not proved to be the threat to their social dominance they had imagined, but had evinced rather the conservatism, subordination or apathy of most of the population. The republicans in power had failed to make a positive appeal to the rural population who numerically dominated the electorate. The social question for them had meant the problems of urban rather than rural poverty. This failure lost them the Republic.[35]

Louis-Napoleon's first ministry composed of representatives of the conservative parties seemed to recognise his accord with and dependence upon them. Subsequently he was able to take advantage of the inability of conservative politicians to agree on an alternative to him as head of state, the growing disenchantment of public opinion with the endless disputes in the Assembly, the intense desire for social order, and his own powerful position as head of the executive, to establish ministries composed of men dependent upon him.

VII

The election of Louis-Napoleon helped to restore business confidence but it remained volatile. The general economic situation remained depressed and misery and discontent widespread, and dangerous, in a political situation which remained very agitated.

Recovery from crisis was most evident in industry, particularly in the production of consumer goods whose purchase could perhaps no longer be delayed. This stimulated artisanal and small and medium scale industry, particularly in the towns. Political uncertainty limited capital investment, whilst building trades, major employers of labour, and much rural industry remained depressed throughout the period 1849-51 because low agricultural prices reduced rural purchasing power. Thus what recovery occurred was limited but nevertheless significant. It was one factor, along with the evident failure of the urban revolutionaries, from June, which caused public interest, and political agitation to transfer its focus from the major cities to the countryside. The urban centres were relatively quiet from 1849. Even strikes were rare, although in Paris, at least until the *coup d'etat*, efforts to develop mutual aid and cooperative societies continued to involve large numbers of workers. Elsewhere, rural and urban artisans in trades more seriously affected by the economic situation continued to involve themselves in the *démocrate-socialiste* movement. These were not class conscious representatives of the working class but rather supporters of the cause of property for all, struggling for the creation of the *Republique des Petits* against the notables.[36]

In the wake of an economic crisis due to poor harvests and high crop prices there now succeeded one very different in character and due to bumper harvests and deflated price levels. This situation, very welcome to the mass of urban and rural poor who purchased foodstuffs rather than cultivating their own, caused severe problems for those who needed to sell in order to purchase whatever they did not produce themselves, or else to pay taxes, rents and interest of loans. In areas which would become politically agitated, income from the basic crops of cereals and wine was reduced whilst in the case of another major revenue earner — silk — prices remained high but not sufficient to compensate producers for the mediocrity of the crop.

The consequences of the crisis for professional groups varied greatly from place to place, between economic sectors and over time. It is not easy to judge the intensity of the crisis in various places. Official reports tended often to minimise social and economic dislocation which might have led to criticism of the administration and more significantly would have considered as perfectly normal in most areas high levels of popular misery. The adverse effects of good harvests are clear in the case of reducing purchasing power or causing unemployment but those in work found food cheaper, and peasants who farmed essentially for subsistence were hardly bothered by abundance. In the Alpine region the mountain communes so miserable in 1847 and 1848, i.e. those least engaged in commercial agriculture found their situation much improved. On the cereal growing plains of the north and Paris basin agricultural labourers profited from both low food prices and the expansion of employment provoked by the large crops. Those who were especially vulnerable it seems were small and medium proprietors, more heavily engaged in commerce, who paid the land tax and taxes on wine and salt, who were likely to have contracted loans to purchase their land, and who now found their income reduced, and this after a number of already hard years. Large scale farmers and proprietors-rentiers complained about declining incomes, but they, and indeed many small scale proprietors in deferential communities influenced by the propaganda of the notables against the communists who supposedly wanted their land, saw a solution to their economic difficulties in

36

political repression. In the south in particular, communities with a more democratic structure and ethos would be increasingly attracted towards an alternative political solution.

The causes of the crisis were thus variously interpreted according largely to class, party and the local interplay of social influence. Even if this was a crisis which significantly eased physical suffering, as hunger disappeared, it contributed to the maintenance of anxiety and social tension. The February revolution had generated hope, and belief in the possibility of reform. The continuation of crisis, political agitation and growing awareness of social inequality generated a widespread desire to resist exploitation, often conveniently personalised by the presence of the rural bourgeoisie sometimes in the shape of the usurer who was often a local notary. The growing number of appropriations for debt directly affected only a small proportion of the population but revealed to the majority the precariousness of their economic and social positions, and the willingness of the rich to exploit their difficulties.[37]

VIII

The majority of moderates in the Constituent Assembly were increasingly aware of their isolation in the country as opinion polarised and decided in January 1849 that the election of a Legislative Assembly should occur in May. In preparation for this, committees representing the various shades of political opinion were established to select candidates and organise propaganda. This was the work of a small minority of political activists. The lists of candidates they established were, if not completely so, far more homogenous than they had been in April 1848. Party divisions were far clearer. The candidates almost everywhere were drawn from the bourgeoisie, but with a clear progression from grande to petit bourgeoisie as one moved from right to left in the political spectrum.

Local campaigners received direction and advice from committees of the Party of Order, and the radical, démocrate-socialiste *Solidarité républicaine*, established in Paris. The basic themes of conservative propaganda were the need to combat the *partageux*, the communists. It associated the republic with the 45 centime tax, and combined hatred of Paris with demands for decentralisation. The moderate republicans so prominent in 1848 were now conspicuous largely by their absence. They had nothing very positive to offer between the two extremes. Moderates now either supported conservative repression or else joined the radicals to defend the republic. Radical candidates fought the election on the social question, promising the right to work, cheap credit and tax reform and appealing more than ever before to the peasants.

During the campaign and on polling day both conservatives and radicals applied pressure of various kinds. That of the latter had of necessity to be mainly informal. Conservatives however could make use of the state apparatus. Police harassment of election meetings and intimidation of militants was not uncommon. The result of the election was a clear conservative success. In two thirds of the departments, especially in the north-northeast, north-northwest, west and southwest, the political preponderance of the grands notables was reaffirmed. In most of these areas the electoral alliance of notables formerly divided over local and ideological issues, indicated their determination to defend their common economic and social power. Their failure in other areas, for example in Haute-Saône, Jura and in Alsace, could mainly be attributed to the survival of their old divisions.[38]

The election of a minority of démocrate-socialistes, and the geographical concentration of their support revealed, however, the existence of a 'red France'. Three areas can be identified in which they gained over 40 per cent of the votes cast, and 154 of 196 seats. These were the centre — west and the north of the Massif Central; the valleys of the Saône, and the Rhône and neighbouring areas — that is regions within the political and economic orbit of Lyon; and the Alsatian departments. A lesser degree of support was received (30-40 per cent of the votes and 41 seats of 170) in the Mediterranean departments, southern Aquitaine and the Pyrénées, and in the Nord. In contrast a large number of departments, particularly in the northeast, in the Paris region, Normandy and the west were barely touched by radical ideas.

A larger proportion of votes tended to be given to démocrate-socialiste candidates in towns than in the surrounding countryside. Even in small centres a middle class group usually existed with sufficient economic independence and familiarity with ideas to serve as militants. They seem to have enjoyed some success wherever the economic position or social influence of the traditional notables had declined, and where new notables drawn from the lower middle class and liberal professions could issue a challenge and gain popular support. Whatever his political label, the successful candidate needed normally to be a well-known personality — further evidence of the political immaturity of this newly enfranchised mass electorate.

It is not easy to relate political behaviour to socioeconomic structures. Similar structures bred varying political reactions. Peasant support for radicals seems to have been more common where small proprietors enjoyed far greater social independence than did sharecroppers, tenants and labourers. Artisans and tradesmen in the larger villages were more likely to vote for the left than were peasants, but exceptions to these statements are legion. Significantly much of the electorate, from indifference or rejection of the political game, failed to vote. Only 6,700,000 of 9,940,000 inscribed on the voting rolls actually participated.

As one would expect the result changed the social character of the Assembly. The predominance of grands notables there was restored, although not to the quasi-monopoly levels of the July Monarchy, because of the influence of middle class radicals. Of 715 deputies, 70-75 were moderate republicans, about 450 conservatives of the Party of Order, and 200-210 démocrate-socialistes. Contemporaries were struck less by the conservative success than by the election of a large minority of radicals. Conservatives were especially concerned at the radical vote of large numbers of peasants, a fact which appeared especially threatening to their social position, and which threw some doubt on the advisability of recurrent appeals to universal suffrage. In reaction to this the use for repression of the apparatus of the centralised state had growing appeal as the only means to curb the 'red menace'. Ideological and political divergences amongst conservative politicians, however, made it difficult for them to agree on an institutional framework for this policy, or to take political initiatives themselves. The President of the republic, controlling the administrative machine, police and army was thus increasingly able to seize the initiative, whilst the ability of parliament to control him was reduced by its internal divisions.[39]

One significant exception to this lack of parliamentary initiative was the electoral law of 31 May 1850 which by introducing new residence qualifications for enfranchisement, succeeded in disenfranchising a substantial portion of the electorate, especially of its urban component. This represented the growing conservative fear that control over the electorate was escaping them. In Paris on 13 June 1849, Ledru-Rollin and some of his démocrate-socialiste supporters had demonstrated in protest against French military intervention against the Roman Republic. The only real result was the removal of thirty deputies from the Assembly, but in the elections to replace these in March 1850, twenty-one démocrate-socialistes had been elected in spite of intense administrative pressure. The new law sought to prevent a repetition of this and constituted a great blow to démocrate-socialistes and their sympathisers who had seen in universal suffrage the vital means by which to reform society. The new restrictions were a major factor persuading reformers to shift from institutionalised politics towards extra-legal means.[40]

Solidarité Républicaine had been formed in November 1848 to organise and link republicans throughout France. Its initial leaders were radical deputies but gradually as they lost prestige due to their squabbles and ineffectiveness, and especially after June 1849 as government repression intensified and obstructed national organisation republicans became more of an extra-parliamentary opposition based on informal or illegal groups which were local in character. It is difficult to detect extra-local contacts at all, given the obvious need for secrecy at the time. What evidence exists suggests the predominant role of three centres of agitation — Paris, Lyon and Marseille.

The press was especially important in this organisational and propaganda network. Following a lull after the May 1849 electoral campaign, activity multiplied towards the end of 1849 when innumerable brochures and newspapers began to reach the countryside — from Paris for example *Le Peuple de 1850* edited by Proudhon and *Le Feuille du Village* by Joigneaux; from Marseille the influential *Le Peuple*. Journalists and local correspondents of the various newspapers not only supplied news and sold newspapers but established local republican groups and maintained contacts with groups elsewhere and particularly with the organisational centre provided by the editors of newspapers like *Le Peuple* or *L'Emancipation* of Toulouse.

The Parisian press was particularly important for supplying information and themes for agitation often reproduced in local newspapers. These, able to take part in the political battle which directly concerned the department, were more influential. Newspapers, often read aloud in workshops, cafés and private meetings, whose themes were further discussed at fairs and markets thus helped to maintain political interest amongst large segments of the community. Government repression designed to counter these influences whilst enjoying a certain degree of success also contributed to maintaining agitation.

Notwithstanding the efforts of men associated with the various newspapers repression was effective in localising the démocrate-socialiste movement. Each local group whilst aware of the themes of nationally presented propaganda had also its own local concerns and problems. Even within local groups there were obvious differences, often for example between the original middle class leadership — doctors, notaries, landowners, primary school teachers, etc. — influential because of their relative wealth, education, experience of the wider world and contacts, their leisure and individual energy, and the rank and file composed of artisans and peasants, some of whom as they gained experience assumed leadership roles. The former were characterised usually by a scrupulous practical legalism, which inevitably led to their sincerity being doubted.

As early as December 1848 the left wing press appears re-orientated from an often revolutionary concern with the urban social problem, that of the worker, to a reformist rural oriented socialism, belated recognition of the need, now that universal suffrage existed, to win over the peasantry. The themes of this propaganda were simple and appealing — free education, tax reform and especially cheap credit and an end to usury. Credit appealed to the hunger of peasants and artisans to acquire property and with it greater security, status and independence.

Land reform was to be achieved not by expropriating the rich but by the gradual accession of the poor to property. Although most republican deputies, confident of success in the general election due in 1852 recommended patience to their followers, repression led to exasperation encouraged by some of the more radical deputies who formed a breakaway group called the 'Nouvelle Montagne' and by exiles who believed it necessary to prepare resistance. Echoes of this, and attacks in the press against nobles, priests, usurers — the *blancs, gros bourgeois* — particularly in the south, generated considerable social fear. The dominant position of the notables was again clearly threatened.41

IX

In assessing the impact of political agitation upon rural societies it is incorrect to think of the peasantry as a unitary class. Peasants were differentiated both geographically and socially. Amongst them status tended to reflect the amount of land owned and the degree of independence this conferred. In many areas as population pressure on resources continued to grow in this initial period of economic modernisation the burden of debt and the common obsession with the problem indicated the insecurity of the rural population.

The politicisation of the countryside can be described best by combining the approach of the social anthropologist with that of the historian. It requires an analysis of village structures and their interpenetration by external forces. In spite of previous commercial development and the links this and other factors established between villages and the external world, the survival of traditional customs and particularly local linguistic forms was indicative of the continuing compartmentalisation of the national society. The community preserved its beliefs and values, and was for its members clearly differentiated from other communities by the peculiarities of its language and particularist sentiment. Despite class differentiation, strong bonds of community generally existed.

Within the village, the individual owed his place above all to the status of his family and to his place within that family. In a face to face community little about an individual's character was not known. It was impossible to ignore the established norms of behaviour, to escape the pressure to conform to the rules established for individuals with a recognised economic role and social status. Marriage within the locality, and the difficulty of establishing oneself elsewhere were powerful forces helping to preserve the inner coherence of the community.

Similar patterns of life created a certain basic unity within the village. There was, in addition, an intense awareness of links of relationship. Economic, social and even political necessities led to recognition of a large network of cousins, to kinship links which might be either reinforced or cut across by the existence of alternative groupings based on age, sex, occupation or cultural affinities.

These were elements of diversity within the community, their significance depending upon the wealth, socially recognised roles and consequent status of individuals and families. Within the community, although most roles were shared, the young especially contributed to the maintaining of social life, the adults dominated economic life, the old defined customary rules of conduct. Fundamental to social differentiation were gradations in wealth both amongst peasants and artisans and between them and the local notables — the larger landowners and the professional men.

Hostilities within the community were to an important extent sublimated by means of the ritualisation of violence according to traditional forms, in particular by the *charivari* including injurious songs and the parading of a straw effigy of the victim at carnival. These customary forms of protest were reluctantly accepted even by the notables and administration against whom they could be and were turned. Given the diffuseness of the policing network and the force of village solidarity particularly in the face of external authority, such means of maintaining conformity were necessary for the limitation of internal violence.

In its relations with the external world, especially the official world, the community was determined to preserve its autonomy. In resisting outside interference unity was increased at the expense of ever present internal discontent and conflict. Relationships with the external world were to a large degree controlled by notables, whose education and experience fitted them for this role. Their importance was magnified in regions where the dispersal of habitat, in the form of isolated hamlets with limited contacts between each other and diverging interests, reduced cohesion within the administrative unit whose interests notables could then represent with less possibility of being challenged. Due to the lack of alternative bonds of community the church often performed a vital cohesive role in such a situation and more generally, religiosity, not necessarily accompanied by actual church attendance was a vital element in popular culture. Communal cohesion was normally far greater where habitat was concentrated either as a large village or even the quarter of a town.

The intermediary role performed by the notables was a considerable source of power. To be performed it required that an individual have roots in two cultural universes — that of the village, and that of the external world. In *Madame Bovary* Flaubert describes a hierarchy of movement with aristocrats and grande bourgeoisie travelling abroad and to

Paris, the petite and moyenne bourgeoisie to Rouen the regional capital, whilst the poor remain generally restricted to the farmyard and village square. Thus most of the population, rooted in one culture, found it difficult to conceive of events other than in terms of the past. External events, described orally, were reduced to distorted rumours, and thus what occurred outside the locality was unimportant unless it directly impinged upon the community — as did taxation for example.

In political terms the structure of the village community and the norms by which a representative notable emerged generally determined a conservative orientation. The reverse might be true in a situation where instead of a relatively closed mental universe the existence of regular currents of trade or temporary migration established a more open society, many of whose members were familiar with the external world and capable of relating it to their own community, as well as of using ideas learnt elsewhere as a basis for the criticism of traditional customs and social relationships. As long as the village culture preserved enough autonomy to retain its vitality it was generally able to absorb external influences, but from the 1840s economic and social change was accelerating and adaptation becoming less easy. Even in the educationally more backward areas south of the line St Malo-Geneva, the growing standardisation of language and use of French rather than patois were key elements in this changing cultured universe. Increasingly the intermediary activity and political power of the traditional notables would be effectively challenged, particularly where articulate groups of individuals, often professional men, were prepared to give a lead in establishing the moral legitimacy of new models and codes of behaviour. This kind of situation was generally more likely to occur where the predominance of small and medium, rather than large properties gave a degree of economic independence to large proportions of the population.[42]

In towns and larger villages republican leaders were usually local notables, not as wealthy as the grands notables dominating the local conservatives, but with sufficient wealth to possess status in the community and justify claims to political authority. In the eyes of its lower class supporters such leadership gave an air of respectability to the movement. This was vital to the effective diffusion of political ideas and organisation. The leaders' own motives were no doubt diverse, ranging from poltical idealism to personal discontent and ambition.

Although there was a growing popular awareness of the connection between local problems and national politics — a process of politicisation which the advent of the republic had accelerated — it remained true that save in times of crisis like the June days regional and especially local concerns took precedence over the political preoccupations of Paris. Ideological debate often only cloaked struggles for power amongst notables. Factions defined themselves in terms of 'symbolic issues' and exploited local grievances to gain support. As long as these local conflicts did not threaten the authority of the state's local representatives they were not interfered with. Politics became a very different matter when reduced from the national to the local level. The electoral results concealed tensions between individuals and groups which the electoral process itself animated. Such factors as kinship, the degree of solidarity amongst the kin, and the allies and dependents upon whose support they could call became vital at the community level. Influential local families and their clients disputed local influence. It is not easy to determine what was due to personal rivalry and what to political opinion. In addition to rivalries within a community, traditional hostilities often existed between villages which were now expressed in political terms. Ted Margadent very effectively sums the situation up: 'Factionalism was a widespread phenomenon in local politics — it was the natural counterpart of a stratified social system whose upper and lower layer were bound together in "vertical" patron-client relationships rather than opposed to each other in "horizontal" class relations.' Even where particular social groups predominate within particular parties it is never possible to simply relate conflict to anatagonism between property owners and proletarians. Such antagonism exists but remains only one element amongst others causing political conflict. The appearance of factions was clearly more likely where the number of potential competitors was greatest, that is in towns and large market villages — in the concentrated habitat so common in the Midi for example.[43]

The difficulty of making political generalisations should be evident. So much depends upon local political conditions, which can be comprehended only in relation to a total economic, social and cultural background, and in relation to established traditions of behaviour and conflict. But in addition to long term economic and demographic developments, the character of political propaganda indicates popular concern with short term economic difficulties. Misery and discontent were common and became politically significant when the discontented were mobilised in support of a particular political orientation.

It was clearly easier to mobilise political support in an urban environment which allowed continual contacts between people, greater personal independence and with its newspapers, travellers, and the meeting places served as a centre of opinion and political activity. The Revolution in 1848 had been urban, spreading from Paris to the main towns of departments and *arrondissements* and then out into the countryside. Although repression, disillusionment and partial economic recovery reduced worker militancy in the larger industrial

44

centres, towns continued to serve as central places for the diffusion of ideas.

Even in a traditional economic system the exchange of products was important. With improvements in communications, production for the market, and the economic activity of a host of small market towns increased. More than ever before the village was integrated into a wider system of relations, a system which at this time, because of the continued shortcomings of the transport infrastructure, remained essentially localised, focused on a central place which provided adminstrative as well as commercial services.

The social contacts of the artisan and peasant were in general not limited to his village but drawn from the whole area a particular marketing centre served. An area defined not only by its economic interconnections but by a uniformity of language, and selection of marriage partners. People attended markets not only to buy and sell but for pleasure — to meet people to gossip. Regular contacts were thus established between people from different villages and additionally between social groups.[44] At market the bourgeoisie, artisans and peasants came into contact. Normally, as can be seen by the patterns of sociability in areas of southern France described by Maurice Agulhon, imitation of the practices of one social group by another occurred — the *cercles* of the bourgeoisie, their informal all male meetings, became the *chambrées* of the artisans and some peasants. Social innovation, including the spread of new political ideas, occurred to an important extent by means of inter-class diffusion which occurred in spite of tensions between social groups. Imitation and the patronage of the politically aware middle class elements were crucial to the transmission of republican and socialist ideas, and created amongst artisans and peasants in many areas a confused but positive ideal of the Republic. Margadant has shown how Montagnards in Béziers for example recruited support from men in nineteen other communes who came to market there.

Thus from the market towns with their complex social structures — their notables, members of the liberal professions, tradesmen, and artisans, their cafés and newspapers — artisans and peasants from smaller more isolated communities arrived home with more questioning attitudes to the society in which they lived, and with a growing belief that something ought to be done. A simplified hierarchy of diffusion can be drawn linking large cities like Lyon and Marseille — from which the radical newspaper *La Voix du Peuple* circulated throughout the southeast — to market towns and from these to smaller communes, to hamlets, and to isolated farms, with the gradual emergence at all levels of local leaders indicative of a gradual democratisation of local leadership, and also the dependence of a movement, fragmented by repression, upon the energy of these local men.[45]

A variety of factors determined how susceptible men were to

radical political ideas. To a large extent it was a question of culture. Where a traditional culture had been preserved more or less whole, particularly where firm religious faith affirmed the necessity of respect for those chosen by God to exercise authority, there seems to have been little room for political radicalism. Where respect for the church had declined this was often in places with relatively good communications more open to outside influences — the market centres. The traditional influence of a culture was also reduced by the spread of literacy particularly amongst the young, which had the added effect of reducing linguistic particularism and making contact with French speaking urban populations easier.

In the Var in 1850, democrats were dominant in most of the towns and market villages, but not in the isolated mountain villages, or in those along the coast which were less integrated into market systems, nor significantly in the more prosperous agricultural areas where the social predominance of paternalistic Legitimist landowners survived. Similarly in the Alpine region the small proprietors of the culturally backward mountain areas were not open to new ideas, those of the foothills and plains more sensible to economic difficulties, more dependent on the market, were more aware of social inequalities and more interested in radical political solutions. In both these areas the factors permitting mobilisation were economic depression, traditional economic grievances and cultural change of which politicisation was a part.

In parts of the Massif Central, large scale temporary migration took men to cities and especially Paris and Lyon, an experience which stimulated the process of cultural modernisation and helps explain the apparent paradox of economically backward, physically isolated regions, voting for the left. Migration, rather than the local market was the means by which money could be accumulated, and which incidentally provided access to alternative political ideas.[46]

Within the community, ideas could be communicated by means of the traditional forms of sociability. These gave vitality to a village otherwise composed of independent family units. Almost everywhere, after their day's work, men met in a workshop, at the blacksmith's forge or at the café. On winter evenings a mixed gathering — the *veillée* — was common. This associational life seems to have been particularly developed in parts of the Mediterranean region, in the larger villages where traditional forms of sociability existed far richer in character than in the concentrated villages of the Beauce or of Lorraine. This region was distinguished also by the degree of segregation of males from females in associational activity and by the existence in the larger, more commercially active settlements of a particular form of voluntary activity — the *chambrée* or *chambrette*. These imitations of the bourgeois private clubs — the *cercles* — united usually 20-25 members, drawn from the same social class, neighbourhood and age group. They met in a private room, often the backroom of a café and gave their members leisure free from their families, cheap drink and access to mutual favours, often including the cost of burial of its members and aid in case of sickness. Visits were frequently exchanged between members of various *chambrées* creating a network of friendship and solidarity. For 1847 it has been estimated that in the departments of Var, Basses-Alpes, Vaucluse, and Bouches-du-Rhône such gatherings had a minimum of 40,000 members.

Even before 1848 the expression of public approval or disapproval, in political as in other matters, had been a normal part of village life present in all forms of collective activity. In a period of more intense political activity, voluntary associations obviously contributed to the diffusion of ideas, and as repression increased provided ideal cover for political organisation. In Blois early in 1849 this function was performed for bourgeois republicans by a literary circle, at Montargis and Besançon by masonic lodges, in the Seine-et-Oise by popular choral societies, in Gâtinais mutual aid societies, in Limousin by the *veillée*. More generally the café served as an organisational centre where strangers, who might be police spies were immediately noticed amongst its habitual clientele.[47]

The weakness of the Montagnard movement was the fragmentation of its organisation, the lack of effective regional and national links. This too was the source of its strength. It was based locally upon pre-existing associations, upon friendship. Men joined these associations for leisure activity and mutual aid functions, both of which attracted members and strengthened the bonds of loyalty between them. Commitment was ensured by conformist social pressures and the threat of ostracism in a relatively small community. Whether or not these associations were created for overt political purposes, grievances against the existing order were likely to be expressed in them and politicisation often followed. Moreover the formal regulations of the typical *chambrée* constituted a valuable experience in organisation.

In terms of political mobilisation this was one feature distinguishing the Mediterranean region from other areas. Due to the concentrated habitat and existing forms of sociability it was possible to more effectively organise larger sections of the rural population, than in other areas of resistance to the *coup d'état* like the Gers and Lot-et-Garonne. This serves to lend emphasis to a basic point made by Agulhon — that if support for the democratic movement was due to the existence of a variety of economic, social and religious grievances and conflicts, the organisational forms which were possible in particular regions in large part dictated the character of their political activity.[48]

Growing repression, particularly after June 1849 stimulated modification of organisational forms by forcing activity underground. In many regions, secret societies were organised, sometimes successfully using the cover provided by existing voluntary associations, sometimes forced to organise independently of these when they became the object of police suspicion. Much of the information we have is based on police reports which tend to exaggerate the threat. In October 1850 they claimed to have uncovered a vast conspiracy associated with some of the more radical Montagnard leaders like Alphonse Gent, which was supposed to be planning an uprising in fourteen departments in the southeast. It is doubtful if an uprising was planned but probable that an organisational network had been developed. A dialectic of organisation, repression and sometimes reorganisation occurred and secret societies proliferated throughout the countryside of the centre, southwest and southeast — spreading outwards from numerous market towns privileged by their superior communications with major regional centres, organised by local militants relying on oral propaganda and a wave of seditious literature. The chronology and the effectiveness of the process varied according to the energy of local militants and the effectiveness of repression. Organisations were established in many localities only after they had died in neighbouring towns.

The tradition of political conspiracy which had evolved during the July Monarchy and earlier — in the south the form of the *carbonari* — combined with ceremonials and organisations borrowed from freemasonry and the artisanal *compagnonnages* to provide models for underground organisation, which together with communal solidarity offered some guarantees against police infiltration. Typically at village level leadership devolved on a youthful representative of the liberal professions, and on some of the more substantial peasants, merchants and artisans, particularly where relatively egalitarian social structures allowed influence to leaders close to the people rather than the traditional notables. Membership would clearly vary according to the social composition of the particular area and normally included only a minority of the adult males but most of the young men, especially in villages where they traditionally acted to protect the collective interest of the community.

A whole range of grievances stimulated political activity, often continuing an old tradition of conflict. Protestants formed the core of support in departments like Gard and Ardèche where factional conflict during the first Revolution and the White Terrors had been particularly intense. Besides such established sociopolitical loyalties the Montagnard programme of social and economic reform was an obvious attraction. Hatred of usurers and tax collectors associated hostility to the exploiting bourgeoisie and to the repressive state.

On tactical questions clear divisions existed amongst Montagnard leadership, between those who enjoined caution to avoid justifying a preventative *coup d'état* by the authorities before the 1852 elections, and those who saw a need to be ready to combat such a possibility. The electoral law of May 1850 was important in shifting the balance toward the latter. Prior to this, confidence had been growing in the possibility of gaining power through the ballot box in spite of repressive political conditions. Now a substantial reduction in the electorate made this less likely. Paradoxically, Montagnards prepared, not mass insurrection on a national scale, but to fully implement universal suffrage in their localities in 1852, by use of force if necessary. They continued to expect a decisive victory at the polls in May 1852 and pinned their hopes for social reform upon this. This anti-democratic legislation did however further stimulate the organisation of conspiratorial networks, so that according to Margadant's estimates by the eve of the *coup* some 700 communes had Montagnard organisations in some form, including about 500 in the southeast, 150 in the centre, and 50 to 100 in the southwest, with in all 50-100,000 members throughout the nation — 'by far the largest conspiratorial movement in nineteenth century France'.[49]

In spite of localism, factionalism, the political immaturity of the masses and government repression, a mass political organisation had been created which participated in a political struggle whose victors would assume control of France. This was more than a series of local struggles — Montagnard organisation, the struggle against repression, and the pursuance of particular goals, the significance of these symbolic issues for both conservatives and radicals served to simplify and polarise the conflict. This process was in effect a sign of the slow transformation of social structures, and the slow growth of political awareness. Conversely it represented the decline of traditional cultures and of habitual subordination as part of a process of modernisation spreading from the towns with the development of mass communications and the intensification of commerce.

X

The slowness with which structures were changing and the even slower transformation of old habits of obedience, meant that in the northern half of France in particular the authority of the traditional notables continued to be recognised. A whole complex of factors combined to produce this result — in areas of technically relatively advanced large scale farming, labourers benefited from low food prices and were less likely to be subject to land and drink taxes than peasants in regions of small scale property. They lived in societies polarised by major differences in wealth, and more hierarchical in character, lacking often the independent artisan and middle class elements essential to the process of cultural diffusion and in which autonomous voluntary associations like the southern *chambrée* do not appear to have taken root. The café lacking the formal regulation of the *chambrée* was less suitable to the work of political propaganda and organisation. Elsewhere, especially in the Breton west the vitality of the traditional culture and especially of religion within it helped to prevent new ideals take root. In departments of the Paris region like Seine-et-Oise, Seine-et-Marne or Marne, unity was conferred on the rural community by a common fear of 'reds', the 'communists' in nearby Paris or Reims. A basic contrast thus existed between societies with a hierarchical structure in which patron-client relationships predominated, and others with more egalitarian structures which permitted the spread of radical ideas. The Party of Order as it took shape was thus able to exploit the fears and ignorance of large numbers of people in all social groups. The political inexperience of the masses can be gauged from the frequent voting for local personalities whatever their political label. If the theory of universal suffrage implies a rational and independently meditated choice by voters the practice was generally very different. Although lacking the kind of organisation typical of modern political parties, the Party of Order, due to the wealth, prestige and influence of its individual members, was able to retain its dominant political position.

1848 had been a considerable shock, and things would never be quite the same again. Revolution had made conservative notables more aware of the interests they had in common. A sense of social solidarity tended to replace former geographical and ideological antagonisms. Formerly dissatisfied middle class liberals, especially in commercial and industrial circles, lived in horror of social revolution, and desired security at all costs. Orléanists and Legitimists allied to defend social order. In this new situation in which their joint social eminence was under attack their outlook on society tended to change – the liberalism of the one, and the traditionalism of the other fused. Few republicans actually attacked the existence of private property, nevertheless conservatives believed that this, the basis of their society, was threatened. Furthermore, they assumed that only individuals motivated by envy and greed could attack what they conceived of as timeless and sacred values. Their explanation of the démocrate-socialiste challenge to their political supremacy remained thus essentially pathological. Given the conservative social and political stance of the Catholic church, it had inevitably been subject to considerable criticism by radicals, which appeared to confirm conservative fears about the growth of atheism. The Holy Trinity of Property, Family and Religion had thus to be defended and 'moral order' to be restored. In this work it would clearly be necessary to influence men's minds as well as to destroy radical organisation. Thus the clergy assumed a major place in conservative ideology, accepted by formerly anticlerical liberals as well as Legitimists. The priest and the soldier became the foundations upon which social order might be restored and the nightmarish vision of 1852 destroyed.[50]

The system of primary education established by the Guizot Law of 1833 had recognised existing social divisions. It sought to provide the masses with an education impregnated with the precepts of morality and obedience, which would fit their lowly place in the social order, quite different from the largely classical culture which was the hallmark of a notable. This confirmed the enormous cultural gulf, which reflected and helped to maintain class differences.

Already before 1833, there had been striking regional inequalities in literacy. To the north of a line St Malo-Geneva, primary education was relatively advanced, to the south backward but with higher levels of literacy in the southeast — the Alps, and Rhône Valley — than in the southwest. Contrasts also existed between urban areas, and agricultural regions more actively involved in commerce, and economically more stagnant zones; between places with Protestant populations, where Catholics too would possess relatively high levels of literacy because of a spirit of emulation, and those without mixed religious populations. Significantly it does seem that it was precisely this kind of commune in the southeast — engaged in commerce, with Protestants present, which due perhaps to the combination of relatively high levels of literacy and good road links tended to have a high level of political awareness. The reduction of linguistic and cultural isolation appears to have been, in most places, a basic prerequisite for an involvement in national politics.

Conservatives generally established a more simple connection between education and politicisation. With evidence of the activity of the relatively few primary school teachers who became active republican militants before their eyes, they tended to see the existing system of primary education as a threat to society. Teachers were accused of spreading socialism instead of preaching resignation to God's will. Once universal male suffrage had been recognised the significance of the *instituteur* seemed greatly enlarged. Carnot, the Minister of Education in the Provisional Government in 1848, had proposed to establish free and obligatory education, and every statement by the left on education appeared to confirm conservative fears that a struggle to control the minds of the young was underway.

Although most teachers were already dominated by the local authorities and behaved with respectful deference towards priest and mayor, even bourgeois anticlericals now felt a need to intensify control, and to ensure that sound moral and religious principles were taught. The education laws of 11 January and 15 March 1850 sought to intensify administrative surveillance of the teacher, to increase the number of priests engaged in teaching by ending the need for them to prove their ability to teach, and increased the participation of bishops in the higher administration of the educational system.[51]

Such measures reflected the deformed vision of religion held by the ruling notables, which combined sincere faith in many cases with the belief that religion was the main safeguard of social order. Religion was impregnated, in inseparable fashion into their general cultural outlook, just indeed as it was for most of the population, though with varying degrees of intensity depending on long established social structures and traditions. Thus in most of Brittany religious faith and the prestige of the clergy were strong, and the Church with its more tolerant attitudes towards popular beliefs and superstitions was in the nineteenth century able to maintain the faith. Here priests were frequently able to assume decisive roles in politics once a mass electorate had been created. The majority of priests preached a religion of fear in which God's judgement and eternal damnation for the sins of this world loomed very large. They blamed dechristianisation for revolution, materialism, and for the blasphemous notion of human equality. In daily life the lust of the peasant for land, the moral disorder propagated by the cabaret, by seasonal migration, and by the *veillée* were all to be condemned, but perhaps the human weakness which awoke an obsessive interest and the most concern on the part of the priest was sexual behaviour. The priest was in a very delicate position. He needed at least to appear to live up to his ideals. His position resulted in social isolation and a feeling of insecurity for which the main compensating factors were an awareness of his own moral superiority, the authoritarian direction of his flock, and in order to prevent further Revolution and its accompanying moral decay, alliance with the principal advocates of social order, the wealthy, upon whose material aid and influence, the success of his parish activity often depended.

In regions in which historically respect for the clergy had not always been too great, in places in which the authority of individual priests was rejected, in towns and villages in which the traditional culture and religion as an aspect of it were in decay, or where the consolation which the priests offered to the miserable, was not sufficient to deny the new hopes offered by the Montagnards, in much of the south where old vendettas opposed Protestants and many liberals to the association of Legitimists with the Catholic church, conflict developed around this whole question of the role of the church in society so that measures designed to further the church's aims in combination with the defence of social order generated opposition which rendered the original objectives in large part self-defeating.[52] Due to this and the fact that moralisation through church and school must anyway be a long term objective, the defence of the social *status quo* had then to take on less subtle forms, which were also, at least physically, more brutal.

Stricter controls on political activity were imposed even before the June insurrection in 1848. Subsequently they became even more repressive, so that by the summer of 1849 legal Montagnard propaganda and organisation were subject to so many forms of interference that it was difficult for them to continue to exist. The removal of mayors, and National Guard officers, suspensions of municipal councils, closures of masonic lodges, *cercles* and cafés, the persecution and harassment of the press and of individuals, including deputies suspected of acting as organisational links between Paris and their constituencies, all contributed towards the creation of an atmosphere of terror. Even the wearing of red scarves or dresses became suspect, while the symbolic action associated with carnival became intolerable. Many erstwhile democrats were frightened into inactivity, others into increased secrecy. To a large extent the whole shape of the démocrate-socialiste movement was being determined by the vigour of and the need to respond to police repression.

During the July Monarchy when politics had been restricted to an elite such widespread measures had been unnecessary, but with the advent of universal suffrage France entered a new political age in which to defend itself against the untoward effects of democracy the old elite was prepared to support the deployment of all the coercive force at the disposal of the state. This dependence of the notables on the state heralded a major change in the balance of power within French society. During the July Monarchy the administration had depended upon the support of the local notables both in parliament and at local level. Now, in a potentially revolutionary situation, provided the state guaranteed their economic power and social status the notables were prepared to accept centralisation and reinforcement of the power of the state.

Upper class recruitment of senior administrators and army officers guaranteed the dependability of the state machine. Landowners were still drawn into those professions which offered increased social status and power rather than business which continued to imply *dérogéance* as before 1789. Thus an administration dominated by landowners sought to secure its control over France. Prefects, procureur-généraux, and generals at the head of their respective hierarchies controlled a massive and dependable machine, which, in most localities, enjoyed the enthusiastic support of local landowners serving as mayors and justices of the peace. Due to the slowness of communications these officials enjoyed considerable initiative, being forced to take decisions in matters which they would in later years refer to Paris. That, in relation to the political question, they shared the common opinions of their class of origin can be seen in the general repetition of these views in their reports, and in their readiness to see conspiracies, even where none existed. It should not however be ignored that in spite of facilitating legislation and the arbitrariness of the prefectoral administration a check was imposed on the intensity of repression both by public opinion and the concern of the legal administration headed by the procureur-généraux to ensure that the rule of law survived.

Due both to the limited effectiveness of centralised controls, and the frequent incompetence of local police, repression depended on use of the army — both of gendarmerie and regular forces. Such action was inevitably harsh but even so rarely resulted in violence. Intimidation was its normal aim. To ensure the government a continued monopoly of the armed forces, in October-November 1851 the remaining units of the National Guard were disarmed and great concern was inevitably caused by continuous démocrate-socialiste efforts to win the sympathies of soldiers.

As already observed, the electoral law of 1850 introduced after frightening radical electoral successes represented a major step in the intensification of repression and also in the replacement of open by conspiratorial politics on the left. By means of stricter residential qualifications, complicated procedures and advice to mayors to be selective in accepting registration the number of electors was reduced from around 9,600,000 to 6,800,000, with the proportionate reduction being far higher in the urban centres of democratic voting strength than in the mainly conservative countryside.

This repressive activity enjoyed considerable success — frightening, discouraging, and in the last resort arresting adversaries. Rural populations often with only tenuous links with urban based militants soon fell away. In Limousin, for example, it was far more difficult to maintain organisation amongst the dispersed population of Creuse than in Limoges. Elsewhere repression was often more effective in the towns than in the countryside because a more numerous police and military presence could be maintained and surveillance easily intensified. Thus in the winter of 1850-1 after the discovery of the Lyon plot republican municipal officials were dismissed, and *cercles* closed in places like Nîmes, Anduze and Sauve in Gard. Where conditions were favourable démocrate-socialiste organisations, particularly secret societies, developed in the countryside rather than in the town. Repression was particularly successful in dismantling inter-regional links. Contacts with regional capitals and with Paris, even with departmental centres, were frequently broken. Démocrate-socialiste organisational networks became increasingly localised and with this the possibility of organising a national movement became remote.

In some regions the discontent, the effectiveness of Montagnard organisation and propaganda, its use of traditional forms of sociability,

54

communal solidarity, conservative factional division and the ineffectiveness of overstretched military resources allowed secret societies to
survive and increased a determination to seek revenge. The limits to the
success of repression are evident in the scale, but also the geographical
setting of resistance to the *coup*. In Limousin, repression was almost
complete before the *coup*. In most areas democratic strength had never
posed a threat. Everywhere the *coup* finally broke the vicious circle of
intensification of repression — organisation of resistance. It was the
final decisive intensification of repression, recognition that success depended upon the at least temporary removal of restraints on the forces
responsible for the maintenance of social order, and that influential
public opinion obsessed with fear of social revolution would support
the necessary moves. Louis-Napoleon could thus seize personal power
whilst posing as the saviour of society.[53]

As the presidential and legislative elections of 1852 came closer, and
as manifestations of republican confidence became more apparent, an
irrational fear spread amongst conservatives. Economic difficulties,
social tensions and political conflicts, an uncertain future in which a
new Terror and peasant *jacquerie* loomed large, persuaded them of the
utility of a military dictatorship. They were disillusioned with the
conservative republic. In July 1851, 446 deputies supported revision of
the constitution to provide for an extension of the term of office of the
President, whom existing constitutional provisions excluded from
another term of office. This was not the two thirds majority required
for revision. From this point Louis-Napoleon could only avoid a return
to private life by means of unconstitutional action.

Once he had secured control over the levers of military command by
placing the ambitious Saint-Arnaud in the War Ministry Louis-Napoleon
was able to act. Key positions in the civil bureaucracy had also been
assumed by his supporters. Although there were relatively few Bonapartists amongst senior members of the administration or officer corps
almost all would obey orders. The Assembly had already shown its un-
willingness to risk a political crisis by disputing the President's control
of the army, both in the case of the dismissal by Louis-Napoleon of
General Changarnier, a monarchist conservatives had trusted, and over
the proposition that it could requisition troops for its own defence.[54]
Opinion in the country was generally antiparliamentarian; and in most
areas dominated by those who desired social order. The President had
throughout 1850 and 1851 in speeches and by means of provincial
tours presented himself as the potential saviour, as a living promise of
good things to all men, only frustrated in his intentions by a squabbling
indecisive Assembly.

On 2 December the *coup* occurred — decapitating potential centres
of resistance particularly in the larger towns, by means of preventive

arrests. These did not spare leading conservative parliamentarians although their subsequent treatment was to be gentler than that which democratic opponents would receive. Some potential opposition on the left was disarmed by proclaiming the restoration of universal suffrage, and even by the dissolution of the conservative, monarchist dominated Assembly for most of whose members neither the poor, nor the democrats, could be expected to have much sympathy. But rather than an anti-royalist *coup*, most of the measures taken signified a preventive assault against democratic organisations. More than anything else this was the culminating act in a long period of repression.

It did however provoke serious resistance, and this in rural areas of the centre, southwest and especially southeast, rather than in the towns. In Paris on 3 December barricades were constructed in the usual areas of insurrection – in the Quartier du Temple, the rues Transnonain, Rambuteau, St Martin, etc. – generally in close proximity to the Hôtel-de-ville. Earlier reverses, economic depression, lack of sympathy for the Assembly, the positive appeal of Louis-Napoleon, and general apathy all contributed to restricting participation to around 1,000-1,200 militants, mainly workers who answered the call of a *Comité Central des Corporations*. The rapid crushing of this, together with a seemingly accidental fusillade which caused heavy casualties amongst jeering middle class spectators on the boulevards discouraged resistance. In Paris, Lyon, Marseille, and indeed in most departmental and *arrondissement* administrative centres the presence of a garrison, obviously prepared to meet trouble, was enough to dissuade possible resistants. The disorganisation caused by preventive arrests destroyed the remnants of nationwide organisation and a chain of command based on deputies in Paris which might have mobilised and coordinated action. To the many democrats who insisted on waiting for a lead from Paris, inspiration never came. The urban-rural linkage which democrats had attempted to create had either been destroyed, or because of military and police pressure could not now be activated. At best, the tenuous links between such centres as Toulouse or Béziers or Orléans and the surrounding countryside were rendered in large part inoperative.[55]

If the larger towns did not move, the countryside did – in the centre, insurrection occurred at Clamecy on 5 December following an appeal by middle class republicans to defend the republic, and spread into the nearby countryside in Nièvre, Yonne and Loiret. In the southwest more widespread risings occurred in Lot-et-Garonne and especially in Gers in response to an appeal from the editors of the newspaper *Ami du Peuple*. Thousands of peasants occupied Auch and Mirande. Less significant movements occurred in Dordogne, Aveyron, and Tarn-et-Garonne. The southeast was the major zone of reistance, with the administration losing control of the entire department of Basses-Alpes to a

Comité départmental de résistance established at Digne and connected with local committees. In Drôme on 6-7 December, 5-6,000 peasants attempted to occupy Crest and in Var too resistance on a similar scale occurred, with significant if less widespread activity in Ardèche, Gard, Hérault and Vaucluse. Elsewhere there were only isolated movements, for example at La Suze (Sarthe) and Poligny (Jura) or minor disorders, as at Anzin (Nord) or pacific meetings.

There seems to have been relatively little geographical continuity between the localities of insurrection and those in which economic protest had occurred in 1848 or in which protest had occurred against the 45 centime tax. Many communes which had voted for democrats in 1849 were clearly not involved in resistance, for all manner of reasons, including the overwhelming presence of troops, a decline in commitment due to repression or disillusionment, the appeal of a Bonapartist solution to their problems, and obviously because insurrection demands a different kind of commitment from voting. An isolated location in a region of hill, forest or *bocage* rather than an open plain with good roads encouraged the belief that a military reaction might not be forthcoming. Equally significant were the prevailing levels of economic discontent and social tension. Thus a number of inter-related factors contributed to determining both the intensity of the will to resist and the practical possibility. Insurrection occurred primarily in small market towns where an exceptional leader, discontent, and the ease with which the few local gendarmes could be overwhelmed encouraged mobilisation.

Population structure in such towns and villages varied between regions. The concentrated villages of the southeast, typically, had a larger proportion of peasants among their residents than market centres in the centre and southwest where many peasants lived in dispersed hamlets, and thus a larger proportion of the insurgents were peasants rather than artisans. In Var however the picture is more complicated, with larger groups of insurgents being provided by villages with relatively homogeneous social structures and a clearly defined common interest — thus the cork workers of La Garde-Freinet with old grievances against their employers and the poor peasants of the northwest of the department long engaged in conflict over rights of usage in the forests of that zone. In the southwest artisans were more likely to predominate — in Tarn for example there was a preponderance of rural textile workers amongst the insurgents.

As one would expect from the traditional role of the young in protecting the community's interests, they rather than their fathers took part in the insurrection. The sons of property owners, and labourers were more active than property owners themselves. The latter were probably less committed to village sociability than the young (or old) men, and more conscious of their family responsibilities. The possession of property whilst giving a certain economic independence also engendered caution and moderation in its possessors.[56]

The role of the middle class elements and of artisans in the diffusion of ideas and organisation has been stressed. It was inevitable therefore that individuals from these groups assumed important leadership roles in the resistance to the *coup*. Often however bourgeois leaders recoiled in face of a decision which would have unleashed forces they were afraid they might be unable to control. There was frequent suspicion tinged with contempt on the part of these 'Messieurs' for the poor and for, in their eyes, the excessively materialistic peasants and artisans to whom they had generally promised so much, in order to persuade them to join secret societies. This fear of *jacquerie* which they shared with conservatives became a good reason for inaction, even where the absence of the military made action possible.[57]

More committed or adventurous leaders followed a fairly homogeneous course of action. Once news of the *coup* reached towns on the major roads, messengers were sent by local *démocrate-socialiste* leaders to supporters in nearby villages. Significantly, the decision to call on militants in Vaucluse to resist was taken at Manosque fair on 6 December where most delegates from the surrounding areas would have been present. The pattern of mobilisation, following that of organisation, tended to correspond to economic and social links created by attendance at market, but with the networks created by militants from such regional centres as Marseille and Toulouse imposed imperfectly upon this. The rapidity with which mobilisation occurred and the numbers involved can only be explained by the existence of a network of Montagnard societies. These, in their various forms, seem to have existed in all areas of insurrection. Not all insurgents belonged to secret societies, but those who did not were generally grouped together with kin, friends and neighbours in a *chambrée*, or a mutual aid society or more loosely in a patron-client type of relationship, all of which served the same political purpose.

In mobilising resistance to the *coup* the prior politicisation of traditional forms of sociability proved invaluable. Everyday ties of dependence, or of friendship together with relative homogeneity of conditions of existence served to establish solidarity, unanimity and a collective response on the part of the community and especially that age group which normally represented the collective interest. In this situation it was hardly necessary for more than a small elite, probably composed of the more literate artisans and young peasants, to have acquired a political awareness in order to mobilise a community, the majority of whose members remained bound within a traditional cultural universe.[58]

The movement almost everywhere began as a municipal revolution.

The sitting councillors either joined the insurgents or were deposed. The article of the constitution which deposed the President of the Republic himself for unconstitutional action was thus applied to his supporters. From the village the plan was then to march to *arrondissement* and departmental administrative centres to seize control in these. The insurgents believed that this was both legitimate action in itself, and that by gaining control of the administration they would further legitimise their activity. The first problems arose where gendarmes resisted disarmament, and violence occurred at village level, possibly involving the paying off of old scores against the representatives par excellence of centralised authority in rural France. The second problem occurred when the small garrisons, combined with armed officials and bourgeois in the larger administrative centres resisted the groups of artisans and peasants moving in from the countryside to reinforce democrats in these centres themselves. At this point the level of violence was raised.[59]

What were all these people protesting about? One wonders how important political ideology was to the mass of artisans and peasants. No doubt egalitarian principles had considerable appeal but one suspects that this was essentially due to their association with pressing economic and social grievances. These originated in hunger amongst the unemployed, and those with inadequate monetary resources to provide for the basic needs of their families even during a period of relatively low food prices. After a series of good harvests this problem in most areas was far less serious than it had been in 1846-7 or even 1848. But low cereal prices, the depressed condition of the wine and *eaux de vie*, and timber markets and diseased silkworms combined to reduce farm incomes, resulting in a reduction of the employment of labourers, and in the demand for artisanal products. Thus many labourers, artisans and property owning peasants were attracted by démocrate-socialiste promises of tax reform and cheap credit. There was considerable anxiety about the possibility of seizure of one's goods for non-repayment of debt. Even if in a depressed economic situation creditors were likely to be less pressing, fear of expropriation remained a potent force. In comparison with areas in Northern France in which industrial development had already begun to relieve pressure on the land by inducing migration, population pressure on resources, resulting in parcellation of land, high land prices, debt, and overabundant labour supply were more likely to be problems in the south. These characteristics of the economic situation combine to suggest that the areas experiencing the greatest difficulty during this period were those normally heavily engaged in and dependent upon commercial activity, which sold cash crops primarily in order to purchase foodstuffs and pay taxes.[60]

The facilities available for the diffusion of ideas made it likely that politicisation could occur in areas where substantial popular discontent was combined with relative openness to outside influence. Clearly the active market centre fits this requirement. Ted Margadant has sought to systematically examine this relationship and considers that if the local economies of rebel districts varied in character, most were heavily engaged in production for the market. Their activities ranged from silk cultivation in Drôme, Ardèche and Gard, vine cultivation in much of Languedoc and Provence, to cork making at La Garde Freinet and tanning at Barjols (Var), and the timber trade in insurgent areas of the Nièvre, Yonne and Loiret. Significantly in the Basses-Alpes the insurgent areas were the economically better off areas in the southwest of the department rather than the desperately poor mountain villages. Market towns with their hinterlands, their economically dependent zones, were the bases for revolt. In most of these areas, a significant proportion of the population enjoyed some social independence due to landownership or else the genuine possibility of acceding to it by inheritance or purchase. Social structure was far less hierarchical in character than in parts of the Paris region for example, the dependence of poor on rich less marked, although poverty and exploitation meant that social tensions survived, particularly amongst the woodcutters and the labourers of the wine producing regions.

Discontent, and even social hatreds are clearly not sufficient causes of political organisation. They are facilitating factors. They caused unrest but no simple correlation exists between areas of economic distress, and those of politicisation, much less of insurrection. Political mobilisation depends upon a social context which facilitates the diffusion of ideas and the organisation of the discontented part of the population. It remains nonetheless true that the success of démocrate-socialiste propaganda directed at artisans and peasants depended upon its simple appeal to material interests. The *Comité de Résistance* of Basses-Alpes which had time to put into practice some of the promises made thus abolished direct taxes and burnt the tax records, the *Comité démocrate républicain* of the commune of Beaumont (Vaucluse) proclaimed the abolition of usury, free education and the division of communal property amongst the poor. It was for the *République des Petits*, the *République des Paysans* that the masses fought — for a more egalitarian society in which there would be no more poverty, exploitation or notables. Bourgeois leaders might stress the political objectives of the movement, but it was the social content of their propaganda which had attracted peasants and artisans over the past three years, and which now, at least in its early stages, created a fanaticism which threatened to exceed their capacity to control.[61]

The insurrection was thus both an attempt to seize control of the state, and a more primitive social revolt expressing resentment against the rich and the bureaucracy which supported them. Insurgents were not class conscious social revolutionaries. They were poor men in a difficult economic situation demanding some guarantees that their economic position in the existing social system would be protected, and that they should be given greater opportunities to improve themselves. The more politically committed — the lawyer, doctor, shopkeeper, *et al* — shared their resentment of the traditional local elites of the grands notables. They demanded greater economic opportunity, and a more democratic political system. Their demands were clearly more formalised than those of the mass of participants.

If the strength of démocrate-socialiste organisation lay in its social roots, excessive localisation was its fundamental weakness. In many areas like the Limousin only isolated fragments of organisation had survived the years of repression. A series of uncoordinated local risings was doomed to failure. Men were mobilised when local leaders heard the news of the *coup*, by which time in more accessible areas revolt had already been crushed. Initially insurgents seem to have been full of confidence, believing that the army would not fire on them. On 9 December, in Basses-Alpes, 3-4,000 insurgents forced regular troops to retire at the *défile des Mées*, but then on hearing of the success of the *coup d'état* elsewhere, becoming aware that the whole of France was not with them as they had previously presumed, their morale collapsed, and resistance was replaced by a desperate desire to reach home and safety. Not until 15 December was Barcelonette reoccupied by the army, but the delay was due only to its isolation. The insurrection had already collapsed. Only the manhunt continued.62

Until a decree of 27 March 1852 restored ordinary laws and judicial procedures a state of siege was declared to exist in over thirty departments, and by thus introducing military law the normal restraints on police actions were removed, most notably by the power given on 2 December to shoot immediately insurgents caught with arms in hand. The work of systematic repression was further facilitated by a series of decrees designed to enable the government to finally put an end to the period of unrest commencing in 1848.

To ensure the loyal cooperation of the administration it was purged. In Ain 446 mayors and their deputies were replaced, in Hérault 22 municipal councils dissolved. This process was authorised formally only on 13 December, but prior to this prefects had not hesitated to remove officials at all levels on whom they could not rely. This action too represented the culmination of a long established policy. The government's desire to control the local roots of politics was more effectively emphasised by the control it assumed through the 1852 constitution over the appointment of mayors and their deputies.

The establishment of an effective authoritarian regime also required control over the press. Circulars of 6 December and 13 December 1851 empowered prefects to suspend or suppress newspapers at will and required editors to submit their proofs for approval. A decree of 31 December transferred press cases from assize to correctional courts. This removed them from the competence of juries which were judged too likely to be sympathetic. Eighty-seven newspapers in seventy-nine departments were suppressed. Fourteen in Paris also disappeared, and to these must be added the numerous newspapers forced out of existence since 1848. If a large and disparate press survived, hardly any of the survivors were republican, and all would be extremely restrained in their criticism of the regime for many years to come.

Obviously aware of the importance of associations of various kinds in the mobilisation of resistance to the *coup* the administration struck hard at them. In addition to a decree of 8 December directed against secret societies the local manifestations of sociability were attacked. In Var, under the state of siege, *chambrées* were banned; in Limoges workers mutual aid associations dissolved. In a largely unsuccessful attempt to prevent the members of these groups simply transferring their meetings to the nearest café a decree of 25 March 1852 and law of 29 December 1851 sought to regulate more closely all forms of public association, and assembly including public drinking places.

But in addition to providing an opportunity for the introduction of a more repressive legal framework for government activity the *coup* and insurrection provided an opportunity to arrest republicans and destroy democratic organisation throughout France, and not simply in regions in which uprisings had occurred. It appears to have been generally believed that the insurrection was only the discovered portion of a more massive uprising planned for 1852 which had prematurely exploded in response to the preventive measures of the government. This justified the arrest of militants even though they had not participated in insurrection. Guilt did not need to be proved, suspicion sufficed. Arrests were most numerous in areas where insurrection had taken place. Here they occurred in an atmosphere of suspicion and fear, as mobile military columns scoured the countryside for republicans, and innumerable, usually anonymous, denunciations reflecting personal or factional hostilities poured into the authorities. In Hérault for example where 2,066 individuals were prosecuted, over 60,000 were denounced. Arbitrariness and brutality were the chief charactersitics of this process. Blame had to be apportioned but this often reflected the balance of local influences, the good will or degree of competence of local officials, or more creditably the continual influence on administrative behaviour of long established codes of practice. The intensity of repression thus varied considerably from place to place, and the insurgent rank and file soon began to benefit from large scale clemencies favoured by a Louis-Napoleon perhaps somewhat horrified by the consequences of his *coup*.[63]

XI

Generally conservatives welcomed the *coup* if with misgivings. The insurrections seemed to confirm government propaganda, and their own fears, about the red menace in 1852. Louis-Napoleon did appear to be the saviour of society. Some discontent was registered amongst Orléanist sympathisers due to the arrest and temporary exile of Parliamentary leaders like Thiers. Indeed eight prefects resigned for this reason, although they do not seem to have been reluctant to direct the repression of republicans until their successors arrived. Some Legitimists, especially in the west where the red menace had never been very real did not disguise their hostility. Many abstained in the subsequent plebiscite, but their influence on the mass vote was limited by the enthusiasm of most of the clergy and lay clericals. The church by means of solemn *Te Deums* publically celebrated the *coup*.

The plebiscite held on 20-21 December 1851 intended to legitimise the extraordinary measures taken indicated, regardless of official pressure, that a large majority of Frenchmen approved of, or at least accepted these measures. A year later the re-establishment of the Empire would receive even greater support. The restoration of business confidence once political uncertainty had ended contributed to the establishment of more prosperous conditions, which together with the crushing of opposition helped maintain a state of indifference to political affairs.

This quiescence could not be preserved for ever. Many of those who, in their desire for social order, rallied to the new regime did so only conditionally. When the danger had passed so their loyalty would waver. The Second Empire would, because of its origins be very much the prisoner of those political groups of notables whose local political influence and positions in the administration continued to give them considerable authority. The *coup d'état*, in permanently alienating most republicans and non-party intellectuals, restricted the field of recruitment of political cadres and made an opening to the left effectively impossible.[64]

The prosperous years of the Second Empire made it easier to retain the support of most of the rural population. In the 1869 elections even the Basses-Alpes elected a government candidate. Emigration removed many of the younger more discontented elements and together with economic growth helped ease population pressure on resources. Wages were higher, land easier to obtain. Even so substantial opposition survived in the countryside – in the eastern part of Côte d'Or, southern Doubs, northern Jura, the Saône, and Rhône valleys and that of the

63

Garonne, and in the coastal regions of Provence and Languedoc. In these areas memories of the repression of 1851 died hard. More generally small groups of republican sympathisers continued to exist especially in the market towns, and were still able to meet regularly in various voluntary associations or more informally. When the Empire collapsed they would provide a firm basis for the establishment of republican influence throughout the countryside.[65]

In other respects much had changed by the 1870s. The establishment of a railway network was a major factor in stimulating a process of economic development, which provided more employment opportunities and reduced the feeling of desperation which had mobilised so many people during the Second Republic. The insurrection in 1851 could be seen as the last great movement of protest by people heavily engaged in commercial production, yet, in terms of their social relationships and patterns of behaviour remaining members of traditional, pre-industrial rural communities. Subsequently the process of modernisation would substantially alter political behaviour. Its focus would move more decisively from the countryside to the rapidly expanding towns, whilst urban norms and values became universal. Its forms would become more institutionalised as the habit of relying on universal suffrage as a means of expressing discontent and demands took firmer root.

Notes

Save where stated, books in French were published in Paris, and those in English in London.

1.   A. Jardin, A.-J. Tudesq, *La France des Notables* I 1973, p. 158; A. Daumard, *La Bourgeoisie parisienne de 1815 à 1848* 1963, pp. xi, 160, 214, 316-7 and *Les Fortunes Françaises au 19e siècle* pp. 9-13 passim; R. D. Price, *The French Second Republic. A Social History* 1972, chs. 1, 2 passim; A.-J. Tudesq, *Les Grands Notables en France (1840-1849)/Étude historique d'une psychologie sociale* I 1964, pp. 343, 435; C. Marcilhacy, *Le diocese d'Orléans au milieu du 19e siècle. Les hommes et leurs mentalités* 1964, pp. 211-2.
2.   A.-J. Tudesq, *Les grands notables op. cit.*, p. 126.
3.   *Ibid.*, 335, 407, 474; II, 1231 and 'Les influences locales dans l'administration centrale en France sous la monarchie de juillet', *Annali della Fondazioni italiana par la storia amministrativa* 1967, p. 386; T. J. Clark, *Image of the People. Gustave Courbet and the 1848 Revolution* 1973, p. 151; H. C. Payne, *The Police State of Louis Napoleon Bonaparte* Seattle, 1966, p. 148; L. Girard *et al.*, *Les conseilleurs généraux en 1870* 1967, p. 68.
4.   A.-J. Tudesq, 'L'opposition légitimiste en Languedoc en 1840', *Annales du Midi* 1956, pp. 391, 407, and *Les grands notables* I, *op. cit.*, pp. 123, 134, 146, 156-7, 162-78, 186, 211; Marcilhacy, *Le diocese . . . op. cit.*, 172, 197-8; A. Armengaud, *Les populations de l'est-Aquitaine au début de l'époque contemporaine (vers 1845-vers 1871)* 1961, pp. 340, 341, 344; G. Dupeux, *Aspects de l'histoire sociale et politique du Lois-et-Cher* 1962, p. 27; Girard *et al.*, *op. cit.*,

pp. 116-7; J. Bécanuer, 'Noblesse et représentation parlementaire', *Revue Française de science politique* 1973, pp. 973, 981, 987; R. D. Price, 'Legitimist Opposition to the Revolution of 1830 in the French Provinces', *The Historical Journal* 1974, passim.

5.   Quoted by Clark, *Image of the People, op. cit.*, p. 150.

6.   T. R. Christofferson, 'Urbanization and Political Change: the Political Transformation of Marseille under the Second Republic', *The Historian* 1974, p. 198; A.-J. Tudesq, *Les grands notables* I, *op. cit.*, p. 211; A. Daumard, *La bourgeoisie . . ., op. cit.*, p. 582; A. Prost, *L'enseignement en France, 1800-1967* 1968, p. 55.

7.   Daumard, *op. cit.*; Tudesq, *Les grands notables* I, *op. cit., p. 320; II, op. cit.*, pp. 862-5; 'La bourgeoisie du nord au milieu de la monarchie de juillet', *Revue du Nord* 1959, pp. 287-9; and 'Les influences locales dans la vie politique Française sous la monarchie censitaire' in A. Mabileau (ed.), *Les facteurs locaux de la vie politique nationale* 1972, p. 345.

8.   A.-J. Tudesq, *Les grands notables* I, *op. cit.*, p. 361.

9.   *Ibid.*, p. 365; Daumard, *La bourgeoisie . . ., op. cit.*, pp. 593, 614.

10.   A.-J. Tudesq, *Les grands notables* I, pp. 366, 371; II, p. 742; *Les influences locales . . ., op. cit.*, pp. 383, 385-6; *Les influences locales dans la vie politique . . ., op. cit.*, pp. 344, 352.

11.   A.-J. Tudesq. *Les grands notables . . .* I, *op. cit.*, pp. 740-1, 858, 970; Daumard, *La bourgeoisie . . ., op. cit.*; J.-P. Aguet, *Les grèves sous la monarchie de juillet*, Geneva 1954, p. 290; A. Jardin, A.-J. Tudesq, *La France des notables* I, *op. cit.*, p. 172.

12.   A.-J. Tudesq, *Les grands notables* II, *op. cit.*, p. 966; A. Endre, 'Meaux et les evenements de 1848. Le banquet de la réforme', *Actes du 71e Congrés des sociétés savantes*, Grenoble 1952, Paris 1952, p. 472; P. Bastid, *Doctrines et institutions politiques de la seconde république* 1945 I, pp. 92-4, 99-100.

13.   J. Merriman, 'Social Conflict in France and the Limoges Revolution of 27 April, 1848', *Societas* 1974, pp. 22, 24; J.-P. Aguet, *op. cit.*; A. Armengaud, *Les populations de l'est – Aquitaine au début de l'époque contemporaine* 1961, pp. 331-40; Jardin, Tudesq, *op. cit.* I, p. 220.

14.   M. Agulhon, *La république au village Les populations du Var de la révolution à la seconde république* 1970, pp. 260, 265; Aguet, *op. cit.*, pp. 392-3; A. Olivesi, *La commune de 1871 à Marseille et ses origines* 1950, p. 2; Jardin, Tudesq, *op. cit.*, p. 22; C. Tilly, 'How protest modernized in France, 1845-1855' in W. Aydelotte (ed.), *The Dimensions of Quantitative Research in History* 1972 p. 220; R. Gossez, *Les ouvriers de Paris. L'organisation 1848-1851* 1967, pp. 10, 28-9.

15.   E. Labrousse, 'Comment naissent les revolutions – 1848 – 1830 – 1789', in *Actes du congrés historique du centenaire de la révolution de 1848* 1948, pp. 11-12; and *Aspects de la crise et de la dépression de l'économie française au milieu du 19e siècle, 1846-51* 1956, passim; A.-J. Tudesq, 'La crise de 1847, vue par les milieux d'affaires parisiens', *loc. cit.*; J. Godechot, 'La crise de 1846-47 dans le sud-ouest de la France', *Études de la Révolution de 1848* 1954, P88f; A.-J. Tudesq, *Les grands notables* II, p. 964; T. J. Markovitch, 'La crise de 1847-1848 dans les industries parisiennes', *Revue d'histoire économique et sociale* 1965, passim; C. Marcilhacy, 'Les caractères de la crise sociale et politique de 1846 à 1852 dans le département du Loiret', *Revue d'histoire moderne et contemporaine* 1956, pp. 6-16; A. Thuillier, 'La crise des subsistances dans le Nièvre en 1846-47', *Actes du 90 congrés national des sociétés savantes* Nice 1965 III, 1966, passim; Aguet, *op. cit.*, p. 392; Jardin, Tudesq, *op. cit.*, p. 240.

16.   Tudesq, *Les grands notables, op. cit.* I, p. 570, II, pp. 936, 966, 984; Jardin, Tudesq. *op. cit.* I, p. 244; Labrousse, *Comment naissent, op. cit.*, p. 13.

17.   R. Gillis, 'Political Decay and the European Revolution 1789-1848', *World Politics* 1970, p. 348.
18.   Tudesq, *Les grands notables, op. cit.*, II, pp. 628, 684.
19.   L. Chevalier, 'Les fondements économiques et sociaux de l'histoire politique de la région parisienne, 1848-70'. Unpublished Thèse pour le doctorat ès lettres Paris 1950 vol. III, pp. 624-5; Tudesq, *Les grands notables, op. cit.*, II, p. 98.
20.   P. Bastid, *op. cit.*, pp. 127-8.
21.   J. M. Merriman, 'Radicalization and Repression: the Experience of the Limousin, 1848-51'. Unpublished Ph.D. thesis, University of Michigan 1972, 51f; S. Coquerelle, 'L'armée et la répression dans les campagnes (1848)', in *L'armée et la seconde république* 1955, pp. 122, 124-5, and 'Les droits collectifs et les troubles agraires dans les pyrénéees', *Actes du 78 Congès des sociétés savantes*, Toulouse 1953, 1954, p. 345 f; Chevalier, *Les fondements, op. cit.*, I, pp. 161-4; Tudesq, *Les grands notables, op. cit.*, II, p. 1037; C. Moulin, 'Les clubs et la presse' in *1848: le livre du centenaire* 1948, pp. 161-4; Armengaud, *Les populations, op. cit.*, p. 346; P. de Saint-Jacob, 'La situation des paysans de la côte d'Or en 1848', *Études d'histoire moderne et contemporaine* 1948, p. 241; L. Clarenc, 'Riches et pauvres dans le conflit forestier des pyrénées centrale vers le milieu du 19e siècle', *Annales du midi* 1967, passim; A. Fel, *Les hautes terres du Massif Central. Tradition paysanne et économie agricole* 1962, p. 142 f; M. Chevalier, *La vie humaine dans les Pyrénées ariègboises* 1956, p. 718 f.
22.   P. Vigier, *La seconde république dans la région alpine* I, 1963, pp. 201, 204; Agulhon, *La république au village, op. cit.*, pp. 42, 107 and *1848 ou l'apprentissage de la république, 1848-1852* 1973, p. 37; Chevalier, *Les fondements, op. cit.*, I, pp. 169, 196, 200, 201, 205; Tudesq, *Les grands notables, op. cit*, II, 1085; A. Soboul, 'Les troubles agraires de 1848', *1848* 1948, p. 9; C. Ardant, *Théorie sociologique de l'impôt* 1965, I, p. 351, II, pp. 767, 771-4. D. Snyder, C. Tilly, 'Hardship and Collective Violence in France, 1830 to 1960', *American Sociological Review* 1972, 520; C. Tilly, 'A Travers le chaos des vivantes cités' in Meadows, Mizuchi (eds.), *Urbanism, Urbanization and Change: Comparative Perspectives*, Reading, Mass. 1969, pp. 392-3; S. Coquerelle, *Les droits collectifs, op. cit.*, pp. 346, 350; T. W. Margadant, 'The Insurrection of 1851', unpublished mss., ch. I, pp. 19-22.
23.   P. Amman, 'La révolution en permanence; les clubs parisiens en 1848', *Information historique* 1973, p. 114; S. Wasserman, *Les clubs de Barbés et de Blanqui en 1848* 1913, pp. 233-4; Moulin, *Les clubs et la presse, op. cit.*, pp. 140-1; A. Pinton, *La province, loc. cit.*, pp. 161-9, 172, 177; R. Gossez, 'Diversité des antagonismes sociaux vers le milieu du 19e siècle', *Revue économique* 1956, p. 450; 'La presse parisienne à destination des ouvriers (1848-1851)' in *La presse ouvrière, 1819-1850* 1966, passim; 'L'organisation ouvrière à Paris sous la seconde république', *1848* 1950, pp. 31-7; *Études critiques: un tournant sands nos études, ibid.*, p. 189; *Les ouvriers de Paris, op. cit.*, pp. 35, 113, 117, 148, 213-4; M. Agulhon, 'La diffusion d'un journal montagnard, "Le Democrate du Var" sous la seconde république', *Provence historique* 1960, pp. 12-13; and *Une ville ouvrière au temps du socialisme utopique. Toulon de 1815 à 1851* 1970, p. 151; Marcilhacy, *La diocèse, op. cit.*, pp. 6-7; Aguet, *op. cit.*, p. 368; F. Dutacq, *Histoire politique de Lyon pendant la révolution de 1848* 1910, ch. I; M.-M. Kahan-Rabecq, *L'Alsace économique et sociale sous le régne de Louis Philippe I*, 1939, pp. 9-10; Dupeux, *Aspects, op. cit.*, p. 131; P. Bastid, *Doctrines et institutions politique de la seconde république* 1945, I, p. 108; C. Tilly, *An Urban World*, Boston, Mass. 1974, pp. 52, 188; W. H. Sewell, 'La classe ouvrière de Marseille sous la seconde république:structure sociale et comportement politique', *Le mouvement social* 1971, pp. 34-5, 37-50, 59-61 and 'Social Changes and the Rise of Working Class Politics in 19th Century Marseille', *Past and Present* 1974,

pp. 76, 182; Merriman, *op. cit.*, p. 87; F. Rude, 'Le mouvement ouvrier à Lyon', *Revue de psychologie des peuples* 1958, p. 235; J. P. Courtheaux, 'Naissance d'une conscience de classe dans le proletariat textile du nord 1830-1870', *Revue économique* 1957, p. 122.

24.   D. C. McKay, *The National Workshops* Cambridge, Mass. 1933, passim; I. Bastid, *op. cit.*, pp. 130, 134, 283; *Markovitch, op. cit.*, p. 256; Price, *The French Second Republic, op. cit.*, p. 168.

25.   Gossez, *L'organisation ouvrière, op. cit.*, p. 32; Bastid, *op. cit.*, p. 138, *Les ouvriers de Paris, op. cit.*, pp. 55, 61 f; P. Vigier, *La seconde république* 1967, p. 22.

26.   J. Vidalenc, 'La province et les journees de juin', *Etudes d'histoire moderne et contemporaine* 1948, p. 92; Agulhon, *La république au village, op. cit.*, p. 457; Tudesq, *Les grands notables*, II, pp. 989, 996 998, 1000, 1001, 1005, 1007, 1040, 1043, 1084, 1106; Gillis, *op. cit.*, p. 367.

27.   Tudesq, *Les grands notables, op. cit.*, II, pp. 1028, 1029, 1030, 1045-6; *Les influences locales, op. cit.*, p. 376 and 'L'administration municipale dans le sud-ouest sous la monarchie de juillet', *Annales du Midi* 1972, p. 484; Vigier, *La seconde république dans la région alpine, op. cit.*, I, pp. 206, 209, 211; II, p. 232; Girard *et al., op. cit.*, p. 43; Bastid, *op. cit.*, pp. 145-6, 163; H. Goallau, *Hamon Commissaire du gouvernement puis prefet d'Ille-et-villaine (3 mars 1848-25 Jan. 1849)*, Rennes 1973, pp. 51-2; Merriman, *op. cit.*, pp. 80-1.

28.   P. Labracherie, 'Le paysan de 1848', in *L'esprit de 1848* 1948, p. 234; Chevalier, *Les fondements, op. cit.*, I, p. 207; Daumard, *La bourgeoisie, op. cit.*, p. 518; Tudesq, *Les grands notables, op. cit.*, II, pp. 1054-7, 1063. Vigier, *op. cit.*, p. 244; Marcilhacy, *Le diocèse, op. cit.*, p. 203; Armengaud, *Les populations, op. cit.*, pp. 352-3; Sewell, *op. cit.*, pp. 54, 60.

29.   Tudesq, *op. cit.*, pp. 1065-7; F. A. de Luna, *The French Republic under Cavaignac*, Princeton, N.J., 1969, pp. 111-13.

30.   Tudesq. *op. cit.*, pp. 1071-2; Merriman, *op. cit.*, pp. 120, 124.

31.   Gossez, *Diversité, op. cit.*, p. 451; *Les ouvriers de Paris, op. cit*, p. 314; Price, *The French Second Republic, op. cit.*, ch. IV; Agulhon, *1848, op. cit.*, pp. 68-9; P. Amann, 'Revolution: A Redefinition', *Political Science Quarterly* 1962, p. 51; F. A. de Luna, *op. cit.*, pp. 219, 222.

32.   P. Montagne, *Le Comportement politique de l'armée à Lyon sous la monarchie de juillet et la seconde république* 1966, pp. 243-4; Olivesi, *op. cit.*

33.   P. Caspard, 'Aspects de la lutte des classes en 1848: le recrutement de la garde nationale mobile', *Revue d'histoire moderne et contemporaine* 1974, pp. 87, 95-6, 103, 106; Gossez, *Diversité, op. cit.*, pp. 440, 442, 446-7. J;-P. Charnay, *Société militaire et suffrage politique en France depuis 1789* 1964, pp. 174, 179, 183; Tudesq, *Les grands notables, op. cit.*, II, pp. 108-13; R. Girardet, *La société militaire dans la France contemporaine* 1953, pp. 57, 60, 88, 104, and 'Autour de quelques probèmes' in *L'armée et la seconde république, op. cit.*, pp. 5-7; P. Chalmin, *L'offiçier français de 1815 à 1870* 1957, pp. 145-6, 190, 237; 'Une institution militaire de la seconde république: la garde nationale mobile', *Études d'histoire moderne et contemporaine* 1948, pp. 37, 41; and 'La crise morale de l'armée française', in *L'armée et la seconde république, op. cit.*, pp. 47, 57; P. Sorlin, *La société française: 1840-1914* 1969, p. 24; L. Girard, *La garde nationale, 1814-71*, 1964, p. 285 f.

34.   Tudesq, *op. cit.*, pp. 1122, 1140-1; Agulhon, *1848, op. cit.*, p. 78.

35.   A.-J. Tudesq, 'La légende napoléonienne en France en 1848', *Revue Historique* 1957, pp. 72-7, 80-2; *L'élection présidentielle de Louis-Napoléon Bonaparte, 10 décembre 1848* and *Les grands notables, op. cit*, II, pp. 1163, 1168, 1180, 1183, 1187, 1196, 1198, 1200; Vigier, *La seconde république dans la région alpine, op. cit.*, I, p. 325; and *La seconde république*, op. cit., p. 82;

G. Fasel, 'The Wrong Revolution. French Republicanism in 1848', *French Historical Studies* 1974, passim; P. McPhee, 'The Crisis of Radical Republicanism in the French Revolution of 1848', *Historical Studies* 1974, passim.
36.　Vigier, *La seconde république dans la région alpine, op. cit.*, II, pp. 87-8; Gossez, *Les ouvriers de Paris, op. cit.*, p. 319 and *La seconde république, op. cit.*, pp. 97-8; Agulhon, *Une ville ouvrière, op. cit.*, p. 311.
37.　A. Corbin, 'Limousin migrants, limousins sédentaires. Contribution à l'histoire de la région limousine au 19e siècle (1845-80)', *Le mouvement social* 1974, p. 117; E. Labrousse, 'Panoramas de la crise' in *Aspects de la crise et de la dépression de l'économie française au milieu du 19e siècle, 1846-1851* 1956, XXI-III-IV; Fasel, *op. cit.*, p. 668; Vigier, *La seconde république dans la région alpine* I, *op. cit.*, pp. 11-12, 265-7; II, pp. 10-11, 26, 28, 41, 72, 130, 163, and *La seconde république, op. cit.*, pp. 92-6; Dupeux, *Aspects, op. cit.*. p. 319 and 'Aspects agricoles de la crise le département de Loir-et-Cher' in Labrousse *Aspects, op. cit.*, p. 68; Armengaud, *Les populations, op. cit.*, p. 374; Clark *Image of the people, op. cit.*, p. 152; Agulhon, *1848, op. cit.*, p. 99; R. Forster, 'Quantitative History', *Journal of Interdisciplinary History* 1974, p. 306; Margadant, *The Insurrection . . ., op. cit.*, IV.
38.　J. Lhomme, *La grande bourgeoisie au pouvoir* 1960, pp. 81-7; Agulhon, *La république au village, op. cit.*, pp. 298-9; Tudesq, *Les grands notables, op. cit.*, II, 1225; Chevalier, *Les fondements, op. cit.*, I, p. 5; T. Zeldin, 'Government Policy in the French general elections of 1849', *English Historical Review* 1959, pp. 242, 300, 352; Dupeux, *Aspects, op. cit.*, pp. 377-8, 383; Armengaud, *Les populations, op. cit.*, p. 375; J. C. Drottin, 'Les élections du 13 mai 1849 à Bordeaux' in Mabileau (ed.) *op. cit.*, pp. 364, 369; Merriman, *op. cit.*, pp. 139, 142.
39.　Tudesq, *Les grands notables, op. cit.*, II, pp. 1212, 1211, 1230; Vigier, *La seconde république, op. cit.*, pp. 63, 68, 71-2, 78.
40.　R. Huard, 'La défense du suffrage universal sous la seconde république: les réactions de l'opinion gardoise et le petitionnement contre la loi du 31 mai 1850', *Annales du Midi* 1971, pp. 335-6.
41.　R. Marlin, *L'épuration politique dans le Doubs à la suite du coup d'état du 2 décembre 1851*, Dôle 1958, p. 8; V. Wright, 'The Basses-Pyrénées from 1848 to 1870. A Study in Departmental Politics'. Unpublished Ph.D. thesis, University of London 1965, I, pp. 143, 224; J. Gaillard, 'La question du crédit et les almanachs autour de 1848', *Études de la Révolution de 1848* 1954, p. 87; M. Dessal, *Un révolutionnaire jacobin: Charles Delescluse 1809-1871* 1952, p. 93; I. Collins, *The Government and the Newspaper Press in France 1814-1881* 1959, pp. 110-17; Tudesq, *Les grands notables, op. cit.*, I, p. 84; Marcilhacy, *Le diocèse, op. cit.*, p. 203; Armengaud, *Les populations, op. cit.*, pp. 379-81; Clark, *Image of the People, op. cit.*, p. 878; Vigier, *La seconde république dans la région alpine, op. cit.*, II, pp. 204, 250, 252, 305-6 and *La seconde république, op. cit.*, pp. 75-7; Agulhon, *La république au village, op. cit.*, pp. 300, 343, and *La diffusion d'un journal montagnard, op. cit.*, p. 13 f; Drouin, *op. cit.*, p. 371; Margadant, *The Insurrection, op. cit.*, ch. 7, p. 14; Merriman, *op. cit.*, p. 169; P. Leuilliot, *La presse et l'histoire. Notes sur la presse en Alsace sous la seconde république et le second empire*, Strasbourg 1965, pp. 13, 16, 19; R. Gossez, 'La résistance à l'impôt: la 45 centimes', *Études de la révolution de 1848* 1953, p. 131 and 'Presse parisienne à destination des ouvriers, 1848-1851' in J. Godechot (ed.), *La presse ouvrière, 1819-1850* 1966, pp. 148, 187; L. Loubère, 'The Emergence of the Extreme Left in Lower Languedoc, 1845-1851: social and economic factors in Politics', *American Historical Review* 1968, pp. 1029-30.
42.　D. Fabre, J. La Croix, *La vie quotidienne des paysans du Languedoc au 19e siècle* 1973, pp. 79, 117, 253-4, 405, 408, 413-9; N. Belmont, *Mythes et croyances dans l'ancienne France* 1973, pp. 53-4, 68 f; A. Soboul, 'La question

paysanne en 1848', *La Pensée* 1948, p. 55; Chevalier, *Les fondements, op. cit.*, III, p. 628; Price, *The French Second Republic, op. cit.*, pp. 242-2; Marcilhacy, *La diocèse, op. cit.*, pp. 5-8; A. Siegfried, *Tableau politique de la France de l'ouest sous la 3e république* 1913, p. 370; Armengaud, *Les populations, op. cit.*, pp. 165, 237, 375; Dupeux, *Aspects, op. cit.*, pp. 21, 157; Corbin, *op. cit.*, p. 118; C. Karnoouh, Le démocratie impossible: parenté et politique dans un village Lorrain', *Etudes rurales* 1973, p. 32; J. Pitt-Rivers, 'Social Class in a French village' in Tilly *An Urban World, op. cit.*, p. 219; M. Jollivet, H. Mendras, *Les collectivités rurales françaises* I, 1971, pp. 22-4; A. Fremont, 'La région: essai sur l'espace Vécu' in *La pensée géographique française contemporaine. Mélanges offerts à André Meynier*, St.-Brieuc 1972, pp. 675-6; L. Trénard, 'L'histoire des mentalités collectives', *Revue d'histoire moderne et contemporaine* 1968, p. 700; L. A. Roubin, *Chambrettes des Provencaux* 1970, pp. 41-3; H. Mendras, *Sociologie de la campagne Française* 1959, p. 101 and 'Un Schema d'analyse de la paysannerie occidentale', *Peasant Studies Newsletter* 1972, pp. 83, 131; Agulhon, *La république au village, op. cit.*, p. 192 amd 'les chambrées en Basse-Provence. Histoire et ethnologie', *Revue Historique* 1971, passim; H. Roulin, 'La communauté villageoise en Châtillonnais', *Etudes rurales* 1972, p. 40; R. Esmonin *et al.*, *La révolution de 1848 dans le département de l'Isère* Grenoble 1949, XIII, XXVI; M. Chevalier, 'La "Guerre des démoiselles" en Ariège: folklore et histoire sociale', *Revue Géographique des Pyrénées et du sud-ouest* 1974, pp. 79-80; A.-J. Tudesq, *La presse et l'événement* 1973, p. 15; T. Shanin, 'Peasantry as a Political Factor' in Shanin (ed.), *Peasants and Peasant Societies* 1971, p. 242; R. Livet, *Habitat rurale et structures agraires en Basse-Provence*, Aix-en-Provence 1962, p. 223 f.

43.   M. Faucheux, 'La Vendée' in L. Girard (ed.), *Les élections de 1869* 1960, p. 148; Margadant, *The Insurrection, op. cit.*, ch. 8, pp. 15,19; Wright, *The Basses-Pyrénées, op. cit.*, I, p. iii; Agulhon, *La république au village, op. cit.*, p. 264; Marcilhacy, *Le diocèse, op. cit.*, p. 44; Armengaud, *Les populations, op. cit.*, pp. 381, 462; Vigier, *La seconde république, op. cit.*, II, pp. 97-8; G. Cholvy, 'Société, genres de vie et mantalité dans les campagnes françaises de 1815 à 1880', *Information Historique* 1974, p. 164.

44.   D. Sabean, 'Markets, Uprisings and Leadership in Peasant Societies in Western Europe 1381-1789', *Peasant Studies Newsletter* 1973, p. 17; Margadant, *op. cit.*, Introduction p. 6, ch. 3, pp. 14-15, ch. 7, pp. 16-18. Girard, 'Introduction' in *Les élections, op. cit.*, XIX; Chevalier, *Les fondements, op. cit.*, III, pp. 628-38; Wright, *op. cit.*, I; Tudesq, *Les grands notables, op. cit*, I, p. 244; Vigier, *La seconde république, op. cit.*, I, p. 199; Loubère, *op. cit.*, pp. 1025, 1036; Marcilhacy, *Le diocèse, op. cit.*, pp. 362-5; Fabre, La Croix, *op. cit.*, p. 449; Mendras, *Sociologie, op. cit.*, p. 21; Jollivet and Mendras, *op. cit.*, p. 163; M. Agulhon, *La vie sociale en provence intérieure au lendemain de la révolution* 1970, p. 473; J. Druker, 'The Workers of the Nord during the Second Republic'. Unpublished M.A. thesis, University of East Anglia 1971, p. 34.

45.   T. W. Margadant, 'Peasant Protest in the Second Republic' *Journal of Interdisciplinary History* 1974, p. 127; *The Insurrection, op. cit.*, ch. 7, pp. 15-17, 20-2; Agulhon, *La république au village, op. cit.*, pp. 204, 242, 481; *1848, op. cit.*, p. 37 and 'Le rôle politique des artisans dans le département du Var de la révolution à la seconde république', *VIIe Colloque d'histoire sur l'artisanat et l'apprentissage* Aix-en-Provence 1965, p. 85 f; Marcilhacy, *Le diocèse, op. cit.*, p. 202; Loubère, *op. cit.*, pp. 1025-6; G. Garrier, *Paysans de Beaujolais et du Lyonnais, 1800-1970* Grenoble 1973, I, p. 226; P. Bozon, *La Vie rurale en Vivarais* 1963, p. 121 f.

46.   A. Chatelain, 'Les migrants temporaires et la propagation des idées révolutionnaires en France au 19e siècle', *Revue des révolutions contemporaines* 1951,

pp. 6, 11-12, 18; Agulhon, *La république au village, op. cit.*, pp. 299, 172; Marcilhacy, *Le diocèse, op. cit.*, pp. 412-4; Vigier, *La seconde république, op. cit.*, II, pp. 440-2; Margadant, *Peasant Protest, op. cit.*; Raulin, *op. cit.*, p. 64; Merriman, *op. cit.*, p. 172; H. Desroche, P. Rambaud, *Villages en développement. Contributions à une sociologie villageoise* 1971, p. 28.

47.   R. Balland, 'De l'organisation à la restriction du suffrage universel en France (1848-1850)' in J. Droz (ed.), *Réaction et suffrage universel en France et en Allemagne* 1963, p. 168; Roubin, *op. cit.*, pp. 29-32, 45, 47, 59-60, 62, 72, 123-4; Margadant, *The Insurrection, op. cit.*, ch. 8, pp. 22, 24, 28, 32-5; Fabre, La Croix, *op. cit.*, p. 249; Agulhon, *La république au village, op. cit.*, pp. 206-14, 422,; II, p. 570; and *La sociabilité meridionale* Aix-en-Provence 1966; Dupeux, *Aspects, op. cit.*, p. 348; Marcilhacy, *Le diocèse, op. cit.*, p. 349; Mendras, *Sociologie, op. cit.*, pp. 29-30; Desroche, Rambaud, *op. cit.*; E. Constant, 'Image du républicain varois à la fin du second empire' in *L'esprit républicain*, Colloque d'Orléans 4 et 5 Septembre 1970, 1972, p. 287; Druker, *op. cit.*; Marlin, *op. cit.*, p. 5; Cholvy, *op. cit.*, p. 158; H. J. Smith, 'Village Revolution: Agricultural Workers of Cruzy (Hérault), 1850-1910' unpublished Ph.D. thesis, University of Wisconsin 1972, p. 34; A.-J. Tudesq, review of Agulhon, 'La république au village' in *Annales du Midi* 1973, p. 115.

48.   Margadant, *The Insurrection, op. cit.*, ch. 8, p. 35; Agulhon, *La sociabilité méridionale, op. cit.*, I, p. 417; Bozon, *op. cit.*, p. 182 f.

49.   Margadant, *op. cit.*, ch. 2, p. 24, ch. 6, pp. 22-3, ch. 7, pp. 6, 10, 24, ch. 8, pp. 1, 6, 8-9, 14; M. Agulhon, *1848, op. cit.*, and *La république au village, op. cit.*, p. 475; T. Zeldin, *France, 1818-1945*, I, 1973, pp. 165-6; M. Dessal, 'Le complot et la résistance au coup d'état dans les départements du sud-est', *1848* 1951, pp. 84, 86; Marcilhacy, *Le diocèse, op. cit.*, p. 348; Vigier, *La seconde république, op. cit.*, II, pp. 162, 384, 385, 387, 392; C. Lévy, 'A propos du coup d'état de 1851 dans l'Yonne', *Annales de Bourgogne* 1953, p. 188; J. Goueffon, 'Le parti républicain dans le Loiret à la fin du second empire' in *L'esprit républicain, op. cit., p. 290; H. J. Smith, op. cit.*, pp. 52-3; E. Reynier, *La seconde république dans l'Ardêche*, Privas 1948, p. 87 f; Corbin, *op. cit.*, pp. 123, 124; Fabre, Lacroix, *op. cit.*, p. 449; Loubère, *op. cit.*, p. 1038; M. Vovelle, 'Essai de cartographie de la déchristianisation sous le révolution française, *Annales du Midi* 1964, pp. 541-2.

50.   Margadant, *op. cit.*, ch. 3, p. 15, ch. 7, pp. 2-3, ch. 8, p. 18; Wright, *The Basses-Pyrenées, op. cit.*, I, pp. 169-70; Chevalier, *Les fondements, op. cit.*, III, p. 646; Tudesq, *L'élection, op. cit.*, pp. 120-1; and *Les grands notables, op. cit.*, I, pp. 335, II, pp. 1210, 1227, 1232-4; and *Les influences locales dans la vie politique, op. cit.*, pp. 343-4; Dupeux, *Aspects, op. cit.*, pp. 359, 363, 377; Loubère, *op. cit.*, p. 1032; P. Amann, 'The Changing Outlines of 1848', *American Historical Review* 1963, p. 950; Mendras, *Sociologie, op. cit.*, p. 30; Jollivet and Mendras, *op. cit.*, p. 162; Armengaud, *Les populations, op. cit.*, pp. 378-9; Vigier, *La seconde république, op. cit.*, II, pp. 240, 244, 247 and 'Lyon et l'évolution politique de la province française au 19e siècle', *Cahiers d'histoire* 1967, p. 197; Agulhon, *La république au village, op. cit.*, pp. 326, 329; *1848, op. cit.*, p. 128 and *Une ville ouvrière, op. cit.*, p. 332; T. Shanin, 'Peasantry: Delineation of a sociological Concept and a Field of Study', *Peasant Studies Newsletter* 1973, p. 6; K. Dobrowolski, 'Peasant Traditional Culture' in Shanin (ed.) *op. cit.*, pp. 297-8; Cholvy, *op. cit.*, p. 161 f.

51.   A. Prost, *L'enseignement en France, 1800-1967* 1968, pp. 8-10, 104, 138-9, 173; M. Gontard, *Les Ecoles primaires de la France bourgeoisie (1833-70)* Toulouse, nd., passim; Marcilhacy, *Le diocèse, op. cit.*, pp. 244, 278-81; Dupeux, *Aspects, op. cit.*, p. 166; Fabre, Lacroix, *op. cit.*, pp. 385-6; Armengaud, *Les populations, op. cit.*, p. 322; Payne, *op. cit.*, p. 117; Agulhon, *1848, op. cit.*, pp. 145-7.

52.   Marcilhacy, *Le diocèse, op. cit.*, pp. 249-50, 412-4, 481, 489; Fabre, Lacroix, *op. cit.*, pp. 342-8, 363-4, 367-70; Goullott, *op. cit.*, pp. 141-3; Siegfried, *op. cit.*, p. 391; Margadant, *op. cit.*, ch. 8, p. 18; P. Pierrard, *La vie ouvrière à Lille sous le second empire* 1965, p. 362 f; T. Zeldin (ed.), *Conflicts in French Society* 1970, passim.

53.   Margadant, *op. cit.*, Introduction, p. 9, ch. 6, pp. 15-16, 18, 19, 22-4, ch. 8, p. 21; and *Peasant Protest, op. cit.*, p. 129; Agulhon, *1848, op. cit.*, p. 113, 117, 124, 151; *La diffusion, op. cit.*, pp. 25-6; and 'Le Baron Haussmann, préfet du Var (1849-1850)', *Provence Historique* 1956, pp. 148, 156, 158, 160; J. J. Darman, *Le colportage de librairie en France sous le second empire* 1972, pp. 84, 102; C. Tilly, J. Rude, *Measuring Political Upheaval*, Princeton, N.J. 1965, p. 51; Marlin, *op. cit.*, pp. 7, 10; Dupeux, *Aspects, op. cit.*, pp. 167, 361-9; Armengaud, *Les populations, op. cit.*, pp. 381-6; Tudesq, *Les grands notables, op. cit.*, I, 406-7, II, p. 1201, and *Les influences locales dans la vie politique, op. cit.*, pp. 358-9; Moulin, *op. cit.*, p. 148; Clark, *Image of the People, op. cit.*, pp. 88, 94; Vigier, *La seconde république dans la région alpine, op. cit.*, II, pp. 221, 229, 282; *La seconde république, op. cit.*, pp. 72, 85, 87; and *Lyon et l'évolution politique, op. cit.*, p. 330; Agulhon, *La république au village, op. cit.*, pp. 320, 331 ff, and *Une ville ouvrière, op. cit.*, p. 317; Leuilliot, *op. cit.*, p. 11 f; Merriman, *op. cit.*, pp. 130, 145, 147-9, 151-2, 156, 164, 174, 176-81, 220; Fabre, Lacroix, *op. cit.*, p. 33; Reynier, *op. cit.*, pp. 89, 91, 100; Huard, *op. cit*, p. 332; Payne, *op. cit.*, pp. 145, 153 and 'Preparation of a coup d'état – administrative centralisation and police powers in France 1849-1851', in F. J. Cox (ed.), *Studies in Modern European History in Honor of F. C. Palm*, New York 1966, pp. 177-81; C. Lévy, 'A propos du coup d'état de 1851 dans l'Yonne', *Annales de Bourgogne* 1953, p. 188.

54.   Charnay, *op. cit.*, p. 173; Agulhon, *1848, op. cit.*, pp. 156-7.

55.   C. Lévy, 'Notes sur les fondements sociaux de l'insurrection de décembre 1851 en provence', *Information Historique* 1954, p. 142; E. Tenot, *La province en décembre 1851* 1865, passim; Vigier, *La seconde république dans la région alpine, op. cit.*, II, pp. 307-11, 325; and *La seconde république, op. cit.*, p. 112; Wright, *The Basses-Pyrénées, op. cit.*, I, p. 313; Marcilhacy, *Le diocèse, op. cit.*, p. 335; Gossez, *Les ouvriers de Paris, op. cit.*, p. 361; Margadant, *op. cit.*, ch. 4, p. 19; Agulhon, *1848, op. cit.*, p. 173; H. J. Smith, *op. cit.*, p. 54; Reynier, *op. cit.*, p. 113; Armengaud, *op. cit.*, p. 390; M. Bruchet, 'Le coup d'état de 1851 dans le Nord', *Revue du Nord* 1925, pp. 84, 86-7; M. Dessal, *Le complot, op. cit.*, p. 83.

56.   Agulhon, *La république au village, op. cit.*, pp. 445-6; *1848, op. cit.*, p. 100; and *Le Baron Haussmann, op. cit.*, pp. 192-3; Dessal, *Le complot, op. cit*; Armengaud, *Les populations, op. cit.*, p. 392; Lévy, *A propos, op. cit.*, pp. 189-90; Marlin, *op. cit.*, p. 27; Corbin, *op. cit.*, p. 121; J.-P. Rocher, 'Les élections dans l'Yonne', *Bulletin de la faculté des lettres de Strasbourg* 1965, p. 363; Margadant, *op. cit.*, Introduction, pp. 8-9, 16-17, 22, ch. 1, p. 23, ch. 5, pp. 24, 26; Loubère, *op. cit.*, p. 1094; Vigier, *La seconde république, op. cit., p. 116.*

57.   Vigier, *La seconde république, op. cit.*, II, p. 330; Agulhon, *La république au village, op. cit.*, p. 396.

58.   Agulhon, *La république au village, op. cit.*, pp. 421-3, 435, 438; *1848, op. cit.*, p. 181; Vigier, *La seconde république dans le région alpine, op. cit.*, II, pp. 314, 325; and *La seconde république, op. cit.*, p. 114; Tilly, *How Protest Modernized in France, op. cit.*, p. 235; Margadant, ch. I, pp. 17-18, ch. 2, p. 24, ch. 4, p. 22; Merriman, *op. cit.*, p. 207.

59.   Agulhon, *La république au village, op. cit.*, pp. 396, 437-8, 452; *1848, op. cit.*, pp. 186-7.

60.   Margadant, *op. cit.*, ch. 3, pp. 17-18, ch. 5, pp, 8, 19-20, 26-8; Lévy,

A propos, op. cit.; Reynier, *op. cit.*, p. 110; Rocher, *op. cit.*, p. 362; E. Wolf, 'On Peasant Rebellions' in Shanin (ed.), *op. cit.*, p. 266.

61.   M. Agulhon, 'Le baron Haussmann, préfet du Var (1849-50) d'après ses memoires', *Provence Historique* 1956, p. 152; 'La résistance au coup d'état en province. Esquisse d'historiographie', *Revue d'histoire moderne et contemporaine* 1974, p. 26, and *La république au village, op. cit.*, p. 427; Lévy, *Notes, op. cit.*, p. 142; Price, *The French Second Republic, op. cit.*, ch. 7, passim; C. Tilly, 'Does modernization breed Revolution?', *Comparative Politics* 1973, p. 442; Vigier, *La seconde république, op. cit.*, II, p. 333 f; Margadant, ch. I, p. 16, ch. 3, p. 22, ch. 4, pp. 1, 3, 5, 19-23, ch. 5, pp. 3, 30.

62.   Dessal, *Un révolutionnaire jacobin, op. cit.*, p. 181; Vigier, *La seconde république, op. cit.*, II, p. 319; Agulhon, *1848, op. cit.*, p. 180; Merriman, *op. cit.*, pp. 128, 192.

63.   L. Puech, *Essai sur la candidature officielle en France depuis 1851*, Mende 1922, pp. 53-5; M. Agulhon, 'Où en est l'histoire de l'insurrection de décembre 1851 en Provence? ', *Feuillet documentaires régionaux.* Centre régional de recherche et de documentation pédagogique, Marseille, nos. 6, 7, 1966; Merriman, *op. cit.*, pp. 203, 205-6; Roubin, *op. cit.*, p. 217; Marlin, *op. cit.*, p. 27; R. Constant, 'Notes sur la presse dans le département du Var sous le second Empire', *Provence Historique* 1960, p. 315; P. G. Vergez-Tricom, 'Les événements de décembre 1851 à Lyon', *La Révolution de 1848* 1920-1, pp. 246-50; Payne, *op. cit.*, pp. 33, 37, 41, 50-2, 70, 109, 153, 282-4.

64.   B. le Clére, V. Wright, *Les préfets du second Empire* 1973, pp. 22-3; Agulhon, *Où en est l'histoire de l'insurrection, op. cit.*, no. 6, p. 3; Lévy, *op. cit.*, p. 142; Payne, *op. cit.*, p. 35; Vigier, *La seconde république dans la région alpine, op. cit.*, II, p. 337, and *La seconde république, op. cit.*, p. 119; J. Maurain, *La politique ecclésiastique du second empire de 1852 à 1869*, 1930, pp. 8, 9, 11.

65.   R. D. Price, 'The Onset of Labour Shortage in Nineteenth Century French agriculture', *Economic History Review* 1975, passim; Vigier, *La seconde république, op. cit.*, II, p. 387; Girard *et al., op. cit.*, p. 135. and *Les élections de 1869* 1960, XIV, XVIII, XIX; Gueffon, *op. cit.*, p. 290; Agulhon, *La république au village, op. cit.*, p. 312; H. J. Smith, *op. cit.*, pp. 55-6.

PARISIAN PRODUCERS' ASSOCIATIONS (1830-51): THE SOCIALISM OF SKILLED WORKERS

Bernard H. Moss

The role played by Parisian workers in the revolutionary politics of the nineteenth century has always generated both interest and controversy. With his intimate knowledge of French politics Marx in 1850 described the emergence of a class conscious and socialist Parisian proletariat under the Second Republic.[1] Most historians, including Marxists, have disagreed with his appraisal, portraying Parisian workers as rather traditional artisans, lacking either a specifically class or socialist consciousness and blending easily into the amorphous mass of artisans, shopkeepers and wage earners known variously as the *sans culouttes*, the crowd or simply the people of Paris.[2] As to the ideology of the organised labour movement, it has appeared either hopelessly vague and utopian or excessively diverse and confused.[3] Historians discussed trade unionism, Republicanism,[4] cooperation[5] and utopian socialism without analysing the relationship among these movements and their concrete meaning for organised workers. When viewed in a broad historical perspective, one project emerges as the final goal of labour action, the formation of producers' associations for the emancipation of all trades from the wage system. It is this movement more than any other that reveals the existence of a socialist and class conscious Parisian proletariat.

The producers' cooperative or association movement has traditionally been given only secondary consideration as the effort of elite workers to raise themselves to property owning middle class status. From its inception, however, the producers' cooperative movement was conceived within the framework of a larger socialist strategy for the collectivisation of capital and the emancipation of entire trades from the wage system. Producers' cooperatives or associations were originally designed with expanding funds of collective 'inalienable' capital to ensure the continual admission of new members and prevent the formation of an emancipated elite. To give associations an advantage in competition with larger capitalist enterprises, workers looked to a democratic and social Republic to provide the necessary leverage in the form of public credits and contracts. Representing the interests of all working people — peasants, workers, shopkeepers and petty capitalists —

the Republic was expected to supply the essential credit that was restricted under a regime of financial privilege. Until the advent of the true Republic, workers could finance themselves by organising a system of mutual credit and exchange in a federation of trades or universal association. Articulated most explicitly by Philippe Buchez and Louis Blanc, the main assumptions of this association strategy for socialism, for workers' ownership of the means of production, were shared by leading elements of labour and Republican movements through most of the nineteenth century.

In describing the origins of French cooperation, historians have insisted upon the influence of the utopian socialists, particularly Fourier. In fact, the first suggestion for a producers' association came not from a bourgeois intellectual, but from a group of Parisian printers who launched *L'artisan, journal de la class ouvriere*[6] following the July Revolution. In proposing association as the remedy for workers' sufferings, these printers manifested a new socialist and working class consciousness. Viewing workers as the only productive class, the source of all wealth, they suggested association as the way to end exploitation by capitalist owners of the means of production. To benefit from the introduction of machinery they advised workers to become their own masters of machinery by pooling their meagre resources and establishing a modern workshop as an association.

The immediate sources of *L'Artisan* remain obscure. Certainly, disciples of Owen, Fourier and Saint-Simon had circulated ideas of economic association, but none of their elaborate theories quite corresponds to this simple and practical suggestion for workers' association. Though these printers were doubtless aware of Saint-Simonian literature, there is nothing in their simple language, awkward expressions, or professed antagonism to middle class journalists to suggest outside collaboration. In the absence of other evidence, one must accept their word that their new consciousness was primarily the result of their own experience since the July Revolution threw the working class into the political and social spotlight.[7]

The assertions of Buchez and his disciples notwithstanding, there is no evidence that Buchez launched his own association programme before 1831.[8] In 1829 Buchez apparently still believed in the useful function of the capitalist entrepreneur. Since the July Revolution, however, the emergence of the working class as an independent force — and perhaps contact with the printers of the *Artisan* — had convinced him that skilled workers were fully capable of owning and operating their own enterprises without the aid of a capitalist. In the course of discussions with Parisian workers, Buchez in 1831 proposed a formula for the emancipation of entire trades from the wage system. He suggested the establishment of public credit banks to supply the initial capital and the formation of a collective, indivisible 'inalienable' capital from re-invested earnings to ensure the continual admission of new members without capital. Buchez thus laid the basis for the collectivisation of all skilled trades in producers' associations.

Doubtless influenced by Buchez, Republican leaders Godefroy Cavaignac of the *Amis du peuple* and Armand Marrast, editor of the *Tribune*, also advocated the formation of associations and public credit banks as means of transferring the instruments of labour to the working class. During the round of general strikes that erupted in the autumn of 1833, several Parisian trades, including tailors, boxmakers, chairmakers and glovemakers, opened their own associations or 'National Workshops'. Formed for the purpose of employing striking workers and applying competitive pressure on employers, these associations came to be seen as a definitive method of trade emancipation. Printers and shoemakers planned huge workshops for the emancipation of their trades, and the shoemakers initiated the formation of a national workers' federation to supply credit to associations. The Republican *Tribune* and *Rights of Man* saw them as the beginning of a new organisation of labour that could only come to fruition under a Republic. After the strikes and associations were crushed by wholesale arrests and prosecutions, the *Rights of Man* convoked labour leaders to draw political lessons from the defeat. Appealing to them to join in the political struggle, they promised that 'the essential duty of the Republic will be to furnish the proletarians with the means of forming themselves into cooperative associations and exploiting their industry themselves'.[9] The alliance of Parisian workers with Republicans was thus founded upon an association strategy for workers' ownership of industry.

Through a process that has remained obscure, the main assumptions of this programme were disseminated throughout the Republican party even before Blanc published his *Organisation du travail* in August 1840. Already in May 1840, François Arago had spoken in the Chamber of the need for a new organisation of labour. During the reformist electoral campaign of that year, the call for workers' associations to 'end the exploitation of man by man' resounded in numerous Republican banquet halls all over France.[10]

The most influential publicists of this programme were of course Blanc and the workers who published the Buchezian monthly *L'Atelier*. Too much perhaps has been made of the differences between their respective programmes. Both looked to the Republic to provide the credit and contracts needed to overcome capitalist competition, accumulate capital and emancipate workers from the wage system. When the *Atelier* first criticised Blanc in 1841, it was a matter of degree rather than substance. Where Blanc had stressed the state's initiative, the *Atelier* advised workers to rely more on their own devotion and efforts. Where Blanc insisted on the establishment of an association monopoly in each trade, the *Atelier* like Buchez wished to preserve limited competition among multiple associations as an incentive for technical innovation. Nevertheless, it continued to share the basic assumptions of the programme whereby the Republic would assist trades toward the collectivisation of industrial capital in associations.[11]

During the Forties the association programme became the dominant social policy of the entire Republican movement, not merely its explicitly socialist wing.[12] While the radicals of the *Réforme* generally shared Blanc's approach, the moderates of the *National* preferred the slightly more liberal socialism of the *Atelier*. Representatives of various utopian schools — Fourierists, Saint-Simonians, revolutionary communists and Icarians — also rallied to associationism as a practical and transitional form of socialism. In 1845 a group of Fourierists, Saint-Simonians, and Republicans joined with labour leaders to form the *Compagnie des industries unies*, a universal association for the establishment of associations in all trades. Beginning with an industry of vital necessity, they planned to extend operations until all trades were included in a complete national circuit of production and exchange.

The following year Republican and labour leaders met to discuss how they could best assist the movement. While Blanc and most of the labour leaders favoured a single association in each trade, the moderate majority, including the banker Michel Goudchaux, Alexandre Marie, Hippolyte Carnot, Louis Garnier-Pagès, Armand Marrast. and the men of the *Atelier* preferred to support multiple associations in each trade. Yet, even the moderates advocated association as the universal regime of the future; in the final analysis both moderate and radical Republicans were cooperative socialists.[13]

Republican associationism reveals the idealistic and contradictory nature of Republican ideology that makes it impossible to characterise simply, as did Marx, as either bourgeois or petty bourgeois. In principle, most Republicans were inclined to favour a liberal democracy of small property owners — independent peasants, shopkeepers and petty capitalists. Regarding the landed and financial aristocracy as the hereditary enemy of this democracy of small producers, they did not see any basic conflict between petty capitalists, the masters of small scale industry, and their workers. Instead of considering capitalist masters as independent exploiters of labour and accumulators of capital, who were continuously rising into the upper bourgeoisie, they would treat them as victims of its exploitation whose interest in association coincided with that of their workers. Thus, a petty bourgeois Republic could be expected to help the workers abolish the wage system and establish a universal regime of association.[14]

Associationism was the Republican response to the rising tide of working class protest that appeared after the July Revolution. Industrial strife convinced idealistic young Republicans of the need to find a way to improve workers' conditions and relieve their suffering. In the working class they found determined and dedicated followers who were willing to sacrifice their lives for the cause of equality. Enrolling workers in the revolutionary sections of the *Rights of Man*, they instructed them in Robespierrist principles that subordinated property rights to the social requirements of security, harmony and equality. With a philosophical tradition that favoured capitalist property, class conciliation and middle class democracy, Republicans built revolutionary organisations that were essentially working class in composition and popularised a programme tending to undermine capitalism and the middle class. The application of democratic egalitarian principles to industrial society led them beyond their middle class framework to an authentic socialist programme.[15]

Why did the association programme appeal to Parisian workers? To what social situation and condition did it respond? The association movement has usually been seen as the revolt of artisanal workers against industrialisation, against machinery, the large factory and managerial authority, and as part of their quest for individual advantage and independence.[16] Some have also detected a return to the corporatism of the guild system. These views rest on the nearly universal assumption that Parisian workers were traditional artisans with a social situation and outlook quite distinct from those of the industrial factory worker. It is certainly true that the activist workers of 1848, 1871 or 1890 tended to come from the traditional crafts — tailors, shoemakers, jewellers, painters, joiners, carpenters, locksmiths, etc. As traditional craftsmen, these workers represented an elite in terms of social status, trade solidarity and political culture at least relative to the new factory worker. But to assume, as many historians do,[17] that the skilled men of 1848 and 1871 were the same as the artisans of 1792 is to overlook the whole process of industrialisation that had transformed them into a suffering working class.

Rather than an exceptional elite of artisans or privileged labour aristocracy, Parisian workers constituted an authentic proletariat, who experienced a greater relative deprivation from industrialisation than the new factory worker. Except for the introduction of a few power tools, few skilled trades were completely transformed by mechanisation. Instead, they suffered from the competition of less skilled and unapprenticed labour producing cheaper and ready made goods in domestic piecework, sweated workshops, subcontracted gangs and prisons and convents. Without eliminating these crafts, industrialisation constantly threatened them with massive seasonal and cyclical unemployment, greater speed, intensity and division of labour, and economic decline at least relative to expanding wealth. Despite their craft status, skilled workers experienced industrialisation as a deterioration, as a process of proletarianisation that tended to unite them with new elements of the working class.

Statistical sources confirm the picture of economic misery for Parisian workers from 1830 to 1848. Reaching a peak of prosperity under the Empire and early Restoration, workers began their relative decline with the onset of industrialisation. From 1830 to 1848, a period of great industrial growth that enriched the capitalist masters, most Parisian trades confronted stagnating wages and recurring crises of unemployment. During cyclical depressions unemployment often affected more than half of the trade. The massive influx of provincial and foreign labour further aggravated the situation. Seasonal unemployment extended in most trades from three to five months, reducing the annual earnings of even elite trades to a bare minimum. The decline of piece rate wages forced workers to increase the speed, intensity and division of labour. While the prices of manufactured goods fell, those of food and rents did not; thus *per capita* consumption of wine and meat declined in this period. Parisian workers experienced a real deterioration of living standards. When Marx wrote in the *Manifesto* about the increasing misery of the working class, he was not referring to a mere theoretical hypothesis.[18]

While thus threatening the status, security and revenues of traditional crafts, industrialisation did not alter the small scale, semi-artisanal mode of Parisian production. In fact, since 1789 and the onset of industrialisation Paris witnessed a marked decentralisation of industry as larger textile, chemical and leather factories relocated in cheaper suburbs or provinces. By 1848 the vast majority of Parisian workers were employed in small or medium sized shops with little mechanisation.[19] Lacking ownership of the means of production, they still possessed the property of their craft acquired through long apprenticeship and professional experience. As craftsmen, they still controlled much of the process of production, applying skill and dexterity to their work, exercising judgement over choice of tools, sequence and quality of work, setting their own pace and rhythm, and finally fashioning a product as an extension of themselves, of their own hand and brain. The artisitic quality and technical autonomy of the craft — the relative freedom from management direction and interference in the work place — gave them a sense of professional capacity and pride and a positive social identification with their trade.[20]

Since skilled workers still controlled the process of production, they could easily see themselves as the only real producers and their employers as superfluous parasites who used their ownership of capital, a symbolic value, to extract part of the real value they alone produced.

Hence, many would conclude that they would never obtain the 'full product' of their labour until they owned their own capital in an association. In those trades where skilled labour constituted the major capital and where workers controlled the process of production, they were fully capable of owning and operating their own workshop. As associationists, they were not so much seeking worker control of the workplace, which they still possessed to some degree, as the end of economic exploitation, the production of surplus value for the capitalist. It was precisely because they still possessed some control over the workplace that skilled workers felt the capacity to abolish the wage system by their own direct efforts.

Against worker impoverishment, the strike weapon had proved unavailing. Under the Napoleonic Code all strikes of workers were illegal and punishable with up to five years imprisonment. Prefects often showed sympathy for workers in labour disputes, but they never hesitated to use the full force of the law when they found their demands to be excessive or politically dangerous. During the Parisian strikes of 1830, 1833 and 1840, involving as many as 100,000 workers, the Government dispatched troops and arrested hundreds of strikers to quell the disturbances. Striking effectively during periods of economic recovery, workers often lost their new advantages during the subsequent downturn. With their craft cohesion, high wages and educational standards, the printers were one of the few Parisian trades to maintain an illegal trade union and engage in regular collective bargaining. Few trades were so exceptionally endowed to overcome both legal and economic obstacles to trade unionism.[21]

Where strikes proved ineffective, the association appeared as the only practical remedy to the workers' material suffering, the only way to guarantee steady employment, decent wages, and the full product of labour. Associationists could show that the introduction of machinery, influx of cheap labour and legal repression made trade union action impracticable. Rather than oppose machinery and technical innovation, associationists advised workers to reap their benefits through the collective ownership of industrial capital. Unlike strikes, commercial societies were legally protected by the code. With partial reform blocked, workers reached out for the solution that would end forever the 'exploitation of man by man'.

The Revolution of 1848 stirred tremendous hopes for the emancipation of labour through association. For labour spokesman Pierre Vinçard, 'the 24 of February was but the political prologue to a serious drama whose conclusion is the complete and radical emancipation of the producers'.[22] The workers who overthrew the Monarchy in the streets wanted a 'democratic and social' Republic that would favour associations with credit and contracts. Not only the formal socialists

79

Blanc and Albert, but even the moderates — Goudchaux, Marie, Marrast, Garnier-Pagès, Carnot and even General Cavaignac — seemed willing that 'workers should form associations in order to enjoy the fruits of their labour' and establishing a Commission for Workers at the Luxembourg, the Provisional Government committed itself to some kind of association programme. As workers assembled by trade to elect their delegates to the Luxembourg and formulate immediate demands for higher wages, shorter hours and an end to sweating subcontractors, they also planned associations for their final emancipation. While workers awaited the formation of a Ministry of Progress to finance their movement, a few associations were begun with the encouragement of the Luxembourg Commission, notably the Tailors Association, which employed over two thousand workers in the Clichy Prison.[23]

Despite the triumph of reaction — the defeat of Luxembourg candidates in the April election, the rejection of the Ministry of Progress and the dissolution of the Commission — the Luxembourg labour delegates continued its work on their own, coordinating strikes and political action and organising their own universal association, the *Société des corporations unies*, seeking the 'end of the exploitation of man by man through the immediate association of producers by the creation of associated workshops'. Beginning with contributions from 50,000 workers, they planned to establish a social workshop in a vital industry, gradually expanding production to other trades until all were included in a complete circuit of collective production and exchange.[24]

Although the repression following the June Days virtually eliminated political and trade unionist activity, it hardly interrupted the workers' association movement. Holding out associations as an alternative to violence, the moderate Republicans in the Assembly voted three million franc credit to associations and granted them concessions on public works contracts. Guided by the socialist principles of the *Atelier*, the official Commission granted the credit to competitive associations that provided for an expanding fund of 'inalienable capital' and the obligation to admit auxiliary wage earners as associates. The Cavaignac Government was sincerely committed to the success of this programme. Only with its demise did official policy turn to neglect and then active hostility.[25]

Pursuing a more centralist direction, the labour delegates took advantage of the favourable climate to promote their own independent association movement. In lieu of a Ministry of Progress, they continued the formation of a universal association to expand and coordinate the movement. At first they launched the *Chambre du Travail* to organise mutual credit and exchange among the newly created associations. When this failed, they agreed to join with Proudhon in his Bank of the People. Annexing syndicates of production and consumption to his

80

exchange bank, they tried to use it to 'centralise the function of production and consumption' in order to 'constitute the free and democratic *corporation* as the absolute and definitive regime of the workers'.[26] Within six weeks more than 20,000 workers, coming from a representative cross-section of Parisian trades,[27] and forty-nine socialist associations had joined. When, fearing the centralist tendencies of the Luxembourg delegates, Proudhon, the quintessential petty bourgeois, liquidated his bank, the delegates continued the project as *La mutualité des travailleurs* under the patronage of Louis Blanc and the 'democratic-socialist party'.[28]

After several other abortive efforts, association delegates finally agreed upon the statutes for a *Union des associations* in November 1849. Initiated by the socialist feminist Jeanne Deroin, the Union proposed to organise mutual credit and exchange among associations until all trades had acquired their own means of production. With 104 member associations the Union was preparing to issue its own labour bonds for this purpose when the government, fearing the resurgence of Republican socialism in May 1850, invaded its headquarters, arrested its leaders and dissolved the organisation.[29] Other projects for universal association followed, including the *Corporations nouvelles*, a central committee of Parisian trades organised by the typographers on the eve of Napoleon's *coup d'etat*.[30] Bound to the Republican party, the association movement shared its fate under the dictatorship of Louis-Napoleon.

Altogether nearly 300 socialist associations from 120 trades with perhaps 50,000 member workers were created in Paris under the Second Republic.[31] Open to all members of the trade willing to make a nominal investment, they were designed with an expanding fund of 'inalienable capital' to ensure the eventual emancipation of the entire trade. Patterned on either Buchezian or Luxembourg models, their statutes proclaimed a socialist aim 'to free workers through the extinction of the wage system', and 'to return to the producers the entire product of their labour'.[32] Through association the bronze workers sought 'the elimination of the intermediary parasites and usury capital through the socialisation of the instruments of labour . . . the emancipation of workers through the abolition of the employer class . . . [and] the realisation of harmony in work, the Republic in the shop and justice in the distribution of social burdens and advantages'.[33]

Established with insufficient capital, associations could only grow on the basis of severe wage deductions and the re-investment of all earnings. In fact, the only tangible advantage of membership in this period of persistent crisis was the assurance of steady employment. Displaying the carpenters' level as the sign of equality, associations usually found their first customers among other socialist workers and associations with whom a few exchanged through the medium of printed bonds. True to Luxembourg principles, the vast majority of trades had only one association. In those small trades where associations proliferated, notably the barbers and cooks, who served as channels of communication for the movement, efforts were made to centralise credit and supplies. Nearly all associations contained provisions for an 'inalienable fund' to be used for the extension of the association movement as a whole.[34]

Without the help of a democratic and social Republic, organised working class and universal association, this movement was bound to fail. For most associations life was hard and short. Lacking credit and customers, many were also beset with administrative problems and disputes. Elected managers did not always possess the requisite managerial and commercial skills. Internal disputes over managerial authority and the distribution of earnings often led to the dismissal of managers and the exclusion or resignation of members. Of the subsidised associations for which we have records, most remained marginal operations, comprising fewer members in 1851 than when they began; fewer than half survived the four years. Of forty-nine trades that started associations in 1849, only twenty-six still had them in 1851. Since new ones were constantly being created, however, there were still 200 in that year.[35]

What kind of trades participated in the movement? Did they, as the traditional argument would suggest, represent only the more independent, well paid or artisanal workers? We cannot determine whether the workers who formed associations were elite in their trades, but we can say something about the kinds of trades that participated. Participating trades were as diverse as the Parisian working class itself — from food, construction, furniture, clothing, leather, metal work, printing and luxury trades, indeed from all industrial groups except chemicals. As for the specific characteristics of participating trades, we can compare them statistically with the average Parisian worker with respect to size of enterprise, daily wage, number of apprentices, rate of unemployment, literacy and nature of residence.[36]

As regards daily wages, associated trades very much represented the Parisian average with few poor workers and very few well paid workers.[37] They were average with respect to unemployment as well, which reached an average of 54 per cent in 1848.[38] Where the traditional view would suggest greater participation among the smaller artisanal trades with many apprentices, independent artisans and domestic workers, the precise opposite is the case.[39] Instead, associated trades tended to come from the more concentrated industries, which admittedly were not very concentrated. In only two respects did the trades constitute an elite, in respect to rates of literacy and permanent residence in Paris.[40] These then were Parisian workers with a high level of education and political consciousness, who had undergone the process of proletarianisation, to which the association movement was an active transformative response.

Thus, the Parisian association movement represented the aspirations of an authentic proletariat for trade socialism, the collective ownership of industrial capital by a federation of skilled trades. With the help of the organised working class, social Republic and universal association, associations could be expected to gradually outcompete capitalist enterprises, accumulate capital and eventually emancipate all trades from the wage system. Since skilled trades represented the vast majority of French workers and still constituted the primary source of capital accumulation,[41] this programme would eventually encompass the socialisation of all industrial means of production.

Past historians, notably Marx,[42] saw this as 'petty bourgeois socialism', an essentially utopian middle class movement. If this was 'petty bourgeois socialism', however, it was not because of its social base, which was primarily working class, nor its objective, which was certainly some form of collectivisation. but its utopian belief that the objective could be attained peacefully within the framework of an essentially middle class Republic, that is, in Marxist terms, without the prior conquest of state power by the proletariat.

Yet, if bourgeois Republicans, transcending their immediate class interest, were sincere about the association programme, and little indicates that they were not, then what was utopian about this belief? When, after June, the petty bourgeoisie and peasantry joined workers in a social democratic alliance, did they not pose a real threat to capitalism that actually drove the bourgeoisie into the arms of Louis-Napoleon? And in 1849 did not many moderate Republicans also join this alliance? What was utopian about Republican cooperative socialism was that the bourgeoisie did not allow it to continue. Why? Because it contained the seeds of true socialism.

Notes

1.   Karl Marx, *The Class Struggles in France (1848-1850)* (New York, 1964), esp. pp. 42-5, 58, 123-6.
2.   The best recent synthesis is Roger Price, *The French Second Republic: A Social History* (Ithaca, N.Y., 1972), esp. pp. 5-12, 108-11. See also Georges Duveau, 'L'ouvrier de quarante-huit', *Revue socialiste*, nos. 17-18 (1948), pp. 73-9; *1848* (Paris, 1965); George Rudé, *The Crowd in History, 1730-1848* (New York, 1964), pp. 164-78, and Georges Renard, *La République de 1848 (1848-1852)*, vol. IX of *Histoire Socialiste*, ed. Jaurès (Paris, 1904).
3.   The standard survey of the labour movement is Edouard Dolléans, *Histoire du mouvement ouvrier*, 2 vols. (Paris, 1947-8).
4.   See Georges Weill, *Histoire du parti républicain en France de 1814 à 1870* (Paris, 1900).

5.   The authoritative work is Jean Gaumont, *Histoire générale de la coopéra-tion en France*, 2 vols. (Paris, 1924), who tended to downplay producers' associations as utopian.

6.   26 Sept.-17 Oct. 1830.

7.   Cf. François-André Isambert, 'Aux origines de l'association buchézienne', *Archives internationales de sociologie de la coopération*, no. 6 (1959), pp. 29-66.

8.   The question of mutual influence between *L'Artisan* and Buchez remains unresolved. See Buchez Mss. f. 201 (letter of 30 Aug. 1829), f. 202 (Athenée des ouvriers), and *Les sociétés populaires de 1830 par un négotiant* (Paris, 1830), p. 40, where Buchez mentions a project for an exchange bank. Cf. *L'Européen*; 17 Dec. 1831, and M. A. Ott, *Traité d'économie sociale* (Paris, 1851), p. 309.

9.   *Procés des citoyens Vignerte et Pagnerre, membres de la Société des droits de l'homme* (Paris, 1834), p. 8. See also *Discours de Cavaignac sur le droit d'association*, 15 Dec. 1832, *La tribune*, 31 Jan. 1833, *La gazette des tribunaux*, 2-3 Dec. 1833, 26-29 Apr. 1834, and *Association des travailleurs, signé Marc Dufraisse* (Paris, 1833).

10.   *Le journal du peuple*, esp. 14 June, 26 July, 2, 9, 23 Aug., 20, 27 Sept., 15, 22, 29 Nov. 1840. *Le national*, 9 July, 17 May 1840.

11.   Armand Cuvillier, *Un journal d'ouvriers: 'L'atelier', 1840-1850* (Paris, 1954), esp. pp. 132-76. *L'atelier*, esp. Oct. 1840, July, Aug., Dec. 1841, Nov. 1842, Oct. 1843. Also, A. Ott, *Les associations d'ouvriers* (Paris, 1837), p. 10; *Traité*, p. 314, C. F. Chevé, *Programme démocratique* (Paris, 1840).

12.   Frederick A. de Luna, *The French Republic under Cavaignac, 1848* (Princeton, 1969), esp. pp. 23-35, has reminded us that many moderate Republicans also had a programme for producers' association. Also, Weill, *Histoire du parti républicain*, pp. 185-93.

13.   Gaumont, I, 160-227. Accounts of the differences between moderates and radicals differ. Cf. Garnier-Pagès, *Histoire de la révolution de 1848* (Paris, n.d.), I, 35-7, II, 294; Dabiel Stern, *Histoire de la révolution de 1848*, 2 vols. (Paris, 1862), II, 570-71; Louis Blanc, *L'organisation du travail*, 5th ed. (Paris, 1848), pp. 270-84, and *Almanach des corporations nouvelles* (Paris, 1852), pp. 112-17.

14.   See the author's 'Parisian Workers and the Origins of Republican Socialism', forthcoming in *The Revolution of 1830*, ed. John Merriman.

15.   *Ibid.*

16.   Cf. Peter Stearns, *European Society in Upheaval: Social History Since 1800* (London, 1967), esp. pp. 138-54; Price, pp. 5-12, 108-11; Duveau, 'L'ouvrier de quarante-huit', pp. 73-9.

17.   Cf. Jacques Rougerie, *Procès des communards* (Paris, 1964), esp. pp. 165-208; '1871', *Le mouvement social*, no. 79 (1972), pp. 54-63.

18.   Jacques Rougerie, 'Remarques sur l'histoire de salaires à Paris au XIX siècle', *Le mouvement social*. no. 63 (1968), pp. 71-108; A. Perdiguier, *Statistique du salaire des ouvriers en reponse à M. Thiers* (Paris, 1849), Also, *Archives de la Seine*, DM^{12} 23, wages, 1830-47.

19.   Computations from the *Statistique de l'industrie à Paris résultante de l'enquête faite par la Chambre de commerce pour les années 1847-48* (Paris, 1851). Cf. George Rudé, 'La populations ouvrière parisienne de 1789 à 1791', *Annales historiques de la Révolution française*, XXXIX (1967), 15-35.

20. ˙ This discussion owes much to the sociological analyses of Alain Touraine, *L'évolution du travail ouvrier aux usines Renault* (Paris, 1955); 'L'évolution de la conscience ouvrière et l'idée socialiste', *Esprit*, XX (1955), 693-97, and Robert Blauner, *Alienation and Freedom: The Factory Worker and His Industry* (Chicago, 1964).

21.   Peter Stearns, 'Patterns of Industrial Strike Activity in France during the July Monarchy', *American Historical Review*, LXX (1965), 371-94. Jean-Pierre

Aguet, *Les grèves sous la Monarchie de Juillet, 1830-1847* (Geneva, 1954).
France, Office du travail, *Les associations professionelles ouvrières*, 4 vols. (Paris, 1897-1904), hereafter *APO*.

22.　*Le journal des travailleurs*, 4 June 1848.

23.　The major work is Rémi Gossez, *Les ouvriers de Paris: L'organisation, 1848-1851* (Paris, 1967), pp. 10-26, 45-79, 100-224, 314-21. Gossez' insistence that the association movement represented a line of retreat that only got underway after the June repression is inconsistent with the numerous examples of earlier projects he cites. Cf. his article 'Présyndicalisme ou pré-coopération? L'organisation ouvrière unitaire et ses phases dans le département de la Seine de 1834 à 1851', *Archives internationales de sociologie de la coopération*, no.6 (1959), pp. 67-89.

24.　*Le journal des travailleurs*, 8-25 June 1848.

25.　Ed. Octave Festy, *Les associations ouvrières encouragés par la deuxième République* (Paris, 1915), esp. pp. 1-10; *Procès-verbaux de Conseil d'encouragement pour les associations ouvrières, juillet 1848-24 octobre 1849* (Paris, 1917), pp. 123-33, 180-6, 407-42. Also, Emile Heftler, *Les associations coopératives de production sous la deuxième République* (Paris, 1899), Bernard Schnapper, 'Les sociétés ouvrières de production pendant la seconde République: L'exemple girondin', *Revue d'histoire économique et sociale*, XLIII (1965), 163-8, and De Luna, pp. 294-9.

26.　P. J. Proudhon, *Banque du peuple suivi du rapport de la commission des délégués du Luxembourg* (Paris, 1849), pp. 36-9.

27.　A trade breakdown of 8,694 worker members given in *Le peuple*, 23 March 1849, was compared to the general distribution in the population found in the *Statistique*.

28.　Gossez, 'Pré-syndicalisme', pp. 74-8; *Ouvriers*, pp. 327-45. *Le travail affranchi*, esp. 17, 21 Jan., 21 Mar. 1849. *Le peuple*, Sept. 1848-June 1849, passim.

29.　Gossez, *Ouvriers*, pp. 345-51; *La République*, 13-15 Nov. 1850. *Le nouveau monde*, 15 July 1849-15 Sept. 1850, passim. *Lettre aux associations sur l'organisation du credit, signé Jeanne Deroin* (Paris, 1851).

30.　Gossez, *Ouvriers*, pp. 351-64. *L'almanach des corporations nouvelles, op. cit.* Also, Gaumont, I, 237-311.

31.　A compilation of 284 associations was obtained from the *Atelier* and *L'économiste français* in Gaumont, I, 256, 279-80. *Le nouveau monde*, Sept. 1849, 15 Aug.-15 Sept. 1850, and Gossez, *Ouvriers*, pp. 319-22.

32.　*Association des ouvriers bijoutiers* (Paris, 1850), p. 5. *Pacte fondamentale de l'association fraternelle des ouvrières chemisières et coutières*.

33.　*Projet d'association destiné à l'industrie du bronze* (Paris, 1850), p. 3.

34.　For a bibliography of statutes see Gossez, *Ouvriers*, pp. 411-23. See also, André Cochut, *Les associations ouvrières* (Paris, 1851); Gilland, *Revue anécdotique des associations ouvrières* (Paris, 1850), and Antonym Romand, *Manuel des associations ouvrières* (Paris, 1849).

35.　Festy, *Associations*, esp. pp. 7-9, 158-63. Also, n. 26.

36.　Sixty-five of 120 associated trades were located in the *Statistique*.

37.　Five per cent of Parisian workers earned more than five francs daily. Forty-four trades had fewer and seventeen had more than five per cent. Fourteen per cent earned less than three francs. Forty-two trades had fewer and twenty-two had more than fourteen.

38.　Thirty had over and thirty under this rate.

39.　Fifty per cent of Parisian businesses were owned by individual artisans with or without aid. Forty-seven trades had fewer and sixteen more. Fifteen per cent of Parisian workers were employed at home. Forty-six had fewer and sixteen more. Five per cent were apprentices. Thirty-three had fewer — eleven none at all — and twenty-two more. Only ten per cent of Parisian enterprises employed more than ten workers. Thirty-nine trades had more and twenty fewer than this average.

40.   Twenty-one per cent of Parisian workers lived in *garnis* or lodging houses. Forty-four trades had fewer and fifteen more. According to employers, eighty-seven per cent could read and write. Nineteen had fewer and forty-three more, including many with total literacy.

41.   T. J. Markovitch, 'Le revenu industriel et artisanal sous la Monarchie de Juillet et le Second Empire', *Cahiers de l'I.S.E.A.*, no. 4 ((1967), pp. 78-88.

42.   Marx, esp. pp. 123-6.

ECONOMIC CHANGE AND ARTISAN DISCONTENT: THE TAILORS' HISTORY, 1800-48

Christopher H. Johnson

The 'springtime of peoples' it may have been, but for tens of thousands of European artisans, 1848 was a troubled time. The machine was taking its toll, especially in the textile industries. Shearmen, then hand-loom weavers succumbed to its onslaught. Reactions varied: the English weaver fell so quickly he barely raised his voice in protest; Silesians rioted, while Alsacians displaced their frustrations in attacks on Jews. Luddism had been endemic, and it went far beyond textile manufactures. Printers broke mechanical presses; carters tore up railroad tracks, shoemakers sabotaged cutting machines; and the revolutions of 1848 saw a good number of factories put to the torch. The struggle against mechanisation was generally fruitless, although occasionally, as with the weavers' strike in Lodève in 1845, it could be used to mobilise working-men for intelligent union action.[1]

The history of the adaptation of machines to industry and their role in generating artisan protest is well known. The process constitutes perhaps the most obvious facet of the industrial transition. It is questionable, however, that it was the most important, especially in France during the first half of the nineteenth century. For side-by-side with technological change were alterations in the structure and organisation of work that affected the lives of artisans no less profoundly than the competition of machines. Even in 'mechanised' industries such as textiles, it might be well argued that the massive expansion of rural out-working was of greater social significance than the installation of water- or steam-driven mule jennies in factory towns. In an arc from Elbeuf to Mulhouse, the countryside of northern France became a vast dispersed workshop toiling for urban entrepreneurs.[2] Besides the broad social change that occurred in the rural world, this process upset the balance of labour resources in many cities, and with more immediate consequences for the social order. Traditional handloom weavers of Reims, for instance, suffered and fought back as employment and wages diminished throughout the July Monarchy.[3] But equally profound changes occurred in industries virtually uneffected by the machine. And when one considers the rather paltry share of mechanised production in France even in 1848,[4] it becomes clear that structural, rather than strictly technological, change and its social effects deserve first rank in the analysis of French economic modernisation in its early phases.

Two points must be made immediately. First of all, structural transformation operates more slowly, less perceptibly than the installation of machinery. The artisan affected by it is not simply wiped out. His craft survives, but his work situation becomes more difficult. Silk workers in Lyon, for instance, faced with increasing competition from cheap rural labour and generally more sophisticated employment practices, were submitted to a variety of subtle pressures; a ferocious pace of work when orders were plentiful followed by long periods of inactivity; increasing deductions for 'faults' in the finished product; and an inability to establish any kind of fixed wage scale.[5] Everyone knows their reaction — the insurrections 1831 and 1834 and a record of sustained radicalism matched by few of their contemporaries. Secondly, a more minute division of labour altered skill levels required in the process of production, and undermined both the artisan's material benefits and his sense of self-esteem without, again, driving him from his craft entirely. The vast majority of industrial work before the advent of the modern age was performed by people with skills the practice of which called for a broad expertise in the making of an entire good. Apprenticeship and long years as a journeyman had developed this skill and made it part of one's being. Over all, one's craft was as much a way of life as a livelihood. Nineteenth century specialisation eroded this situation. One of many examples is that of the clock makers of eastern France whose work increasingly involved little more than fashioning standardised parts. To make an entire timepiece on one's own was a luxury left only to the finest craftsmen. Thus, in contrast to the direct impact of the machine, structural transformation deeply affected the working lives of people without eliminating them from the industrial scene. For some, the central problem was competition of people 'foreign' to their craft, now no longer protected as a legal corporation. For others skill requirements — and wages — declined due to new ways of organising production.

When viewed from the perspective of structural change, a variety of anomalies about the social and economic development of nineteenth century France can be clarified. Lévy-Leboyer and others have argued persuasively that the tendency of French capitalists to avoid expensive machinery if possible was not due to timidity but to solid economic rationality: French industry could compete more effectively on the international market with quality goods and this meant a high percentage of outlay for hand labour in the final cost price.[6] Why install clumsy power looms in the 1830s when their low quality product would sell for half as much again as the same English good? It was thus to imaginative labour use that one must look in order to develop greater efficiency.

Many scholars also question why the French working class was so radical before and during 1848, if industrialisation had moved so slowly? One answer, of course, would be that ideals of liberty and social equality were motivated less by economic forces than by the new concepts of human rights bequeathed by the Enlightenment and the French Revolution.[7] A subcategory of this problem is our understanding of the French Revolution of 1848. If Marx was wrong in stressing conflict between labour and capital as the central antagonism in 1848, then much of his social theory is thrown open to question. But as so often occurs in great debates, the arguments are presented with goals other than the development of scientific history in mind and well before all the facts are in. Among the most pressing questions to be answered remains: what happened to non-mechanised artisan industry in nineteenth century France?[8] The point to be made in this essay is that capitalism progressed rapidly in this area before 1848 and created circumstances for working people within it moving them towards radical action. These working people were artisans in the sense that they were still handworkers. But hand work is not necessarily non-capitalist work. A process of proletarianisation was occurring during the July Monarchy, and its consequences would be manifest in 1848.

From several points of view, the clothing industry, specifically tailoring for men, provides an excellent example of the general trend. Workers in this industry were among the most vocal and well-organised militants throughout the July Monarchy and Second Republic. They rallied to various utopian ideologies, especially Cabet's Icarianism, and must be regarded, along with the carpenters and printers perhaps, as the leading trade in the French union movement.[9] While they may not have produced working class leaders of the stature of Martin Nadaud, Joseph Benoit, or Pierre Vinçard, the tailors had more than their share of heroes: Grignon, leader of the great strike of Paris of 1833; Firman Favard, Cabet's chief organiser for Paris; Albert Troncin, martyr to the union cause accused of organising the general strike in 1840; Bérard, one of the principal promoters of worker association in France. In 1848, tailors led the way in cooperation for production among workers. Master tailors and cutters had their own associations, among them one of the first *syndicats patronals*. In the press, tailors published a number of trade journals, and one of them, the *Journal des Tailleurs*, became the voice of master tailors' economic and social interests. Two tailors also figured among the handful of editors of *l'Atelier*, the famous worker newspaper published during the forties. While Paris, where tailors constituted the largest single trade, took the lead in all movements, tailors in Nantes, Bordeaux, Lyon, and several smaller provincial cities contributed to artisan protest to a degree that far surpassed their actual numbers.

The sheer volume of such agitation was impressive. By and large, these outward signs of discontent have been studied, but their causes remain obscure. Certainly the competition from machines was of minimal importance. Thimonnier had patented a sewing machine by the 1830s, but it had little direct application to the precise work demanded in the production of most articles. While a factory making 'vêtements sans couture' was established in Paris during the early 1830s and a cutting machine was tried later on, they had no impact on the trade.[10] It is rather to structural change that one must look. So massive was the transformation in tailoring between 1800 and 1848 in this respect, that it is hardly possible to speak of the same industry from one date to the next. Simply put, it amounts to the history of the rise of capitalism within one of the purest artisan crafts of the age.

Under the old regime, tailoring was almost exclusively a service industry. The customer purchased the cloth from a draper when he wished to have clothing made and took it around to his tailor to be cut and sewn. It was nearly unknown for a tailor to maintain his own stock. Most tailors were small scale craftsmen who sold only their skills. Masters normally employed few men and were not wealthy people.[11] Their clientele came from the upper levels of society. Most Frenchmen made their own clothes, although a minority in the cities purchased used tailor-made garments from *fripiers*, old clothes dealers who touched up the cast off clothing of the rich.

The first major changes in tailoring occurred during the Revolution and Empire. Wealthier tailors in Paris began to establish their own stocks or at least presented the customer with a folder of samples. The former came to be termed 'merchant tailors', while the latter formed a category of 'échantillonneurs'. Both distinguished themselves from the majority of small masters still working *à la façon*. The customer gained several advantages by patronising this new species of tailor. He saved time and money in avoiding the cloth merchant. He never purchased more cloth than was needed for the article to be made and could usually be assured that quality conformed to price. Since tailors increasinly bought in volume from their suppliers, the cost of the cloth was reduced as well. Finally, merchant tailors bought and sold on credit and their larger shops were usually mortgaged. Some even borrowed money to purchase the businesses of retiring masters.[12] Unfortunately we do not possess precise figures on the growth of such operations, but by 1848, they totally dominated bespoke tailoring.[13] The Empire was the moment of transition: a barely perceptible revolution was occurring, one which clearly involved the assimilation of capitalist practices among a more prosperous minority of tailors. Industrial liberty, consequent to the abolition of the guilds in 1791, was steering the industry into a new world.

Sources are unanimous about the prosperity of tailoring during the later Revolutionary period and the Empire.[14] A number of factors produced this result. In the first place, there is an element rather peculiar to the clothing industry: new political orientations generally called forth new styles of dress. Moreover, the Empire, at least, put a premium on pomp and show. Court styles evolved yearly, and a properly dressed notable was obliged to visit his tailor more often to keep abreast. The military *éclat*, the fancy dress balls, promenades, all made the era of the Empire a goldmine for the businesslike tailor. Paris was the centre of the universe. Military officers patronised private tailors, and civilian courtiers, bureaucrats and ordinary bourgeois aped their manner of dress. It was not without reason that, in 1832, Guillaume Compaing, editor of the *Journal des Tailleurs* would look back with nostalgia to an age when something other than the *habit noir* was in vogue.[15] But the demands of 'society' alone do not explain the prosperity of tailoring during the Empire. While few historians would now describe it as a truly progressive era for the French economy, many artisan industries, especially those of Paris, could not help but benefit from the protection they received from Napoleonic industrial policy and the Continental System.[16] Moreover, the labour supply was restricted due to military service. Finally, this period, as well as the middle years of the Restoration, saw the creation of new wealth among businessmen in Paris and various provincial centres. Textiles, metallurgy, machine building, tanneries, paper mills, porcelain and many other industries and commercial houses pushed towards greater productivity. Their owners, investors, salesmen, and even foremen could afford more clothes more often. This demand factor, derivitive of nascent industrial capitalism, contrived with these other elements to produce a kind of 'golden age' for tailors from roughly 1800 to 1825.[17] Merchant tailors and *échantillonneurs* did exceptionally well, but small traditional masters also prospered. Wage earners in the trade benefited from these happy circumstances, and access to shop ownership was a quite reasonable expectation for many of them.[18]

This generation of relative ease came to an abrupt end with the crisis of 1827-32. A detailed history of this economic depression has yet to be written, but the variety of distress surrounding the revolution of 1830 provides clear evidence as to its severity.[19] In the tailoring industry it was a true crossroads. The *Journal des Tailleurs*, founded in August 1830, spoke often of the industry's precipitous decline, of bankruptcies among overextended tailors (one, at least, went insane), and of growing dissatisfaction among the underemployed journeymen.

One of the key problems had been the influx of young tailors to Paris from the provinces and foreign countries during the earlier period of prosperity. By the 1840s two-fifths of all tailors in Paris were immigrants to France, coming mainly from Germany and the Austrian Empire. Xenophobic antagonisms were thus added to the strains of already overcrowded conditions.[20] During the crisis, which worsened after the revolution of 1830, the scramble for work forced wages down. The austerity of the new regime further upset tailors; almost for the first time, political change did little to stimulate the thirst for new styles. About the only positive influence of the revolution was a new demand for National Guard uniforms.[21] An overall impression of what happened to tailors during this period can be gleaned from bankruptcy statistics for the Seine department: 1831 and 1832 were disaster years for small merchants, the category that included merchant tailors.[22]

Thus began stage two in the modernisation of tailoring. This collapse, however, was not the most important fact of the era. In the context of the crisis itself, a new phenomenon, one destined to transform the craft entirely, entered the picture. This was *confection*, the production of ready-made clothing. In its most basic definition, 'the manufacturers called *confectionneurs* are those who make, or have made, men's clothing in advance and in a certain number of sizes and models, articles which are displayed for direct sale or are shipped to the departments or foreign lands'.[23]

A preliminary sense of tailors dismay over the onslaught of *confection* may be gained by moving briefly two decades ahead, to the Revolution of 1848. On 13 March 1848 a mass meeting of master and journeymen tailors sought to bring the two levels of bespoke tailoring into greater harmony. While differing on other issues, both agreed that the main threat to their industry came from *confection*. Finally, a voice demanded the floor. 'I am a *confectionneur*. Let me speak to you', cried M. Franck, owner of one of the largest ready-made houses in Paris; but he was drowned out by 'great agitation' in the hall.

'*M. le Président*. Let him speak.
From all sides. Let him speak. [Silence is reestablished.]
M. le Président. The citizen who takes the floor carries out a courageous deed; it is proper that *confection* be represented here and that it present its case.
A voice. It is the workers' galleries that are interrupting! [M. Leclerc asks them to listen to M. Franck.]
M. Franck. I do not come here to defend the *confectionneurs*; it is rather the general interest, the Republic, that I come here to defend [the agitation is at its height again; interpellations are directed at the speaker from all over the hall].

M. le Président. Messieurs, I ask for silence in the name of the dignity of our corporation. Let the speaker speak, you will be able to respond.

A voice. Let him not speak of politics.

M. Franck. The guilds are abolished. Today the corporations are all the working people! You believe that in increasing wages, you will improve your lot — this is an error . . . [An explosion of murmurs from all parts of the hall. The speaker tries to speak but he is interrupted from all sides. He is forced to give up the floor.] [24]

Such violent emotion turned to action during the June Days as warehouses and workshops of *confectionneurs* were attacked. One of the largest, located on the Place de la Bastille, and operated by the brother of P. Parissot, owner of *La Belle Jardinière*, Paris' largest department store, was burned to the ground on 24 June.[25] Everywhere in France, tailors raged against the ready-made industry. The master tailors of Lyon summarised a generation of frustration in the condemnation of *confectionneurs* that they addressed to their counterparts in Paris.

'You are as aware as we of the catastrophe besetting our industry and feel its evil effects. It was among you that first saw the light of day these soulless speculators who see only money in life, who have no other religion than gold, who have abnegated all sentiments of humanity, who have substituted the word traffic for that of commerce, machine for that of workers so as not to have to pay any attention to their needs, who push us toward the centralization of commerce, in other words toward the total negation of the motto that adorns our public buildings.'[26]

What, precisely, was *confection*, and how did it develop? The first *bona fide Maison de confection* was founded in 1828 by Ternaux, a highly successful Parisian draper. Its retail outlet, called *Le Bonhomme Richard*, must also be regarded as France's first department store. Both the timing of this development and the profession of its creator are significant. The year 1828 witnessed the first pangs of the depressed condition that would haunt the tailoring industry for several years thereafter and Ternaux found it possible to attract workers at lower than normal wages. As a prosperous merchant-manufacturer in woollens he had the wherewithal to make important fixed capital outlays and to produce large quantities in advance. This was a predictable response of emergent capitalism but was regarded by tailors as merely an incursion into their trade by outside elements. Ternaux' experiment failed in the midst of the deepening crisis three years later, no doubt evoking smiles of secret satisfaction among merchant tailors.[27]

Ironically, however, the latter made their own contributions to the

origins of *confection* and in ways that relate to capitalist attitudes in
their camp as well. Beginning around 1825, when customers failed to
claim their orders, 'special merchants' (probably *fripiers*) bought the
left goods at reduced prices and resold them in the markets of Saint-
Jacques or the Temple.[28] This seems to have been a fairly significant
commerce, although no statistics are available. More important, perhaps, were the advances in pattern making evident during the twenties:
Guillaume Compaing, F. A. Barde and several other merchant tailors
pioneered the development of pattern calculations rooted in geometry.
While their goal was to increase the precision of bespoke tailoring (and
reduce the number of time consuming fittings), it is obvious that their
work was of immediate value in the production of garments cut to standard sizes.[29]

The first volume business for *confectionneurs*, however, was in loose
fitting clothes such as smocks, jackets and dressing gowns. More closely
fitted articles seem to have been produced mainly for export.[30] Although adequate statistics are lacking, all indications point to the mid-
1830s as the period of initial expansion. In general, despite the *Bonhomme Richard* attempt (or perhaps because of its failure) Parisian
confectionneurs concentrated on the French provinces, sending out
their own travelling salesmen or selling to other travelling merchants.
The 1840s were clearly the years of 'take-off'. Department stores now
proliferated in Paris, especially along the *quais*, and the full range of
men's clothing — including suits and riding coats — began to appear on
the racks. Mannequins (another bespoke tailor invention) became
widely used, newspaper advertisements began to appear, and the caver-
nous 'grands magasins de nouveautés' emerged as yet another wonder of
Paris. A sure sign of success, department stores had to endure the barbs
of caricaturists. De Beaumont left an impression of the immensity of
the *Ville de Paris* in this interchange between one of its employees and
a customer:

> 'You'd like to buy a cotton cap, Sir? It's not here, Sir. You will find
> the cotton cap counter in the fifth gallery. When you reach the
> one-hundred-and-thirty-third gas lamp, turn to the right and the fifth
> counter on the right will be the one you want!'
> 'The devil you say . . . it's that far? In that case I'll take a cabrio-
> let!'[31]

Only in 1848, however, can we begin to sense the enormity of the
transformation that had occurred in the French men's clothing industry. The enquiry on Parisian industry conducted by the Chamber of
Commerce (1847-8) supplemented by that of the *Journal de Tailleurs*
(1848) and of Lémann, a later owner of *La Belle Jardinière* (1857),
provides the first concrete data available. In 1847, Parisian tailoring as a

whole had gross sales of over 80 million francs and, of that, *confection* took some 28 million. Thus, expanding from nothing a generation earlier, ready-made clothing had captured over one third of the total business. The share was really higher than that because the Chamber of Commerce listed the gross income of *appiéceurs* (5.5 million), sub-contractors who worked proportionately more for *confectionneurs* than bespoke tailors, separately. Bespoke tailors accounted for some-thing more than 60 per cent while *fripiers* made up the remainder. The division of employees between the two main branches was more even, with bespoke tailors holding the edge, 9,765 to 7,445. *Patrons appié-ceurs*, most of whom were master tailors without shops, and their slightly larger number of workers totalled 7,953. The fact that *confec-tion* employed more workers in proportion to the value of its output should not come as a surprise since the pathway to success in this business was the exploitation of cheap labour. This is made abundantly clear in the percentages of female labour employed in each branch — only 26 per cent in bespoke tailoring as opposed to a full 60 per cent in *confec-tion*. Moreover, while bespoke tailoring still managed to maintain two thirds of its work force in the shop (despite tremendous pressures to the contrary), the overwhelming majority (83 per cent) of *confection*'s employees worked *en chambre*. The sweating system had already reached alarming proportions in Paris, especially when one realises that only 280 out of the 3,393 subcontracting 'bosses' (*patrons appiéceurs*) were actually shopowning entrepreneurs. The great mass of them were home workers just like their employees.[32]

Behind these figures lies a history of human endeavour, frustration and misery. The *confectionneurs* were a new breed in an ancient craft. They were wealthy, confident and self-congratulatory.[33] If we are to believe hostile sources, none of them came from tailoring itself.[34] A few, no doubt, were former *fripiers*, especially the smaller *confection-neurs* who dated from the late twenties and early thirties. But the earlier business experience of individuals we know something about, such as Lémann or Ternaux, was in textiles, and the authors of the 1848 Chamber of Commerce report claimed that the success of *confec-tion* 'caused woollens and stuffs manufacturers to take an interest in it'. Moreover, forty-one of the 223 *confectionneurs* listed in Paris for 1848 were still involved in other areas of manufacturing, none of which were bespoke tailoring. The line between the two branches was rigid. This was not for moral reasons. Very few merchant tailors made enough money to risk their fortunes on *confection* while drapers were often wealthy men. As *confectionneurs* they did remarkably well also and were clearly big businessmen. A simple comparison of volume of business and number of employees among master tailors and *confec-tionneurs* tells us a great deal.[35]

	Master Tailors	Confectionneurs
Employing more than 10	202	121
Employing 2-10	1,205	90
Employing 1 only	735	21
Work alone	870	0
Totals	3,012 employ 9,765	223 employ 7,445
Gross Returns above 200,000 F.	14	25
Gross Returns 100,000-200,000	42	30
Gross Returns 50,000-100,000	137	35
Gross Returns 25,000- 50,000	270	42
Gross Returns 10,000- 25,000	466	40
Gross Returns 5,000- 10,000	400	30
Gross Returns 1,000- 5,000	950	30
Less than 1,000	730	1

It is obvious from these figures that there were a few *confection-neurs* who were small operators and certain merchant tailors who were very prosperous, but these numbers reveal an inverse ratio in terms of the scale of business between the two branches of the industry. The typical master tailor cleared perhaps 2,500 francs per year and employed one cutter, a few sewers, and gave work out to *appiéceurs*. A typical *confectionneur* made possibly ten times as much and controlled a small army of workers either in his direct employ or as *appiéceurs*.

This kind of success was achieved on the basis of an outlook generally foreign to that of most tailors and a series of practices that took full advantage of the socioeconomic circumstances besetting the industry after 1830. The essential philosophy underlying *confection* was 'to attract the majority of consumers by producing cheaply'. This would be achieved, according to Lémann, a leading *confectionneur*, by 'ordering new, light, different, and above all lowpriced stuff; and since the cloth is cheap and cannot rival those of superior quality, it is necessary to call on other industries such as *lace, bonneterie*, and ribbon-making to give cheap clothing an attractive appearance, a coquetterie, an elegance that belies its real value'.[36] Lémann's disarming honesty is appreciated, but there were other secrets in the *confectionneurs*' craft that he either ignored or denied. On the subject of materials, he side-stepped the issues of when and what sorts of stuff were purchased. *Confectionneurs* bought at the end of the season, picking up bin ends and seconds; and in its very origins, *confection* grew out of drapers' needs to put their own unsold cloth to use.[37]

But it was in this area of labour use that *confection*, at least during the July Monarchy,[38] found its clearest advantages. Here a look at the work structures of the entire craft and the nature of its labour supply will be necessary.

Traditionally tailoring had three categories of workers. The cutters comprised a small minority of highly skilled artisans who could receive as much as two thousand francs per year (twice the wage of the average tailor) and were often hired on a yearly contract. Virtually none were paid by the piece. These men made up an elite unto themselves, differing only slightly from the outlooks of their masters whom they hoped to follow into the ranks of independent shop owners.[39] Shops also kept one or two day-wage workers whose work varied from basting to repair jobs. These men were called *pompiers* (literally, firemen); they enjoyed job security, although they gained only moderate wages, and possessed considerable experience in the trade.[40] Finally, the traditional shop employed *ouvriers tailleurs*, who did the sewing and whose image — sitting crosslegged bent over their work on a large platform — is among the best-known from the artisan past. They were the true working class, and the vast majority of the tailor population. Before the advent of the merchant tailor nearly all worked in the shops of their masters. But by the 1820s, increasing numbers toiled in their own dwellings, and the phenomenon of the subcontractor had appeared. Three levels of workers existed, with the differentiation being based merely on the masters' perception of their skills. The best of them did more difficult work in finer materials, with less demanding jobs going to the lower categories. Nearly all received piece wages, which simply depended on the type of garment they were sewing. (Riding or morning coats and suits ranked at the top, while vests and trousers were turned over to the young and/or least skilled men.[41]) In general, daily wages varied between three and five francs during the first half of the century.[42] Downward pressures on piece wages existed from 1830 on, but this was not, nor had it ever been, the main worry for the *ouvrier tailleur*. Irregularity of employment menaced them much more. Tailoring had one of the longest *morte-saisons* (lay-off periods) in artisan industry, running from four to six months, half in midwinter and half in midsummer after the new styles were out. In March or September all hands were occupied, but only in the most prosperous years would employment be maintained for more than a handful on a year-round basis. As the ranks of tailors swelled, the main issue was never *if* one would find work, but for how long. The same problem existed for workers outside the shops but was compounded by the fact that most of them were *ouvriers* of the second and third ranks. Here also was the bulk of what female labour entered men's tailoring before 1830. Master tailors employed outworkers only in the heavy season; before 1830 they probably maintained no more than one fifth of the work force even then.[43]

Such was the anatomy of work in tailoring on the eve of the advent of *confection*. The crisis of 1827-32 and a weak stylistic response to the political revolution combined with normal seasonal lay-offs and an emergent putting out system in bespoke tailoring itself to provide fertile ground for its development. The primordial factor in the early success of *confection* was clearly the irregularity of work in bespoke tailoring. Ready-made clothes, by definition, could not follow *la mode* directly; producing in advance, *confection* had to be ready when each new buying season commenced; its natural rhythm was nearly the inverse of made-to-order shops and willing hands were available during the latter's off-season. Available, and cheap. Tailor shops themselves paid those workers they kept on roughly two thirds the high season rate. *Confectionneurs* found it possible to get off at least as cheaply.[44] Overall, the inquiry of 1847-8 found that the average daily wage over the whole year for male bespoke tailors was 3.86 francs, while workers in *confection* gained only 3.26. Both figures include cutters and *pompiers*, who seem to have received about the same wages in both branches.[45] From one point of view, *confection* could be regarded as a blessing for worker-tailors since it provided alternative employment for bespoke men and greater regularity of pay for those who worked fulltime in it. It also served a curious function in 1832 and 1833. Strikes for higher wages among bespoke tailors occurred in the fall of both years. These have received minute attention from historians because of their tactical sophistication and especially because of the worker cooperative organised during the 1833 strike. But the famous report of worker tailors of 1862 also remarks that the striking workers, not wishing to work (for master tailors) without an increase, preferred to take work from the *confectionneurs* and carry it out in their own lodgings.[46]

A second labour factor important in the rise of *confection* was its use of *ouvriers en chambre*. The typical *confection* establishment maintained a team of cutters and a small number of *pompiers* in the shop. The rest of its work was done on a putting out basis.[47] Commissioned agents from the firm oversaw these operations in a fashion quite similar to that of the textile domestic system, an exercise, of course, familiar to many of these budding drapers-*confectionneurs*. And as with textile putting-out in the 19th century,[48] a system of subcontracting operated side by side with the direct management of sweated labour. The use of *appiéceurs*, often master tailors who had failed to maintain their own shop, multiplied with the emergence of *confection*. Spawned by an earlier age of capitalist bespoke tailoring, these *marchandeurs* now contributed heavily to the success of a competing mode of production. Worker-*appiéceurs* and many 'master'-*appiéceurs* were the business' marginal people. They jumped back and forth from *confectionneur* to bespoke tailor depending on the season and received the lowest pay of any element in the industry. A global view of their conditions of existence may be observed in figures from 1848. There were, at that time, 3,393 *patrons appiéceurs*, a tenfold increase at least from 1830. Only 549 of them employed two or more workers (24 more than 10) while two thirds provided jobs for a single worker. The great mass of these bosses, therefore, were in reality merely workers themselves. Gross return figures bear this out as well with only ninety of them generating more than 5000 francs in business. Their adult male workers, who numbered only 1,267, averaged 3.05 francs a day, the lowest wage of all tailors.[49] Women comprised the mass of their workers, however, totalling over 3,200, and were clearly the key to the whole enterprise. This form of *marchandage* grew under the stimulus of *confection*, but bespoke tailors obviously adapted to it also, for the enquiry of 1848 assumes that the labours of *appiéceurs* were about evenly divided between the two branches.

The final, and perhaps primordial, aspect of labour savings for *confectionneurs* (and in reaction, for bespoke tailors as well) was the employment of women. No specific figures exist on the numbers of females employed in tailoring for men as of 1830. But all sources imply that they were inconsequential. Only the most menial sewing jobs (especially vests) were given to women, who seem to have worked only part-time at home. But by 1848, nearly half of the 22,000 worker-tailors in Paris were women, as were some 866 of the *patrons appiéceurs*. Their numbers and wages were as follows:

| | Women working for | | | |
	Bespoke Tailors	Confectionneurs	Appiéceurs	Totals
Number (incl. girls)	2,839	4,454	3,222	10,515
% of work force	28%	60%	71%	48%
Wage Earners[50]	2,382	4,448	1,312	-
Average Daily Wage	2.04	1.35	1.58	1.58

Thus in *confection* itself and among *appiéceurs*, a category of workers given massive stimulation by *confection*, women clearly dominated the work force by 1848. But the percentage of women workers in bespoke tailoring was quite significant as well. Despite outcries against it from made-to-order tailors at all ranks, female labour provided one means to combat the competition of *confection*. Wages of women in general were less than half those of men although bespoke tailors paid proportionately better than the other branches. The fundamental figure is that of *confectionneurs*, and one can easily appreciate the role of female labour in their final cost prices.

Cheaper materials, cheap labour, volume production and mass marketing: such were the bases of *confection*'s ascendancy. By the mid-1840s, the voice of the merchant-tailors, the *Journal des Tailleurs*, was well aware that *maisons de confection* had 'invaded a large part of the affairs of Paris'.[51] Other newspapers — especially those of the left such as *L'Atelier*, Cabet's *Le Populaire* and Leroux's *Revue Indépendante*, attacked the 'concentration' and 'monopoly' practices inherent in their operations. But while the *confectionneur* sometimes took on the image of evil incarnate, his newly won place was founded securely upon the economic realities analysed above. Charles Compaing expressed both the irrational prejudices and the grim realism of bespoke tailors in his newspaper's most vigorous attack on *confection* during the July Monarchy:

> 'Confection, this competition false in its claim to give at half price products of the same value, hostile in that tailors' business practices are held up in comparison to it! The *grand mot* is always: reductions 30% below the going price; but note well that there is no going price in clothing and that tailors are far from realizing a profit of 30%!
>
> 'Thus confection is decidedly a separate trade. The worker who prostitutes his talent on cheap goods not only degrades himself but destroys his future; pride once forgotten, abilities weaken . . .
>
> 'Yet what frustration, because he and his fellow merchant tailors had themselves accepted capitalist ethics.
>
> 'To be sure, we are far from contesting the freedom of commerce, guilds are no longer in season. anyone can do this or that commerce without giving proof of his capacities; useless it is therefore, dangerous even, to employ any means to impede a competition necessary to certain classes of consumers.'[52]

What Compaing recognised in this final line was that *confection* was here to stay because it had found markets among the middle and lower middle income groups for whom made-to-order clothing was inaccessible. The demand factor is the crucial constant in the rise of *confection*. The proliferation of prosperous petty bourgeois, of market orientated peasants, and of skilled workers spawned by the nascent industrial revolution in France, when tied with efficacious distribution procedures and easier means of communications, created the market it sought. Moreover, a fact that bespoke tailors only occasionally admitted even to themselves, *confection* had made headway among the rich as well. There were several reasons for this. Delays due to numerous fittings had always been an inevitable complaint against tailors. For the man in a hurry, the *confectionneurs* provided the answer.[53] Moreover, concern over quality seems to have declined

during the July Monarchy. The *Journal des Tailleurs* rued the era end-
lessly. A 'société des riches' was formed as early as 1831 to protest
formally the slovenly standards that were invading the clothing industry
and to issue an appeal to their fellow aristocrats of wealth to return to
good taste.[54] The department stores of the forties were generally sump-
tious affairs. Compaing, in remarking that 'one cannot buy a suit like
an umbrella', was still awestruck by these 'veritable palaces' with their
fancy changing rooms and their smooth salesmen.[55] But even if a rich
man recognised, with Compaing, that ready-made suits 'fit like a raincoat', he still could safely buy his raincoat, cloak, occasional jacket or
trousers, and any number of items that previously he would have left
to his tailor from these stores and clearly at cheaper prices. Finally,
there is the importance of *confection* for the French provinces. Marseille, Niort, Reims, and many other provincial towns saw their tailoring
industries undercut by the arrival of the ready-made merchants.[56]
Lémann claimed that the demand in the provinces was the real basis for
the triumph of *confection* (especially as rail connection developed) and
that their main customers were wealthy people.[57]

From all points of view, then, by 1848 capitalism had set full sail in
the French clothing industry. In so doing it substantially recast the lives
of all who were tied to that industry. Our final task is now to re-exam-
ine the larger issues posed earlier and see what the tailors' experience
tells us about them.

First, there is the question of worker-tailor militance. Before 1848,
there is little direct evidence of worker protest against *confection* itself.
The enemy was not perceived to lie above and beyond their craft, but
within. Master-worker conflict is the most obvious fact of the tailors'
history during the July Monarchy. Aguet has enumerated thirty-one
tailors' strikes in France during this period[58] and the breadth and
sophistication of their union organisation was without parallel. Certainly it was natural to strike out at the proximate enemy: for the journeymen, who else but their masters refused them work in the off-season?
Who else pressured them during the rush periods? Who else sought to
replace as many of 'their' jobs as possible with outside, often female,
labour? And who else attempted to keep their piece wages at a level
below what they had earned in the twenties? Other kinds of problems
intervened. While merchant tailors tightened their belts, many small
masters succumbed to the competition of confection and fell into the
ranks of workers, usually, however, as *appiéceurs*, thus glutting the
labour market with more cheap labour as their former employees
scrambled to survive. The big bespoke houses became bigger and were
forced to introduce the streamlining and impersonality that marked the
establishments of *confectionneurs*. But they appear to have trimmed
down the number of people actually working in their shops. What was

occurring, of course, was a levelling process of major proportions. Few tailors were forced to leave their craft but a majority, be they small master or worker, led increasingly insecure, poorly renumerated, and perhaps above all, less dignified lives.

Tailors were skilled and literate. They had a reputation for reflection and intelligence. Their pride in craft was intense, perhaps in part due to the fact that they had traditionally served a demanding social elite. But their wages had never been high and their margin of existence was consequently narrow. The circumstances of the thirties and forties tended to crush pride and push them to the edge of poverty. As early as 1833, Cabet, whose knowledge of the tailors' world was intimate, published a typical workers' budget in which receipts and the cost of bare necessities barely offset each other. In 1848, wherever in France one finds statistics, the mass of tailors are found in the same position. Such conditions, especially coming on the heels of the high expectations produced by thirty years of prosperity, were the breeding ground for revolt.

A final point should be emphasised. These proletarianised artisans, the men who continued to work for the bespoke tailors, were the militants of the 1830s and 1840s. There were no strikes against *confectionneurs* or *appiéceurs*. It is possible that 'tailors' listed in the cadres of Cabet or among the militants of 1848 came from the latter categories, but one indicator — women in the tailoring business — reveals none in the forefront of militant activity. The feminists of forty-eight lamented the plight of the *giletière*, but female needleworkers' social action occurred almost exclusively among *couturières*, workers in ladies' garments.[59]

It is equally interesting to follow merchant tailors' reactions to the silent revolution occurring in this trade. Three stages before 1848 are perceptible. The first lasting until around 1837, was marked by indifference toward confection and a typically capitalist condemnation of their unruly and unappreciative workers. The second witnessed the dawning of an understanding of ready-made's implications and a quasi-paternalistic, quasi-'professional' drive to encourage their workers to contain their antagonism. The third, beginning in 1845 found the merchant tailor fully in the grips of *confection*'s impact, and a kind of panic began to set in. Finally, the revolution of 1848 carried them to the hope that *confection* could be extirpated altogether, and, while still seeking the upper hand with their workers they proposed 'corporate' measures of worker-master alliance. The workers for their part, shifted their main antagonism to *confection* but never put their trust in their masters either. They went over, *en masse*, to the concepts of socialist worker association.

This process can be traced most easily through the *Journal des Tailleurs*. It was primarily a technical and trade journal but its editors also included information and opinion on the tailoring business and on labour relations. After the founding of the *Société philanthropique des maîtres tailleurs*, an association of the major merchant tailors of Paris, in 1833, it reported the group's meetings and defended it without criticism. Finally in 1848, the *Journal* took on the subtitle, 'the Monitor of the Corporation', and devoted itself almost exclusively to discussing the programmes developed by master tailors. In short, it represented the outlook and attitude of the more prosperous tailors for over twenty years and is a precious source.

Phase one in the thinking of master tailors saw little change in their outlook from the 1820s with the exception of normal concern over the gravity of the continuing depression and complaints about the lack-lustre styles of the new regime. A few houses of *confection* existed, to be sure, but the *Journal des Tailleurs* ignored them. This is especially interesting because we know from other sources that important contracts for National Guard uniforms went to *confectionneurs*[60] and the *Journal* was intensely interested in the possible commerce for bespoke tailors that the expansion of the Guard represented. Obviously the confident merchant tailors gave little serious thought to these upstarts. As for the workers, the journal greeted the founding of the *Société philanthropique des ouvriers tailleurs* in the summer of 1831 with pleasure in view of its stated function as a mutual benefit society and house of call. It also assumed that 'once the workers are back in the job, they would abandon their political discussions and no longer think of joining the Saint Simonians, Amis du Peuple, etc . . . Tranquillity would come to them as peaceful and laborious Frenchmen who ask only for the work and the freedom for which an honest artisan has the right to ask.'[61] Such a viewpoint could hardly approve worker coalition for collective redress of grievances, and the *Journal* predictably opposed the strikes of November 1832 and their massive successor one year later. But while condemning worker attempts to impose an 'iron authority' over the masters, the *Journal* thought that better daily wages might be procured by developing greater efficiency in the shops and thus faster production for the same piecerates through improved methods. It argued that larger shops, being better equipped and organised, were preferable to small ones and even seemed to be inviting small masters to return to worker status.[62] Such an attitude clearly represented merchant tailor interests. There were hints of the impact of *confection* in these discussions although the *Journal* never referred to it specific-ally. Falling prices due to the thirst for *bon marché*, a fairly obvious reference to the competition of cheap goods, provided an excuse for opposing the strike of 1832. The paper also counselled master tailors to reduce outworking, avoid speed-up in high season, and pay equiva-lent rates in low, all conflict laden issues that *confection* accentuated. It was nevertheless assumed that such reforms could be made without cost; a blithe self-assurance still seemed to dominate the merchant tailors' mentality.[63]

Master tailors of Paris had much less to worry about, at least from their workers, over the next several years. The workers' *Société Philanthropique* was dissolved under threat of law, and police repression of all association after 1834 kept worker tailors generally at bay. It was otherwise in the provinces, however, as twelve of the fifty strikes recorded by Aguet for 1834-8 occurred among tailors. Widespread organisation, apparently modelled on that of Paris, was apparent as well.[64]

A careful examination of ten justice files on these strikes and on the pursuit of tailor unions yields no reference to *confection*, but this was the period of rapid expansion of ready-made commerce into the provinces and the nature of worker grievances (downward pressure on wages) implies that masters were feeling the competition.[65]

But in Paris itself an important change was taking place in merchant tailors' atttitudes toward their workers as well as toward their methods of operating their businesses. By 1838, *confection* was a clear danger and virtually every proposal for reform reflected it. The *Société Philanthropique des Maîtres Tailleurs de Paris*, born as a masters' syndicate to offset worker pressures, was radically reorientating its goals. Compaing, in a long article on this group, emphatically denied that it was a 'coalition against the worker'. Instead its funds were to be used to 'assist the workers of its members, whether in case of sickness or lack of work; a doctor is attached to the society . . .'.[66] Compaing went on, however, to list a variety of other functions that the Society should perform. Delays in responding to new styles could be reduced if the Society would set out guidelines well before each season. They should agree to extend the work season to give their workers 'more regular employment'. The Society should limit and control credit sales, standardise prices for the clients of the same shop, and use its influence to improve the quality of the cloth available in Paris. They should seek to develop greater uniformity in methods of production to avoid costly retraining when workers moved from one shop to another. The relevance of all these proposals to the conditions imposed by confection is obvious. Finally Compaing issued a renewed cry for better professional training of workers and reminded them of the proud heritage of their craft. The latter theme would increasingly become a hallmark of his paper, a sure indication of a deterioration in this regard.[67] The year 1840 showed, however, that professionalism could have more than one meaning. As in 1832-3, workers took advantage of a post-depression revival to strike for higher wages in the bespoke tailoring industry. Beginning in April, this action had stimulated a virtual general strike in Paris by September. Several leaders of the worker tailors were arrested despite the fact that their industry had already settled.[68] Our concern here is with what the merchant tailors attempted to do. Their Society met in full force and dealt collectively with their ungrateful charges. To contain the strike, they took an interesting course: they went to the Prefect of the Seine and sought the legal imposition of the *livret* on all worker tailors.[69] The *livret* was a marvellous means of black listing troublemakers and of controlling the work force more effectively. They were unknown to tailoring heretofore. But they were also an official badge of qualification, a kind of journeyman's certificate. Workers certainly resented them, but they did tend to guarantee them greater job security (if they remained 'bons garçons', of course). What is significant in this case is that the master tailors were looking in two directions in seeking obligatory *livret* usage in their craft: toward worker tailors whose syndical activities they wished to impede and toward the *confectionneurs*, the better part of whose workers (many of them being unapprenticed) could not hope to qualify for the 'right' to carry a *livret* as a recognised tailor. While the strike of 1840 failed, the merchant tailors also lost their campaign for the *livret*. In a curious dialectical twist, the only winners in this situation were the *confectionneurs*.

But it was only one of many victories over the next five years: *confectionneurs*, their *commis*, their department stores, their *appiéceurs* would spread like a net over the trade. If Compaing had earlier spoken circumspectly about them and even rosily predicted that there was room for both *confection* and bespoke tailoring even in January 1845, only a month later he would write of the 'invasion' of *confection* and call for the outright suppression of *appiéceurs*. He cried out against the deterioration of workers' skills due to over-specialisation or to accepting cheap and nasty jobs from *confectionneurs* in the off-season. Two years later we find him frantically supporting a bonus system developed by the merchant tailor Janssens to reward his men for good work. The hope was to offset declining pride in craftsmanship and the enormous turnover in shopworkers. In the same article he raised the general alarm against *confection* quoted above.[70] Thus on the eve of the February revolution, bespoke tailoring was in crisis, and really for the first time, was fully aware of it. Yet the merchant tailors retained a belief, bred by decades of operation as medium sized capitalists, in the free enterprise system. The revolution shook this opinion but did not dispel it.

1847 had not been a particularly prosperous year for tailors, (nor was it for most Frenchmen), but 1848 was a disaster. According to the enquiry of the Paris Chamber of Commerce, the returns in the entire industry declined a massive 52 per cent and employment was halved. Bespoke tailors suffered the most, their figures being 58 per cent and 57 per cent, while *confectionneurs* saw their business drop 42 per cent and their employment 44 per cent. The latter figures, however, are somewhat misleading because 'the crisis had little effect on the small *confectionneurs*' whose business declined only 28 per cent due to their capture of an important share of National Guard uniform work.[71] This means, then, that the large houses absorbed a disproportionate share of the loss, a fact also underlined elsewhere.[72] To what extent employment was drastically curtailed among large *confectionneurs* remains somewhat open to question. In an extremely detailed report prepared after the June Days, Parissot of *La Belle Jardinière* claimed he paid more to workers in the first six months of 1848 than the same period of 1847 and tried to lay no one off, despite an important diminution of sales.[73] No source denies, however, that the revolution worsened the situation of all connected with the tailoring industry.

There was nevertheless one important avenue of relief, the preparation of the new, lower priced National Guard uniforms, now for the first time an expense absorbed by the state rather than individual guardsmen.[74] And it was in this context that the fundamental socioeconomic principles of the worker-tailors first appeared. Their masters' reactions followed. In analysing the opinions of each we can begin to gain a sense of these artisans' ideologies. They were not concepts pulled from the air, but grew out of a generation of change in the concrete circumstances of their trade. For the workers the 'social workshop' established at the old debtors' prison of Clichy to manufacture uniforms for the National and Mobile Guards became the focal point of their hopes. Petitioned on 6 March 1848,[75] it was definitively authorised by the provisional government (due to the personal intervention of Louis Blanc) late in the month and began operations on 1 April. Clichy turned out to be the most successful worker cooperative of the forty-eight era.[76] Original financing came from the government in the form of a loan, and the fifty charter associates and all who later joined them were obliged to contribute nothing, a situation distinguishing it from most other cooperatives of the period. Wages were low (two francs per day) but equal for all. Profits were ploughed back into the operation and used to repay all debts including those owed to the government. By 11 June, 1,500 men worked in the establishment and it had produced 22,927 tunics and trousers for the guards. As of that date (the last for which we have information before the government contracts were withdrawn in the wake of the June Days), it had made a gross profit of 35,741 F. It survived the midsummer crisis and continued without the benefit of government support or contracts, paid off all original loans (including 11,500 francs from the master tailors), maintained a large work force of associates and even sent piece work to non-associates on the outside, and made handsome profits on lower priced goods. By mid-1849, the association had moved to a more convenient location at 23

Rue Faubourg St Denis (the former seat of Proudhon's Banque du Peuple). When M. Gilland, a journalist, went there to interview Bérard, the current director, he found the workers contented, the warehouse full of cloth, and pictures of Barbès and Jesus Christ (as worker-republican) on the walls.[77] The experience of Clichy stimulated other cooperatives among tailors and probably played the most important role of any cooperative in promoting the idea of worker association during the Second Republic. Cooperation dominated the minds of the journeymen tailors of Paris to such an extent that most other programmes of social reform fell by the wayside. What should be underlined is that worker tailors, while willing to cooperate with their masters on certain broad questions relating to their trade (opposition to *confection* above all), stood aloof from them and in fact really sought competition with them in their devotion to worker cooperative principles. Over and again, when asked by their masters to join various programmes they were sponsoring, the latter were rebuffed.[78] Naturally from past experience, the workers suspected the entreaties of goodwill of their superiors; even after they received their loan from the *Société Philanthropique des Maitres Tailleurs*, the men at Clichy were convinced that this apparent generosity was motivated mainly by the masters' hope to keep the guard contracts out of the hands of the *confectionneurs*.[79]

Workers found in cooperation what they thought to be a solution to the forces crushing them over the past generation. By running their own affairs, they might re-establish their sense of dignity as skilled artisans. Their confraternity with fellow workers was realised in the equal pay policies of Clichy. How different were capacities anyway? Simultaneously, however, their willingness to accept only moderate profits would allow them to outcompete the capitalists. Cooperation thus seemed to be a way to maintain and make triumphant a moral economics that enhanced and strengthened human dignity in a world of capitalism by beating the latter at its own game. This is the kernel of all cooperative thinking. Its strength in France and its impact on later French Socialism — so convincingly demonstrated by Bernard Moss[80] — is rooted in experiences such as the one we have described for the tailors: a broad exposure to capitalism without being decapitated by it. The peculiarities of French Socialism are in the long run derivative of the peculiarities of French capitalism, and an understanding of the structural transformation in artisan industry takes us a long way toward explaining them.

Master tailors, of course, were the men in the middle and emerge as the tragic figures in the story. The more successful of them lept at capitalism when the opportunity arose in the first third of the century. They continued for years unaware of the forces undermining this position. Their small scale brethren slipped away into the ranks of the *appiéceurs*. Their workers suffered and rebelled. The masters first tried to crush them, then to mollify them with philanthropic acts and talk of craft pride. Only in the later forties did the realities of their situation become fully apparent.

In 1848 we find the bespoke tailors in the worst business slump they had ever experienced, workers rejecting them out of hand, and the monster of *confection* no less menacing. Their reactions underline their tragic situation. Their Society discussed nothing but the 'organisation of work' and the means to contain *confection*. The masters sought to tie themselves together and many talked of broad master-worker co-operatives. The term 'corporation' reappeared. The Society hoped to emerge as the voice and regulator of the entire body of Parisian tailors. Capitalism, in name and concept was attacked: the source of all misery for 'patrons and workers alike' was 'unlimited free competition'; 'all were falling under the capitalist yoke'.[81] All of the consequences and advantages of *confection*, low and unregulated wages, *appiéceurs*, home production, off-season lay-offs, female labour, department stores, *bon marché* itself, became subjects of attack in reform proposals. But − and here remains the fundamental contradiction in their mentality − two generations on the margins of modern capitalism prevented them from developing any really new perspectives on the main issue, free competition. In concluding a report to the government in 1848, the *Société des Maîtres Tailleurs* felt obliged to remark that 'if we demand these rights be recognised, it is still far from our thought to eliminate legal competition, for competition is necessary to the French genius for innovation; what we want to destroy is the homicidal competition as it existed under the egotistic and corrupt regime that we have just overthrown'.[82] Politically, master tailors were democratic republicans; the collapse of their business in 1848 did not shake their faith in the revolution. But bigness and cut-throat competition had to be controlled. *Marchandage* was of course officially abolished by the Provisional Government. This, however, was the only measure taken that seemed to limit the power of *confection*. Master tailors tried other devices themselves, such as erecting a cloth buying service for all members of the Society,[83] but they could not control the march of capitalism in their industry.

The experience of 1848 for the tailors, as with many other artisan industries, clarified a number of questions only vaguely understood beforehand. Capitalism did indeed create two great classes and mechanisation was not necessarily the only cause behind the process. The true capitalists in tailoring, the *confectionneurs*, retained their faith in Orléanism, went on to Bonapartism, or simply combined the two, while the proletarians (for the word was surely applicable by then) opted for cooperative socialism. The petty capitalists had hoped to cajole the workers into programmes emphasising corporate solidarity in the political context of a kind of middle class republicanism. They failed and would continue to fail. In the long run, their fate, especially in France where small business and quality production always maintained an allure, was not simply extermination. But by the end of the nineteenth century and then in the twentieth, corporatism had taken on a concrete political meaning, and many of the descendants of the *Société Philanthropique des Maîtres Tailleurs* responded to its appeal.

This examination of the tailors' history during the first half of the nineteenth century renders clues that assist in building a composite picture of the transition in France from traditional economic and social life to a modern industrial society. This artisan industry experienced the emergence of capitalist practices in two stages, first among the bespoke tailors, then in the rise of the ready-made business, without the least bit of mechanisation. The entire trade benefited from the first, or petty-capitalist stage; it is not unreasonable to view the period before 1827 as a golden age. The second stage saw the intrusion of major capital and production and marketing practices that were unmistakably 'modern'. All elements in the trade were hurt by it, although it took a decade, at least, for the victims to recognise fully the source of their discontent. This discontent was all the more bitter due to the earlier prosperity and the rising expectations that accompanied it. Throughout the thirties, masters and men in bespoke tailoring were at loggerheads, but their conflicts over wages and conditions of work were only symptomatic of the larger transformation that *confection* was bringing about. The very gradualness of this change assured that no part of the tailoring industry would collapse entirely nor that the day to day work would be altered radically. Thus, unlike the sabre stroke that killed the English handloom weaver, the bespoke tailor-workers suffered from a 'cancer' (the very word was used) that engulfed their trade without impairing its essential functions. In defence, worker tailors, after flirting perhaps with this or that utopian doctrine, settled upon large scale cooperation of production to try to meet the threat. Their masters also banded together and resurrected corporate ideals. The fundamental point, however, is that they all had time to do so. Neither group was involved in some hopeless, last ditch effort doomed to inevitable failure. The masters may, perhaps, be called 'reactionary', but certainly the great mass of the proletarianised artisans who rallied to cooperation were nurturing a body of social thought, whether termed syndicalism fifty years later or worker control today, that has maintained an honoured place in modern socialism. In the minds of these worker-tailors of the forty-eight era — and of the shoemakers, cabinetmakers, printers, and score of other handwork craftsmen — there were locked memories of an artisan tradition; they did not discard them but rather adapted them to new conditions created by the rise of capitalism in their trades. Whether or not their orientation was 'progressive', remains to be seen.

Notes

1.   F. E. Manuel, 'L'introduction des machines en France et les ouvriers: la grève des tisserands de Lodève en 1845', *Revue d'histoire moderne* (1935), pp. 211-25, 352-72. See also Charles Ballot, *L'introduction du machinisme dans l'industrie française* (Lille, 1923); Fernand Rude, 'L'arrondissement de Vienne en 1845', in Rude, ed., *La Révolution de 1848 dans le département de l'Isère* (Grenoble 1949), p. 230 ff. E. P. Thompson, *The Making of the English Working Class* (London 1963); Duncan Thomas, *The English Handloom Weaver* (Manchester 1969); P. H. Noyes, *Organization and Revolution: Working Class Association in the German Revolutions of 1848-1849* (Princeton 1966).
2.   A. Demangeon, *La plaine picarde* (Paris 1905), p. 265 ff. J. Sion, *Les paysans de la Normandie orientale* (Paris 1909), pp. 301-17; Mme Kahan-Rabecq, *La classe ouvrière en Alsace pendant la Monarchie de Juillet* (Paris 1939), ch. 3.
3.   Marc Vincent, 'La situation économique et la condition des travailleurs dans le département de la Marne d'après l'enquête de 1848 sur le travail agricole et industriel', in G. Laurent, ed., *Le Département de la Marne et la Révolution de 1848* (Châlon-sur-Marne, 1948), pp. 93-5.
4.   No writer on the French economy during the first half of the nineteenth century denies this. The question is whether or nor industrialisation and mechanisation are necessarily synonymous.
5.   See the recent work of Robert Bezucha, 'The "Pre-industrial" Worker Movement: The *Canuts* of Lyon', in R. Bezucha, ed., *Modern European Social History* (Lexington, Mass. 1971), pp. 93-123.
6.   This line of analysis owes much to Lévy-Leboyer's great work, *Les banques européenes et l'industrialization internationale dans la première moitié du XIXe siècle* (Paris 1964), especially p. 74 ff.
7.   This is the impression left in the work of those adhering to the 'Cobban school's' attack on the Mathiez-Lefebvre tradition of French Revolutionary historiography. On the first half of the nineteenth century, see Alfred Cobban, 'The Middle Class in France, 1815-1848', *French Historical Studies*, 5 (1967), pp. 41-56.
8.   On the need for research in this area, see Charles and Richard Tilly, 'Agenda for European Economic History in the 1970s', *Journal of Economic History*, Special Issue (1971), pp. 184-98.
9.   See Christopher H. Johnson, *Utopian Communism in France: Cabet and the Icarians, 1839-1851* (Ithaca, N.Y. 1974), especially ch. 4; J.-P. Aguet, *Contribution à l'histoire du mouvement ouvrier français: les grèves sous la Monarchie de Juillet (1830-1847)* (Geneva 1954), and Octave Festy, 'Dix ans d'histoire corporative des ouvriers tailleurs d'habits (1830-1840)', *Revue d'histoire des doctrines économiques et sociales*, 5 (1912), pp. 166-99.
10.   *Journal des Tailleurs* B.N. V.28638-58, 1 March 1831; Archives Nationales (hereafter A.N.) F12 2318 dos 'Machines à coudre'.
11.   See especially Maurice Garden, *Lyon et les lyonnais au XVIIIe siècle* (Paris n.d. [1973]), pp. 340-42. On the tailors under the old regime: 'Les Tailleurs d'habits', *Rapports des délégués des ouvriers parisiens à l'exposition de Londres en 1862* (Paris 1862-4), p. 327 ff. B.N. V.38241; *Journal des Tailleurs*, 1 Aug. 1850; Martin St. Léon, *Histoire des corporations de métiers depuis leur origine jusqu'à leur supression en 1791* (Paris 1897).

12.   *Journal des Tailleurs*, 21 Nov. 1830, 1 Apr., 1 May 1831, 1 Feb. 1833; Chambre de Commerce de Paris, *Statistique de l'industrie à Paris résultant de l'enquête faite par la chambre de Commerce pour les années 1847-1848* (Paris 1851), pp. 293-4; *Exposition de Londres*, p. 342.

13.   Chambre de Commerce, *Statistique*, p. 293; *Journal des Tailleurs*: all post-revolutionary issues in 1848 indicate this influence over the made-to-order trade. The word 'bespoke' simply means tailor-made and is employed here to distinguish this mode of production from 'ready-made' clothing — *confection* in French.

14.   See especially *Exposition de Londres*, pp. 343-4, and Durand (Pierre Vinçard) *De la Condition des ouvriers de Paris de 1789 jusqu'en 1841* (Paris 1841), pp. 59, 86-7, 90, 101-4, 120.

15.   *Journal des Tailleurs*, 1 July 1832. See also issue of 16 May 1831.

16.   Louis Bergeron, 'Problèmes économiques de la France napoléonienne', *Revue d'histoire moderne et contemporaine*, 17 (1970), pp. 467-505.

17.   It is quite probable that many other artisan industries experienced similar conditions during the first quarter of the nineteenth century. More research will be necessary to prove it, but such a boom followed by much more difficult times over the next generation may be one of the key explanations for the massive growth of artisan protest in general during the 1840s.

18.   Piece wages increased significantly after 1700. The reporters on the London exhibition of 1861, who review the history of the tailoring trade with great insight, estimate that the average worker gained 5-6 francs for the sewing of a suit in 1805 and 20-22 towards 1830. The time required approximately doubled, but this still represents an appreciable increase. *Exposition de Londres*, p. 344.

19.   The essential study remains Paul Gonnet, 'Esquisse de la crise économique de 1827 à 1832', *Revue d'histoire économique et sociale*, 33 (1955), pp. 249-91. See also John Merriman, ed., *1830 and the Origins of the Social Question in France* (New York, forthcoming), and Lévy-Leboyer, *Les Banques*, pp. 479-87.

20.   Chambre de Commerce, *Statistique*, p. 289. *Journal des Tailleurs*, 21 November 1830, 16 November 1833 and 1 November 1848. See also André Cochut, *Les Associations ouvrières* (Paris 1851) and Durand (Vançard), *De la Conditions*, pp. 130-5.

21.   *Journal des Tailleurs*, issues of later 1830 and 1831. Only on 16 June 1832 could the editor begin to hope for a 'rebirth of commerce' .

22.   Comments based on an analysis of the 'Statistique des faillites', Seine, F[20] 722.

23.   Chambre de Commerce, *Statistique*, p. 297.

24.   *Journal des Tailleurs*, 1 April 1848.

25.   P. Parissot to the Ministre de l'Agriculture et du Commerce, 11 July 1848, A.N., F[12] 2337.

26.   Molnar, *Projet d'adresse à la Société philanthropique des marchands tailleurs de Paris par celle de Lyon* (Lyon 1849), p. 3.

27.   Henriette Vannier, *La Mode et ses métiers: Frivolités et luttes des classes (1830-1870)* (Paris 1960), pp. 101-2.

28.   Lémann, confectionneur, *De l'industrie des vêtements confectionnés en France: Réponse aux questions de la Commission permanente des valeurs* (Paris 1857), p. 13.

29.   Compaing promoted his own 'méthode de la coup' in every issue of the *Journal des Tailleurs*. His major technical work was *Traité de la coupe des vêtements* (Paris 1830). Barde's study by the same title went through several printings in the thirties. Also a M. Dartmann published a *Manuel des Tailleurs* in 1831 and patented his method. A.N., F[12] 2388.

30.   Chambre de Commerce, *Statistique*, p. 297; Lémann, *Vêtements confectionnés*, p. 13.

31. On the development of *confection* in these years see above all Lémann, pp. 13-16. De Beaumont's lithograph is reproduced in Vannier, *La Mode*, p. 102.
32. Chambre de Commerce, *Statistique*, figures drawn from pp. 285-305. Lémann, *Vêtements confectionnés*, indicates that the gross returns of *confection* had increased to 38,000,000 francs by 1856. It should also be noted that 1847 was somewhat an off-year. Compaing estimated, for instance, that ten years before the sales of tailoring had amounted to nearly '100 million'. *Journal des Tailleurs*, 1 June 1839.
33. Bespoke tailors and *confectionneurs* agreed about this, if nothing else. See Lémann, *Vêtements confectionnés, passim*, and *Journal des Tailleurs*, 1 Aug. 1850.
34. For example see *Journal des Tailleurs*, 16 Nov. 1844, 1 Jan, 1845, 1 Feb. 1847, 1 and 16 Aug. 1850; Ch. Callebaut, *A messieurs les Maîtres et Ouvriers Tailleurs* (Paris 1848), 3; Molnar, *Projet*, p. 2.
35. Chambre de Commerce, *Statistique*, p. 286. The *Journal des Tailleurs* made its own inquiry in 1848, and, perhaps naturally, produced figures showing an even greater split between the two branches. Issue of 1 Sept. 1848.
36. Lémann, *Vêtements confectionnés*, p. 31.
37. Cochut, *Les Associations*, p. 30, is clearest on this question.
38. Lémann argues vociferously that *confectionneurs* paid wages equivalent to those of bespoke tailors at the time of his report (1857). *Vêtements confectionnés*, p. 52 ff. This position is challenged by the worker-authors of the report of 1862. *Exposition de Londres*, p. 346 ff. The Chambre de Commerce de Paris enquiry, cited below, leaves no doubt about the question for the July Monarchy.
39. *Journal des Tailleurs*, 16 Feb. 1837; Chambre de Commerce, *Statistique*, p. 295.
40. Chambre de Commerce, *Statistique*, p. 296. *Journal des Tailleurs*, 16 March 1848.
41. *Journal des Tailleurs*, 16 March 1848.
42. The *Journal des Tailleurs* and the *Statistique* of the Chambre de Commerce agree on this range for the 1847-8 era. Wage statistics do not exist for earlier times but both indicate that wages had not increased since 1830 and were, in all likelihood, lower on the average than twenty years before. All other commentators on the tailors agree. Calculation of wages was very difficult because of the uncertainties of time consumed in producing various garments. The only solid figures available are piece rates. The figures, of course, are averages for days *worked*; the lay-off periods are not averaged in.
43. *Morte-saison* estimates are given in Lémann, the *Journal des Tailleurs*, the workers' report of 1862, Cochut, and the Chambre de Commerce *Statistique*. All agree that three months was the absolute minimum period in bespoke tailoring but that six months was not unusual. See also Grignon, *et al.*, in *Lettres adressées au journal La Tribune par des ouvriers* (Paris 1833), p. 5, for a classic statement of workers' dread of the off-season. Outworking, to which we shall return in greater detail, is rued by the *Journal des Tailleurs* in early 1830s, but it is still thankful that a large majority remain in the shops.
44. On the basic logic of *confection*'s advantages in this respect, see especially Cochut, *Les Associations*, pp. 30-1; Chambre de Commerce, *Statistique*, pp. 297-8; and Lémann, p. 16.
45. Chambre de Commerce, *Statistique*, p. 289.
46. *Exposition de Londres*, p. 345.
47. Chambre de Commerce, *Statistique*, p. 298.
48. See, for instance, Canton de Tourcoing, 'Enquête au le travail agricole et industriel', (1848), Archives départementales, Nord, M 547/1, for a detailed discussion of such questions.

49.   On *appiéceurs*, see *Journal des Tailleurs*, 16 Jan. 1845; Cochut, *Les associations*, pp. 29-30; and especially Chambre de Commerce, *Statistique*, pp. 301-5. The last, in fact, notes that the average income of the *patrons appiéceurs* was slightly lower (3.01 francs) than the wage of the workers.

50.   A varying proportion worked in the family and were not included in the wage figures of the Chambre de Commerce enquiry. The wage earning *appiéceurs* are also relatively few because wives and daughters of *patron-appiéceurs* figure prominently in the total number. This of course does not lessen their importance in the work force. Figures in this table are drawn from *Statistique*, pp. 285-305.

51.   *Journal des Tailleurs*, 1 Feb. 1845.

52.   *Ibid.*, 1 Feb. 1847.

53.   Lémann notes that some *confectionneurs* promised twenty-four hour service, even for garments to be made to order. *Vêtements confectionnés*, p. 14.

54.   *Journal des Tailleurs*, 1 Apr. 1831.

55.   *Ibid.*, 1 Nov. 1844.

56.   Tailors in Grenoble actually tore down the stalls of ready-made salesmen in 1844. A.N., BB[18] 1421 dos. 8243. In Marseille, Reims, and Niort, see the 'Enquête sur le travail agricole et industriel', A.N. C948, 960, 966. Also the list of petitions to the Comité de Travail in 1848 (A.N., C934), reveals the signifi cance of *confection* as a grievance among provincial tailors.

57.   Lémann, *Vêtements confectionnés*, pp. 14-15.

58.   Aguet, *Les Grèves, passim.*

59.   Vannier, *La Mode*, pp. 111-16.

60.   Lémann, *Vêtements confectionnés*, p. 14.

61.   *Journal des Tailleurs*, 1 July 1832.

62.   The *Journal* had already discussed this issue, discouraging workers from attempting to set up on their own because of the dangers of commerce, April and May 1831.

63.   61. *Ibid.*, 16 March 1832 (reprinted 1 Nov. 1833 and 16 Nov. 1833). On these strikes and other worker-master conflict during this era, see Festy, *Le Mouvement ouvrier au début de la Monarchie de Juillet (1830-1834)* (Paris 1908), pp. 77, 136-7, 139-40, 221-6, 233-49; Festy, 'Dix Années', pp. 166-78; Grignon, *Reflexions d'un ouvrier tailleur* (Paris 1833); Aguet, *Les grèves*, pp. 75-83; *La Tribune*, issues of Nov. and Dec. 1833, Jan.-Feb. 1834; and for a sense of the impact of the worker-tailor's spirit on other trades, Bonnet, *Réponse d'un ouvrier typographe à une lettre des maîtres tailleurs* (Paris 1833).

64.   Aguet, *Les grèves*, pp. 130-65; Festy, 'Dix années', pp. 178-90.

65.   A.N., BB[18] 1230 dos. 1994 (Poitiers) 1239 dos. 3612 (Nimes), 1366 dos. 4838 (Nantes, Niort, Bordeaux, Lorient, St. Malo).

66.   *Journal des Tailleurs*, 1 March 1838. The physician was Charles Place, who apparently devoted his life to industrial medicine. He wrote an interesting study of diseases and malformations common among tailors, *Hygiène des Tailleurs* (Paris 1835).

67.   *Journal des Tailleurs*, 1 March 1838 and 1 Feb. 1839.

68.   On the great strike of 1840, see Aguet, *Les grèves*, pp. 196-8; Festy, 'Le mouvement ouvrier à Paris en 1840', *Revue de l'Ecole libre des sciences politiques*, 6 (1913), pp. 266-97; *L'Atelier*, Sept. and Oct. 1840, May 1841.

69.   The *livret*, invented by Napoleonic legislation, was a little notebook that many workers were forced to carry in which their previous employment and their comportment as workers were indicated. For the *Journal des Tailleurs'* retrospective justification of the masters' action, see its issue of 1 Nov. 1848.

70.   *Ibid.*, 1 Jan. 1845, 1 Feb. 1847.

71.   Chambre de Commerce, *Statistique*, p. 298.

72.   Lavigne, *Aux Tailleurs d'Habits: maîtres, coupeurs et ouvriers* (Paris 1848), p. 1.

73.   'Notes remises par les industriels des 8e et 9e arrondissements, après une conférence avec le Général Cavaignac', A.N., F^{12} 2337.

74.   The whole question of the structuring, manning, and equipping of the National Guard, as well as the election of its officers was an important political debate during the early revolutionary period. See especially *Le Populaire* and *Le Réprésentant du Peuple* during March and April 1848.

75.   A.N., BB^{30} 316.

76.   On Clichy, see above all, Cochut, *Les Associations*, pp. 33-49 and *L'Atelier*, 11 June 1848 and 29 Nov. 1849.

77.   *L'Atelier*, 29 Nov. 1849.

78.   The principal source remains the *Journal des Tailleurs*, all issues for 1848.

79.   This, at least, was the opinion of Bérard, *L'Atelier*, 29 Nov. 1849.

80.   'Origins of the French Labour Movement: The Socialism of Skilled Workers', unpub. Ph.D. Diss., Columbia University, 1972. For the various co-operative efforts of tailors see Cochut, *Les Associations*, pp. 40-9; Jean Gaumont, *Histoire générale de la Coopération*, I (Paris 1924), pp. 260 ff; and the excellent brief discussion by Rémi Gossez in *Les Ouvriers de Paris*, I: *L'Organisation* (Paris 1967), pp. 160-6.

81.   'Petition des tailleurs d'habits à l'Assemblée Nationale', [1848] A.N., C 2257.

82.   J. Perrody, *et al.*, 'Rapport adressé aux Citoyens Réprésentants du Peuple, membres du Comité des travailleurs, par la commission centrale des patrons et ouvriers tailleurs d'habits' [1848], A.N., C 2234. One should not be misled by the 'commission centrale'; Perrody was then president of the old Société Philanthropique which had adjusted its title to include workers. Lavigne, *Aux Tailleurs d'habits* and Callebaut, *A Messieurs*, repeat the same theme. They were both masters.

83.   *Journal des Tailleurs*, 1 Aug. 1852.

THE PARIS CLUB MOVEMENT IN 1848

Peter Amann

Most often the French revolution of 1848 has been studied by way of
the activities and policies of the central government, a preoccupation
readily explained in terms of a traditional definition of the historian's
task, the ubiquity of the French administrative apparatus, and the
tempting richness of the sources documenting French officialdom. This
preoccupation was once so much taken for granted that even today
historians rarely question this curious approach to the study of revolution. Though the Provisional Government, the Executive Commission
and General Cavaignac's para-presidency were, directly or not, the products of revolution, none of these governmental organs were in any
meaningful sense 'revolutionary'. The best we can say is that in 1848
successive French national governments were all responding to extraordinary conditions, that they were indeed 'coping with revolution' —
an admission that the locus of 'revolution' was to be found somewhere
else. Historians, in short, have tended to tell about the exploits and
shortcomings of the fire brigade when they thought they were talking
about the great conflagration.

Current attempts to deal with the social history of the Second
Republic are raising a different set of problems. Few historians would
question that a thorough and up to date analysis of French society at
the mid-nineteenth century mark, such as that recently provided by
Professor Price, is invaluable as a prerequisite to understanding the
revolution of 1848.[1] To return to the tired fire metaphor: this sort of
social history assesses just how, where and why the social edifice was
inflammable. Possibly — though the social revolutions of our own age
have dampened some of our deterministic ardour — social analysis can
even suggest the practical limits of change in a given society. Where
such social history falls short, or requires a leap into blind faith, is in
relating the realities of social structure to the actual short term course
of the revolution.

I am arguing in this roundabout way for a study of revolution in
terms of behaviour that is peculiarly revolutionary, namely that associated with what Trotsky called 'the irruption of the masses on the stage
of history'. What distinguishes a revolutionary from a non-revolutionary
period is a sudden political mobilisation of significant social groups

115

previously passive or inert. If we mean to understand a revolution as something more than a chronicle of violence, we must know how the political institutions functioned through which the newly mobilised worked. In 1848 the most conspicuous and most characteristic of these institutions was the revolutionary club movement, though the clubs never were the exclusive vehicle of revolutionary participation.[2]

The degree of mobilisation of the masses in the Paris of 1848 could be schematically represented by a four-tiered pyramid, with the broad base the graphic equivalent of the large number of those marginally touched by the revolution and the apex standing for the infinitely smaller numbers of the totally committed. On this first, bottom tier we would find all those who registered and voted, about three quarters of the adult male population. One tier up can be found those voters who also obeyed the call to enroll in the Paris National Guard when the latter was opened to 'the people'. About every other male ended up in the democratised Guard. In this same scheme, the membership of the revolutionary clubs and of the trade unions would make up the third tier, comprising no more than one of every four male Parisians. Unlike voting which took a minimum of trouble, or National Guard duty, usually confined to one or two nights a month, club and, to a lesser extent, union participation took several evenings a week, requiring a genuine change in everyday habits. Finally, the few thousand activists in positions of leadership within the club and union movement, men for whom revolutionary participation had become a way of life, occupied the peak of the pyramid. This essay will explore briefly these two last tiers.

In terms closer to the concerns of traditional political history, an examination of the club movement, as of other revolutionary institutions, helps reveal the political dynamics of the French revolution of 1848.[3] Our generation of historians may be too ready to be impressed by familiar ideological controversies. We have tended to ignore what may have been the major drama of the period between February and June 1848: the national government's drive to reassert, in the face of a challenge from improvised revolutionary institutions, a traditional monopoly of power.[4] The 'irruption of the masses on the stage of history' (and their inclination to stay there!) had not only caused the overthrow of the monarchy, but severely curtailed the power and authority of the newly installed republican regime. Even had these new governors been more closely attuned to the revolutionary mood, any nineteenth-century French government would have inherited a potent tradition of bureaucratic centralisation unlikely to accommodate revolutionary institutions. For four months the French national governments waged an unceasing campaign, at times surreptitious, at others open, against the institutions created or captured by the revolutionaries — not merely clubs and trade unions, but the democratised National Guard, the mercurial Garde Mobile, the uncurbed revolutionary press, independent municipal police forces, unreliable National Workshops — in order to reduce them to obedience or to destroy them. The collapse of the June insurrection also marked the definitive triumph of the central government over its revolutionary rivals. Certainly the tensions of the spring of 1848 can only be understood if we also take into consideration the history of the forces that challenged the government.

If, as I have suggested, political mobilisation is a central aspect of revolution, and of the French revolution of 1848 in particular, the emergence of some sort of revolutionary institutions needs no explanation. What does require explanation is the emergence of a particular kind of revolutionary vehicle, the club movement. Why, in the specific circumstances of Paris in 1848, did the revolutionaries choose clubs (or popular societies, as they were known interchangeably) rather than workers' councils, a revolutionary militia, or a revolutionary party — three alternatives which, singly or in combination, have had some success in the twentieth century.

The answer seems to lie in a mix of very concrete social conditions and historical experience. Workers' councils — soviets — require large scale industry concentrating hundreds, preferably thousands, of workers. Save for a few large engineering and cotton printing works in the suburbs, Parisian industry was dispersed among literally tens of thousands of small workshops employing, on the average, half a dozen skilled workers.[5] In this setting, workers' councils would have been completely ineffectual, though a dynamic trade union movement learned to cope with this mass of dwarf firms. History, rather than economic structure, was the impediment to the predominance of a revolutionary militia. Revolutionaries were up against the existence of an entrenched, middle class National Guard with a strong cohesion of its own which the flood of lower class entrants was unable to breach. Only in districts of eastern Paris where the middle class was numerically weakest, and only under the impetus of another popular insurrection — June 1848 — did some National Guard units become 'revolutionised'. As to the chances for a monolithic party in 1848, it would be too facile to shrug off the possibility as hopelessly anachronistic: there is no inherent reason why such a party could not have been invented at this time — save that it ran counter to the whole weight of the revolutionary tradition. Where popular spontaneity was credited with the revolutionary successes of 1789, 1792, 1830 and February 1848, revolutionary regimentation was blamed for such dismal failures as the insurrection of the Seasons of 1839, that had been long on organisation but short on support.

117

The popular societies offered what seemed a painless compromise between spontaneity and regimentation, by promising to bring revolutionaries together without unduly impinging upon their individual autonomy. Locally implanted for the most part, the clubs also catered to the well-known Parisian reluctance to step beyond one's immediate neighbourhood. And as an institution, no doubt it was hallowed by history: where it had taken two years after 1789 for popular societies to take hold, their rediscovery in 1848 was almost instantaneous. Yet the ideological carry-over from the First to the Second Republic should not be exaggerated. There is no indication that the folk memory was either critical or precise. At most 5 per cent of club names deliberately evoked the revolutionary past; and if there were three Club des Jacobins in 1848, no one apparently remembered the Club des Cordeliers. The rhetoric of club posters and announcements rarely appealed to the precedents of 1793, though historical evocations fitted the overblown style popular in 1848. The only seeming exception — frequent bows in the direction of Robespierre's proposed Declaration of the Rights of Man (1793) — misleads: the Declaration's popularity owed more to its use as a test of republican orthodoxy among the secret societies of the July Monarchy than it did to vivid memories of 1793.

If the revolutionary tradition had its share in persuading the revolutionaries of 1848 that popular societies were a 'good thing', the republican underground of the Orléans Monarchy provided a much more tangible legacy. The importance of clubs as the prime expression of popular sovereignty had been stressed by such neo-Babouvist organisations as the émigré *Société démocratique française* of London and the secret *Travailleurs égalitaires* in Paris. Clubs, they agreed, were to become the building blocks for administering post-revolutionary France.[6] More immediately, one of the most important clubs in 1848, the *Société des Droits de l'Homme*, borrowed its leadership, name, organisational structure and ethos from its defunct predecessor of the 1830s. A number of other popular societies incorporated structural features — mainly the subdivision into 'sections' or 'cells' — lifted directly from the secret societies of the July Monarchy.

This impression of continuity between a pre-February republican 'resistance' and the nascent club movement in 1848 can be substantiated. Among thirty-six clubs organised between 25 February and 10 March 1848, I could trace the political antecedents of seventeen club founders or presidents. The largest single group — ten of seventeen — was comprised of militant veterans of the illegal republican underground, socially divided evenly among men of working and middle class extraction. A second group of founders, four of seventeen, had been members of the legal republican opposition, though some of these had begun their political careers as flaming revolutionaries. The last group of three was identified with established utopian sects — Icarian, Fourierist and Christian-Socialist — an identification that was to limit their membership and influence. These classifications do not necessarily represent categories insulated from each other. For example, Dr Alphonse-Victor Baudin, founder of the *Club démocratique de l'Avenir* in early March (and known to generations of French republicans as the martyr of 2 December 1851), had actively participated in most of the July Monarchy's secret societies. In 1848 he was also an active Icarian appearing at the side of Etienne Cabet, the father of the 'school'; earlier Baudin had associated successively with Saint-Simonians, neo-Babouvists and the *Ecole sociétaire* founded by Fourier.[7]

Baudin, philanthropic physician and club leader, raises the question of the social and professional origin of club cadres. Of 178 club presidents identified, I was able to classify about half by profession and, with occasional misgivings, by class. Of the 178, 23 per cent were manual workers; 22 per cent intellectuals (writers, journalists, professors); 21 per cent bourgeois (employers, proprietors, managers, *rentiers* — though this last category is problematic); 18 per cent white collar workers (ranging from clerk through book-keeper to priest); 9 per cent members of the 'popular bourgeoisie' of wineshop owners, rooming house operators and modest greengrocers; and 5 per cent university students. No doubt, these statistics should be greeted with healthy scepticism: our sources tend to single out the educated, the accomplished and the propertied. Even if we allow for this bias, the fact remains that the Paris middle class (at its most inclusive definition, no more than one third of the population) furnished two thirds of the club presidents, compared to the working class (two thirds of all Parisians) that provided no more than one third of the club presidencies.[8]

All this does not necessarily prove that clubs were essentially bourgeois or petty-bourgeois institutions, but merely that the middle class must have enjoyed certain competitive advantages over their proletarian rivals. Two explanations suggest themselves. In the first place, club leadership enshrined the supremacy of the word, of public speaking. Club offices were therefore likely to go to the articulate. Though some orators may be born, more are made and in the nineteenth century they were turned out by French secondary education, a bourgeois preserve, with its classical rhetorical tradition. In the second place, the special circumstances of 1848 removed the elite of the working class from the competition for the popular societies' leadership. The creation of the Luxembourg Labour Commission may have resulted in the first official recognition of the French labour movement; it also resulted in tying up 730 delegates of the Paris crafts in nightly meetings.

This is not to go to the other extreme to claim that the popular societies were exclusively working class organisations in the sense that *corporations ouvrières* evidently were. Contemporary observers, though generally noting the proletarian dominance in most clubs, did distinguish between, say, Armand Barbès' *Club de la Révolution* where mostly middle class veterans met, and the *Club républicain des travailleurs* (headed, incidentally, by a notary's clerk) flatly described by contemporaries as 'a gathering of four hundred weavers and machinists'. Where the *corporations* were restricted to skilled craftsmen, popular societies usually welcomed all comers willing to subscribe to their programme. This meant that clubs, compared to trade unions, reached both up and down the social scale: up into the middle classes, and not merely in selecting officers; down into the ranks of the unskilled with no access to the organised crafts. My guess is that both middle class (for ideological reasons) and labourers (for reasons of political apathy) were under-represented among the club rank and file.

I would argue, in the absence of hard evidence, that there must have been considerable overlapping between club and trade union membership, though no one really knows just how great the percentage of the organised was in the spring of 1848. We do know that popular societies, most often closely tied to a particular neighbourhood of the capital, generally met three to five evenings a week, while *corporations ouvrières*, city wide and organised along trade lines, met only very intermittently. Tinsmith lampmakers, for instance, held only twelve general meetings between the February and June Days, which works out to an average of once every ten days.[9] There was nothing to prevent a craft conscious tinsmith from devoting the rest of his evenings to his neighbourhood club. Such dual affiliation also made psychological sense in that the objectives of the trade union and club movements were complementary rather than competitive. Though political rivalry between the two sets of organisations divided them occasionally, by and large, the *corporations* concentrated on questions of full employment, collective bargaining, wages, hours and working conditions, while the popular societies always stressed revolutionary politics.[10]

Whatever the overlap, the latter does not erase a useful distinction between clubs and trade unions in 1848. At the most elementary level, a cabinetmaker about to join a popular demonstration like that of 17 March had to decide to march behind the banner of his craft or behind that of his popular society. The distinction also appeared on a collective level: the Revolutionary Committee, *Club of Clubs*, organised to manage the election campaign of April 1848, distinguished between delegates chosen by member popular societies and those sent by trade unions.

Perhaps more important even than their ties to the labour movement was the clubs' symbiotic relationship with the revolutionary press. In 1848, the press as much as the clubs and the unions was a symptom of revolutionary mobilisation: hundreds of new newspapers — many admittedly stillborn — were founded after February; just before the June Days the combined press run of all Parisian newspapers had risen from 50,000 to 400,000.[11] Popular societies had good reason for seeking the sympathetic collaboration of revolutionary newspapers: clubs needed publicity to attract members and to disseminate resolutions and decisions. Newspapers also served an important coordinating function by apprising individual popular societies of what others were doing.

In practice, such collaboration took a number of different forms. Least common was the co-option by a club of an established, prerevolutionary newspaper: the only such case was the relationship of Xavier Durrieu's *Le Courrier français* to Blanqui's *Société républicaine centrale* of which Durrieu was vice president. Until the government's campaign against Blanqui cooled his ardour. Durrieu faithfully published the minutes, announcements and resolutions of Blanqui's club in the otherwise staid columns of his paper.[12] More common, but often unsuccessful, were attempts by a single club to float its own newspaper. Few of these sheets were able to compete with more professionally edited papers. Only an exceptional and experienced polemicist like François Raspail managed to combine the presidency of the *Société des amis du peuple* with the editorship of *L'Ami du peuple en 1848*. An informal 'interlocking directorate' between professional journalists and club leaders often worked more smoothly. For example, Théodore Thoré, chief editor of a major revolutionary daily, *La vraie République*, also figured prominently among the cadres of the *Club de la Révolution. La vraie République*, though devoting little direct coverage to the club's sessions, generally reflected its political concerns.

In yet another category were journalistic ventures that catered to widespread sentiments for closer cooperation among Parisian popular societies. The earliest of these promotions, *La Voix des Clubs* (later title: *La Sentinelle des Clubs*), reproducing mainly club minutes and announcements, owed its existence to a veteran police spy who was duly unmasked. More serious, more effective and more durable was *La Commune de Paris, Moniteur des clubs*, the official organ of the *Club des clubs* and of its affiliated popular societies. Even after the arrest of its publisher editor, Joseph Sobrier, involved in the 15 May affair, a makeshift staff was still printing 5,000 copies daily — respectable by 1848 standards.

During the weeks preceding the June insurrection, the polarisation of public opinion reinforced the role of revolutionary newspapers and their editors. The latter were, for example, invited to participate in selecting a slate of candidates for the special elections of 4 June and in dealing with the question of the famous Banquet of the People shortly afterwards. As official pressure on clubs increased, founding a special newspaper again appeared as a solution. In June the *Club de la Révolution*, for instance, founded *Le Travail* enjoying press runs of up to ten thousand copies.[13] The Blanquist *Club du Peuple* headed by Alphonse Esquiros, himself a journalist and writer of note, put out *L'Accusateur public* in five thousand copies.[14] A number of other examples could be cited. Revolutionary clubs and revolutionary press alike underwent the crisis of the June Days; neither fully recovered.

Unfortunately, to define the clubs' relationship with other revolutionary institutions may be easier than to answer prosaic questions about the dimension of the club movement. Three problems must be distinguished: (1) the number of popular societies; (2) the total number of members or participants; (3) the fluctuations in both the numbers of clubs and of clubbists. Let me try to deal with these one at a time.

How many clubs were there? The answer to this apparently simple question relies as much on the historian's arbitrary criteria for inclusion and exclusion as it does on the accidents of documentary survivals. As to the latter, in the files of the Bibliothèque historique de la Ville de Paris I came across several admission cards to clubs — such as a *Club des Minimes* — that have otherwise left not a trace of their existence. Chances are that there were many more — but how many? — that did not even leave a stray admission card. As to criteria for inclusion on my master list of popular societies, obviously a revolutionary club in the heart of Paris admitting all sympathisers and dealing with general political issues poses no problems. But what about a *Société républicaine des commerçants locataires*? I chose to exclude it from my count as a special interest group, but was I justified in also barring the *Club démocratique des hommes de lettres sans emploi* that linked the defence of unemployed white collar workers with that of socialist reform? I chose to veto the literally dozens of electoral committees and clubs grouping provincials of a given department or region but residing in Paris on the grounds that these were not 'general admission' clubs. But in real life was a *Club des ouvriers alsaciens*, presided over by that veteran revolutionary, Aloysius Huber, that different from the (included) *Club du progès*, chaired by the same Huber on different nights of the week? And what was the proper geographical demarcation line to draw? Staying within what were then the Paris city limits would have eliminated some of the largest and most active clubs, such as the *Montagnards de Belleville* and the *Société républicaine de Batignolles-Monceaux*. Yet by taking in all the *intra-muros* suburbs — as I did — I also let in sleepy agricultural villages like Auteuil and Vaugirard, much less urban than Sèvres and Boulogne whose location beyond the capital's fortification put them beyond the pale. Given the particular criteria that I relied on, I can vouch for no less than 203 popular societies at the height of the club movement in mid-April.

Unsatisfactory as they are, these estimates are models of precision compared to the ludicrous projections and guesses to which we are reduced when it comes to numbering club members and sympathisers. Few reliable membership figures seem to have been kept; fewer have survived. Membership figures cited in what were clearly publicity releases in the revolutionary press may or may not have been accurate: there is no particular reason to think that they were. Journalistic estimates are generally confined to a handful of the best-known clubs and rarely distinguish between members and spectators whose sympathies may have been elsewhere. Several tortuous methods of juggling with these highly unsatisfactory figures lead me to assume a rockbottom minimum of 50,000 to 70,000 clubbists — a somewhat more inflated figure of 100,000 strikes me as every bit as plausible.[15] However hazy these calculations, the range indicates that the clubs were in any case a mass phenomenon in which a significant minority of the adult male population took part.

What is perhaps equally important is to be aware of the instability of the club phenomenon. The figures of 203 clubs and their 80,000 sympathisers (give or take 20,000) apply for the relatively brief period preceding the April 1848 elections. A week before these elections were held, the demonstration of 16 April set off an anticommunist hysteria which checked the momentum of the popular societies. Between mid-April and early May, somewhere around one half of all Parisian clubs disbanded for reasons that are easier to surmise than to document. The disaster of the *journée* of 15 May in which the surviving clubs were heavily committed once again halved their number: only some fifty popular societies survived into June 1848. Judging from published lamentations about declining membership, consolidations of as many as four clubs into one, the collapse of club membership may have been even more dramatic than the fall in the number of popular societies themselves. A couple of dozen clubs were permitted a modest rebirth in August after several weeks of blanket prohibition following the defeat of the June insurgents. Nonetheless the June Days marked the end of the club *movement*: isolated, hemmed in by restrictions written into the club law of 28 July 1848, continuous police surveillance and judicial repression, the popular societies were well on the way to early extinction.[16]

Yet how can we account for the decline of the club movement long before official repression can be blamed? Declining revolutionary fervour, 'political demobilisation' of the masses seems a dubious answer. Political demobilisation cannot account for the fact that electoral support for the club-supported revolutionary candidates was greater in June (when only thirty-three clubs were left to cooperate in the *Commission centrale pour les élections démocratiques*), than in the April elections (when there had been 149 popular societies to float the *Comité révolutionnaire, Club des clubs*). Steadily rising newspaper circulation and the very scope of the June insurrection itself testify that popular apathy was hardly the problem. The club movement probably foundered, not because its adherents had grown weary, but because it offered no credible answers to the most pressing problems of the day: catastrophic unemployment and the victory of political reaction through democratic means.

If we are to assess the role of the popular societies without imposing our own standards, it is only fair to test them against their own stated objectives. Their dominant appeal was to republican unity and fraternity. This call to unity was ideological and often defensive: the clubs called on all good republicans to gather together in order to defend the conquests and realise the promises of February 1848 against a host of open and secret enemies. Fraternity was another constant, but its definition varied from club to club. In some cases, would-be members were invited to believe that the advent of the republic had already rendered classes obsolete; other popular societies defined fraternity as an incipient form of class solidarity, pitting a virtuous majority of workers against a handful of vicious bourgeois exploiters. A second, related, theme presented popular societies as instruments of ideological education for the newly enfranchised, as a market place of ideas where an informed public opinion would be moulded. In this respect, most clubs looked beyond the mere mechanics of civic participation to the substance of social reform, particularly to reform raising the position of the workers. A third major theme was the clubs' promise to channel their members' desire to participate effectively in electoral politics, which impending elections made into an immediate issue. The popular societies catered to the obvious hunger for political involvement. By banding together members would be able to select and support the best democratic candidates. A final theme was the club ambivalence toward the Provisional Government. In one sense, that government, proclaimed by the people in arms, embodied the legitimacy of the February Revolution – and as such it deserved support. In another sense, it was a government that had had to be coerced into proclaiming the Republic in the first place, a government including men whose conversion to republicanism was suspect. Therefore the proper stance for the popular institutions produced by the revolution was what the *Club démocratique des Quinze-Vingt* tersely defined as 'the surveillance and support of the new government'.[17]

These themes were reflected to differing degrees in the day by day activities of the popular societies. The clubs sought, first of all, to exert pressure on the government, pressure which could run the gamut from petitioning respectfully to threatening renewed insurrection. Though

Rousseauean terminology was never invoked in 1848, the clubs acted as though they saw themselves rather than the Provisional Government, as the embodiment of the 'general will'. Delegations, manifestos, demonstrations, threats all made the same essential point: that the change of regime from monarchy to republic was a beginning and not an end; that the role of the Parisian masses, organised in clubs, was to ensure that 1848 would be a year of social as well as of political revolution. The popular societies long remained oblivious to their narrow dependence on the very authorities whom they habitually chastised. The clubs were vulnerable on two counts. As most of their meetings were held in public buildings, their status as tolerated guests could be terminated any time by executive *fiat*; second, though temporarily unenforced, a string of anti-club laws remained on the statute books that might again be put into effect. When the government came to withdraw its toleration, secretly in May, publicly in June 1848, the clubs discovered that without legal standing they faced a bleak future.

The search for unity, fraternity and political effectiveness took place on at least two different levels: the adaptation of individual popular societies to the requirements of democratic mass politics; and, on a higher level, the attempts to funnel all clubs into a powerful political machine to coordinate the revolutionaries' campaign. Neighbourhood clubs by and large sought to intervene in the electoral campaign, first, in preparing the election of cadres in the newly democratised Paris National Guard, later in examining and nominating candidates to the National Assembly. Listening to political speeches, interrogating would-be candidates, debating the issues, criticising the procedures for voting – such were the questions that took up the bulk of club sessions in the weeks prior to the national elections of 23 April. At the same time the individual clubs, under the leadership of Barbès' *Club de la Révolution*, sponsored the umbrella organisation of the *Comité révolutionnaire, Club des clubs* which, in tandem with the trade union movement, was to oversee the revolutionaries' campaign effort. As it turned out, the *Club des clubs*, through managerial incompetence and excessive ambition, did very badly. Its successor, created for the special elections of 4 June, showed greater skill and could point to some visible successes at the polls.

The theme of civic education, indoctrination, propaganda or what have you, was much less prominent in practice than club programmes would have led one to expect. Usually ideology was introduced from the outside, by candidates soliciting endorsement, or, in discussions of Robespierre's Declaration of the Rights of Man, by the authority of the *Club des clubs*. Occasional admonitions by club officers suggest that the rank and file suffered from a short attention span when it came to finely honed theories or elaborate schemes of social renovation. Only

125

a handful of clubs headed by ideologues, whose doctrines served as their organisations' *raison d'etre*, were exceptions to this rule.

Though on-going revolutions may be inherently unpropitious to ideological speculation, the priority given to practical political considerations is nonetheless striking. Apparently the explanation must be sought in part in a dilemma confronting club leaders and activists. However sympathetic they were to 'socialism', however responsive to its catchwords, club militants were genuinely perplexed by the welter of competing doctrines. Occasionally they voiced the hope that open discussion among social reformers and theorists would lead to an early consensus on a common socialist programme. But, understandably, these same leaders of the popular societies were reluctant to 'waste' their own club sessions and to confuse their own membership by hosting such a debate. Hence as long as ideological babel prevailed among rival socialist 'schools', club leaders, opting for the better part of courage, prudently confined themselves to a common denominator of socialist generalities.

This is why and how the popular societies came to play a major role in what might be called 'mythical' indoctrination, if we accept Sorel's definition of a political myth as a cluster of emotion laden ideas that lead men to act. The clubs' contribution to clarifying such slogans as 'organisation of labour' or 'social and democratic republic' may have been nil, but they helped enshrine these catchwords as political myths in the Sorelian sense. Where in February probably no more than a few thousand veterans of the republican underground and of the socialist coteries had responded to them, by June the clubs — no doubt aided by other organs of revolutionary opinion — had transformed these phrases into rallying cries for half of Paris.

The 'civic education' of the popular societies bore results in another area as well, though indoctrination was no doubt reinforced by the lessons of day by day experience. Even in the first weeks after the February Revolution, club leaders appear to have been aware of the ideological conflicts that divided the Provisional Government's members. By contrast, the rank and file, guided by a visceral republicanism, seems to have been oblivious of the cleavages among men all of whom proclaimed their republican convictions. As late as the April elections, this original enthusiasm for all republicans remained intact. By the time of the special elections of June, however, the clubs had taught their adherents to distinguish and discriminate between revolutionary and conservative republicans, between what a few months later would be labelled 'red' as against 'blue' republicans. The ambiguous result of this polarisation was a new political line up emerging in June 1848; winning candidates were either avowed socialists or frankly anti-republican conservatives.

Yet these propaganda 'successes' were incidental by-products of the clubs' dominant concerns: direct action and electioneering. It was the tension between these two latter modes of activity that haunted the club movement. Organising successful street demonstrations requires an ambiance very different from that of a well-run political machine tuned for effective participation in conventional electoral contests. In this respect, the dilemma of the Parisian popular societies foreshadows analogous contradictions that have plagued revolutionary parties in the twentieth century. The club movement dealt with its polarity by tacking back and forth between confrontation in the streets and routine campaigning, a zigzag course determined pragmatically rather than by ideological considerations or conscious planning. This explains why the club movement from its beginnings at the end of February to its abrupt terminus in June went through a number of distinct phases.

1. From the first week of March, when the popular societies emerged as a mass phenomenon, through the great club and trade union demonstration of 17 March, the club movement favoured direct pressure on the still shaky Provisional Government. What the popular societies hoped for was to commit the government to a genuinely revolutionary course, which implied a transitional dictatorship during which basic social reforms would be undertaken and rural France won over to the new republic. During this first phase, the clubs of Blanqui and of Cabet assumed the revolutionary leadership, while the trade unions were content to follow in their wake. The *journée* of 17 March, which impressed observers with the sheer number and massive organisation of the demonstrators, failed to achieve the hoped for results, though the failure was not clearly perceived at the time.

2. Appeased by minor concessions, the popular societies shifted their effort from street demonstrations to electoral politics, once the final dates for National Guard and National Assembly elections had been set. The foundation of the *Comité révolutionnaire, Club des clubs*, which was to coordinate the revolutionaries' political campaign by ultimately enlisting 149 Parisian clubs, dates from this period. So does the ascendancy of Barbès' *Club de la Révolution* and the decline of the *Société républicaine centrale* of Blanqui whom the well-publicised 'revelations' of the Taschereau document helped to isolate. Despite formal cooperation within the *Club des clubs*, club and trade union movements were at odds over means, though they agreed on ends: the *Club des clubs* was in virtual rivalry with its nominal ally, the *Comité central des ouvriers de la Seine*, sponsored by the unions under Louis Blanc's patronage. The disastrous *journée* of 16 April, a street demonstration hemmed in by armed force, was organised by the *corporations ouvrières* without the assistance of the popular societies.

3. Following the workers' defeat of 16 April, the revolutionaries'

failure at the polls on the twenty-third, the post-election 'massacre' of workers in Rouen and Elbeuf, the clubs again switched to direct pressure. The opportunity — the tragic plight of the Poles whose movement for independence encountered Prussian and Austrian repression — arose for the popular societies to regain some of their lost prestige by embracing an immensely popular cause. The clubs opted for direct pressure on the National Assembly which had already betrayed its overwhelming conservatism. The result was the *journée* of 15 May, a comedy of errors, that led to a wave of repression, depriving the popular societies of their best-known leaders. Unlike 17 March, 15 May showed unmistakably that a policy of direct confrontation was bankrupt.

4. On the basis of this lesson, and of supplementary elections announced for 4 June, the club movement reverted to conventional politics. Under the leadership of the *Société des Droits de l'Homme*, a *Commission centrale pour les élections démocratiques* sponsored a slate of exclusively socialist candidates, which organised labour was also content to follow. Under the shadow of 15 May, the clubs were extremely suspicious of renewing any mass action, which explains their opposition to the famous Banquet of the People that despite its popular appeal, they succeeded in postponing.[18] The 'moral victory' of the elections (four socialist winners for eleven seats at stake; four runners-up, all socialists) of 4 June seemingly justified club prudence.

5. During the last ten days preceding the outbreak of the June insurrection, the popular societies seem to have lost the political initiative among the revolutionaries. The crisis over the National Workshops which became the symbolic issue for lower class Paris eluded them, particularly since they had lately concentrated on conventional politics. Disorganised by their eviction from public buildings, the clubs do not seem to have played a major part in preparing the impending popular uprising. Though a few popular societies, such as the *Montagnards de Belleville* and the *Société républicaine de Batignolles-Monceaux* can be distinguished on the barricades, National Guard units were better adapted to street fighting than the clubs. Though club activists tended to be singled out in the repression following the rebel defeat, most of them had participated as individuals or members of the National Guard rather than in obedience to club instructions.[19]

Why did the Parisian club movement fail in 1848? If we accept what I take to be Professor Price's conclusion that the aims of the revolutionaries were simply not consonant with the realities of French society, or Professor Fasel's recent suggestion that urban obsessions doomed them in an overwhemingly rural society, the question may be rhetorical.[20] The club tail could hardly be expected to survive the death of the revolutionary dog. Let us therefore retreat to a more modest question: why was the club movement not more effective?

On the most basic level, the very psychological success of the clubs made their practical effectiveness very problematical. The popular societies provided a sense of civic participation and personal significance to tens of thousands of ordinary people with no practical experience of politics. Anarchical mass movements may be exhilerating for most participants, but they make clumsy instruments for achieving limited and well-defined objectives. More recent revolutionary leaders may have succeeded in taming and channeling revolutionary enthusiasm of the sort that fuelled the club movement: one thinks of the subordination of the masses to the hero-leader or their *encadrement* by a revolutionary vanguard claiming the sanction of 'History'. Yet, as has already been noted in passing, the modern revolutionary party as a focus of popular energies had not been invented; and the urge to democratic self-expression was too strong in 1848 to be manipulated by charismatic leaders. Even an Auguste Blanqui, the most powerful personality among the Forty-Eighters and the one who inspired the most intense loyalties, took for granted that his proper role was as chairman of his club; he showed no inclination to play the Führer.

The popular societies may also have erred in their reading of the revolutionary situation such as it emerged in 1848. The clubs tended to slur over the fact that in February the insurgents had triumphed only because the Monarchy had lost its nerve (or, according to a more charitable interpretation, preferred defeat to the horrors of civil war) and because the sizeable and armed Parisian middle class turned out to be unwilling to defend their supposedly bourgeois king.[21] The reluctant or benevolent neutrality of the old line National Guard may be explained in that the street fighters of February never made explicit social demands which would have stiffened the resistance of all those with wealth and status to lose. The clubs that mushroomed after the instauration of the Second Republic did make just such demands. As it turned out, they were never able to wear down the Provisional Government, the majority within which was determined to preserve the existing social order. Had the clubs really managed to leap over the official hurdle, they would have encountered the concentrated force of the possessing classes in much the same way that the June insurgents would have been defeated by the mobilised middle class had they overcome General Cavaignac's regulars.[22]

Finally, in more conventional terms, the political effectiveness of the club movement may have been up against built-in limitations. It may well be misleading to construct a curve of rising effectiveness, low in April, much higher in June – but artificially cut off by the repression that followed that month's abortive second revolution. Several considerations that speak against such an interpretation should be kept in mind. First and foremost, Paris was not the nation and, save for a few provincial cities like Lyon, Marseilles and Limoges, the club movement was essentially confined to the French capital. Even had the clubs succeeded in monopolising the slate of candidates from the department of Seine, thirty-four revolutionaries in a National Assembly of 900 members would hardly have overwhelmed the conservatives. When it came to campaigning, the popular societies were really aiming at a moral victory only. A second consideration is less generally acknowledged: the Parisian revolutionaries, despite two years of trying, were never able to surmount what seem to have been intractable political realities. Granted that the club movement itself was neutralised after June 1848, nonetheless the revolutionaries continued to organise for the various elections held, gaining in experience and, probably, in sophistication. Nonetheless, in the half dozen general and special elections held between 1848 and 1850, the electorate supporting revolutionary candidates fluctuated consistently between two fifths and one half: conservatives and 'demo-socs' remained almost evenly matched, though the former generally retained an edge of 1 to 5 per cent of the vote. There is no compelling reason to suppose that, had the club movement survived, it would have overcome this opposition. What campaigning could achieve, it seems, was limited not only because Paris was not France, but also because revolutionary republicanism never really triumphed even on its home ground.

If we broaden our focus from the Second Republic to French history since the eighteenth century, the club movement appears in a still different light. As a historical phenomenon, revolutionary clubs on a mass basis occurred on three distinct occasions: in the 1790s, in 1848, and in 1870-71 during the Prussian siege and the Paris Commune.[23] In short, the club movement seems to have been symptomatic of the three most profound revolutionary upheavals of what the French call 'contemporary history'. Equally striking, as a historical phenomenon, the club movement occupies a sharply defined epoch. Popular societies do not seem to have played a role in that great revolutionary upheaval of seventeenth-century France, the Fronde.[24] They had no importance in any of the three or four twentieth-century crises that mobilised great masses of people in ways that may be described as revolutionary or at least pseudo-revolutionary: 1934, 1936, 1944 and 1968. In his masterful analysis of the power elite that dominated France during much of the nineteenth century, Andre-Jean Tudesq speculated that this elite, whom he labels the Great Notables, was characteristic of a transitional society. Enjoying landed wealth, prestige and visibility, the notables served as intermediaries and brokers between the individual and the state at a time when corporate solidarity was already eroded and traditional hierarchies had lost legitimacy, but before modern mass organisations had taken root.[25] In France, Tudesq suggested, this period of transition extended from the late eighteenth century to the 1870s, precisely the time span during which, in moments of major revolution, popular societies flourished. Difficult as it may be to prove, is it not plausible that the function performed by the Great Notables in periods of relative social stability — binding men together by means of an elaborate network of patron-client relationships — may have been taken over by the club movement during moments of acute social crisis? Certainly what the popular societies sought to establish were patterns of social solidarity and social effectiveness in the midst of rapidly changing political and social structures. In any case, the new era of parliamentary democracy, mass parties and, somewhat later, a mass labour movement founded on large scale industry, relegated Great Notables and revolutionary clubs alike to the dustbin of history.

Notes

1.   Roger Price, *The French Second Republic: A Social History* (Ithaca, 1972).
2.   This article draws on my book, *Revolution and Mass Democracy: the Paris Club Movement in 1848* (Princeton, 1975) to which the reader is referred for a fuller and more documented account. It is published by kind permission of Princeton University Press.
3.   The following monographic studies, varying in scope and perspective, may be cited: for the labour movement, Rémi Gossez, *Les ouvriers de Paris*, vol. I, *L'Organisation* (1848-1851) (Paris, 1967); for the revolutionary press, Gossez, 'La presse parisienne à destination des ouvriers (1848-1851)', in 'Bibliothèque de la Révolution de 1848', vol. XXIII: *La presse ouvrière, 1819-1850* (Paris, 1966); for the Paris National Guard, Louis Girard, *La garde nationale* (Paris, 1964). for the *Garde mobile*, P. Chalmin, 'Une institution militaire de la Seconde République: la garde nationale mobile', *Etudes d'histoire moderne et contemporaine*, II (1949), pp. 37-82; for the *ateliers nationaux*, Donald C. McKay, *The National Workshops* (Cambridge, Mass., 1933). Suzanne Wassermann's studies, 'Le club de Raspail', *La Révolution de 1848*, V (1908-1909), pp. 589-605, 655-74, 748-62 and *Les clubs de Barbès et de Blanqui en 1848* (Paris, 1913) are still useful as monographic treatments of the clubs named.
4.   I developed these ideas some years ago in a somewhat different and more elaborate form in 'Revolution: a Redefinition', *Political Science Quarterly*, LXXVII (1962), pp. 36-53. By emphasising 'revolutionary behaviour' of which the government's drive for a monopoly of power is only a corollary, I have brought my then redefinition closer to common usage. Moreover, the Chinese Cultural Revolution, at least as I understand it, has undermined my once childlike faith in a universal 'governmental dynamic' transcending all ideologies. On a more modest scale, my model still strikes me as relevant for nineteenth-century France.
5.   The basic source is *Statistique de l'industrie à Paris pour les années 1847-1848* (Paris, 1851) which, particularly for the suburbs, may be supplemented with Rémi Gossez' *thèse de droit*, 'Circonstances du mouvement ouvrier, Paris — 1848', (Université de Paris, 1951).
6.   Georges Sencier, *Le babouvisme après Babeuf* (Paris, 1912), pp. 274-5.
7,   *Dictionnaire biographique du mouvement ouvrier français*, ed., Jean Maitron *et al.*, 1ère partie: *1789-1864*, I, pp. 168-9, supplemented by my own

file on Baudin.
8.   For methodological detail, see Amann, *Revolution and Mass Democracy*, p. 41, n. 14.
9.   Gossez, *Les ouvriers*, p. 156.
10.   *Ibid.*, pp. 48-79.
11.   Gossez, 'Presse Parisienne', p. 184.
12.   Wassermann, *Les clubs de Barbès et de Blanqui*, pp. x-xi.
13.   Gossez, 'Presse parisienne', p. 139.
14.   *Ibid.*, pp. 143-5.
15.   For greater detail as to how I reached these figures, see Amann, *Revolution and Mass Democracy*, p. 35, n. 4.
16.   The popular societies resuscitated in August 1848 are less interesting in and of themselves than that they are as objects of systematic judicial repression which has left considerable documentation in the National Archives, BB[18]. I am preparing an article on this subject.
17.   *Le Courrier français*, 4 March 1848; for a more documented treatment, see Amann, *Revolution and Mass Democracy*, pp. 50-55.
18.   Cf. Amann, 'Prelude to Insurrection: the Banquet of the People', *French Historical Studies*, I (1960), pp. 436-44, and *'Du neuf* on the Banquet of the People. June 1848', *French Historical Studies*, V (1968), pp. 344-50.
19.   The most telling direct testimony is by F. Pardigon, *Episodes des journées de juin 1848* (London, 1852), pp. 69 ff. Pardigon, a law student at the University of Paris, was at that time president of the *Club du Deux Mars* at the Sorbonne and on the exective board of the *Commission centrale pour les élections démocratiques*, founded by the clubs at the end of May 1848.
20.   George Fasel, 'The Wrong Revolution: French Republicanism in 1848', *French Historical Studies*, VIII, pp. 654-77.
21.   Cf. William L. Langer, 'The Patterns of Urban Revolution in 1848', in Evelyn M. Acomb and Marvin L. Brown, Jr., eds., *French Society and Culture since the Old Regime* (New York, 1966), pp. 97-100, 110-12.
22.   This is the case convincingly made by Jean Vidalenc, 'La province et les journées de juin', *Etudes d'histoire moderne et contemporaine*, II (1949), pp. 81-144.
23.   Isabelle Bourdin, *Les sociétés populaires à Paris pendant la révolution* (Paris, 1937), takes the story to 1792 only, but it can be pursued in less detail in Albert Soboul, *Les sans-culottes parisiens en l'an II* (Paris, 1958), pp. 614-48. For the clubs of 1870, we have only the tendentious Gustave de Molinari, *Les clubs rouges pendant le siège de Paris* (Paris, 1871); and for the Commune of 1871, Eugene Schulkind, 'The Activity of Popular Organizations during the Paris Commune of 1871', *French Historical Studies*, I (1960), pp. 394-415. The structure and role of political clubs during the early years of the Fifth Republic owes nothing to those of the period 1789-1871. See Jean-André Faucher, *Les clubs politiques en France* (Paris, 1965), which is devoted to contemporary clubs stemming from dissatisfaction with the ideological and practical bankruptcy of the established left-wing parties.
24.   I am venturing these generalisations on the basis of having examined two leading analytical works on the Fronde: E. H. Kossmann, *La Fronde* (Leiden, 1954) and A. Lloyd Moote, *The Revolt of the Judges: The Parlement of Paris and the Fronde* (Princeton, 1971).
25.   Tudesq, *Les grands notables en France (1840-1849)*, (Paris, 1964), II, pp. 1230-41, esp. pp. 1230-31.

THE REVOLUTIONARY POLICE OF 1848

Patrica O'Brien
University of California, Irvine

The police is a nineteenth century bureaucratic innovation. In Western Europe during the nineteenth century, ordinary citizens and the army came to be relieved of the burdens of policing, as neutral and professional peace-keeping organisations were created. With the rationalisation of the policing function, military and volunteer forces were gradually rejected because of their exclusively repressive character; the recognition of the efficacy of prevention in providing security for the lives and property of the members of the community was the basis for the bureaucratisation of police duties. This process is worth examination because the development of the police in France has much to tell us about the changing pattern of social conflict and is a good indication of the changing moral consensus of the French middle classes in the age of revolution.

In France the modern police was created by Napoleonic decree in 1800. Yet despite the erection of the scaffolding of a new policing organisation, it was not until after the mid-nineteenth century that the construction of a modern and professional civil force was completed.[1] The municipal police, the police responsible for the daily peace-keeping activities in the city, has been consistently overlooked by historians attempting to explain the pattern of development of the modern French police. The Prefect, rather than the *sergent de ville* or the *gardien de la paix*, has commanded historical attention: the political and secret activities of the modern police far more frequently have been the object of historical concern than the duties and performance of the footpatrolman on his beat.[2] But it is precisely this agent of the law who stood between the public and the legal system on a daily basis and whose activities reflected administrative attitudes toward the problems of urban society in the first half of the nineteenth century.

The revolution of 1848 and the Second Republic constitute a crucial period in the institutional development of the modern police in France. At that time the police underwent a crisis in philosophy and in organisation. By examining the changes that took place before, during, and after the revolution, certain conclusions can be drawn regarding the process of rationalisation of internal peace-keeping activities. Between February and May 1848, the revolutionary Prefect of Police,

Marc Caussidière, was responsible for the experiment which sought to create a police organisation fundamentally different from its July Monarchy predecessor. Caussidière's identification with the radical faction of the Provisional Government has long obscured the importance of his innovations for a modern police administration. These innovations were more than just the products of the factional rivalries in the Provisional Government and the Prefecture of Police was more than just 'an essentially negative power bloc, withholding obedience yet without clear aims of its own'.[3] Such explanations tend to oversimplify the dynamics of the struggle between the Prefect of Police and the moderate members of the Provisional Government by overlooking the significance of Caussidière's concept of the role of the police in a modern democratic state. To the contrary, the Prefect of Police was not merely using his position as leverage in disputes with his colleagues and he did have 'clear aims' for his municipal force: according to Caussidière's own rhetoric, he was rejecting the 'police of repression' in favour of a 'police of conciliation'.[4] In essence, he was articulating a system of neutral peace-keeping. What was at stake here was a critique of the existing police structure and a desire to devise within the revolutionary context a new police force which would be neutral and trustworthy in its enforcement of the law. It is true that the issue of reform was complicated by Caussidière's political activity as well as by his apparent rejection of professional standards. Yet Caussidière himself argued that both his political involvement and his lack of professionalism reflected the same 'democratic' principles that were the foundation of his justification of neutrality. In looking beyond Caussidière's own justifications and explanations, what is to be undertaken here is an examination of the philosophy and actual operation of Marc Caussidière's new revolutionary police in the context of what they replaced and of what in turn replaced them.

At two o'clock on the afternoon of 24 February 1848, Marc Caussidière and a group of fellow revolutionaries took possession of the Prefecture of Police. Caussidière, claiming to be operating under the directive of a citizens' committee at the office of the radical newspaper, La Réforme, declared himself jointly with Marie Joseph Sobrier, his comrade from the secret societies, new head of the Paris police. The two men seized control of police headquarters with the professed intention of reorganising the entire police system. After three days Sobrier resigned the post and Caussidière assumed sole direction of the police of Paris.

The revolutionaries who entered the courtyard of the Prefecture on 24 February met with no resistance from the July Monarchy police in their takeover. The Prefect of Police, Gabriel Delessert, had already fled the city and the Municipal Guard, the *sergents de ville*, and the troops of the line who were present disarmed on the request of the National Guard.[5] The police of the July Monarchy, because of their insufficient numbers,[6] had been rendered completely helpless with the defection of the National Guards and the disintegration of army support. Of the forces under the direction of the Prefect of Police deployed throughout Paris, only one corps offered any significant resistance to the revolutionary movement on the streets: the elitist Municipal Guard moved against barricades, often on their own initiative without orders from the Prefect of Police or the *commissaires*. Their actions were reported by a judicial inquiry in March 1848: the enquiry showed that the Municipal Guard continued to function, however ineffectively, without being able to count on military or civilian support and after communication with police authorities had broken down.[7] The Municipal Guard, whose full force was 3,900 men, was too small alone to act effectively. In several cases, its actions were responsible for the increased antagonism and fervour of the revolutionary crowd. The Municipal Guard was the only policing force that put forth such a concerted effort to impede preparations for the revolution. The discipline, regimentation, and elitism of the corps are possible explanations for the sustained performance. The autonomy of the officer corps was a key to the Municipal Guard's ability to respond to the revolutionary threat.[8] In contrast to the Municipal Guard, the other municipal forces had failed to act because they were dependent on the *commissaires* who were often more concerned with the political implications of their involvement than with the maintenance of order.[9] By 24 February any kind of police opposition to the progress of the revolution had completely disappeared. Alexis de Tocqueville, as an eye witness to the events, reported that

'Throughout the day, I did not see in Paris a single one of the former agents of the public authority: not a soldier, not a gendarme, not a policeman; the National Guard itself disappeared.'[10]

The police in 1848 as in 1830, although an expanded and improved force,[11] had demonstrated their inability to respond to the revolutionary threat. In both periods the police served as targets for the discontented of the population and were attacked as agents of the government. It is in this area that Georges Duveau was incorrect: Duveau claimed that 'there is no evidence to suggest that the rioters invariably acted with such ferocity to the Municipal Guards'.[12] There is a variety of evidence that indicates, to the contrary, that the workers 'who treated Municipal Guards with great humanity'[13] were the exception and not the rule. It is wise to ignore, as Duveau doubtless did, tales of wanton slaughter of the Municipal Guards by the revolutionary population; equally without weight are histories in which the Municipal Guards were responsible for 'carnage' and 'appalling butchery'.[14] Yet in a search for reliable evidence it is difficult to exclude the findings of the judiciary inquiry in March 1848. Twenty agents of the July Monarchy police, who had been incorporated into the revolutionary administration, presented uniform testimony concerning the encounters of the crowd and the Municipal Guard.[15] *Sergents de ville* and *commissaires* were objects of public discontent but no branch of the police was a more frequent target of the revolutionary crowd in February 1848 than the Municipal Guard.

As one of his first official acts, Caussidière disbanded all the units of the unpopular July Monarchy police. In 1830 similar action was taken by the new administration created by the July revolution. Yet by the autumn of 1830 the police system of the Restoration had been reestablished, albeit with new names and new personnel; the structure and duties of the police were altered not at all. This was not the case in February 1848. It is true that in dismantling the police force of the July Monarchy Caussidière did retain members of the old force in his new police.[16] But in spite of the presence of members of the July Monarchy organisation in his administration Caussidière set out deliberately to create the image of being a revolutionary who intended to implement a revolutionary programme of municipal policing. He described the Prefecture as a 'sanctuary of permanent justice' in which fraternity would replace fear.[17]

Caussidière's flamboyant rhetoric notwithstanding, his attitudes and activities were very little different in certain areas from those of his predecessors. In his first proclamation announcing the release of all political prisoners, Caussidière was explicit about his policy toward those who had committed 'crimes against persons and against property': they would be prosecuted to the full letter of the law.[18] In defending property, he remained faithful to his repeated commitment to preserve the 'moral order': 'I devoted every effort to the destruction of social vermin, to stop theft, rape, murder, arson, all that by moral authority and in the certainty that I would not bend before my duty'.[19]

Inspite of his rhetoric and the fears of his opponents, Caussidière was no socialist. He spoke of the 'true instinct of the people' as guiding his actions.[20] Yet he never allowed those instincts to alter his understanding of the law. In critical periods, for example, he mediated rent disputes by instructing tenants to respect the contractual claims of their landlords. His delegates were present in the more politically explosive neighbourhoods of the Faubourg St Antoine, du Temple, Saint Martin, Saint Marceau, and the Marais attempting to bring 'to a proper understanding the rich and the poor'.[21] He was continually concerned with placating the fears of the middle classes regarding the revolution and

Marx rightly recognised in Caussidière a 'defender of bourgeois honour'.[22] He supported his predecessor's policies regulating prostitution and prohibiting gaming houses: he spoke of his duty to give to the new government 'a stamp of integrity, of splendour'.[23]

His efforts to create an image of integrity and splendour for 'the great democratic and social Republic' were a failure. Many felt that Caussidière's own background made him an unlikely candidate for such a task. He took pride in pointing out that his preparation for prefectoral responsibilities was gained in the secret societies of the July Monarchy. In 1834 his work in the mills of Lyon and Saint Etienne was terminated by a prison sentence of twenty years received for his participation in the April disturbances of that year. It was suggested by his accusers that he had not only been an activist in the disturbances but that he had also been responsible for the murder of a policeman.[24] Amnestied after five years, Caussidière resumed his activities in the secret societies. By 1847 he had become a member of the Society of the Seasons and he toured France as a wine broker selling subscriptions to *La Réforme* and raising money for the society's activities.[25] Such a background did not recommend Caussidière as a defender of law and order to his more moderate collagues in the Provisional Government.

Yet the real distrust of the revolutionary police was not caused by the political history of the new Prefect of Police. Caussidière had created a policing force known as the Montagnards to replace the *sergents de ville* of the previous administration: it was the image of this new corps that was the source of genuine misgivings about the reliability of the revolutionary police. The Montagnards were absolutely essential, Caussidière claimed, to his conciliatory programme: 'by organising the Montagnards, I surrounded myself with intelligent comrades, sincerely devoted to the Republic, and they constituted an active force capable of keeping in awe all disturbances of the peace.'[26] Daniel Stern saw the new force as a 'veritable army corps' concerned primarily with Caussidière's personal safety and maintaining him in power.[27] From the first, even the manner of dress of 'Caussidière's janissaries' was regarded as alarming. *La garde rouge*, as they were popularly called, wore blue shirts with red sashes and red caps and carried long sabres. There was no uniformity in dress and the corps at best seemed to be a colourful and undisciplined lot.[28] Louis Blanc called their appearance 'energetic';[29] others only considered it dangerous.[30]

More than its manner of dress, the corps' composition was the source of real concern. All ex-*sergents de ville*, whose reputation was infamous on the barricades, were to be excluded from the corps and a completely new body was composed of unemployed patriots and barricade fighters. Membership in the new corps was opened to those who could show a certificate of jail registration as a political prisoner, a proof of participation on the February barricades, or an honourable discharge from the army. All grades to that of captain were to be determined by election, not appointment. The names of the four newly created companies were the Montagnard, the company of February, the Lyonnaise, and most frightening of all, the company of Saint Just. Each citizen in the guard was to receive a salary of 2 francs 25 centimes per day, regardless of rank. The new corps was in these ways attempting to create a thoroughly democratic police organisation.

In acknowledging the objections of those who felt that democratisation meant the loss of discipline and standards, Caussidière recognised the inclination to rowdiness of the new groups but pointed out that their 'independent spirit' was the best insurance for a system of justice.[31] This independence of spirit was interpreted by the corps' most vociferous critics as outright depravity. Adolphe Chénu, a former member of the revolutionary police who had been discredited and dismissed by Caussidière, took pleasure in recounting tales of moral turpitude of both the Prefect of Police and the Montagnards and in emphasising their negligence in their duties.[32] Critics spoke of drunken orgies at the Prefecture of Police;[33] and Pornin, commandant of the Montagnards, was especially singled out for his questionable conduct. In prints illustrating one of Chénu's works, Pornin was depicted with his wooden leg and his wild looks in the stature of a depraved and drunken bandit chief.[34] These works were able to capitalise on the hostility, distrust and fear that the new corps had created in Paris from the end of February until the middle of May 1848.

At base, the criticism of Caussidière's Montagnards reflected the bourgeois fear of *les classes dangereuses*: the fear of this new police was being confounded with the fear of the lower classes in the city. It was widely known in Parisian society that these ex-barricade fighters, political prisoners, and members of secret societies received an 'exceptional pay'.[35] Complaints have been cited among anti-republicans that the high wages of these men were the cause of an increase in prostitution and venereal disease in the city: 'A whole new class of smart young men had money to spend.'[36] The Montagnards, many of whom had only wooden shoes in their first days of service in the corps, were indisputably regarded by some as being from a class without means and without morals.

There were, on the other hand, contemporary accounts that spoke favourably of the new corps. Louis Blanc, for one, had only words of praise for Caussidière's police: 'As for the public security, never was it better protected than by the vigilance of Caussidière's Montagnards, who in order to put it in the Prefect's own language succeeded very well "in making order out of disorder".'[37] The variety of accounts makes it difficult to arrive at a fair assessment of the Montagnards' contribution. To attack the Montagnards was to strike at the very core of Caussidière's policy of conciliation. Caussidière defended his own men by pointing to the record: only one murder had been committed during his term of three months and there had been a marked decline in thefts.[38] In judging the veracity of his claim, the historian is faced here with a real problem. With the documents that are left to us from this period, there is no effective way of assessing the accuracy of his figures because Caussidière himself was responsible for the official record. There are, however, several qualifications of his achievement which must be mentioned. The importance of revolutionary idealism as a crime deterrent was only passingly considered by Caussidière, who instead chose to emphasise as an explanation the effectiveness of his men. There is also the possibility that the records were less well kept or that crimes were less frequently reported to the police in the three months of Caussidière's service. Although he attempted to maintain the office staffs of the Prefecture of Police and the *commissariats* at their full complement, Caussidière was forced to admit that affairs were often conducted in a disorderly fashion. The Prefect of Police looked at the record and concluded that the drop in crimes against persons and against property was due to his philosophy of policing: 'It must not be supposed . . . that the thieves walked about with their hands in their pockets because the republic had been proclaimed.'[39] Nor must it be supposed on the basis of the evidence that Caussidière has provided that crime dramatically decreased because of a reorganisation of the police force.

Just as the claims of the Prefect of Police must be questioned, the attacks made by the corps' critics must be qualified. In every case, those who attacked the new police had personal as well as political grievances against the new Prefect of Police: these animosities undercut the credibility of their attacks. Yet the words of praise bestowed on Caussidière by one of his most dependable critics, *Le Constitutionnel*, can be taken as somewhat more reliable: the newspaper acknowledged that 'each day the streets of Paris are becoming more tranquil . . . We sincerely congratulate citizen Caussidière for this very marked progress toward the public order. As he perseveres, he will contribute, more than one thinks, to the restoration of confidence and credit.'[40]

Indeed one of the most striking facts about the new corps was its ability to function at all, given its insufficient numbers. Because of the limited funds coming from the Hôtel de Ville, which Caussidière called 'a regular game of rackets',[41] he was unable to maintain what he considered to be a sufficient patrolling force. Caussidière himself admitted that Paris was 'without one really organised corps'.[42] By mid-May the Prefect of Police was in command of the officially recognised Montagnards and the *gardiens de la paix* and the successor to the Municipal

Guard, the Republican Guard. These forces were not always distinguishable from one another to the general public because of the constant interchange of personnel among the units and because of the lack of uniforms for all the recruits. Division of duties, moreover, was not clearly delineated. Further confusion was created by the proliferation of armed forces under the control of other members of the government. The mayor of Paris had set up his own policing force, the counterpart of the Prefecture's *gardiens de la paix*. The main purpose of the mayor's force was to police the police. Caussidière recognised that the attempt by the mayor of Paris to establish a separate force was a direct challenge to his prefectoral powers and he accused the government of attempting to undermine his position. Caussidière reminded the Minister of the Interior of the Napoleonic law delineating supervision of the municipal police and he demanded that the Minister, Lédru-Rollin, 'put a stop at this attempt at jugglery'.[43] Lédru-Rollin, Caussidière's colleague from *La Réforme* as well as his ministerial superior recognised the validity of the objection put forth by the Prefect of Police and immediately ordered Mayor Marrast to terminate his recruitment operations. This incident is a good indication of the ongoing distrust and antagonism between the Prefect of Police and the Hôtel de Ville.

Because of the weakened state of the military on the morrow of the February revolution (only 9,822 troops on 24 February), the government set about creating a new, militarily organised, highly regimented fighting force known as the Mobile Guard. This corps, like the Montagnard police, had been drawn from the barricade fighters of February. Designated by Marx as the 'lumpen-proletariat',[44] these troops, mostly young, unemployed workers, were 15,000 strong by June and proved themselves to be among the government's most reliable striking forces in the June fighting.[45]

In addition to the formation of the Mobile Guard, after 1 May attention was again directed seriously to increasing the military presence in the city: regular troops had expanded from under 10,000 at the end of February to 25,000 by 23 June.[46] The government's original ambivalence regarding the size of the fighting force had been transformed by the end of June into accusations that the expansion was insufficient.[47] There can be no doubt after examining the kind of investment that the government was making in re-establishing a military policing force that the philosophies of peace-keeping of the Prefect of Police and the central government were fundamentally different. Furthermore, the prefectoral right of supervision and deployment of military troops in the city and the consultation between the head of the Paris police and military leaders was undercut by the government's support of military autonomy. Caussidière made no effort to — nor was he in a position to — offset or control the growing military presence. Yet he

140

was aware of its implications for his own position: *'Gendarme* number one, I was reduced to that. Yes, the Prefect of Police, who represents a minister, was reduced to the state of a *gendarme.*'48

Being undercut by an increasingly powerful military presence was not Caussidière's only problem. He contributed to the further weakening of his own powers by refusing to use police spies and by disavowing openly the use of secret police agents. With the mushrooming of the club movement — by March there were more than 300 clubs of every shade of political affiliation — the government's attitude toward the *droit de réunion* was becoming more cautious. The Prefect of Police did not consider the clubs as a threat to public order but, on the contrary, a healthy indication of the people's right to free expression. Caussidière dissociated himself from the use of undercover agents of any sort and the Minister of the Interior assumed direction of the secret police. This meant the removal from the Prefect's jurisdiction of the force entrusted with all political espionage and surveillance: the effect was not only the weakening of the Prefect's power but also the creation of a rival police organisation. Caussidière claimed that the informer system and the *police de provocation* were remnants of the 'old school' approach to police administration and he looked upon this police division and its new director, Pierre Carlier,49 as the avowed enemy of his organisation with its agents spying on the Prefecture.

The lack of trust was the most striking feature of the expansion of policing organisations from February to May. Added to the confusion of an increasingly strong military presence and three competing organisations under the separate directions of the Prefect of Police, the mayor of Paris, and the Minister of the Interior, was the conflict, which often became public, over jurisdiction and legal rights. The duplication of activities and the absence of any coordinating power further paralysed cooperation among branches of government and contributed to the depletion of the government's limited resources. The proliferation of policing organisations was itself partly the result of the nature of the newly conceived police role: Caussidière had undermined his own position by divorcing the new police from its political functions and by making the organisation suspect through the apparent rejection of standards of professionalism.

Even the issue of neutrality seemed a false one for Caussidière's critics within the government. On 29 April, Caussidière was elected representative of the people, standing twentieth in a field of forty-nine. Caussidière attempted to explain this apparent inconsistency in his claims to neutrality by pointing out that he was able to separate his duties as an elected official from his performance as Prefect of Police. This only increased the tensions between him and moderates in the government. His association with Sobrier further contributed to the deterioration of his position. Sobrier, Caussidière's colleague from *La Réforme* and his co-delegate at the Prefecture for three days in February, was charged with conspiracy and his headquarters on the rue de Rivoli were seized: Caussidière was implicated because he had provided munitions and uniformed guards to protect Sobrier's establishment.[50] His equivocal attitude toward Blanqui was also compromising. It is likely that Caussidière realised that arresting Blanqui would have caused dissension among his own men.[51] In any case, Caussidière's failure to arrest Blanqui at the beginning of May on the government's request was a good indication of the continuing deterioration in relations between Caussidière and his superiors.

Caussidière's resignation from the Prefecture of Police came on 16 May, after over two and a half months of rumours and suspicions. The immediate cause of his departure was his failure to act against the demonstration of 15 May. Caussidière claimed that he had received no orders from the government, that he had been excluded from the decision making process, and that when he did send troops (one hundred Republican Guards), they were requested by government representatives to return to the Prefecture.[52] Yet Caussidière had failed to take action against the two other major demonstrations in the city, those of 17 March and 16 April, and he defended his lack of action in a manner consistent with his avowed democratic principles: 'the people assembled in a body are always great and generous.'[53] What was at issue here, then, was not Caussidière's failure or refusal to obey orders but rather his pursuit of a policy which Peter Amann has labelled 'political non-intervention'.[54] According to Caussidière's own explanation, it was the neutrality of the police and not the survival of the regime that was his first concern. But his pursuit of neutrality had inevitably assumed a political character. His withholding of obedience was considered at best inadequate by the government which felt that the sympathies of its Prefect of Police were with the crowd of Paris. In addition the lack of professionalism obscured the justification of neutrality: in the end, Caussidière's 'bizarre army' only intensified the bourgeois fear of the lower classes and by its failure reaffirmed the indispensability of the military in protecting property and maintaining order in the city.

The experiment in the brotherhood of revolutionary policing had failed. With Caussidière's forced resignation, the Provisional Government ordered the Mobile Guard, the National Guard, and the troops of the line on 16 May to disband the Montagnards: by May 20 the force has been completely suppressed. Caussidière had attempted in his testimony before the National Assembly to defend the honour of his men: the reminder that the Montagnards were the patriots of the February barricades only caused an uproar among the conservative body.[55]

142

There is no proof, despite assertions to the contrary,[56] that Caussidière's Montagnards were ever able to win the public trust. The administration that succeeded Caussidière's on 16 May was from the first dependent on the army:[57] the commitment to an independent civilian force collapsed with Caussidière's administration. On 8 April 1849 the organisation of the municipal police as it had existed during the July Monarchy was quietly and without official publicity re-established.[58] This meant that the attempted reorganisation of the municipal police during the first months of the Provisional Government had been completely abandoned. The only real difference between the *gardien de la paix* of the Second Republic and the *sergent de ville* of the July Monarchy was in the style of the uniform.

Much the same process took place with the *gendarmerie*. By the end of 1848, the recruitment policies, discipline and pay scales of the old Municipal Guard had been re-established.[59] As in 1830 the commitment to an elitist semi-military force emerged battered but essentially unchanged from the revolution of 1848. The methods of ensuring law and order in Paris under a state of siege were not very different from those developed during the July Monarchy: in both periods the *régime mixte* consisted of an inadequate civilian force and a relatively large military concentration. The attempt at revolutionising police procedures had failed resoundingly before the first barricades went up in June. It had taken the post-revolutionary police organisation somewhat longer to snap back to its original form and function following the 1848 experience than it had in 1830. But it did snap back and with barely perceptible alterations. If the municipal police was larger and the Republican Guard was smaller than their July Monarchy counterparts,[60] the municipal organisation was still too insufficiently staffed to provide on its own for the maintenance of law and order in the city. The necessity of the military as a repressive policing force had been temporarily reaffirmed by the revolutionary experience because the problem of peace-keeping continued to be regarded as one of internal war.

Caussidière was not alone in his recognition of the need for reform: his philosophy was significant of the growing concern among administrators with the problems of neutrality and accountability of the institution. In spite of the differences in politics and rhetoric, this constitutes a fundamental similarity between Caussidière's administration and that of his predecessor, Delessert. Although it was not until 1854, under the personal direction of Napoleon III, that structural reforms were undertaken, agitation for the reorganisation of municipal policing continued after the failure of Caussidière's experiment. Caussidière had emphasised that only a civil force was able to guarantee the rights of citizens: 'A well-organised police force is the mainspring of the public

143

security; it gives impulse to trade, confidence to capital, and consequently provides, more than any other department, work for the people.'[61] Less than two weeks after Caussidière's resignation, a plan very similar in philosophy to Caussidière's and calling for the reorganisation of the police was published in Paris.[62] Noting the advantages of the London model, Horace Raisson called for a 'purely civil' police as indispensable to the needs of a great city: 'the police, for too long a time annoying, henceforth ought to appear *preventive and protective.*'[63] Raisson himself had served in the July Monarchy administration and was acknowledged as a leading expert on the history of the French police. The similarity of his rhetoric with Caussidière's is as good an indication as any of the shifting base of attitudes toward the policing function.

Tocqueville said about the performance of the police in the revolution of 1848: 'We [Frenchmen] are strange people: we cannot do without the police when we are orderly, and as soon as we start a revolution, the police seem useless.'[64] There is a sense in which Tocqueville's observation is false. If anything, the revolution highlighted for reformers the indispensability of a responsive policing system. It is true that the revolution and the institutional chaos which followed changed little in urban policing methods. Indeed, the failure of Caussidière's experiment ensured, temporarily at least, the supremacy of the military principle of policing. Yet many of the issues that Caussidière had raised in his rejection of repressive policies were again considered and some of his innovations were preserved in the municipal police reforms of 1854.

Marx saw 'security', the protection of persons and property, as 'the supreme social concept' of bourgeois society.[65] Caussidière's 'revolutionary' programme of 1848, therefore, has to be understood not only within the context of the internal struggle of the revolution but also within the context of the changing institutional needs of French society in the nineteenth century.

Notes

1.   The growth of civil policing is examined by me in 'Urban Growth and Public Order: The Development of A Modern Police in Paris, 1829-1854', unpublished dissertation (Columbia University 1973).
2.   Even as the social historian has lowered his gaze to scrutinise the activities of mobs and crowds, he has only occasionally widened his field of vision to consider the movements and motives of the forces of coercion with which the crowd did battle. Richard Cobb's *The Police and the People: French Popular Protest. 1789-1820* (Oxford 1970) is an exception to this in its treatment of the assumptions and habits of the police. Yet Cobb is at all times more concerned with the police as social historian, as reporter of popular protest, than he is with the nature of the changing response of the force of order to the popular movement. Recent scholarship in police studies continues to deal with the activities of the secret and

political police and prefectoral administration: Howard C. Payne, *The Police State of Louis Napoleon Bonaparte, 1851-1860* (Seattle, 1966); Edward A. Whitcomb, 'Napoleon's Prefects', *American Historical Review*, 79 (October 1974); and Bernard LeClère and Vincent Wright, *Les Prefets du Second Empire* (Paris, 1973).

3.   Peter Amann, 'Revolution: A Redefinition', *Political Science Quarterly*, 77 (1962), p. 46.

4.   Marc Caussidière has left us with his own analysis, which must be read with caution, of his term at the Prefecture: *Secret History of the Revolution of 1848. Memoirs of Citizen Caussidière*, 2 volumes (London, 1848).

5.   Caussidière's assertion that the takeover was peaceful and without bloodshed — *Secret History* I, p. 65 — was substantiated from an unfriendly quarter by Lucien Delahodde, *History of the Secret Societies and of the Republican Party of France from 1830 to 1848* (Philadelphia, 1856), p. 464. Caussidière had correctly accused Delahodde after the February Revolution of spying for the government of the July Monarchy in the secret societies.

6.   APP-Db31. By 1848 there were 300 *sergents de ville* and 180 officers of the peace. These numbers, when combined with the office personnel, brought the size of the municipal police to a total of 600. The Municipal Guard in 1848 consisted of 3,900 members.

7.   AN-BB[30] 296. This is a series of special reports made by the *commissaires* of Paris to the Cour d'Appel de Paris, commission rogatoire, on the February revolution. The reports were responses to a questionnaire of 1 March 1848, that was attempting to ascertain the points of attack and resistance in each quarter, the names and addresses of participants in the fighting, a list of the wounded, actions taken by the armed corps, and any statements of information which residents might wish to contribute to the official record.

8.   *Ibid.* The Municipal Guard responded most effectively and met with greatest violence in the Champs-Elysées, Montmartre, Bonne-Nouvelle, and Saint Martin des Champs quarters. Place Vendôme and Place d l'Hôtel de Ville were the locations where the *gendarmes* were reported to have charged the crowds. In every instance, whether aided by the army or alone, the Municipal Guard was forced to retreat.

9.   *Ibid.* The lament of commissaire Noël of the Quartier des Invalides was not untypical of the justifications by his colleagues of their failure to take action. 'Je n'ai reçu de M. le Préfet de police aucune recommandation particulière de l'exécution de l'ordre qu'il m'a adressé le vingt février et que je depose'.

10.   Alexis de Tocqueville, *The Recollections of Alexis de Tocqueville*, ed. J. P. Mayer (New York, 1959), p. 75.

11.   The rationale of police expansion is treated in O'Brien, 'Urban Growth'. The municipal police increased during the July Monarchy from 97 to 480 members; the Municipal Guard nearly doubled in the period to its maximum strength in 1848 of 3,900 members. Of greater significance was the expansion of military presence in the city from about 11,000 in 1830 to 40,000 in 1848.

12.   Georges Duveau, *1848: The Making of a Revolution* (New York, 1968), p. 27, n. 1.

13.   *Ibid.*

14.   Delahodde, *Secret Societies*, p. 465: 'the mounted guards . . . were shot down like dogs by the infamous populace!' The Municipal Guard is presented as victim in *Histoire de la légion de la garde républicaine — extrait de la décision journalière du 15 juin 1906* (Presse Regimentaire, 1908), pp. 83-96. Certain accounts, however, accuse the *gendarmerie* of unjustifiable brutality and of inflicting injuries on innocent passers by: *Histoire populaire de la révolution de 1848, avant, pendant, après* (Paris, 1848), p. 5. Blame was also placed on the Municipal Guard for inciting the crowd to riot because of the corps' 'aggressive and insolent'

attitude on 22 February: Xavier comte de Montepin and Alphonse Bernard, *Les Trois journées de février* (Paris, 1848), p. 13.

15.   AN-BB[30] 296. The *commissaire* of the quartier Champs Elysées reported that the Municipal Guard post in his area was barricaded against the crowd on the twenty-fourth and that several gendarmes were wounded in the fighting. In the Arsenal district several National Guardsmen were reported to have joined the crowd in shouting 'A bas la garde municipale, nous n'en voulons pas'. A battle ensured and the *gendarmes* were forced to retreat. In the quartier Chaillot the barracks of the allée des Veuves had to be evacuated in order to avoid an armed confrontation with the hostile population.

16.   Twenty *commissaires* willing to serve the new goverment were maintained in their posts: their testimony of their conduct in the February revolution is found in AN-BB[30] 296. Although Caussidière had no choice but to rely on some of Delessert's agents to keep the bureaucratic machinery in running order, he clearly considered the service of these new *commissaires* a liability: *Secret History*, I, pp. 84-5. Certain *sergents de ville* continued to be maintained on the payroll as well, though Caussidière never acknowledged this fact. Louis Canler, a member of the July Monarchy municipal force, served as an undercover agent for Caussidière and has provided an account in his memoirs of the continuity in personnel: Canler claimed that Caussidière was shrewd enough to know what services he could expect from the former *sergents de ville* that he could not expect from his own Montagnards. A special entry was reported to have been used by these agents who came out of hiding to collect their salaries: Louis Canler, *Mémoires de Canler, ancien chef du sûreté* (Paris, 1882), II, p. 229. Similar testimony is given in Rey and Féron, *Histoire du corps des gardiens de la paix* (Paris 1896), p. 146, n. 1.

17.   Caussidière, *Secret History*, I, p. 184.

18.   Reprinted in Alfred Delvau, *Les Murailles révolutionnaires* (Paris, 1852), p. 27. *Le Moniteur* refused to print Caussidière.s and Sobrier.s first proclamation, even when intimidation was attempted.

19.   *Le Moniteur Universel* (17 May 1848), p. 1064. In circulars to his *commissaires* Caussidière urged them to concern themselves with the 'public morality': APP-Aa427. Préfecture de Police, 10 March 1848. He justified his new Republican Guard as a 'moral' guarantee against disorder: *Secret History*, II, p. 90.

20.   Caussidière, *Secret History*, I, p. 29.

21.   *Ibid.*, I, p. 255.

22.   Karl Marx, *Class Struggles in France, 1848-1850* (New York, 1964), p. 46.

23.   *Le Moniteur Universel* (17 May 1848), p. 1064.

24.   Cour des Paris, *Affaire du moi d'avril 1834. Réquisitoire de M. le Procureur-Général présenté à la cour le 8 décembre 1834* (Paris, 1834). *Procédure interrogatoire des accusées* (Paris, 1835), IX (Saint-Etienne), pp. 241-54. In his interrogation, Caussidière claimed that he had only pushed the policeman and he used the opportunity to complain about his maltreatment at the hands of the police.

25.   APP-Ea20. Dossier Caussidière. His involvement in the secret societies is also described in volume one of his *Secret Society*.

26.   Caussidière, *Secret History*, I, p. 129.

27.   Daniel Stern (pseud. of Mari, comtesse d'Agoult), *Histoire de la révolution de 1848* (Paris, 1862), I, p. 494.

28.   Minister of the Interior Lédru-Rollin officially requested the historical painter Raffet to sketch the corps on 28 February in the courtyard of the Prefecture of Police. The rendering gives a good indication of the variety of uniforms: reprinted in Rey and Féron, *Gardiens*, pp. 128-9. The authors' comment on p. 141: 'les costumes bizarre excitent encore notre étonnement.'

29.   Louis Blanc, *Histoire de la révolution de 1848* Paris, 1870), I, p. 292.

30.   In Gustave Flaubert's novel, *L'Education sentimentale*, Frédéric Moreau and the Maréchale, walking through the streets of Paris and enjoying the euphoria following the February revolution, were frightened only by the 'men of Caussidière' with their sabres and their scarves. (Paris, 1964), p. 295.

31.   Caussidière, *Secret History*, I, p. 101.

32.   Adolphe Chénu, *Les Conspirateurs* (Paris, 1850).

33.   *Ibid.*, pp. 116-7. Delahodde, *Secret Societies*, p. 468: 'The court, the offices of the employees, the halls all were thronged by a wild-looking set of men, hideous, offensive to the very smell, lounging upon cushions, or howling among the drinking pots. Nothing can give any idea of the spectacle unless it is a camp of drunken and rampant Cossacks.'

34.   Chénu, *Les Montagnards de 1848, encore quatre nouveaux chapitres, précédés d'une réponse à Caussidière et autres démoc-socs* (Paris, 1850). Pornin answered these attacks in a ghost-written work by Noël Castera, *La Vérité sur la Préfecture de Police pendant l'administration de M. Caussidière* (Paris, 1850). Pornin denied all the charges made against him and his men by Chénu and Delahodde. He denounced even the portraits in Chénu's book as false: Pornin pointed out that they showed him with long hair which he had not worn since 1829 and they showed his wooden leg on the wrong side. Another work by Jules Miot answered the same charges of immorality and drunkenness and went so far as to assert that Caussidière only drank black coffee at the Prefecture: *Réponse aux deux libelles: les Conspirateurs et la Naissance de la République de Chénu et de Delahodde, d'après les lettres, pièces et documents fournis et publiés par Caussidière, ex-Préfet de police, Lubati, ex-officer d'état-major de la garde républicaine, et d'autre ex-fontionnaires de la Préfecture de police, avec des révélations curieuses sur la vie de Delahodde, par le citoyen Jules Miot, représentant du peuple* (Paris, 1850). Caussidière answered these accusations in his memoirs before some of them were even in print: *Secret History*, I, p. 80.

35.   Stern, *Histoire*, I, p. 494. The Montagnards were supposed to be receiving 2.25 francs per day, although late paying procedures and bureaucratic wranglings often obstructed salary payments. According to a government investigation on wages and working conditions conducted between 1840 and 1845, the average wage for male workers in Paris was 2.09 francs per day: these reports are examined in E. Levasseur, *Histoire des classes ouvrières et de l'industrie en France de 1789 à 1870* (Paris, 1904), II, pp. 257-61.

36.   Cited in Priscilla Robertson, *The Revolution of 1848: A Social History* (New York, 1952), pp. 56-7.

37.   Blanc, *Histoire*, p. 295.

38.   Caussidière, *Secret History*, I, p. 187. Robertson surprisingly accepts Caussidière at his word: 'In checking crime Caussidière was highly successful. During his three months in office there was only one murder in the city, and theft was greatly reduced': *Revolutions*, p. 56.

39.   Caussidière, *Secret History*, I, pp. 187-8.

40.   *Le Constitutionnel* (9 April 1848).

41.   Caussidière, *Secret History*, I, p. 227.

42.   *Ibid.*, I, p. 228.

43.   *Ibid.*, I, p. 268.

44.   Marx, *Class Struggles*, p. 50.

45.   Rémi Gossez, 'Diversité des antagonismes sociaux vers le milieu du XIXe siècle', *Revue Economique* (1956), pp. 439-58; Pierre Chalmin, 'Une institution militaire de la seconde république: la garde nationale mobile', *Etudes d'Histoire Moderne et Contemporaine* II (1949), pp. 37-82; Frederick de Luna, *The French Republic under Cavaignac* (Princeton, 1969), pp. 134-5. These corps, as Gossez shows, shared much the same fate as the Montagnards in being confounded with

les classes dangereuses.

46.   Peter Amann puts the literature on military developments in analytical perspective: 'Writings on the Second French Republic', *Journal of Modern History* XXXIV (1962), pp. 409-29. The best single work on military strength and strategies is de Luna's *The French Republic.*

47.   For the debate and the criticism of Cavaignac on this point, see de Luna, *The French Republic*, pp. 167-8.

48.   *Le Moniteur Universel* (17 May 1848), p. 1064.

49.   Carlier had been the head of the municipal police during the July Monarchy and for this reason he was doubly suspect by Caussidière. APP-Ea20, Dossier Carlier.

50.   Garnier-Pagès complained that the house in the rue de Rivoli looked like 'a branch of the prefecture', *Histoire de la révolution de 1848*, VII, pp. 81-2. Caussidière claimed that Sobrier had been planning to set up a rival police and that it was upon discovery of the plot that Caussidière had withdrawn support, *Secret History*, II, p. 200. For the best account of Sobrier's conspiring before 15 May, see Peter Amann, 'A *Journée* in the Making: May 15, 1848', *Journal of Modern History*, 42 (1970), pp. 42-69.

51.   Several contemporary observers credited the rumour that Blanqui had agents and supporters in the police ranks: Jacques Arago, *Histoire de Paris: ses révolutions, ses gouvernements et ses événements de 1841 à 1852*, II, p. 114; Stern, *Histoire*, I, p. 495. Canler, a former agent of the July Monarchy police, claimed that he was commissioned to aid in the arrest of Blanqui because Caussidière knew that he could not trust his Montagnards on the mission: Canler, *Mémoires*, II, pp. 229-33. The claim that there was a conspiracy in the ranks, whether true or not, provided an excuse to Caussidière for his failure to take action against the left at the beginning of May.

52.   *Le Moniteur Universel* (17 May 1848), pp. 1064-5; *Le Voleur* (5 June 1848), pp. 495-6.

53.   Caussidière, *Secret History*, I, p. 181.

54.   Amann, 'Revolution', p. 49.

55.   *Le Moniteur Universel* (17 May 1848), p. 1064.

56.   Rey and Féron, *Gardiens*, p. 143. The authors contend that the first bad impression made by the Montagnards was replaced by a sentiment of trust, as the corps tracked down wrongdoers and thieves in the city. No documentation is given.

57.   AN-F[7] 1072. On 12 June 1848 the Minister of the Interior advised General Bedeau, commandant of the Mobile Guard, that the new Prefect of Police, Trouvé-Chauvel, was in need of 100 military men to be stationed at the Prefecture.

58.   Rey and Féron, *Gardiens*, p. 165; 'Ni *Le Moniteur*, ni les journaux judiciaires, ni la collection officielle des ordonnances de la Préfecture de Police ne font mention de cette mesure.'

59.   Jean-Baptiste Duvergier, *Collection complète des lois, décrets, ordonnances, règlements, et avis du Conseil d'Etat* (Paris, 1849, XLIX, 27: decree of 1 February 1849, re-established the directorial organisation of the former Municipal Guard and defined the jurisdictional rights of the ministries; XLIX, 377; decree of 27 October 1849, re-established the privileges of the former officer corps.

60.   The Republican Guard was set at 2,600 in 1848, as compared to 3,900 in the last days of the July Monarchy. The force of the *gardiens de la paix* was whittled down by stages from 2,500 in 1848 to a low of 940 declared in the budget of 1849: this was still almost double the 480 footpatrolmen of the July Monarchy.

61.   Caussidière, *Secret History*, II, p. 173; *Le Moniteur Universel* (17 May 1848), p. 1066.
62.   Horace Raisson, *De la Police de Paris, Nécessité de réorganiser son personnel et de moraliser son action* (Paris, 25 May 1848).
63.   *Ibid.*, p. 20. Italics added.
64.   Tocqueville, *Recollections*, p. 142.
65.   Karl Marx, 'On the Jewish Question', *Writings of the Young Marx on Philosophy and Society*, trans. and ed. by Lloyd D. Easton and Kurt Guddat (Garden City, 1967), p. 236.

CIVIL-MILITARY RELATIONS IN PARIS, 1848

Jonathan M. House

Paris during the revolutionary events of February through June 1848 provides an unusual opportunity to study civil-military relations and the role of armed force in controlling civil disorders. An essay of this length cannot hope to recount military actions in any great tactical detail. Instead, it focuses upon the reasons for the collapse of the French Army during the February Revolution, and upon the relationships between a wide variety of paramilitary groups and a series of political crises. An understanding of the composition and of the political reliability of these groups is central to a more complete analysis of political events. This essay will therefore deal with the regular army during the February Days and with the many military formations which arose after that revolution, before turning to the role of these formations in the political confrontations of March through June.

The composition and use of military forces in Paris during the February Revolution go far to explain the initial success of that revolution. By 1848, the French Army closely approximated the ideal of a long term force which was both professional and apolitical. Politically conscious officers and men did indeed exist, but the July Monarchy's efforts to improve material conditions and to repress radicalism amongst the troops had eliminated overt political activities. Furthermore, the Algerian colonial war provided an outlet for personal ambitions which might otherwise have opposed the existing government. However, this political passivity did not mean that the army strongly supported the July Monarchy. The Revolution of 1830 had shown many army officers the danger of supporting a regime seriously threatened by domestic opposition. Excessive devotion to the Bourbons had split the French officer corps and had caused much disorder within the army as a whole. Consequently, many soldiers tended to place stability, unit integrity, nationalism, and personal career ahead of loyalty to any particular government. Below the level of the highest commanders, the army was not heavily committed to Louis-Philippe.[1]

Alongside an apolitical army was a thoroughly political National Guard. Recruited from bourgeois volunteers, the Guard had a primary function of protecting property during revolutionary upheavals, so that the regular army could deal with centres of rebel resistance. Unfortunately for Louis-Philippe, however, the National Guard of the Seine was as reformist as it was monarchist. A long tradition of Guard liberalism was reinforced by the expansion law of 1837, which allowed large numbers of *petit-bourgeois* citizens to enlist in the National Guard legions. These guardsmen, lacking the vote and suffering in any economic crisis, were always eager for an opportunity to liberalise the government's policies. During the February Days many National Guardsmen proved unable to differentiate between a reform demonstration and a revolution. As a result, these guardsmen unwittingly helped overthrow the monarchy instead of simply liberalising it. The king reportedly remarked afterwards 'the bourgeois of Paris would not have overthrown me if they had not believed me unshakable'.[2]

The July government was fully aware of these political tendencies in the National Guard and had avoided using the militia since 1841. As the February political Banquet approached, several officers warned the cabinet that the Paris legions would not support the government against the reformers. Most government and military leaders expected the National Guard to remain neutral, calculating that regular forces could handle the situation unaided.[3]

Contemporary observers, and more recently Albert Crémieux,[4] attributed the military failure in February primarily to the absence of National Guard support for the army. The important point, however, was not the Guard's neutrality but its active intervention against the army. Some guardsmen were in fact loyal to the government or at least neutral, yet the persistent opposition of other militiamen not only paralysed Louis-Philippe's will but greatly hindered army efforts to control the crowds.

Long before the National Guard appeared on 23 February the July Monarchy was endangered by a faulty command structure, rigid planning, and political limitations upon military action. Operational command of Paris lay between three men: Lieutenant General Tiburce Sébastiani headed the regular army garrison as Commandant of the First Military Division: Lieutenant General Jean-François Jacqueminot commanded the National Guard of the Seine: and Police Prefect Delessert controlled the Municipal Guard (the hated military police force of 3,200 men) and other police units. Sébastiani and Jacqueminot were both competent, but apparently both owed their appointments to political influence. Jacqueminot's frequent illnesses limited his contact with and hence his influence over the guardsmen; during the February Revolution his Chief of Staff often had to act in his stead. In early February, War Minister Trézel sought in vain to superimpose the famous Marshal Bugeaud d'Isly as joint commander of all forces in Paris. Instead the Duke de Nemours became an informal and largely ineffectual arbitrator between the three commanders.[5]

At a lower level, most of the brigade and major unit commanders in Paris were overaged brigadiers whose military experience dated in many cases to the Napoleonic Wars.[6] Like their commanders, they were more noteworthy for their politics than for their military prowess.

Many previous upheavals in Paris, especially those of the later 1830s, had followed a set pattern. Whether or not large riots developed, the core of each insurrection was a small, clearly identifiable secret society which attempted to seize the government buildings and then hold out until the previous regime became discredited. This type of secret society, with its radical socialist beliefs, was the natural enemy of the bourgeois National Guard. With militia support assured, the regular garrison had only to react rapidly in order to suppress such a *coup*.

The existing plan for the military control of Paris, adopted in 1839, was specifically designed to combat this form of insurrection. Marshal Maurice-Etienne Gérard, the author of the plan, calculated that 6,500 regular soldiers would suffice to protect the seat of government, although in fact the July Monarchy maintained a much larger garrison in the capital. These troops, in cooperation with any National Guardsmen available, were to occupy seven strategic points and twenty-seven outposts, sending out patrols of twenty-five men to locate and pin the rebels until larger forces could be brought up to smash resistance.[7] This plan, however, was intended to combat the specific type of threat posed by a secret society, and proved largely ineffective against the massive, amorphous and socially respectable reform demonstrations of February.

On the evening of 21 February 1848, General Sébastiani called a meeting of his senior commanders to prepare for the disturbances expected the next morning. Sébastiani had 33,400 regular troops in Paris and Versailles, in addition to 3,600 Municipal Guardsmen and gendarmes. In each barracks he had stored not only ammunition and rations, but tools with which to dismantle barricades. Sébastiani was not, therefore, unprepared for a military clash. What concerned him was not military defeat but civil bloodshed, for excessive force on the part of the garrison could produce unnecessary violence against the reform leaders. This in turn might provoke public disapproval of the regime and possibly revolution on a scale which no military preparations could control. On instructions from the government, General Sébastiani had changed the entire intent of the 1839 plan, deciding to treat the reform Banquet not as a problem in military repression but rather as a delicate political crisis in which bloodshed must be avoided at all costs. Speaking to his colonels and brigadiers, the commandant reviewed the 1839 plan but strongly emphasised the need for moderation in the use of force. In order to avoid unnecessary violence, local commanders were to use police commissioners, summonses, and the

152

other mechanisms of civil law before physically dispersing crowds.[8]

The emphasis which Sébastiani, the Duke de Nemours, and the royal government placed upon moderation severely hampered the royal forces during the February crisis. Since the regular army was neither trained nor equipped to disperse demonstrations peacefully, commanders were unable to do much beyond passively holding their positions. Even when the demonstration changed into rebellion, the orders to avoid violence and observe legal procedures restrained many officers from vigorous action. It is significant that, because of the divided military command in Paris, the Municipal Guard was not represented at the 21 February meeting and received no special instructions. As a result, the Municipal Guardsmen were much more active and combative than were the line infantrymen, controlling some disorders but provoking others by their vigour.

The final handicap under which the government forces laboured in February was the confused manner in which the 1839 plan was implemented. Even if that plan were inappropriate, its correct execution would have deployed the available forces rapidly, discouraging violence by the demonstrators. Since, however, the opposition political leaders had cancelled the Banquet the night before, the government and its commanders were caught off balance by the large crowds which appeared on the morning of 22 February. The occupation of strategic points and the mobilisation of the National Guard were therefore fragmented and confused.

Throughout 22 and 23 February, the regular troops struggled to control crowds, vandalism and intermittent armed resistance in many parts of Paris. Civilians frequently cheered the army and concentrated their attacks against the Municipal Guard. Individual National Guardsmen, as already indicated, constantly hampered the regulars and aided civilian efforts to disarm troops. Meanwhile the commanders became confused by the diffuse nature of the threat, by constant rumours and poor communications, and by the alternating paralysis and interference of the civilian government. Small detachments were shifted from point to point to meet imaginary threats, thereby contributing to the confusion, exhaustion and demoralisation of the soldiers involved. Cut off from their barracks, the troops began to run short of rations and other supplies.

By the evening of 23 February most government leaders believed that the change in ministry had resolved the crisis. The Duke de Nemours and the various commanders continued to move army and loyal National Guard units about, despite the delicate political situation and the increasing weariness of the soldiers. At 8 p.m. on 23 February, the tension culminated in a confrontation on the Capucines Boulevard. Three companies of the Fourteenth Line Infantry Regiment, part of a heterogeneous force protecting the Foreign Ministry building, refused to allow a crowd of demonstrators to pass. Someone fired a shot, and without orders the soldiers responded with ragged vollies which killed fifty-two civilians.[9] This incident converted a waning disorder into a full insurrection during the night. Citizens constructed barricades and looted several barracks. The army fought more vigorously against a clearly identifiable opponent, but outnumbered units abandoned outposts and fell back upon the central reserve at the Tuileries Palace.

During the night the king belatedly appointed Marshal Bugeaud as joint commander, and Bugeaud set out to restore the situation. Early on 24 February, the marshal despatched three strong columns to clear barricades along important arteries. Even in this extremity, however, Bugeaud felt compelled to observe the legal formalities and to publicise the reform cabinet, hoping to rally the population without the use of force. As a result of these restrictions, one column under General Marie-Alphonse Bedeau became stalled in the Boulevard Poissonière. Faced by a seemingly endless series of barricades and surrounded by civilians who appealed to them individually, Bedeau's troops became indecisive and passive. At the same time, de Nemours and the new ministers persuaded Bugeaud to renounce force and recall his columns, arguing that further bloodshed would only discredit the new cabinet. Everywhere local officials and prominent citizens urged troop commanders to avoid conflict. In the ensuing retreat and confusion, civilians disarmed a large part of the Paris garrison. Deserters, stragglers and small detachments were forgotten and scattered. The last royal commander, Marshal Gérard, saw no alternative to withdrawing his disintegrating army from Paris. Some officers contemplated armed opposition to the republic, but both troops and barracks were scattered throughout the city. making impossible any reorganisation or resistance. Bugeaud and other influential commanders urged junior officers to support the moderate Provisional Government in order to prevent social chaos and foreign invasion.[10]

Divided leadership, inappropriate plans, and political considerations had made control of the reform demonstrations difficult. National Guard opposition, confused leadership, and the demoralisation of the army made such control impossible. The army's failure and withdrawal in February not only made the republic possible, but helped to create the political and military situation which dominated Paris for the next four months.

The garrison of Paris restored its organisation if not its discipline within a few days after the February Revolution. Stragglers returned to their units rapidly. In the army as a whole waves of mutiny and troop disorder, briefly in February and then again in late March, affected thirty-two out of 180 combat units in metropolitan France. The

Provisional Government and the new heads of the War Ministry were concerned by the unreliability of the army and took steps to improve troop conditions and to move undisciplined units away from the potential influence of civilian radicals. In point of fact, most of these troop disorders were not politically motivated, except insofar as soldiers took advantage of the uncertain political climate to air their personal grievances. The most common complaints were the sudden changes in garrison location and the reimposition of discipline after the laxness of early March. The efforts of the War Ministry, of troop commanders, and of non-commissioned officers restored order during April, while the army expanded its ranks in preparation for a possible war in Italy or Germany.[11] This recovery was greatly aided by the willing cooperation which officers gave to the new republic.

The direction of the War Ministry was crucial to the return of discipline and to the expansion of the army. The first War Minister of the republic, Gervais Subervie, was a retired general who had been appointed in default of a more prominent commander. Subervie proved unimaginative and immobile, and so on 19 March the Provisional Government 'promoted' him to a sinecure as chief of the Legion of Honour. The ministers then named General Eugene Cavaignac, the famous republican who was then governor of Algeria, as War Minister. Cavaignac, however, refused to become associated with a regime which would soon be replaced by the National Assembly and which appeared to distrust the army.[12]

The Commission for the Organisation of National Defence, a board of prominent generals created to prepare France for war, had been a prime mover for Subervie's dismissal. Reporting directly to the provisional cabinet, this commission was extremely influential during March and April. Gradually, however, control of the War Ministry passed from the commission as a whole to two of its members. François Arago, chairman of the Defence Commission, was already overworked as a member of the Provisional Government and as Minister of Marine when Cavaignac's refusal forced him to succeed Subervie in the War Ministry. Most military administration therefore devolved on Lieutenant Colonel Jean-Baptiste Adolphe Charras, who became in succession secretary of the Defence Commission (9 March), Under-Secretary of State for War (5 April), and acting Minister (11 May). At the age of thirty-eight, Charras had a reputation both as a confirmed republican and as a brilliant commander in Algeria. He owed his rapid rise in 1848 to his long association with the reform journal *Le National*, but he had the respect of most generals as well as of the moderate politicians.[13] Although his own politics verged upon socialism, Colonel Charras was convinced that the army needed a return of discipline and Paris needed a return of order, including a strong garrison.

Charras implemented a variety of cabinet decisions designed to retire forcibly those generals who were considered too old or too royalist to remain in command. These retirements excited much resentment amongst the generals involved, but most of the younger officers accepted them as an inevitable consequence of the change in regime. Large numbers of promotions and the prospect of foreign war assured the loyalty of NCOs and junior officers.

For three weeks after the monarchy collapsed, War Minister Subervie and the new commanders in Paris maintained a number of army units on the outskirts of the capital, as well as two cavalry regiments at the Ecole Militaire in the centre of the city. General F. F. Duvivier, the army commandant for central Paris, planned a garrison of four to six regiments for the specific purpose of maintaining civil order. The moderate faction of the Provisional Government was equally eager to have reliable armed forces, if only to halt the daily crime and rioting which plagued the capital. This intention was reinforced by demands from the National Guard's commanders and periodicals that the regulars should resume the daily picket duties which tired the militia. Only the need to rearm the troops and repair the looted barracks prevented the immediate return of the army to the centre of Paris.

There was little public reaction to the 14 March announcement of this garrison, although many journals and politically active citizens believed that the army belonged on the frontier rather than in the capital. Then news of revolution in western Germany and in Vienna in mid-March made war seem less probable, and the 16 March demonstration raised the possibility of an armed counter-revolution. It was thus no accident that one major demand of the radical clubs on 17 March was the expulsion of all regulars from Paris. The weakened Provisional Government had to acquiesce in this, halting the movement of new units towards the capital and removing the cavalry from the Ecole Militaire.

In the absence of a garrison, the Provisional Government had to cope not only with continued disorders in Paris but also with a variety of paramilitary organisations of unpredictable political motivation. Historians have generally neglected the study of these armed groups, perhaps because of the scanty documentation available, yet such paramilitary forces played a central role in Parisian political events.

There were firstly several irregular units which arose spontaneously in the power vacuum of late February. The 'Republican Guard of the Hôtel-de-Ville' surrounded the seat of the new government for three months. Amongst the 400 (later 600) men of this Guard were a few extreme socialists and professional revolutionaries, but 'Colonel' Rey, the former officer who headed them, managed to isolate and eventually to eliminate these radicals. The Provisional Government recognised this unit to the point of giving its officers formal rank, and until 15 May the Republican Guard proved fairly reliable.[14]

The self-appointed Police Prefect Marc Caussidière recruited his own paramilitary police force from former political prisoners and February insurgents. Although Caussidière's own loyalties and motives were often suspect, his 'Montagnards' did not as a unit oppose the government. Caussidière purged the Montagnards of known criminals, and used the remaining men to greatly improve daily order in Paris. The political inclinations of the Montagnards are indicated by the loyal service which the majority gave during the the June Days as part of the reorganised Republican Guard.[15] This political moderation was not at all characteristic of the third and smallest of the irregular organisations, the 'Lyonnais' force recruited by the experienced revolutionary Marie-Joseph Sobrier. Caussidière and Foreign Minister Alphonse de Lamartine attempted at various times to recruit Sobrier for their respective political factions, but the actions of the Lyonnais in any crisis remained unpredictable.

Numerous other paramilitary groups of a more ephemeral nature — Polish and Belgian nationalists, egalitarian female artillerists, and others — complicated the situation in Paris.

Although public opinion had forced the evacuation of the army and the dissolution of the Municipal Guard, common crime and minor disorders required a larger police force than the Montagnards could provide. In late March the Provisional Government ordered the creation of the *Gardiens de Paris*, a body of unarmed policemen. Caussidière apparently defeated Mayor Armand Marrast in a major bureaucratic battle for control of the *Gardiens*,[16] but this body of several hundred men remained loyal to the Provisional Government, and could be armed in a crisis.

The largest full time military force in Paris was the Mobile National Guard. On 26 February the cabinet opened enlistments for 24 (later 25) battalions of one-year volunteers. This force was intended not only to supplement the army and the police forces but to absorb the active youths who had led the February demonstrations, and who might continue to agitate if not otherwise occupied. Eventually 16,000 volunteers, encadred with junior officers and NCOs from nearby infantry regiments were lodged in the barracks of Paris.

Many contemporaries expressed concern about the political reliability of this force, which seemed to be composed of unemployed street urchins and radical insurgents. In fact, however, the average National Guardsman was probably an artisan's apprentice or helper more inspired by a brief and glamorous military career than by complicated social theories.[17] Apparently realising this, the Provisional Government concerned itself with the supply of Mobile uniforms and weapons in order to satisfy youthful ambitions, rather than worrying about the reported politics of a few recruits. There were indeed radicals in the Mobile, and the four battalions in the Ecole Militaire went so far as to organise their own political club, but this club, like most indications of apparent radicalism within the Mobile Guard, proved harmless. Police reports indicated that when a Mobile did express a controversial opinion, he was often influenced by drink and bravado, and not by any serious belief.

The Mobile Guard did, however, constitute a problem of discipline and public order, since until the volunteers could be trained and equipped they were a mass of adolescents with high wages and few responsibilities. Inevitably the 'green epaulettes' brawled, drank and consorted with prostitutes in a manner which alarmed the public and the Prefect of Police. The problem was complicated by the fact that the Mobile Guard was not subject to military law, so that an offender had ·to be expelled by a board of his peers and then tried in civil court. By early April, however, its organisation had advanced sufficiently for the volunteers to police the city during the National Guard elections. Thereafter the increasing demands for Mobiles to guard buildings and suppress disorders kept these troops busy if not entirely disciplined. The Provisional Government had sufficient confidence in the Mobile Guard to despatch its battalions to control disorders in Amiens and Rouen.

An additional problem in the Mobile Guard was the choice of commanders. Although the army provided training cadres, the volunteers had the right to elect their own leaders, up to the rank of major, in the normal fashion of the National Guard. Not only were many instructor sergeants from the army elected captain, but the War Minister had to disallow the election of deserters, lunatics and incompetents who had impressed their peers in the Mobile. Fortunately for the government, General Duvivier and the later commanders of the Mobile Guard provided strong personal leadership and closely supervised their inexperienced subordinates.

Up to this point, I have discussed the military forces in revolutionary Paris with little reference to events, and the Provisional Government has appeared primarily as an administrative body. When considering the National Guard, however, one must return to political events and to partisan factions. As the largest and most diverse military force in the capital, the National Guard of the Seine formed a pivot for political rivalries. The Provisional Government was united in its desire to make the National Guard a representative citizen militia, and therefore opened enlistment to all adult males. Since, however, processing and arming new recruits took time, the main burden of policing Paris during early March fell upon the moderate bourgeoisie of the old National Guard.

Many of these overworked citizens mistrusted the republic from its birth, and when the expansion of the Guard necessitated a complete reorganisation of units, the militia reacted. The proximate cause of their demonstration on 16 March was the dissolution of the elite companies, the units preferred by richer and more motivated guardsmen, but in fact the issue was the general tendency of political events. Unable to oppose a parade of guardsmen, the Provisional Government did attempt to protect itself from the popular counter-demonstration the following day. Most participants in this latter parade were only expressing their opposition to the National Guard, but leaders of the radical political clubs seized the opportunity to pressure the Provisional Government to delay national elections and ban the regular army from Paris. The government sought to counter this pressure by hurriedly arming a number of Mobile battalions and sending them to the Hôtel-de-Ville on the morning of 17 March,[18] but the radical clubs appeared too strong, and all factions of the cabinet had to accept the club demands.

In the wake of 17 March, the moderate members of the Provisional Government feared that the popular Interior Minister Alexandre Ledru-Rollin would combine his influence with that of the more radical political clubs, producing a violent change in the new regime. All factions believed that the next confrontation would come on Sunday, 16 April. In addition to the official National Guard officer elections of 5-10 April, Louis Blanc and the radical Auguste Blanqui announced that militia staff officers would be elected at a 16 April rally on the Champ de Mars. Without wishing to overthrow the Provisional Government, Blanc promoted this 'election' to hasten social innovation. Despite the disapproval of the revolutionary Armand Barbès, the combined influence of Blanc, Ledru-Rollin and Blanqui seemed to menace the Provisional Government. Only at the last moment did Blanc and Ledru-Rollin realise the danger of publically supporting the clubs.

Foreign Minister Lamartine and the moderate politicians Marrast and Arago laboured to prepare for this confrontation. Contrary to reports at the time, the cabinet did not attempt to keep arms from the new lower class recruits of the National Guard. Some bourgeois officers of the Guard did obstruct the expansion in this manner, but Marrast in particular wished to attract artisans and labourers into the National Guard in order to offset the influence of the radical clubs.[19] This paralleled Emile Thomas' policies in the National Workshops. The moderate leaders repeatedly encouraged employees of the Workshops to join the Guard and to seek election as officers. The minutes of the Provisional Government during the week before the Champ de Mars meeting betray a mounting concern to obtain and distribute arms for the entire National Guard.[20] Immediately after the National Guard elections, Marrast as mayor of Paris held a series of reviews and receptions to gain the loyalty of the newly elected officers. Police reports indicated that he was not entirely successful in this effort,[21] but certainly the moderates did not fear the lower class element in the legions unless that element was provoked by the radical leadership. In any case, many guardsmen who responded to the drums on 16 April were uncertain whether the threat came from the political right or left and acted to protect the existing government.

The moderates also needed to assure the loyalty of the major paramilitary forces. In the Republican Guard, Colonel Rey was vulnerable only to his friend Barbès, who opposed the rally. The Mobile Guard became increasingly restless in early April because its uniforms were not yet completed. Despite this situation, the volunteers retained great respect for General Duvivier and for the Provisional Government. Furthermore, the Mobiles were predisposed to resist disorders because of their experience protecting the city during the National Guard elections. Caussidière apparently negotiated for a political alliance with both the radicals and the cabinet, but in the event his most serious action was to immobilise the Montagnards and *Gardiens de Paris* on 16 April.

The actual plan for the control of the radical rally was prepared by the new Commandant of the National Guard, General Amable G. H. Courtais, and his staff. To assure absolute discipline, and despite Marrast's efforts to recruit lower class National Guardsmen, Courtais based his plan upon three units which, because of the class structure of their communities, retained a high proportion of trained and equipped guardsmen from the July Monarchy. As part of Marrast's reviews for the new officers, Courtais ordered the First and Second Banlieue (Surburban) Legions to assemble at the Hôtel-de-Ville on 16 April. From there, these legions were to advance westward and block the advance of any demonstration moving from the Champ de Mars towards the Hôtel-de-Ville. The Tenth Legion from southwest Paris would then cut off the tail of the radical procession.[22] In the event, the demonstration was fragmented by the hurried arrival of Mobile columns from side streets, but Courtais' plan indicated a more sophisticated solution to the problem of controlling large, nonviolent crowds.

Alphonse de Lamartine later wrote a dramatic description of General Nicholas Changarnier and Armand Marrast preparing to defend the Hôtel-de-Ville while Lamartine himself persuaded a hesitating Ledru-Rollin to call out the National Guard.[23] Certainly 16 April posed a great threat to the life of the Provisional Government, and the moderate leaders were quite relieved when elements of the Mobile and National Guards arrived before the radical procession could reach the Hôtel-de-Ville. Furthermore, some National Guard staff officers who were members of the quasi-socialist *Société Démocratique Centrale* delayed the issuance of vital orders. Even without Ledru-Rollin and the Guard staff, however, loyal officers and agents of Marrast were assembling a large portion of the militia. Armand Barbès. newly elected colonel of the Twelfth Legion, opposed a change in government from either political extreme. He therefore accepted the responsibility of leading his potentially radical guardsmen to the Hôtel-de-Ville without orders. Respect for the Provisional Government and distaste for further political disorder apparently motivated the thousands of militiamen who blocked the clubs.

The triumph of 16 April gave the moderates a momentary advantage, but by no means ended the danger of a violent change in government. For days afterwards, large portions of the National and Mobile Guards had to act to control strikes and minor disturbances. At the end of the month, a serious insurrection arose in Rouen when the Assembly elections produced a conservative majority. Blanqui joined with the newspaper *La Réforme* in condemning the suppression of Rouen as class warfare.[24]

Under these circumstances, the moderates in the Provisional Government used their temporary power to make their armed forces more reliable. Colonel Rey purged the Republican Guard of Blanquist radicals. A parade to present republican flags to the colour guards of various regiments indicated that the National Guard favoured and many citizens would tolerate the presence of the regular army in the capital. On 21 April, the Provisional cabinet voted with 'Albert' Martin dissenting to create a garrison of five regiments in Paris.

Nevertheless, the Mobile and National Guards remained the major instruments of government power and civil order in the capital. Most of the army was required elsewhere to control the provinces, defend Algeria and deter Austria from war. The militia's performance on 16 April gave every reason for confidence in the outcome of future confrontations. To indicate its respect and gratitude, the Provisional Government approved a request by National Guard colonels that the militia alone should protect the new Assembly.

With the apparent support of the National Guard but with opposition from a considerable number of Parisians, the National Assembly and the Commission of Executive Power took office in early May. The more conservative members of the Commission may have questioned Colonel Charras' politics, but all accepted the existing structure of military command.

Contrary to statements made after the debacle, the Executive Commision was fully aware of the dangers inherent in the planned 15 May demonstration for Polish liberty, but sought to avoid a clash by allowing the parade to proceed peacefully. A meeting between military and civilian leaders on 14 May established troop dispositions in case the demonstration became violent. General Joseph Foucher, the First Military Division Commandant, divided the small regular army forces between guard pickets and an emergency column at the Ecole Militaire. The new head of the Mobile Guard (Duvivier having been elected to the Assembly), General Jacques Tempoure, persuaded Arago, Lamartine and other leaders to approve his own plans. With the exception of four battalions near the Assembly palace, the Mobile Guard would be confined to barracks so as not to alarm people by an excessive concentration of troops. If the National Guard assembled in force, most of the Mobile battalions would report to the Place de la Concorde and form strong columns to proceed as necessary. General Courtais was designated joint commander for the day. Courtais intended to distribute one thousand men from each National Guard legion to protect key points.[25]

Unfortunately for the Executive Commission, General Courtais neglected to commit his plans to paper, so that many of the National Guard detachments remained in their own neighbourhoods. Furthermore, many guardsmen preferred to join or at least observe the demonstration, rather than spend another day on guard duty. Shirking duty in this fashion did not necessarily indicate a desire to overthrow the government, but it did mean that the Guard detachments upon which Courtais depended were both slow to organise and badly understrength on the morning of 15 May.

As a result, the First Legion guardsmen assigned to protect the vital bridge closest to the Assembly palace did not arrive in time, and their places were taken by a small group from the Fourth Legion. The Assembly's president, Philippe Buchez, sent the Eighth Mobile Battalion to reinforce the National Guard, but even this was inadequate in the face of the huge crowds. General Courtais was so intent upon avoiding violence that he decided to allow 'delegates' from the crowd to present their petition to the Assembly. Against the express orders of President Buchez, Courtais ordered the Mobile Guard battalions to unfix bayonets. Both Courtais and Tempoure, who had come to investigate, were temporarily immobilised in the mob which then invaded the building and declared the Assembly dissolved. At about the same time (1 p.m.), the unofficial deputy commander of the Mobile, Lieutenant Colonel J. V. Thomas, gave the alarm. Thomas and eventually Tempoure assembled a mixture of Mobile and National Guard units which cleared the remaining invaders from the Assembly.[26]

Most of the crowd had by that time moved to the Hôtel-de-Ville to proclaim a more radical government. More through incompetence than any conscious treachery, Colonel Rey of the Republican Guard allowed the radical leaders to enter the building. Elements of the National

Guard artillery arrested the insurgents about 4 p.m. as General Foucher arrived with a mass of militia and with the few army battalions he had available.

This fiasco not only damaged the reputation of the Executive Commission but left the military control of Paris an open question. Early on 16 May, a large force of Mobile and National Guardsmen, backed by regular army artillery, forcibly dissolved the Montagnards and Lyonnais. Without waiting for authorisation from the Executive Commission, Colonel Charras ordered nineteen infantry battalions to the Paris area by railway and forced marching (15-16 May).

The responsibility for the 15 May failure clearly lay with the confused and hesitant military leadership. The Executive Commission arrested General Courtais while his chief of staff had to resign under suspicion of negligence. Colonel Rey and two other officers of the Republican Guard were sacked, while General Bedeau replaced the blameless Tempoure as commander of the Mobile Guard. Charras' friend General Cavaignac finally arrived from Algeria and assumed the War Ministry (17 May), forcing further resignations when he insisted upon unity of command in the capital.

Paris was far from quiet during the month after 15 May. Crowds of people, advocating all manner of causes but especially Bonapartism and socialism, endangered property and public order almost every night in June. The forces used to control these mobs grew from the local National Guard legions to large portions of the Mobile and army garrisons. Troops arrested more than one thousand citizens during the nocturnal disturbances. As a result, the Executive Commission easily won legislative approval (5-7 June) for a Law on *Attroupements* which virtually outlawed public assemblies, leaving the armed forces free to disperse crowds with a minimum of legal formalities.

Police Prefect Trouvé-Chauvel and the Executive Commission were extremely concerned by these nocturnal disorders, but they expected the major clash to occur at a 14 July popular celebration in Vincennes. The local commander of Vincennes prepared to defend his fortress where radical leaders were imprisoned.

Colonel Charras, who remained as Under-Secretary of War, worked to create a politically reliable garrison in the capital. During the Assembly investigation after the June Days, Charras echoed the common belief that the War Ministry had avoided using units which had been affected by the February Revolution, for fear that such units would prove unreliable in future insurrections. In point of fact, at least ten 'February' units were present in the Paris-Versailles area when the June insurrection began. It seems much more plausible that Charras suspected the units which had mutinied in March and Aparil, rather than those disarmed in February. After many troop movements, only one battalion (First of the Twenty-First Line Infantry) out of all the mutinous regiments was present in the Paris-Versailles garrison, and only three other units of formerly undisciplined troops were called in even at the height of the crisis.[27] Despite practical difficulties such as a shortage of barracks, Charras eventually assembled a force of 29,000 trustworthy soldiers in greater Paris.

As for the Mobile Guard, public opinion greatly exaggerated the possibility of a mass defection during May and June. On 15 May, every Mobile battalion continued to obey its officers and enthusiastically defend the government even when the regime was apparently collapsing. The Executive Commission was quite aware of the great moral authority which the National Assembly and the army cadres exercised over the volunteers. The Interior Minister was so convinced of Mobile reliability that in early June he proposed to double its ranks as a useful means of absorbing unemployed labourers.[28]

A new Republican Guard, recruited after careful screening from the dissolved irregular units, was only just organising itself when the June insurrection began. As remarked above, these troops proved both effective and loyal.

The National Guard of the Seine, however, was another problem entirely. Once the more conservative elements of the Assembly and of the Executive Commission determined to eliminate the National Workshops, those legions (especially in eastern Paris) with artisan and labourer majorities could hardly be trusted to support the government in a crisis over this issue. The Executive Commission could reasonably rely upon the more bourgeois units, especially in the Second, Tenth and Artillery Legions (the latter recruited throughout Paris at about the time the elite companies were dissolved, and notably loyal in its politics on 15 May). Nevertheless, General Cavaignac did not expect the Guard to do more than protect its own houses. Even if the militia proved loyal, its new commander, Clement Thomas, was extremely unpopular with his men and lacked the formal training for his duties. Cavaignac concluded that in the event of a major insurrection he could count only on the Mobile and regular garrisons.

On 9 June the army and the Mobile Guard relieved the National Guard of all picket duties. The militia was continually in action against nocturnal disorders, but ceased to figure in War Ministry planning.

Cavaignac's plan for the impending clash was only an elaboration of Tempoure's 15 May dispositions: of the thirty-six regular and twenty-four Mobile infantry battalions, fifteen were to guard the fortifications of Paris, the Luxembourg Palace (seat of the Executive Commission) and similar important points. Thirty-three battalions would concentrate at the Place de la Concorde under the command of General Lamoricière, and the remaining twelve would assemble at the Hôtel-de-Ville under Bedeau. Once these concentrations were complete, the local commanders would despatch strong columns to reduce rebel resistance.[29] Although the Executive Commission grudgingly approved it, this strategy was later widely criticised for two serious weaknesses. Firstly, a great deal of time would pass while the troops were concentrating, allowing the insurgents to raise more support and more barricades. The rebellion would therefore be much more difficult to suppress. Secondly, a corollary effect of Cavaignac's plan was to deprive the National Guard of any moral or physical support from the army. Scattered in small groups or isolated in their houses, loyal militiamen would be unable to resist any rebels in their neighbourhoods. This, however, was the natural consequence of the decision which Cavaignac and the Executive Commission had taken to rely solely upon the army and the Mobile.

Demonstrations against the dissolution of the National Workshops escalated rapidly on 22 and 23 June. At first the Executive Commission regarded the insurrection as another street mob, and ordered Cavaignac to send troops to protect the government buildings. As a result, certain units were in incorrect positions when they received orders to implement Cavaignac's plan, and the concentration of forces was disjointed. There is no proof, however, that Cavaignac delayed this concentration so as to discredit the Executive Commission and gain political power for himself. On the contrary, the order to assemble the garrison arrived at the First Division Headquarters at 9.30 a.m. on 23 June, and the troops marched as rapidly as various barricades and ambushes would allow.[30]

An essay of this length cannot attempt to recount the events of the June Days. Two observations are, however, important to an analysis of civil-military relations. First, regardless of Cavaignac's intentions, the battle was *not* fought in a purely military manner with the object of smashing the rebels. Until the final stages of the contest, troop commanders frequently appealed (with some success) for the insurgents to rally to the government. Local officials often intervened to discourage violence and mistreatment of prisoners. It is true, however, that as the battle wore on, atrocities such as the murder of General Bréa under a flag of truce became increasingly common on both sides, provoking extreme reactions. Furthermore, the young and inexperienced Mobile Guardsmen were deeply affected by the carnage, their initial bravado giving way to mindless savagery. The important point to note is that during the June Days, as in all previous clashes of 1848, government politicians and soldiers used appeals to reason and formalities of law before resorting to force against their fellow citizens. The battle produced hatred and bloodshed, but should not be regarded as an instance of premeditated class warfare, except insofar as the Assembly's actions provoked the crisis.

Secondly, the command and therefore the tactics of the government forces were by no means as uniform nor as centrally directed as later analysts believed. With poor communications and a constant attrition amongst general officers, the battle often dissolved into hundreds of local actions. Although the army operated in larger units in June than in February, each street was cleared by a few hundred men, and each battalion commander had a different manner of attacking barricades. Civilian leaders as well as Cavaignac and Charras were forced to intervene personally in order to inspire and direct troops against specific obstacles. Such personal leadership, in keeping with the traditions of the French Army in Algeria, was more effective in terms of troop morale and practical accomplishments than was the passive central direction of February. The June insurrection was not, however, an example of centralised military command functioning smoothly and without political interference. Rather, each phase of the battle involved close interaction and occasional friction between politicians and generals.[31]

The military failure in February 1848 made the Second Republic possible and set the stage for the unstable political situation which prevailed in Paris for four months. The military success in June did not point to Louis-Napoleon's victory in December, but did determine future events in a variety of other ways. The radical republicans were clearly defeated, while both the Executive Commission and the Parisian National Guard became discredited as political forces. The loyalty of the Mobile Guard and of the regular army not only placed Cavaignac in power but went far to determine the conservative direction of the republic.

Between the two clashes of February and June, each crisis of Parisian politics brought with it a confrontation of paramilitary and militia forces with each other and with the politically active citizens of Paris. The moderate faction of the Provisional Government, together with the War Ministry leaders and the local troop commanders, were therefore concerned with the need for reliable armed forces to defend the regime at home. It would be an exaggeration to portray this concern as the over-riding preoccupation of political leaders, since fiscal, social and diplomatic policy posed problems of equal importance to the struggling regime. Nevertheless, the quality of military leadership and planning, the political effects of military repression in civilian disorders, and the attitudes of the various armed forces, were crucial to the political crises and hence to the life and direction of the political regime.

Notes

1.　Douglas Porch, *Army and Revolution: France 1815-1848* (London and Boston, Routledge & Kegan Paul, 1974), p. 139. Pierre Chalmin, 'La Crise Morale de l'Armée Française', *L'Armée et la Seconde République*, vol. XVIII of *Bibliothèque de la Révolution de 1848* (La Roche-sur-Yon, Imprimerie Centrale de l'Ouest, 1955), pp. 42-4.

2,　Quoted in Alfred Cuvillier-Flaury, *Portraits Politiques et Révolutionnaires*, 2nd ed. (Paris, Michel Lévy Frères, 1852), vol. 1, p. 23.

2.　Louis Girard, *La Garde Nationale, 1814-1871* (Paris, Plon, 1964), pp. 272-3, 311 and *passim*; Comte de Rambuteau, *Memoires of the Comte de Rambuteau*, translated by J. C. Brogan (New York, G. P. Putnam's Sons; London, J. M. Dent and Co., 1908), pp. 209, 240-1.

4.　Albert Crémieux, *La Révolution de Février* (Paris, Bibliothèque d'Histoire Moderne, 1912), pp. 144-5. Crémieux provides the best tactical account of the February Days.

5.　de Rambuteau, *op. cit.*, pp. 233-5; Louis Antoine Garnier-Pagès, *Histoire de la Révolution de 1848* (Paris, Libraire Pagnerre, 1861-72), vol. 4, p. 298.

6.　Based upon fifteen cases drawn from the General Officer files, second series, Archives Historiques de la Guerre (AHG).

7.　AHG, MR 2001. The plan is reproduced in Garnier-Pagès, *op. cit.*, vol. 5, pp. 402-8.

8.　Troop strengths based upon AHG, Situation Générale de l'Armée au 1er Janvier, 1848 (Ms.). On 21 February meeting, see Archives Nationales (AN), BB[30] 297: deposition (no. 510) of General Antoine Prévost. See also Gabriel Vauthier (ed.), 'Rapport sur les Journées de Février adressé à Villemain par le général Sébastiani', *La Révolution de 1848*, vol. 8, no. 46 (1911), p. 322.

9.　The best analyses of the Capucine massacre are in Crémieux, *op. cit.*, pp. 191-6, and Crémieux, 'La Fusillade du Boulevarde des Capucines le 23 Février 1848', *La Révolution de 1848*, vol. 8, no. 44 (1911), pp. 99-124.

10.　Cf. Bugeaud to General Pélissier, 3 April 1848, quoted in Paul Azan, '1848: le Marechal Bugeaud', *Revue Historique de l'Armée*, vol. 4, no. 1 (1948), p. 20. General Bedeau and Lamoricière gave similar advice: see Archives de la Sarthe, Fords Cavaignac, 1 Mi 2/R 28, Lamoricière to Cavaignac, 28 February 1848.

11.　Witold Zaniewicki, *L'Armée Française en 1848*' Thèse de Troisième Cycle (Paris, 1966), vol. 1, p. 48 and following. This is the best analysis of troop disorders and of the regular army in 1848.

12.　Frederick A. de Luna, *The French Republic Under Cavaignac, 1848* (Princeton, New Jersey, Princeton University Press, 1969), pp. 119-21. As a personal and political biography of Cavaignac, de Luna's work is excellent. The book is inadequate in its treatments of civil-military relations and of the June Days, however.

13.　On Charras, see his papers (AHG, F[1] 79) and personnel file (Celebrities file 26bis). Contemporary accounts of Charras: Jules Ambert, *Portraits Républicains* (Paris, Librairie Internationale, 1870); Charles-Louis Chassin, 'Charras: Notes Biographiques et Souvenirs personnels', *Revue Alsacienne*, 5th Year (1882) pp. 337-50, 385-402. More recently the scholarly study of Adrian Jenny, *Jean-Baptiste Adolphe Charras und die politische Emigration nach dem Staatsreich Louis-Napoleon Bonapartes* (Basil and Stuttgart, Verlag von Hellsing und Lichtenhahn, 1969).

14.　Alphonse Balleydier, *Histoire de la Garde Républicaine* (Paris, Pillet Fils ainé, 1848), pp. 12-14; Charles de Lavarenne, *Le Gouvernement Provisoire et l'Hôtel-de-Ville Dévoilés*, 2nd ed. (Paris, Garnier Frères, 1850), pp. 86-8.

15.   cf. the reports of the reorganisation commission, AN, C 932^A, no. 1811 and no. 2282.
16.   Alfred Rey and Louis Féron, *Histoire du Corps des Gardiens de la Paix* (Paris, Librairie Firmin-Didot, 1896), pp. 150-1. For public debate on this controversy, see AN, C 934. Police report for 14 April 1848 (no. 2739).
17.   On social composition of the Mobile Guard, see the indications in AN, F^9 1090. On motivation and conduct, see Pierre Chalmin, 'Une Institution Militaire de la Seconde République: la garde national mobile', *Etudes d'Histoire Moderne et Contemporaine*, vol. 2 (1948), pp. 37-82.
18.   On the arming of the Mobile, see AHG, X^D 385, 1st Military Division Commandant to Director of Artillery, 16 March 1848; X^M 49, Mobile Guard Commandant to mayors of arrondissements, 16 March 1848 (no. 37). On its deployment, see: X^M 49, Mobile Guard Commandant to commander of Second Mobile Guard Battalion, 18 March 1848 (no. 40).
19.   Elias Regnault, *Histoire du Gouvernement Provisoire*, 2nd ed. (Paris, Victor Lecou, 1850), p. 255 and *passim*; B. Sarrans, *Histoire de la révolution de Février, 1848* (Paris, Administration de Librairie, 1851), vol. 2, p. 398. See also the Marrast circular quoted in National Guard Order of the Day for 4 April 1848. AN, F^9* 1252.
20.   AN, 67 AP 9: Procès-Verbaux des Déliberations du Gouvernement Provisoire, pp. 133, 138, 145.
21.   AN: C 934, Police report for 14 April 1848, no. 2739.
22.   Louis Girard, *la IIe République* (Paris, Calmann-Lévy, 1968), p. 110; Garnier-Pagès, *op. cit.*, vol. 7, p. 383.
23.   Assemblée Nationale (Quentin-Bauchart, rapporteur): Commission d'Enquête sur l'insurrection de 23 Juin, *Rapport* (Paris, Imprimerie Nationale, no date), vol. 1, p. 17.
24.   André Dubuc, 'Les Emeutes de Rouen et d'Elbeuf', *Etudes d'Histoire Moderne et Contemporaine*, vol. 2 (1948), pp. 263-75; *La Réforme*, 1 May 1848, p. 1. See also Jacques Toutain, *La Revolution de 1848 à Rouen* (Paris, Editions René Debresse, 1949), pp. 75-85.
25.   Commission d'Enquête, *op. cit.*, vol. 1, p. 199. Tempoure's plan is reproduced in AN, C 932^A, no. 1415.
26.   Haut Cour de Justice Séant à Bourges, *Affaire de l'Attentat du 15 Mai 1848* (Paris, Imprimerie Nationale, 1849), vol. 2, depositions of General Jacques Tempoure, pp. 446-8, and of Captain François Barjaud, pp. 452-4. For an excellent analysis of 15 May, see Peter Amann, 'A Journée in the Making/ May 15, 1848', *Journal of Modern History*, vol. 42, no. 1 (1970), pp. 42-69.
27.   Units determined by comparison between Crémieux, *op. cit.*, pp. 505-14; Zaniewicki, *op. cit.*, vol. 2, pp. 32-3; and Commission d'Enquête, *op. cit.*, vol. 2, pp. 46-56.
28.   AN, F^9 1072, Under-Secretary of Interior to General Bedeau, 10 June 1848. F^9 1072, Mobile Guard Commandant (Damesme) to Interior Minister, 15 June 1848 (no. 1602).
29.   General Doumenc, 'L'Armée et les Journées de Juin', *Actes du Congrès Historique du Centenaire de la Révolution de 1848* (Paris, Presses Universitaires de France, 1949) is a good if oversimplified summary of Cavaignac's plan.
30.   Archives de la Sarthe, Fonds Cavaignac, 1 Mi 2/R22: First Military Division Report for 23 June 1848. Zaniewicki, *op. cit.*, vol. 1, pp. 74-6 and vol. 2, Graphs XVII-XXII, has made an extensive study of the speed and difficulties of troop concentration on 23 June.

31.   The full history of the June Days from the government's side has yet to be written. In addition to the Commission d'Enquête, Zaniewicki, and de Luna (Chapter 6), all cited above, two important sources are: Speeches of Barthelemy Saint Hilaire and Eugène Cavaignac to the National Assembly, reprinted in *Le Moniteur Universel*, 26 November 1848, pp. 3352, 3354-8. Mobile Guard after-action reports in AHG, F¹ 15.

THE PEOPLE OF JUNE, 1848

Charles Tilly
and
Lynn H. Lees

Citizens!

On the February barricades, the men we had installed as members of the provisional government promised us a democratic and social republic. They made us pledges, and, trusting their words, we abandoned our barricades. In four months, what have they done? They have violated their oaths, for they have not kept their promises. We, the citizens at the post of the Eighth *mairie* demand:

a democratic and social republic;
the free association of labour aided by the state;
indictment of the representatives and ministers;
immediate arrest of the Executive Commission;
We demand the immediate removal of the army from Paris.

Citizens, believe that you are sovereign.
Remember our motto: Liberty, Equality, Fraternity.[1]

As this poster, and others like it, went up on the walls of Paris in June of 1848, the authors supported their commitment to the 'democratic and social republic' from behind their barricades. They fought in the name of justice for the fulfilment of promises which had, they believed, been made to them during the February revolution. But other citizens viewed the claims of the street fighters rather differently. Many saw in the bloody struggle of June 1848, not an attempt to redeem the Second Republic, but a demonic assault upon it. The Prefect of Police, for example, was convinced that the men behind the barricades planned 'the overthrow of our entire society' by means of arson, massacre and pillage. Alexis de Tocqueville and many of his existing republican colleagues saw in the conflict a threat to the existing social structure and division of property, a threat which they implacably opposed: '. . . . the insurrection was of such a nature that any understanding with it became impossible immediately, and from the first it left us no alternative but to defeat it or to be destroyed ourselves.' Tocqueville

170

seemed thereby to echo Marx's judgement that the insurrection was the moment when 'the first great battle was joined between the two classes that split modern society'. In fact, observers holding a variety of political positions saw in the street battles of June an elemental form of social conflict, pitting the 'haves' against the 'have nots'; by the depth of that division they explained (and sometimes justified) the carnage of the brief civil war and the repression which followed it.[2]

Since then, the June Days have continued to occupy a special place among the many Parisian insurrections of the nineteenth century. That is partly because of their violence, and partly because of their symbolic significance for historians of the Left. Some historians have found in the insurgents' hunger, or their desire for work, both the motive and the justification of the movement. Others have traced the claims of the street fighters to socialist theories, or to greed aroused by demagogues.[3] The work of Peter Amann and of Rémi Gossez on political clubs, newspapers, and workers' organisations has added much necessary detail to our picture of Paris during the Second Republic.[4] Yet many questions about the June Days remain unanswered. Moreover, the people on the barricades — their identities, their motives, and the world in which they lived — have been lost in the ideological quarrels of academia. Why did a large body of Parisians try in June to overthrow a republic that many of them had helped to establish only four months before? Massive unemployment combined with the closing of the National Workshops led to active discontent, as most historians have asserted; but can these economic pressures account for the rebellion? Is it legitimate, moreover, to argue that the June Days were a rising of the workers against their masters? To what extent did the events of June continue that pattern of urban insurrection which appeared in 1789 and endured into the nineteenth century, a pattern which George Rudé and Albert Soboul have analysed so admirably?[5] An examination of the people involved in the June Days will deepen our understanding of the processes producing conflict in France during the middle years of the nineteenth century.

To be more precise, the close study of the June Days' participants is likely to help answer three sets of general questions:

1) To what degree, how directly, and how did this rebellious movement (and do rebellions in general) result from economic crisis?
2) Did the June Days represent a typical or crucial phase of a standard revolutionary process?
3) To what degree did the participants in this rebellion (and in rebellions in general) consist of people at the margins of orderly social life?

171

All three questions are controversial, although recent work on European rebellions has set important limits to the controversy.

General Conditions for Revolution

The idea of a standard revolutionary situation in which an economic catastrophe raises the desperate and rootless poor against their betters, for example, has probably disappeared forever. In our view, economic crises are only likely to stimulate rebellion under very special circumstances: when they place the powerful in the position of withholding or extracting resources from organised groups of persons who have established claims on these resources. Shortage without an apparent culprit does not incite rebellion. Crisis does not bring collective action from the unorganised masses; on the contrary, it depresses their capacity to act. But in some circumstances organisation and opposition come together. The traditional food riot illustrates on the small scale the sort of process we have in mind: it did not tend to occur where people were hungriest, but where merchants, officials and wealthy individuals were (or appeared to be) diverting supplies on which the local community had a prior claim.[6]

The food riot, however, remains one of the most localised forms of political conflict, precisely because of its tie to the rights of particular communities over their supplies of food. Even in 1789, about the strongest case that can be made for *direct* effect of the subsistence crisis is that it preoccupied the Parisian crowd and that it facilitated the overturning of a great many municipalities which failed to meet their local responsibilities. To push the analogy of 1848 with 1789 in this regard, as C. E. Labrousse has done, one would have to establish that some such connection also appeared in 1848.[7]

We doubt it. If the subsistence crisis of 1846-7 had something to do with the revolution of 1848, it was most likely not through any direct effect on Parisian hunger, and certainly not through the fall of provincial municipalities. Instead, the strongest possibility is some delayed effect on the demand for the products of Parisian industry. That remains to be proven.

If we put aside the idea of a direct link between the agricultural crisis of 1846-7 and the revolution of 1848, however, Labrousse's more general contention still holds up for 1848: 1789, 1830 and 1848 saw the convergence of political and economic crises. The two crises continued to play a fundamental part in shaping working class political action up to the June Days. The appropriate metaphor for the way they came together is not the two sharp blows that break a rock. It is the funnel and the stream of milk — the one channeling the other. The revolutionary regime helped *create* the organisation of the unemployed,

172

notably by forming the National Workshops to absorb the unemployed, but also by temporarily promoting the organisation of the associations which became the *foci* of political action among the poorer workers. (We must clearly distinguish between the manifestly political clubs of 1848, with their relatively middle class constituencies, and the workers' mutual aid societies and similar organisations, which eventually became important vehicles of political action.[8] It is the latter which added the extraordinary element to the organisational scene before the June Days.)

As for the process of revolution, we do not see any standard sequence of events or stages which must somehow play itself out in each transfer of power, except those which are inherent in the definition of revolution itself: the breaking of an existing political system into at least two parts, a struggle (long or short) between the parts, re-establishment of a single system. Reflection on revolution as a struggle among contenders for control over an existing governmental apparatus, however, leads us to several interesting hypotheses about the revolutionary process: 1) the level of conflict is likely to be much higher after the first major actions of the revolution than before, because the emergence of 'dual sovereignty' (in Trotsky's phrase) challenges the position of every contender, and thus generalises the struggle; 2) the contest between the fragments is likely to activate an exceptional proportion of the population on one side or another, as compared with involvement in politics outside the revolution; 3) the successful revolutionary coalition is likely to generate important resistance as it attempts to reassert routine central control over the whole population after seizing the governmental apparatus: this is likely to show up as a shift in the locus of conflict from the centre to the periphery as the revolution proceeds; 4) the initial revolutionary coalition is likely to dwindle, because the initial seizure of control requires a larger coalition than does the maintenance of control, because the divergence of the longer run objectives of the various contenders is likely to become more obvious and pressing once the work of dislodging the enemy from power is finished and because those contenders who mobilised rapidly in response to short run crises but remained relatively underorganised are also likely to demobilise more rapidly than other contenders, and therefore to lose ground in the next round of political manoeuvring.[9]

Some readers will find these hypotheses pretty obvious. Yet they also contradict some widely held notions: revolution as the quick release of tension built up over a long time, revolution as the work of a single class or an entire nation in opposition to an old elite, revolution as the consequence of weakening elite control over the masses.

Obvious or not, these generalisations hold rather well for the French revolution of 1848. There we witness a tremendous widening of political organisation, involvement, action and conflict *after* the revolutionary seizure of power; the conflicts divide into two different categories: 1) struggles among groups within the revolutionary coalition, especially pitting portions of the bourgeoisie against organised segments of the working class in Paris and other major cities; 2) provincial resistance (most notably in the opposition to the 45 centime surtax) to new demands from the centre.

Although the process of revolution draws people into political consciousness, the process is not irreversible. From 1849 through 1851, we witness the gradual, deliberate demobilisation of most groups within the initial revolutionary coalition; the repression of the great insurrection of 1851 completed that demobilisation. And in the June Days themselves we see the most acute phase of the separation of the organised Parisian working class from the revolutionary coalition. After the establishment of the National Workshops had sealed the membership of the organised working class in the coalition, the dissolution of the Workshops then broke that seal. The conflict at this point was particularly fierce because the workers had not yet lost their coherence. Instead, the workers of Paris actually continued to mobilise within their own associations, within the Workshops and within the National Guard during the months following the fall of the July Monarchy.

This analysis has some clear implications for the personnel of the February and June Days, not to mention the several important *journées* in between. In no case should we expect Louis Chevalier's 'dangerous classes' to have played an important part. Nevertheless, if both the widespread mobilisation and the fragmentation of the revolutionary coalition we have described were actually occurring, there should have been some important differences between the participants in February and June. First, the participants in the initial seizure of power should have resembled the organised activists of earlier rebellions: a sprinkling of intellectuals, journalists, lawyers and other professionals, a contingent of shopkeepers, a large number of craftsmen from the older organised trades. In June we should discover a more exclusively working class population, a broader participation among workers in the newer industries, a decline in the role of the shopkeeper. Second, we should find the activists of February standing on a base (an underground base, to be sure) of liberal and republican organisations, while in June we should see the strong influence of the workers' societies, the National Guard and the Workshops — not the clubs. It will take more close study of the participants in February 1848 and of the day to day political participation of the workers thereafter to confirm or deny these hypotheses definitely. We will offer some evidence that they are correct.

Paris in 1848

Let us first look more closely at the city in which the process played itself out. Louis Chevalier's picture of Paris at the time is grim. He describes a milieu of poverty, overcrowding and rapid migration, within which workers had to function as best they could. Death rates were high. About a third of all births were illegitimate. Crime, prostitution and disease flourished.[10] Nevertheless, these conditions were rife in many European industrial cities; some of those cities were politically active, and others quiescent. Moreover, the rapid migration which intensified these problems was not a purely negative phenomenon. The movement of people into the capital — a net flow of 230,000 between 1831 and 1846 — was a sign of vitality and expansion. The attraction of higher wages and varied employments remained strong, despite the appalling hardship for many urban workers. The needs of a large, wealthy market of consumers created jobs for people of all skills and talents.

A substantial group of the Parisian labour force was unskilled: the *journaliers*, the *terrassiers*, and the many varieties of casual labourers who found intermittent jobs in several sectors of the economy. This group was badly paid and poorly organised. Its members were not typical, however; the vast majority of Parisian workers were artisans employed either in small workshops or in their own homes.

We divide the artisans into three categories: 1) an elite of well paid, highly skilled workers — *mécaniciens*, fine metal workers, printers, and some of the craftsmen making *articles de Paris*; 2) workers in the sweated trades — predominantly furniture, clothing and sections of other industries where work was put out. Here wages were low and the scale of production extremely small. Moreover these trades were generally not as well organised as other Parisian crafts; 3) the remaining trades, which varied widely in the level of skill required and in working conditions.

One additional group, factory workers and others employed in very large firms in the transport and service sectors, must be identified. In 1847, about 30,000 workers in the Seine had jobs in firms using mechanical power or employing over twenty persons. These 'factories' — many of which are more accurately described as large workshops — were located primarily in the building, metal working, textile, chemical and leather working trades and in the transport industry.[11] (It must be remembered, however, that each of these sectors included firms whose scale of organisation was small.) The existence of these large firms, in conjunction with the rise of railway companies in the Paris region, indicates that in several industries forms of organisation were changing: the scale of production was becoming larger. Although we do not assert that a factory proletariat made the June Days revolt, we will offer evidence linking participation to the scale of industrial organisation.

It is first necessary to trace the impact upon Parisian industry of prosperity and depression during the 1840s. As the national economy expanded, the skill of the labour force and the availability of financing provided a solid base in Paris for many luxury crafts, the building trades, and the metal working industries. At the same time, economic changes triggered by industrialisation were forcing the local labour force to adapt to new conditions that signalled the relative economic decline of the central city. More specifically, trades which were expanding their production for a mass market found it more profitable to leave Paris for the suburbs or the provinces, where wages and rents were lower; the exodus of textile and chemical firms was particularly marked. Although operations that required highly skilled labour could still flourish in the high wage Parisian economy, more and more workshops decentralised their production, allowing the routine stages of work to be done outside the city and leaving only the difficult tasks to Parisian artisans.[12]

In effect, then, industries were thriving at the expense of their workers. Even the skilled elite was hit hard by the realities of Parisian economic life. Many were employed in crafts closely tied to the fluctuating demands of the Paris market. Not only were they affected by the periods of *morte-saison* that stopped work in a large variety of industries between three and four months annually, but some of these workers found that migration from the provinces and from abroad brought in competitors willing to work for lower wages. By 1847, for instance, foreign workers made up 40 per cent of the labour force in tailoring; links were close between a) dilution of the trade by outsiders, women or children and b) sweated labour for declining piecework rates. Sections of the clothing and furniture trades were particularly affected. The structure of Parisian industry in 1848, then, was a mixture of skilled and unskilled trades and home, workshop and factory production.[13]

Against this background came the events of depression and revolution. The agricultural crisis of 1846 and 1847 brought in its wake sharp (but not uniform) declines in business activity. The depression gathered momentum in Paris after the events of February, which had a cataclysmic effect on the economy. The wheels of commerce slowed: during the spring they seemed about to stop. Comparing the year 1848 with 1847, the Paris Chamber of Commerce reported an average decline in industrial employment. Moreover, the highest rates of unemployment and contraction (all over 58 per cent) were recorded for the furniture, building, and metal industries — sectors which, as we shall see, were over-represented among the insurgents.[14]

There were at least 150,000 unemployed in Paris by the time of the June Days even if we do not take into account the small masters working alone whose businesses had collapsed. The National Workshops offered only a partial refuge for these people. From March to 12 May, when enrolments were stopped, the number of men included rose from 14,000 to about 113,000; over 100,000 continued to receive support until early July. Even if no men from outside Paris were admitted to the workshops — an unrealistic assumption — at least 40,000 unemployed Parisian workers and their families were not reciving the government dole.

Moreover, the workshops scarcely protected those within from the depression: the wage of eight francs weekly was inadequate to support even an unmarried worker, and the state provided the men with no more activity than a day or two of digging per week. Interrogations of the June Days prisoners show that they used the workshops as stopgap support, regularly looking for other work and collecting their pay when there was none to be found. Participation in the brigades was apparently rather casual, an occupation of last resort. While day labourers, who made up some 13 per cent of the workshop members, might adapt to this life, it was both difficult and unrewarding for the rest. The final prospect of being deported to the Sologne or drafted into the army in exchange for token support and employment must have been the final indignity for many artisans who rightly considered themselves to be the elite of French labour.[15] The pressures upon such men, which drew many into the June Days, were far more complex than the economic hardship of a subsistence crisis.

The General Pattern of the French Revolution of 1848

The events that were crucial to the shifts of power in 1848 formed part of a much larger series of struggles. The period from 1848 to 1851 enveloped much of France in political conflict. In the course of a study covering the years from 1830 to 1960, we have attempted to count the number of people in France taking part in violent incidents (that is, events in which someone seized or damaged persons or property over resistance) in which at least one of the groups involved had fifty or more persons. If our estimates of the number of incidents taking place in France as a whole and in the department of the Seine are graphed for the years 1846-52, the increased scale of violence during the period becomes obvious (see Figure 1).

The pattern of conflict in the Seine followed very closely that of the country as a whole. For example, food riots similar to those in the countryside broke out in the winter of 1846-7 in the Faubourg St

Figure 1   Number of Violent Incidents per Quarter, 1846-52

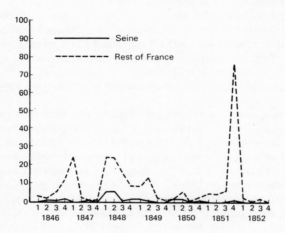

Antoine. But there was no accumulation of violent incidents either in the capital or in the provinces before 1848; the revolution itself signalled the major increase in the scale of collective action. Our graph shows the surging of conflict during the first two quarters of 1848, in both the Seine and the rest of France. We see a broadly parallel movement between the Seine and the rest of France, with the provinces appearing to magnify the fluctuations which occurred in Paris. We also observe the generally downward drift of collective violence from the suppression of the June Days to 1851 – despite some significant interruptions to the trend outside of Paris. Most notably, the graph shows the resurgence of provincial conflicts (especially tax rebellions) in 1849 and the great, violent resistance to the *coup d'état* of December 1851. Then all is silent. By that time, the revolution was over and defeated.

As Peter Amann has suggested, when one ruler – attacked but generally accepted as legitimate – is replaced, his successor has the immediate and difficult task of building a new government which most of the population will again accept.[18] In the case at hand, the revolution was far from over when the revolutionaries dismantled the barricades of February. One could make a case for the persistence, or

178

recurrence, of 'dual sovereignty' over France as a whole into 1849, or perhaps to the *coup d'état* itself.

One major element of the contest in the Parisian region was the great increase in violent activity after the installation of the new regime. Beginning with the revolutionary days, Paris and its hinterland experienced repeated cases of arson, major attacks on the railroads, clashes between groups of workers, others between workers and employers, and numerous political demonstrations, some of which turned into violent struggles with the police or with political rivals. With increasing frequency, casual assemblies grew into political crowds which marched on public buildings shouting slogans: 'Vive Barbès', 'Vive Bonaparte'. Local residents stormed a police station at La Villette; men in the railway crews at Choisy tried to eject German workers; a crowd of hat makers attempting to enforce a common wage and price scale attacked uncooperative workshops. Bonapartists, Legitimists, and Socialist-Republicans were rounded up by the police for demonstrating on Paris streets. This crescendo of activity mounted during early June and reached its penultimate resolution on the barricades.[19]

Behind these public scenes lay a newly mobilised population responding to a changed political climate. For the first time in decades the government permitted men to write, to assemble, and most important of all, to organise with complete freedom. The political life that Orléanists had tried so hard to limit to the *juste milieu* now extended to the entire population. Over 259 deputations of citizens, clubs and unions called on the government in March and April. The press multiplied overnight: 171 newspapers appeared in the capital between the revolution and mid-June; late in May the number of copies printed monthly reached a peak of almost 400,000. In addition, there were political groups for all to join. By late March, the government counted 147 such groups in Paris and its suburbs. While some of these were undoubtedly small and shortlived, others drew several hundred at a minimum to their meetings. These clubs and popular societies played an important role in helping to develop and define members' political commitments.[20]

Even before 1848, there had been a distinct revival of militancy among Paris workers. In 1840, the tailors, joined by sections of the building trades, attempted a general strike and mounted large demonstrations. Printers, masons and carpenters formed associations and pressed claims on wages and hours. Not only did strikes continue after the revolution, but new clubs, committees, and corporate organisations sprang up on all sides in the congenial climate of the republic. The masons and painters each formed a club and a Fraternal Association. other parts of the building trades had their own groups or at least a strike committee. The need to elect delegates for the 'workers' parliament', the Luxembourg Commission, and then to enforce its decisions brought artisans together and stimulated a sense of corporate identity and common purpose. At the same time, the wish for government contracts and plans for the revival of trade and employment usually implied the creation of a central organisation that would hire men and contract for work.[21] To be sure, this mobilisation of the Parisian working class was widely diffused, but it seems to have been most intense in several specific sectors, most of which played an important part in the June Days. Again we find the mechanics, the railroad workers, leather workers, and men from the building and metal trades leading the ranks of both the corporations and the insurgents.

Direct links from the barricades to specific railway crews, construction gangs, and workers in the large engineering firms can be established. M. Cavé, who employed 600 people in 1841 in several engineering workshops, testified before the official enquiry that a number of his men had joined the fighting, led by about ten militants who forced the others to follow. In the affairs of his workshop we begin to see some of the connections between political action and workers' organisations during the Second Republic. Not only had Blanqui visited Cavé's firm in March to speak to the workers, but some of Cavé's men had participated in the demonstration of 15 May. A group of his employees had organised a union under the guise of a *société de secours mutuel*; apparently almost all of the others had joined, although Cavé claimed that many were coerced into belonging. Some of the militant workers had attended unnamed political clubs; moreover, the leaders of the fledgling union were in contact with similar workers' organisations elsewhere. A demand that the working day be shortened appears to have been made, and other issues may also have been in dispute. Clearly, the men in his *ateliers* had begun to organise and had plunged into the radical political activities of 1848.[22] In the same way, militant printers, jewellers, tailors, shoe, hat and cabinetmakers were active both in their own trades before June and in the insurrection. Conversely, workers who belonged to more poorly organised trades that sometimes relied on government privileges and regulation — domestic servants, bakers and other sections of the food industries, and some categories of transport workers — were under-represented in the rising.[23] Perhaps it was the intensity of the depression or perhaps their faith in a republican government, but after February many workers turned to the state for the solution of their economic problems. A mechanic from the Sixth and Eighth *arrondissements*, who identified himself only as 'Alexis', asked the provisional government to back a large issue of new bank notes, to order 100 warships for possible piracy against the English, and to see that all canal and railway construction was completed. His ideal was the 'organisation of labour, building yards, and national workshops everywhere, even in the forests, today or tomorrow if possible'.[24]

These demands for state organised workshops to employ artisans were widespread in Paris as unemployment mounted. Although not often explicitly defined, the phrase *l'organisation du travail* appears again and again in election posters, both for workers' candidates and for others trying to win workers' votes. Most important of all, the corporations' delegates to the Luxembourg Commission, who organised themselves into the *Comité central des ouvriers du département de la Seine* in order to unify electoral and other activities, defined as one of their four aims 'to prepare for the organisation of labour, notably by the detailed study of each trade's techniques'.[25]

Nevertheless, the government and the assembly did nothing to assuage growing alienation from the regime. After the arrest of 130 men for their part in the demonstration of 15 May, police began regularly to round up members of the ever more frequent crowds that loitered in the squares and chanted political slogans. These crowds formed daily, fed by the workshops, which brought thousands of artisans out onto the streets to collect their pay and to grumble about their situations. By 22 June, almost 1,300 people had been arrested in these evening sorties. While some were linked to the parties of Louis Napoleon, Henri V, or Barbès, over 1,000 were identified simply as members of the street corner crowds, which were predominantly working class in composition.[26]

Delegates of the corporations to the Luxembourg Commission refused to hide the growing chasm between the government and the ranks of militant, politically conscious workers. The typographers refused to participate in the government sponsored *Fête de la Concorde* because, they said, too much of the working class was without bread or work and because 'our representatives have received in an almost mocking manner the proposals made to them for the Organisation of Labour'. After the election, the *Comité radical des travailleurs du Nord* condemned the idea of a fraternal Banquet in support of newly elected representatives, for, they pointed out, the proposal had declared the assembly inviolable. This would compromise the principle of popular sovereignty, which they were determined to defend. Their aim as good republicans and that of 'le peuple' should be the foundation of a new social order. Therefore, they 'reserved the right of control and surveillance over the actions of those *républicains du jour* or *du lendemain* who profess to know more of the institutions that fit a republic than those [of us] brought up and nourished at republican springs'. The insurrection was still 'le plus saint des devoirs'.[27]

When faced with this openly expressed hostility, government ministers authorised the calling into Paris of large numbers of troops because the garrison had been reduced to only 5,000 men during the short period of postrevolutionary harmony. By 1 June, the number had risen to 20,000 with increases concentrated in the weeks following the demonstrations of 16 April and 15 May. As a further sign of official premonitions, Cavaignac successively replaced all regiments that had been disarmed in February. Authorities were clearly clamping down on some of the political forces engendered by the February revolution.[28] But the government's attempt to re-establish control over the Parisian population inevitably met resistance from men who were not willing to relinquish influence over the state, which they thought that they had won in February.

Thus Paris became polarised, with organised insurrectionary groups of workers increasingly opposed to the self-proclaimed executors of the revolution. The polarisation reached its extreme in June and ended in the near destruction of the insurrectionary side. The events of the June Days themselves are well known; our brief review will merely recall the terms of the conflict.

The June Days

The trigger for the whole affair was the government's decision to rid itself of the National Workshops by sending those enrolled either into the army or into the provinces, where numerous workshops resembling those of Paris had formed to absorb the unemployed. The government's move, announced on 21 June, produced an immediate, hostile reaction throughout eastern Paris. On 22 June, a morning demonstration of several hundred workers led straight to the Luxembourg palace. There Marie, the Minister of Public Works, made it clear that the government would enforce its edict. The men led by Louis Pujol, lieutenant in the National Workshops and member of Blanqui's club, the *société républicaine sociale*, then rejoined the assembled crowd. They angrily reported the bad news. Soon large bands of hostile men carrying National Workshop banners were marching down the streets. 'Down with Lamartine!' 'Down with Marie!' 'Down with Thiers!: 'We won't go!'

The marchers spread news of an evening meeting at the Pantheon. By 7.00 p.m. the police reported that a 'tumultuous' crowd of 5,000 had assembled. The number grew through evening parades through the Eighth and Twelfth *arrondissements* and around the Hôtel-de-Ville. A group of 8,000 to 10,000 crossed the Faubourg St Antoine: 'Down with traitors!' 'Down with the National Guard!' 'Bread or bullets!' 'Work! Work! Bread! Bread!' Finally all reconverged on the Pantheon. There, in the torchlight, Pujol shouted his defiance of the government, and demanded vengeance. The next morning another meeting was to produce decisive action. Meanwhile the guardians of peace and order did little to forestall the approaching confrontation. Only a few battalions were ordered to guard the Luxembourg and the Hôtel de Ville. The National Guard was not called.[29]

On 23 June, men began to pour into the Pantheon area shortly after 7.00 a.m. Shouts of 'To the barricades!' were heard by the police who, with good reason, feared the 'very bad intentions' of the crowd. By 8.15, they estimated that 3,000 had assembled. Again flags from the National Workshops, as well as a few uniforms of the *garde mobile* and the *garde républicaine* were recognised. The demonstration then spilled out into the other parts of Paris. Over 1,000 men went to the Place de la Bastille, marched around the column, and listened to speeches urging the overthrow of the government. Another band, said to be 1,500 to 2,000 men from the workshops, paraded along the Boulevard St Martin. Soon an immense crowd along the Rue du Faubourg St Denis was building barricades from overturned carriages and carts. A gunshop near the river was raided, and cries of 'To arms! To the barricades!' echoed through the streets. By late morning a rash of barricades in the Cité, in the Eleventh and Twelfth *arrondissements* on the left bank and in the Fifth, Sixth and Eighth north of the river signalled the beginning of the insurrection.[30]

When the National Guard was finally called up during the late morning and early afternoon, the *rappel* produced willing soldiers from the western quarters. Few men responded in the east, where men in National Guard uniforms joined, or even commanded, men behind the barricades. In many areas guards were 'slow to appear' and showed little enthusiasm for shooting at their neighbours. But local responses to the uprising were ambiguous: fear of the insurgents soon began to affect the residents of some barricaded sections. The quarter of the Marais was reported to be 'in panic' and rumours of pillage circulated in the area east and south of the Sorbonne.[31]

Scattered fighting between guardsmen and insurgents broke out shortly after 1.00 p.m. on 23 June. It was followed quickly by more systematic attacks on the barricades by the army and the *garde mobile*. General Cavaignac, the Minister of War, received command of the troops in Paris; he proceeded to direct a three-pronged assault on entrenched positions along the boulevards, near the Pantheon, and around the Hôtel de Ville. Yet little was done to stop the rising elsewhere, Cavaignac and the other generals preferring to mass their own strength and then to force their way through the twisted streets of Paris, using artillery where necessary. Military strategy thus set the seal on what was to become a miniature civil war.[32]

Early on 24 June, the insurrection continued to spread. Barricades were reported in the Seventh *arrondissement*, while the Fourth was invaded by men looking for arms and supplies. Fighting also broke out in the suburbs in the north and east, beyond the *octroi* wall. Meanwhile the National Guard, usually understrength, patrolled in its own quarters and handled local skirmishes, leaving the army and the *garde mobile* to follow generals Damesne, Duvivier and Lamoriciére in attacks upon the major rebel strongholds. Only Damesne reported a success: the clearing of the Pantheon area. By this time, the Assembly, although thoroughly alarmed by the collapse of civilian authority in Paris, ratified the effective transfer of power to the military by proclaiming a state of siege and giving Cavaignac sole authority.

But insurgents had already begun to lose the test of strength. The army and the *garde mobile* demolished their citadels of resistance — slowly at first, then more rapidly. Many parts of Paris were quiet by the morning of 25 June; opposition began to 'melt away', men from the barricades retreating into houses and back streets. By that time, the work of tidying up after the holocaust had already begun: guardsmen patrolled cleared areas and went to search lodging houses in the Hôtel de Ville and St Martin-des-Champs for caches of weapons. Suspected suppliers of arms were arrested before the fighting had even stopped. By nightfall the rebels had been beaten in the Fifth *arrondissement*; a gloomy calm had settled over the Twelfth. Finally, on 26 June, the hopelessness of continuing became apparent. The last centres of resistance, in the Temple and the Faubourg St Antoine, gave up.[34]

In defeat, the insurgents held to their hopes. Rondot, chief of the Fifth Battalion, Fourth (Suburban) Legion reported on his meeting with the 'rebel commander of the Eighth Arrondissement'.[35] According to Rondot:

'He told me the reason for the revolt was that they wanted the *democratic* and *social* republic. I asked for an explanation of "social". He said he meant the right of workers to band together on their own in order to undertake public works and private jobs as well. The overall explanations that the unlucky leader gave me were quite satisfactory. He complained bitterly of the calumnies *Le Constitutionnel* is spreading about their cause. He swore that public and private property had been respected, that the inscription Death to Thieves is written on the façade of every property.'

And Rondot gave the rebels a chance to disperse without bloodshed.

A very large number of people fought in the June Days. Over 25,000 troops were stationed in or near Paris when the rising broke out, and the battalions of the *garde mobile* brought the total force available immediately to about 37,000 men. Then two more regiments, with additional squadrons of artillery and cavalry, came in by rail on 23 and 24 June. The number of National Guardsmen who fought with the regular troops is less clear. The official size of the legions had increased

184

to 237,000 men since the Guard opened its ranks to workers. But the vast majority of its members did not answer the *rappel*, from political conviction, from fear or from a desire to guard their own property. The mayor of the Twelfth *arrondissement* reported, for instance, that only a few hundred initially assembled out of a group normally 15,000 strong. The commissioner of police in the Marais counted only 1,500 of 24,000 in the Eighth Legion. Possibly 6,000 men were available in dispersed groups from the companies of the east, while an estimated 12,000 guardsmen came out initially from the western *arrondissements*.[36]

Most of this force was available for use only in the home territory of its members. Nevertheless, the number of guardsmen who appeared grew steadily as the insurgents were beaten. The deficiencies of the capital's militia, moreover, were made up by men from the provinces, who flocked to Paris after being notified of the rising. Beginning on 24 June, a steady stream of volunteers came into the city. Although most arrived too late to do anything but patrol and then return home, over 120,000 rushed to defend law and order from the Parisian threat. The February republic was therefore able to raise a considerable force in a very short time.[37]

Devotion to the 'democratic and social republic' is much more difficult to measure. Here most of the evidence is conjecture. The informal groups of streetfighters can never be counted with precision; participation rates rose and fell with the time of day and the proximity of the troops. Because the fighting took place in residential areas, men could easily move from their homes to the barricades and back again. The lines separating insurgents, sympathisers and onlookers would have been hard to draw even for an eye witness. Moreover, they probably changed from hour to hour: the casual, intermittent nature of much participation is evident from interrogations of the prisoners. There is simply no way of determining exactly how many people joined in the rising, because participation was informal and could mean so many things. Thousands of National Guardsmen materially aided the rising by not answering the *rappel*; few of them were prosecuted for doing so. How do we tally passive sympathy, or passive resistance? At this point, the historian trying to count his subjects throws away his pen in despair.

Yet we can be somewhat more specific. Both Trouvé-Chauvel, the Prefect of Police, and General Cavaignac estimated the number of insurgents at between 40,000 and 50,000 men. Ignorance in such matters usually produces exaggeration, however, so their tally should be accepted only as a maximum. At least 15,000 people (and possible several thousands more) were picked up during the fighting, many to be released soon after. Arrest records were kept for 11,616 people. But of these only 4,500 were either transported or jailed for participation in the rising (see Table 1). A figure of 50,000 insurgents therefore seems much too high. A more realistic estimate would begin with the 4,500 convicted, then add another 1,500 for those who were killed. Zealous investigations implicated no more than another 5,000 to 9,000 people, most of whom were innocent. While many who were involved undoubtedly escaped the authorities, there is no reason to assume that their number exceeded the figure for those who were held and released. A range of 10,000 to 15,000 participants is, therefore, a reasonable guess.[38]

The four day battle between thousands of insurgents and the forces of order produced enormous losses. The numbers of casualties in the revolutions of July 1830 and February 1848 had been small, reflecting the ease with which the governments fell. Not so during the June Days; the Prefect reported 1,400 dead. The figure should be regarded as a minimum measure of the carnage. The number of wounded taken into the hospitals within a day or two of the fighting passed 1,700. Since many others were cared for at home to escape detection, this figure is again incomplete. Casualties in the army (708 killed and wounded) and the *garde mobile* (114 killed and 475 wounded) are probably accurate, but the full extent of the violence done to the insurgents cannot be reckoned. For a few days, eastern Paris was an occupied territory. The generalised feeling that all were guilty until proven innocent gave the forces of order free rein. Renan reported that the *garde mobile*, 'drunk with blood', was responsible for a series of atrocities which reminded him of the wars of religion. Two or three days after the fighting stopped he heard 'incessant shooting' from the Luxembourg, where prisoners had been taken. Although dwarfed by the Commune, the June Days took a toll of at least 4,000 casualties from among the 70,000 to 100,000 participants on both sides.[39]

Participants in the June Days

So far we have scrutinised the exterior of the June Days, but have not probed beneath the skin. The June Days left a well preserved skeleton which will also reward careful study. In addition to a lengthy official inquiry, there are police and prefects' reports, arrest and judicial records, and even detailed interrogations of most of the 11,000-odd persons charged with taking part in the insurrection. The documentation is comparable to the vast residues left by the repression of the insurrection of 1851 and the Commune, making the June Days one of the best documented rebellions to occur anywhere.

We have not exhausted the material, by any means. But we have surveyed the chief collections of relevant documents at the Archives Nationales, the Archives Historiques de L'Armée, the Archives Départementales de la Seine and the Archives de la Préfecture de Police. We have taken an especially close look at some sources permitting a description of the mass of the insurgents: the individual dossiers of the persons charged with participating in the June Days, and the summary registers prepared to keep track of those dossiers. The largest part of our effort went into coding into machine-readable form each of the 11,616 descriptions of individuals in the *Liste générale en ordre alphabétique des inculpés de juin 1848* and into a statistical study of their characteristics. We also devoted considerable attention to the close examination of approximately one per cent (every fifth dossier in every twentieth carton, for a total of 123 persons) of the individual dossiers in the Archives Historiques de l'Armée at Vincennes.[40] We shall present the results of these analyses in order of increasing specificity: general characteristics of those arrested, distribution by industry and occupation, place of origin, residence in Paris.

To be sure, the employment of judicial records as the basis for this sort of description makes us adopt the perspective of the authorities, in ways we cannot always control. Because those who escaped the authorities also escape the historian, we can only examine those who were arrested. The records bear the imprint of official assumptions and prejudices; they reflect the procedures used to locate suspects. It is clear from the dossiers of the prisoners that overzealous guardsmen dragged off to jail many people who had no connection whatsoever with the rising: bystanders, workmen without alibis, or men mistakenly identified by supporters of the regime.

The majority of those arrested were picked up on the streets or in adjoining houses as the government forces cleared insurgent areas. While most of those rounded up casually were eventually released, those unlucky enough to have been caught with powder stained hands or bullet filled pockets stood little chance of escaping prosecution. The rest of the 11,616 were ferreted out by watchful administrators, energetic guardsmen or police who were sent from house to house interrogating residents. Louis Jacques Voisambert, a shoemaker in his late fifties, one day found that his stall had been raided. Police had learned of his political leanings, and they found enough radical literature in his possession to arouse suspicion. After local witnesses linked him to the rising, he was arrested. Eventually the court sentenced him to twenty years hard labour. After 7 July, over 4,000 people were located in this way. Moreover, the net of suspicion was spread all over France. Police stopped anyone without papers and questioned anyone absent during June who returned home.[41]

Let us look first at an actual participant in the fighting. Raymond Capdegelle, *ouvrier mécanicien*, was born in Bordeaux and had come to Paris several years before the revolution, moving at some point into the

Table 1   Results of the Judicial Proceedings for the June Days

Decision	First Decision Known		Last Decision Known	
	Number	Per Cent	Number	Per Cent
freed	6,658	57.3	6,708	57.7
transported	4,247	36.6	742	6.4
jailed	31	0.3	165	1.4
died before sentencing	36	0.3	49	0.4
trial before *Conseil*				
de Guerre	211	1.8	27	0.2
pardoned	6	0.1	3,504	30.2
dropped charges	359	3.1	353	3.0
no information	68	0.6	68	0.6
total charged	11,616	100.1	11,616	99.9

Sixth *arrondissement* in St Martin des Champs.[42] He was twenty-eight and married, but also had a three year old daughter by another woman, who had since died. Capdegelle worked as a locksmith for a contractor of carpentry located in the Faubourg Poissonière. Although his employer complained that Capdegelle was too interested in politics he was well enough satisfied with his services to have employed him for several years. Like many of his compatriots, Capdegelle had ambiguous political loyalties in the period before the revolution. He had joined the National Guard after the ranks were opened to workingmen, but he continued to attend the clubs even though his concierge claimed that he disapproved of the 'extravagant' things said at the meetings.

One extra ingredient must be noted; by the spring of 1848, our mechanic, like so many others, was unemployed, and he enrolled in the National Workshops. There is no record of his response to the demonstrations of April and May, but with his dual commitment to the guard and the workshops Capdegelle was drawn inevitably into the events of June. When his company was called out on 24 June, he announced that he was going out to fight with the guard. Yet after he and two or three hundred of his company met at the Marché St Martin, they determined to march on the National Assembly with the intention of 'forcing an end to the shedding of blood'. After this point, Capdegelle's part in the rising becomes less clear. When questioned by the authorities he claimed to have left his company when he saw barricades being erected and then to have been disarmed by the rebels. After wandering around the streets for hours, he was arrested; he was transported several months later.

Others arrested for fighting in the June Days were quite similar to

Capdegelle. Table 2 provides a preliminary description of all 11,616 persons arrested. In our tabulations for both arrests and convictions, the same industries, the same parts of the city, the same age groups predominated. Either the authorities maintained their initial biases throughout the entire repression, or they had a pretty good idea who had taken part in the insurrection from the beginning.[43] Given the nature of the repressive process and the sheer numbers involved, we

Table 2   Characteristics of Persons Arrested for Participation in the June Days, by Industry

Industrial Category	Number of Persons	Per Cent of Total*	Per Cent of 1856 Labour Force	Ratio† Column 2/ Column 3	Per Cent Married**	Median Age***
Textiles	343	3.1	4.9	.63	67.7	30
Clothing	1,035	9.2	17.2	.53	56.9	33
Luxury trades	210	1.9	3.5	.54	83.6	32
Printing, paper	441	3.9	3.0	1.30	54.5	30
Ordinary metals	1,324	11.8	2.9	4.07	57.4	31
Fine metals	240	2.1	1.9	1.11	72.7	35
Food	461	4.1	6.7	.61	51.3	31
Furniture, wood	674	6.0	4.0	1.50	63.1	31
Leather	168	1.5	0.6	2.50	56.8	32
Carriage making	195	1.7	1.0	1.70	58.0	31
Chemicals	148	1.3	0.9	1.44	54.5	34
Basketry	133	1.2	1.2	1.00	66.7	32
Construction	2,055	18.4	6.6	2.79	58.1	32
Transport	528	4.7	2.1	2.24	58.2	34
Retail trade	791	7.1	4.7	1.51	68.0	34
Professions finance students	311	2.8	13.6	.21	56.9	34
Military	497	4.4	4.5	.98	54.3	30
Services & others	1,640	14.7	20.6	.71	57.3	34
Not reported	422	–	–	–	63.3	32
TOTAL	11,616	99.9	99.9	–	59.4	32

*   Per cent of total with occupations reported = 11,194
**   Per cent of total with marital status reported = 2,860
***   For those with age reported = 11,065
†   A ratio above 1.0 indicates more arrests than purely proportional representation would produce.

believe that both the arrests and the convictions give a good picture of the participants in the rebellion. In the analyses that follow, we shall report results sometimes in terms of arrests and sometimes in terms of convictions; we shall in every case indicate which population is under examination.

The typical insurgent was a male worker employed in the metal, building, furniture or clothing trades. He had a wife and children and was between the ages of twenty and forty. Although he lived in eastern Paris, he probably had not been born there. In addition, our typical participant was very likely to be a member of either the National Guard or the National Workshops.[44]

The specific occupational titles one encounters most frequently in the dossiers of the June Days are the 693 *journaliers*, 570 *masons*, 474 *menuisiers*, 448 *marchands*, 446 *cordonniers*, 317 *ébénistes*, 295 *tailleurs*, 268 *mécaniciens* and 261 *serruriers*. These figures, however,

Table 3   Arrests per 10,000 Workers by Industry (Paris only)

Industry	Number of Arrests	1848 Survey as Base	1856 Census as Base
Textiles	274	75	68
Clothing	863	96	61
Luxury Trades	168	47	58
Printing, Paper	378	226	154
Ordinary Metals	1022	410	426
Fine Metals	200	119	125
Food	337	323	61
Furniture	576	159	176
Leather	138	302	283
Carriage Making	131	95	159
Chemicals	110	113	150
Basketry	90	166	92
Construction	1521	366	279
Transport	344	?	199
Retail Trade	633	?	164
Professions, Finance, Students	237	?	21
Military	249	?	67
Services	363	?	30
Other	737	?	147
Not Reported	279	–	–
TOTAL	8658	170	102

must be related to the structure of the Parisian labour force. Tables 3 and 4 compare the number of persons living in Paris in each of a number of occupational-industrial categories who were arrested and the number who were convicted in June 1848 with the corresponding numbers of workers enumerated in two different surveys — the Chamber of Commerce survey of Paris in 1848 and the census of 1856 — via rates per 10,000 workers in that category.[45] Comparison of the arrests with the base population (Table 3) de-emphasises the roles of the textile, clothing and furniture industries; they all had a large share of the total Parisian labour force and not such a large share of arrests. It also produces low rates for the various specialty industries of Paris. The comparisons also leave us uncertain about the intensity of participation among chemical workers and carriage makers. Among the industries not covered in the 1848 survey but enumerated in 1856, transport and retail trade appear to have had more than their fair share of insurgents.[46]

Table 4   Convictions per 10,000 Workers by Industry (Paris Only)

Industry	Number of Convictions	1848 Survey as Base	1856 Survey as Base
Textiles	107	29	27
Clothing	307	34	22
Luxury Trades	60	17	21
Printing, Paper	151	90	62
Ordinary Metals	439	176	183
Fine Metals	66	39	41
Food	126	121	23
Furniture	257	71	78
Leather	49	107	100
Carriage Making	45	33	52
Chemicals	47	48	64
Basketry	34	63	35
Construction	538	129	99
Transport	117	?	68
Retail Trade	229	?	59
Professions, Finance, Students	75	?	7
Military	114	?	31
Services	143	?	12
Other	283	?	56
Not Reported	76	—	—
TOTAL	3265	65	39

When it comes to convictions (Table 4), construction, leather, metal working, and the graphic arts again stand out. The furniture making industry, in which a high proportion of all those arrested were convicted, shows up more strongly than it did in the tabulation of arrests. Within the industries for which we have no 1848 labour force data, transport and retail trade again have high rates. From these comparisons and from the finer breakdown by individual craft, it appears that shopkeepers, cabinetmakers and printers held their own, but men from many other skilled crafts — particularly tailors and shoemakers — had virtually abandoned the politics of violent protest. In contrast, rates of participation in the metal, building and transport industries were several times higher than those of the clothing or Parisian specialty trades. Although only 13 per cent of all workers had jobs in these three sectors in 1856, 35 per cent of the persons convicted in 1848 came from these three industries.[47]

Balance against the high involvement of some kinds of manufacturing workers that of white collar workers, professionals and *patrons*. Very few joined in the insurrection. To be sure, a few people of distinctly bourgeois status were convicted for their parts in the June Days — students, intellectuals such as M. Dupont, professor at the Lycée Corneille, or *patrons* like M. Grenon-Meunier, architect and entrepreneur in the building trades; he owned a house worth 200,000 francs but he had also joined the National Workshops.[48] But these men were exceptions. Of occupations carrying a higher social rank than that of artisan, only shopkeepers were implicated with any frequency. Although it is impossible in most cases to distinguish between *ouvriers* and *patrons* on the basis of arrest registers alone, our study of a one per cent sample of individual dossiers turned up only five *patrons*, four of whom were freed after interrogation. It would appear, therefore, that the political alliances between wage earners and the petty bourgeoisie, which had been operative since the 1790s, were breaking down. Virtually all employers cast their lot with the provisional government. Those who opposed it were drawn primarily from male dominated trades with relatively large units of production. The connection between scale and form of industrial organisation and participation in the June Days can be seen much more closely when we classify the thirteen industries covered by the 1848 Chamber of Commerce survey according to the average number of workers per *patron* and the ratio of males to females in the trade and then compare the results with Tables 3 and 4.[49]

192

RATIO OF MALE TO FEMALE WORKERS

	High	Low
A Building Leather Metals		**B** Carriage making Textiles Chemicals Printing
C Furniture Basketry Food		**D** Fine Metals Articles de Paris Clothing

NUMBER OF WORKERS PER *PATRON* — High (cells A, B), Low (cells C, D)

workers/*patron*: high = 7.5 + (7.5 is the median; average number of
                                   workers/*patron* = 5.3)
                   low = under 7.5
males/females: high = over 5 males/female employee
                   low = under 5 males/female employee

With the exception of the furniture trade, those industries with a low
number of workers per *patron* had the lowest rates of participation in
the June Days, while those trades with both a high number of workers
per *patron* and a high male/female ratio were the most active ones. Conversely, the presence of females, particularly when coupled with smaller
than average firms, inhibited participation. Domestic production also
had an inhibiting effect; cells C and D had the highest proportion of
domestic production. Trades with a high proportion of females but a
relatively high number of workers per *patron*, where less work was put
out, form the intermediate group with medium rates of participation
(cell B). Although the furniture trade and the textile industry do not
fit this pattern, in the eleven other trades surveyed, the convergence between the amount of participation in the June Days and position on the
table is striking. Crafts with large amounts of domestic production and/
or many females in the trade were not as politically active as crafts
based upon medium sized or large workshops where the labour force
was predominantly male. This argument does not imply that factory
labourers led the June Days revolt. Rémi Gossez has shown that workers
in the large factories of the *banlieue* were less militant in 1848 than sections of the Fabrique de Paris.[50] Nevertheless — even though our

information does not identify the size of firm within which each arrested man was employed — the complicity of industries that, on the average, had the largest units of production is clear.

Another dimension must be added to this explanation of worker militancy: that of the amount and kind of organisation within the trade. All the industries in our cell A — building, metals, leather — and the mechanised sections of the transport industry are sectors identified by Rémi Gossez as being among those with the most advanced forms of organisation in 1848 — *corporations, syndicats,* and *federations d'industrie.*[51] Moreover, organisations of another sort linked those on the June barricades to one another. Close ties between arrested men and the National Guard and National Workshops can be demonstrated. In our detailed examination of one individual dossier out of a hundred (123 persons), we found that three fifths of the persons charged belonged either to the National Guard or to the Workshops (43 per cent had joined the Workshops and 34 per cent the Guard; 16 per cent of those arrested had dual membership). It is clear, furthermore, that substantially more of the convicted than of the freed were members of either the Guard or the Workshops (in our sample: 76 per cent of the convicted, 58 per cent of the freed). The police and the judiciary must have thought that these institutions were implicated in the rising, for a man's chance of being released were greatly lessened if he was identified as a member of either group. And woe to him who had joined both: in our small sample, 14 of the 20 persons with dual membership (70 per cent) were transported, while over 75 per cent of those who belonged to neither were freed.

Although membership in mutual aid societies and similar working class organisations was only infrequently discussed in the interrogations of prisoners, Rémi Gossez has located many insurgents who also belonged to workers' groups. In contrast, we found very few men who were linked to the clubs. The tie between the June Days and the workers' societies seems to have been much closer than the link between the clubs and the insurrection. Simple arithmetic, to be sure, is enough to prove that most of the men in the Guard, Workshops and workers' societies did not fight on the barricades. But it is clear that members who did join the revolt bear a major share of responsibility for the June Days. In addition, many thousands of others materially aided the rising by refusing to take their places in the Guard.[52]

Gossez has also pointed out the prevalence among the insurgents of workers who had come up from the provinces and settled in the city. As was true of the population of Paris as a whole, the majority of the insurgents were migrants to the city (Table 5). About a quarter of those convicted were born in the Seine, but the remainder came from elsewhere. A sizeable contingent (about 9 per cent of the arrested and of

Figure 2   June Days Arrests per 10,000 Population in Department
            of Birth

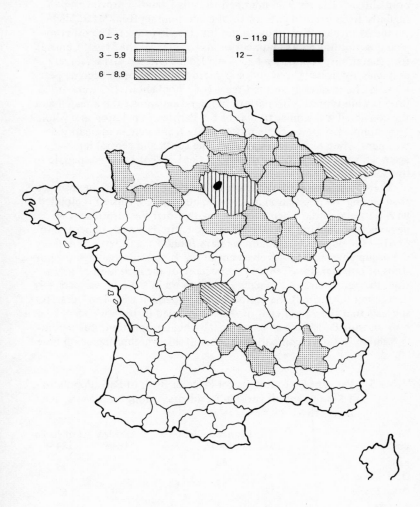

195

the convicted) had moved into Paris from neighbouring departments: Seine-et-Oise, Seine-et-Marne, Oise. An additional 5 per cent had been born abroad. The rest had migrated to Paris from the provinces, particularly from departments north of a line running from Mt St Michel southeast through Burgundy to the Jura (see Figure 2). The other region contributing a large number of insurgents was the Massif Central; for generations, young men had come from there to Paris seasonally or permanently, usually to work on construction jobs or to become petty traders. The masons from the Creuse (of whom about 150 were arrested) were typical. This pattern of migration among the arrested and the convicted was similar to that of the Parisian population as a whole. The capital also drew people most heavily from a circle of nearby departments stretching north and east. The south and central regions, again with the exception of the Massif Central sent far fewer people to the Seine.[53]

There were seemingly far fewer native Parisians among the insurgents than among the population as a whole, but that conclusion is clouded with several doubts. When compared with either the birthplaces of persons who died in Paris in 1833 or the entire Parisian population of 1861 — the only two estimates we have found for this large period — the group charged with involvement in the June Days had high proportions of outsiders (see Table 5).[54] Because of the high level of migration, the percentage of Parisians actually born in the city was probably decreasing throughout the period. The comparison with 1861 therefore suggests that the 75 per cent of those convicted in 1848 who had been born outside Paris were an exceptionally high proportion. But the uncertainties in such a comparison are manifold: whether the death-based

Table 5   Per cent Distributions for Place of Birth of Paris Population, 1833-66, and of Parisian Residents Among Insurgents, June Days, 1848

Birthplace	Total Paris Population			Arrested	Convicted
	1833	1861	1866	1848*	1848*
Paris	50	36	33	24	25
Other Seine	2	59	61		
Other France	41			70	69
Abroad	4	5	6	6	5
Unknown	3	−	−	−	−
TOTAL	100	100	100	100	100
Number of Parisians with Known Birthplaces				7922	3066

*   Persons with Known Birthplace only

figures for 1833 represent the city as a whole depends on the lifecycles of migrants, on earlier fluctuations in migration and on prevailing patterns of fertility and mortality. The figures for 1861 and 1866 include the entire population — women, children, the aged, and so on. But the appropriate base for a comparison of birthplaces, as the age and sex distribution of the insurgents suggests, would be the male population of working age. So the question remains unresolved: many migrants, but perhaps no more than was true of the working population of the city as a whole.

One other factor must be taken into account: length of residence in the Seine. There is no evidence to indicate, and much to disprove, that men *newly* arrived in Paris formed the backbone of the rising. Although migration into Paris had been at a high level for decades, it had declined sharply by the end of 1846. Virtually all migrants living in the capital in June 1848 had been there for a minimum of a year and a half, and most for a much longer time. Balzac has shown through his portraits of César Birotteau and Célestin Crevel how deeply provincials could become integrated into the economic and social life of the city. On a different level of society, by 1840 more and more formerly seasonal migrants were remaining permanently in Paris or staying for several years at a time. Regional differences among workers had already become less noticeable, and assimilation, as revealed in mixed housing and occupational patterns, was far advanced by the middle years of the Second Empire.[55] Case histories of migrants arrested drawn from our one per cent sample of dossiers indicate that few had come recently to the capital. Information allowing us to calculate a minimum length of residence in Paris was available on 53 per cent of those born outside the city (N = 100). Among both the arrested and the convicted two thirds had been in Paris for at least three years. Moreover, one third of those convicted had lived in the capital for at least a decade. Most of the insurgents were, therefore, well settled in Paris. After several years of residence, they had joined local institutions and had established families. The contribution of migrants such as these to the political struggles of the Second Republic is a sign of the increasing integration of the Parisian working class, rather than proof of a threat to public order coming from disoriented outsiders.

Wherever they came from originally, most of the insurgents in the June Days were recruited locally. About 75 per cent of those convicted lived in Paris within the *octroi* walls. Another 17 per cent came from other parts of the Seine, predominantly from communes adjoining the city to the north and east, where fighting had also taken place. Although a few people without settled addresses or with homes in nearby departments fought in the uprising, their contribution was dwarfed by that of resident Parisians.

In this regard and several others, the insurgents resembled the *gardes mobiles* despatched against them. According to the analyses of Rémi Gossez and of Pierre Caspard, both consisted very largely of workers, living in Paris but born elsewhere.[56] There were, nevertheless, some significant differences. If we compare Caspard's statistics concerning the *garde mobile* with our own evidence concerning the arrested, we find the average *garde mobile* much younger, more recently arrived in Paris, less likely to be married. By comparison with Caspard's industrial breakdown, we find construction, printing, cloth trades and shopkeepers more heavily represented in the insurrection than among its conquerors; leather, luxury trades and the liberal professions contributed a relatively large share to the *garde mobile*. Leatherworking stands out as more deeply split than any other major industry, for it contributed large numbers both to the insurrection and to the *garde*. Marx and Engels' characterisation of the regime's makeshift soldiers as a *lumpenproletariat*, observes Caspard, seems to have erred. Instead, the *garde mobile* came especially from the least privileged (and most unemployed) members of privileged trades. Their opponents, the insurgents of June, drew more heavily on the ordinary workers of intensely organised, large scale industries.

The Geography of Participation

The insurrection drew men from all parts of the city into the barricaded areas, but, as could have been expected, the largest contingents were drawn from the scenes of combat. Two thirds of the convicted men lived in the five *arrondissements* of heavy fighting. The Eighth *arrondissement* contributed over 1,000, and the Twelfth over 500 to the total of those jailed or transported. When the size of local populations is taken into account, the unequal distribution of both arrests and convictions emerges clearly. Several areas in the east stand out for their high rates of involvement: especially Popincourt, Quinze Vingts, Hôtel de Ville, Faubourg St Antoine and Faubourg St Jacques; all were familiar neighbourhoods for nineteenth century rebellions.

For lack of labour force data at the level of the quarter, Figure 3 lays out the conviction rates by *arrondissement*. Calculated in terms of the resident labour force, the rate of convictions for the Ninth and Twelfth was very high: over 300 per 10,000 workers. Rates for western Paris remained at fifty or less. Thus as one would have expected, there was a close correspondence between areas of heavy fighting and those of high participation.

The map of the insurrection traced by these statistics is a familiar one. It is the traditional topography of Parisian rebellions. Yet we may reasonably ask what *else* went with an area's high or low propensity to

Figure 3

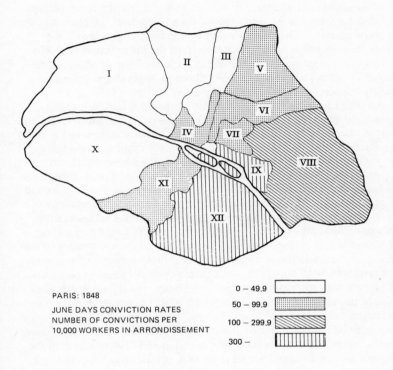

PARIS: 1848

JUNE DAYS CONVICTION RATES
NUMBER OF CONVICTIONS PER
10,000 WORKERS IN ARRONDISSEMENT

0 – 49.9

50 – 99.9

100 – 299.9

300 –

rebellion. In order to get at that question, we have accumulated a certain amount of information about the *arrondissements* and quarters of Paris, and then carried on a series of statistical analyses correlating the characteristics of the areas with each other, and with the frequencies of arrests in 1848.[57] Arrests tend to be frequent where fabricants are numerous, workers' societies abundant, unemployment high, and prior violent conflicts plentiful.

In contrast, the level of migration into an area between 1841 and 1846 shows no relationship at all to the frequency of arrests in 1848, and it is negatively related to the number of *fabricants* and to the levels of unemployment and business activity. The number of clubs is also negatively related to these measurements of industrial size and strength, as well as to the number of arrests. All in all, the results give the impression of an important division between the areas and effects of the clubs and the workers' societies. The clubs are tied to non-industrial activity; they either discourage the local population from the insurrection or shield them from its repression. The workers' societies flourish where unemployed industrial workers, especially those in larger shops abound. Their presence forecasts high rates of arrest in June 1848.

Although we have fewer items of information about each of the forty-eight quarters of Paris, the larger number of units and the smaller scale of the individual unit permit us to pay more attention to the levels of correlation we find. This time we rely on the number of rooming houses (*garnis*) in the quarter as a measure of the concentration of dependent workers in the area. Following the lead of Louis Chevalier, we take the death rate from cholera in 1849 as a measure of the extent of genuine poverty. The correlations run lower than in the analysis of *arrondissements*, but they are consistent. We again see an association between clubs and a relatively prosperous, non-industrial population, and some tendency for arrests to be rare where clubs are frequent. Conversely, the covariation of rooming houses, cholera, workers' societies and arrests in 1848 appears again. Leaving aside for correlation of the arrest rate with the absolute number of arrests, the strongest relationships in the table tie arrests to areas with a high concentration of poor but organised workers.

It may be helpful to recast the strongest relationships among characteristics of quarters in the form of a causal model. The numbers in the diagram are standardised partial regression coefficients. They indicate, loosely speaking, how much change in the variable at the end of the arrow is associated with a unit of change in the variable at the arrow's origin. (The starred coefficients are at least twice their standard error, which is a conventional level below which similar results could easily be produced by chance.) Here is the diagram:

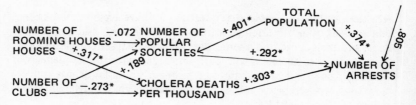

200

This model does not have overwhelming explanatory power; the coefficient of determination (R^2) for number of arrests is .352. Nevertheless, it brings out some relationships which lie hidden in the correlation matrix. To the extent that cholera does stand for poverty, it confirms the association of the clubs with relative wealth, and with none of the other variables in the set. Now we see the apparent association between rooming houses and rebellion dissolve into two components: relative poverty and the organisation of popular societies. The geography of the rebellion corresponded, in a general way, to the geography of poverty and the geography of working class political and economic organisation.

The variables of our analyses of *arrondissements* and *quartiers* describe the world of the organised artisan, the journeyman living in furnished rooms, and the workshop member living in areas that had been hosts to earlier collective protests. All of these elements tended to draw local men into the June Days. Where other factors were dominant, however, participation was inhibited. In the areas where the number of migrants who arrived during the 1840s was comparatively high (predominantly the less crowded areas of western Paris) or where the number of master craftsmen and entrepreneurs was relatively large, the propensity to revolt was lower. The presence of clubs also inhibited men from joining the uprising. In this case, differences in Parisian social and economic milieux led to different forms of political action. While the clubs were certainly militant in many ways, their militancy was closer to the existing structure of power and their alliances with the bourgeoisie were much stronger than in the case of the workers' societies. Their contribution to the June Days was small. Too many of them recruited their members from levels of society above the one which produced the June Days: intellectuals, professionals, students, all groups which were under-represented among the insurgents. Only 4 per cent of the suspects whose dossiers we examined were identified as club members.

Conclusions

While every social class was represented to some degree on both sides of the barricades, the vast majority of the men opposing the government came from a specific social and economic milieu and were members of workers' organisations. The 'haves' and 'have-nots' were not all out on the streets locked in hand to hand combat, certainly, but the opposing forces represented substantially different social groups. Even if many artisans and journeymen fought for the government with the National Guard, the central cadres came from higher social ranks — from property owners, professionals, shopkeepers and their employees. Marx's analysis of the June Days was essentially right.

Despite the passivity of the majority, a determined minority, drawn disproportionately from trades with the largest firms, remained mobilised outside the governing coalitions; they came not from the elite artisans of the luxury trades but from crafts with mixed skill levels, sectors supplying the basic needs of an industrialising economy. These men were willing to reassert — by violence if necessary — their right to oversee public policy and to share public goods. Much of the credit for this survival of political impulses belongs to the organisations which provided a forum for articulate workers and a focus for their energies. At the same time, these groups helped to define and to exalt the claim for a democratic and social republic. That claim brought together the varied commitments to guaranteed employment, altered labour relationships, and political influence which animated Parisian workers in 1848. The June Days resulted from this collective commitment — and more directly from the government's violent denial of the claims and rights which that commitment asserted.

The uprising possessed important elements both of typicality and of uniqueness. On one level, the June Days were part of a standard sequence of mobilisation and demobilisation which takes place after revolutions: contenders for power fight to define and to control the new regime. Politicisation generated by the February revolution both reached its climax and began its decline in June of 1848. The burgeoning, incongruously linked groups of the February coalition finally broke apart; they turned upon one another in a desperate struggle. 'Dual sovereignty' could not be maintained, but the people of June resisted being thrown on the scrap heap of history. The workers' societies, however, were the weakest of those vying for power; after a heavy dose of republican repression, they, like their ancestors, the *sans-culottes*, were forcibly removed from the revolutionary stage. To point to the June Days as part of a typical revolutionary sequence is not to assert that they were only a pale echo of earlier revolutionary events in France. The spring demonstrations and the final battle of 1848 did not merely repeat the great *journées* of 1789-95. Both the issues and the participants had changed. The sections and the *sans-culottes* had given way to the trade societies, the mechanics, and the construction workers of an increasingly proletarianised labour force. Protest in France was becoming modern.

Notes

The Canada Council and the National Science Foundation provided the essential financial support for this research. Priscilla Cheever, Muhammad Fiaz, Freddi Greenberg, Judy Kammins, Virginia Perkins, Sue Richardson and Cyrus Stewart gave us indispensable help in carrying out the analyses; we thank them warmly. For criticism of earlier drafts of this paper, we are grateful to Peter Amann,

202

Andrew Lees, Joan Scott, William Sewell and Edward Shorter. This paper is a revised and extended version of Lees and Tilly, 'Le peuple de juin 1848', *Annales; Economies, Sociétés, Civilisations*, 29 (Sept.-Oct. 1974), pp. 1061-91.

1. *Rapport de la commission d'enquête sur l'insurrection qui a éclaté dans la journée du 23 juin et sur les évènements du 15 mai* (Paris, Imprimerie de l'Assemblée Nationale, 1848), II, p. 290.
2. *Ibid.*, I, p. 358; Alexis de Tocqueville, *Recollections of Alexis de Tocqueville*, J. P. Mayer, ed. (New York, Meridian, 1959), pp. 150-9; Karl Marx, *The Class Struggle in France, 1848-1850* (New York, International Publishers, 1935), p. 56.
3. Explanations of the June Days differ markedly according to the political persuasion of the historian offering them. In general, historians on the left stress the elements of class conflict and the economic pressures of hunger and unemployment [Georges Renard, *La République de 1848, Histoire Socialiste (1789-1900)*, t. ix, Jean Jaurès, ed. (Paris, J. Rouff et Cie. 1906); Jean Dautry, *1848 et la IIe République*, (Paris, Ed. sociales, 1957)] or the effect of socialist theories and organisations [Georges Duveau, *1848: The Making of a Revolution* (New York, Pantheon, 1967)]. Conservative historians have concentrated more exclusively on a description of the events themselves, explaining them by a combination of ideological and political factors [Pierre de la Gorce, *Histoire de la Seconde République française*, I (Paris, Plon-Nourrit, 1925); Charles Seignobos, *La Révolution de 1848 – Le second empire, Histoire de France contemporaine*, E. Lavisse, ed., t. vi (Paris, Hachette, 1900-11)]. See also Charles Schmidt, *Les journées de juin* (Paris, Hachette, 1926); George Rudé, *Debate on Europe, 1815-1850* (New York, Harper Torchbooks, 1972), pp. 213-27.
4. See particularly, Petter Amann, 'A *Journée* in the making : May 15, 1848', *Journal of Modern History*, 42, no. 1 (March, 1970), pp. 42-69; Rémi Gossez, *Les Ouvriers de Paris, I: l'organisations, 1848-1851*, Bibliothèque de la révolution de 1848, t. XXIV (La Roche-sur-Yon, Imprimerie Centrale de l'ouest, 1967); Rémi Gossez, 'La Presse Parisienne à destination des ouvriers, 1848-1851', *La Presse ouvrière, 1819-1850*, Jacques Godechot, ed., Bibliothèque de la Révolution de 1848, t. XXIII (La Roche-sur-Yon, Imprimerie Centrale de l'ouest, 1966), pp. 123-90.
5. Albert Soboul, *Les sans-culottes parisiens en l'an II* (Paris, Librairie Clavreuil, 1958); George Rudé, *The Crowd in the French Revolution* (Oxford, Clarendon, 1959); George Rudé, *The Crowd in History* (New York, Wiley, 1964).
6. See Louise A. Tilly, 'La révolte drumentaire, forme de conflit politique en France', *Annales: Economies, Sociétés, Civilisations*, 27 (1972), pp. 731-57.
7. C. E. Labrousse, '1848-1830-1789: Comment naissent les révolutions', *Actes du Congrès historique de centénaire de la Révolution de 1848* (Paris, Presses Universitaires de France, 1948), pp. 1-20; 'Panoramas de la crise', in C. E. Labrousse, ed., *Aspects de la crise et de la dépression de l'économie française au milieu du XIXe siècle*, Bibliothèque de la Révolution de 1848, tome XIX (La Roche-sur-Yon, Imprimerie Centrale de l'ouest, 1956).
8. Rémi Gossez, *Les ouvriers de Paris, op. cit.*
9. More extensive statements in this reasoning (and some evidence to support it appears in James Rule and Charles Tilly, '1830 and the Unnatural History of Revolution', *Journal of Social Issues*, 28 (1972), pp. 49-76, and Charles Tilly, 'Revolutions and Collective Violence', in Fred I. Greenstein and Nelson Polsby, eds., *Handbook of Political Science* (Reading, Mass., Addison-Wesley, forthcoming).
10. Louis Chevalier, *Classes laborieuses et classes dangereuses à Paris pendant la première moité du XIX siècle* (Paris, Plon, 1958).

11.   A. Audiganne, 'L'Industrie française depuis la révolution de février', *Revue des Deux Mondes* (1849, II), pp. 992-3; Louis Chevalier, *La Formation de la population parisienne au XIXe siècle* (Paris, Presses Universitaires de France, 1950), pp. 121-7, 131-4.

12.   Maurice Lévy-Leboyer, *Les Banques européennes et l'industrialisation internationale dans la première moitié du XIXe siècle* (Paris, Presses Universitaires de France, 1964), pp. 116-8, 345-8.

13.   Chambre de Commerce de Paris, *Statistique de l'industrie à Paris résultante de l'enquête faite par la Chambre de Commerce pour les années 1847-1848* (Paris, Guillaumin et Cie., 1851), pp. 48-51, 63-7, 76-8, 114-7, 130-5, 158-60; Chevalier, *Formation*, pp. 91, 114-8.

14.   Chambre de Commerce, pp. 38-41; see also Ernest Labrousse, 'Panoramas de la crise', *Etudes: Aspects de la crise et de la dépression de l'économie française au milieu du XIXe siècle, 1846-51*, Bibliothèque de la Révolution de 1848, t. XIX (La Roche-sur-Yon: Imprimerie Centrale de l'Ouest, 1956), iii-xiv.

15.   Donald Cope McKay, *The National Workshops: A Study in the French Revolution of 1848* (Cambridge, Mass., Harvard University Press, 1965), pp. 26-9, 159; Stein, III, pp. 351-3.

16.   For more detailed information on our procedures, see Charles Tilly, 'Methods for the Study of Collective Violence', in Molly Apple Levin and Ralph W. Conant, eds., *Problems in the Study of Community Violence* (New York, Praeger, 1969). Recent reports of this work include Charles Tilly, 'The Changing Place of Collective Violence', in Melvin Richter, ed., *Essays in Social and Political History* (Cambridge, Mass., Harvard University Press, 1970); Charles Tilly, 'How Protest Modernized in France, 1845 to 1855', in William Aydelotte, Allan Bogue and Robert Fogel, eds., *The Dimensions of Quantitative Research in History* (Princeton, Princeton University Press, 1972); Edward Shorter and Charles Tilly, 'Le déclin de la grève violente en France de 1890 à 1935', *Le mouvement social*, 79 (July-September, 1971), pp. 95-118; 'Les vagues de grèves en France, 1890-1968., *Annales: Economies, Sociétés, Civilisations*, 28 (1973), pp. 857-87. Our estimate of the number of violent incidents taking place in France from 1845 to 1854, runs as follows:

Year	Number of Incidents	Number of Participants (thousands)
1845	4	1
1846	27	41
1847	33	11
1848	126	271
1849	27	49
1850	15	5
1851	93	97
1852	2	0.3
1853	0	0
1854	3	5

17.   Sources for Parisian incidents: *Le Moniteur universel*, 2 October 1846, 3 October 1846, 16 September 1847; *Le Droit*, 2 October 1846, 3 October 1846, 5 October 1846, 30 October 1846, 31 October 1846, 3 September 1847, 5 September 1847, 8 September 1847, 14 September 1847, 16 September 1847, 17 September 1847, 30 September 1847.

18.   Peter Amann, 'Revolution: A Redefinition', *Political Science Quarterly*, LXXVII (1962), pp. 36-52.

19.   General sample incidents, nos. 405, 425, 446, 491; see also *Archives Nationales*, BB[18] 1461, 1468, 5265, BB[30] 363.

20.   Daniel Stern, *Histoire de la révolution de 1848, 3 tomes (Paris, 1850-3)*

II, pp. 419-29; Gossez, 'La presse parisienne', pp. 183-5; *rapport d'enquête*, II, pp. 99-102.

21. Henri Sée, *La vie économique de la France sous la monarchie censitaire, 1815-1848* (Paris, F. Alcan, 1927), pp. 122, 126-31; see also Jean-Pierre Aguet, *Les grèves sous la monarchie de juillet, 1830-47* (Geneva, E. Droz, 1954); Pierre Quentin-Bauchart, *La crise sociale de 1848: les origines de la révolution de février* (Paris, Hachette, 1920), pp. 274-5; Gossez, *Ouvriers*, pp. 127-9.

22. *Rapport d'enquête*, I, pp. 258-9; Lévy-Leboyer, p. 349.

23. For a detailed description of workers' organisations in Paris during the Second Republic, see Gossez, *Ouvriers*, particularly pp. 112-20, 136-45, 160-220.

24. Charles Richomme, *Journées de l'insurrection de juin, 1848: journal de la rue* (Paris, Vve L. Janet, 1848), p. 46.

25. A. Delvau, ed., *Les Murailles révolutionnaires* (Paris, C. Joubert, 1851), pp. 362, 476-9, 563-5; see also Boutin, pp. 183, 211; Richomme, pp. 166-7.

26. *Archives Nationales*, C. 934, no. 2692, 'Etat des principales arrestations politiques du 15 mai au 22 juin, 1848',; *rapport d'enquête*, II, pp. 193-5, 199-200.

27. Richomme, pp. 138-9, 148-9.

28. *Rapport d'enquête*, II, pp. 49-54.

29. *Archives Nationales*, C. 933, nos. 2427-8, 2452, 'rapports sur la journée de 22 juin'; *Le Siècle*, 23 juin 1848; *Moniteur*, 2 décembre 1848; Daniel Stern [Marie. C. S. de F. comtesse d'Agoult], *Histoire de la révolution de 1848* (Paris, G. Sandre, 1853), III, pp. 153-6; *Rapport d'enquête*, II, pp. 212-4; Maxime du Camp, *Souvenirs de l'année 1848* (Paris, Hachette, 1876), pp. 238-9.

30. *Archives Nationales* C. 933, nos. 2447-2451, 'rapports sur la journée de 22 juin', nos. 2454-2472, 'rapports sur la 23 juin'; Stern, III, p. 157.

31. *Archives Nationales*, C, 933, nos 2454-2497, 'rapports sur la journée de 23 juin'.

32. *Archives Nationales*, C. 933, nos. 2554-2591, 'rapports sur les journées de 23 et 24 juin'; *Moniteur*, 2 décembre 1848. See also de la Gorce, pp. 331-68.

33. *Archives Nationales*, C. 933, nos. 2556-2574, 'rapports sur la journée de 23 juin'; no. 2965, 'rapport sur la journée de 24 juin'; *Moniteur*, 2 août 1848.

34. *Archives Nationales*, C. 933, nos. 2968, 2975, 2980, 'rapports sur les journées de 25 et 26 juin'; *Rapport d'enquête*, II, pp. 248-50.

35. *Archives Historiques de l'Armée*, F[1] 9.

36. *Moniteur*, 25 juin-21 juillet, 1848; 3-4 décembre 1848; *Rapport d'enquête*, II, pp. 53-4; *Archives Nationales*, C. 933, nos. 2428, 2484, 2497, 'rapports sur les journées de 22 et 23 juin'; Louis Girard, *La garde nationale, 1814-1871* (Paris, Plon, 1964), pp. 294, 313-4.

37. Jean Vidalenc, 'La province et les journées de juin', *Etudes d'histoire moderne et contemporaine*, II (1948), pp. 102-3.

38. *Rapport d'enquête*, I, pp. 298, 358; Stern, III, pp. 270-1; *Archives Nationales*, F.[7] 2585-6. 'Liste générale en ordre alphabétique des inculpés de juin, 1848'; *Archives de l'armée*, 'justice militaire, 1848; non poursuivis'; Seignebos, p. 105.

39; *Moniteur*, 22 juillet, 2 and 8 août 1848; *Rapport d'enquête*, I, p. 363; P. Chalmin, 'Une institution militaire de la seconde république, la garde nationale mobile', *Etudes d'histoire moderne et contemporaine*, II (1948), p. 68; Ernest Renan and Henriette Renan, *Nouvelles lettres intimes, 1846-50* (Paris, Calmann-Levy, 1923), pp. 209-10; de la Gorce, I, p. 393; *Archives Nationales*, C. 933, no. 2730, 'Le nombre des morts et blessés'.

40. There are several versions of the list, in Archives Nationales F[7] 2585, F[7] 2586 and Archives Historiques del'Armée AA, A. There are small discrepancies among the three huge registers, but all three contain about 11,700 names. The

register in F^7 2585 ends with number 11,671 while F^7 2586 ends with 11,693, for an apparent difference of 22 persons. However, our detailed reworking of F^7 2586 revealed a considerable range of numbering errors; our final total is 11,616 persons — 77 persons (or 0.7 per cent) less than the apparent total. Since we have not made a person-by-person comparison of the registers, it is still possible that the lists are identical. We employed F^7 2586 because it contains more items of information concerning each *inculpé* than F^7 2585, and because it was more convenient to have it microfilmed than the copy at Vincennes. We coded each entry onto perforated cards, retaining the birthplace (but not, unfortunately, the name of the person — that was a mistake) in alphabetical form as well as in numerical code. We performed the verifications, tabulations and computations with a tape version of the 11,616-card deck. George Rudé, Rémi Gossez, and most likely Georges Duveau have all used these sources before, but their analyses were not as intensive or detailed as our own. Most recently, Roger Price, in *The Second French Republic* (London, B. T. Batsford, 1972) has worked with F^7 2585. Our results differ from his in several respects: he, for example, has counted 11,727 people; also see n. 45.

41.   *Moniteur*, 16 October 1848; 26 March, 7 and 10 April 1848; A. N. C. 933, nos. 2961, 2980. 2985, 'rapports sur la journée de 26 juin 1848', no. 2701, 'Etat et répartition des prisonniers'. See also Archives Historiques de l'Armée, A 1-125, 'Justice Militaire, 1848'.

42.   AHA, A 65, no. 4834, Capdegelle. Unfortunately, our view of these men comes from official interrogations, which took place after jail and the prospect of transportation had decisively dampened most men's militant enthusiasms.

43.   For more exact comparability with the base population, later tables will deal only with the 8,635 persons known to have lived in the city of Paris in 1848, excluding the 1,926 surburbanites, the 368 from other departments, the 387 living in barracks or other group quarters and the 300 for whom we have no certain address; the totals will therefore be smaller than in Table 2. (There were only 273 women in the original 11,616 suspects.) For information on police procedures and attitudes, see R. C. Cobb, *The Police and the People, French Popular Protest, 1789-1820* (Oxford, Oxford University Press, 1970), pp. 27, 29.

44.   These and subsequent general remarks about the composition of the insurgents summerise tabulations of the *liste générale . . .* which we have not presented in detail here.

45.   Both of the sources have significant disadvantages. The Chamber of Commerce survey ignored both shopkeepers who did not manufacture some of their wares and the whole range of service industries. It also neglected solitary workers who did not run their own shops: itinerants, peddlers, part-time craftsmen and the like. Those exclusions, for example, probably inflated the rates for the food industries. The 1856 census (the first one to provide relatively detailed and reliable enumerations of the labour force) has the serious disadvantage of coming eight years after the insurrection. It is unlikely, nevertheless, that the two bases erred in the same direction from the 'true' 1848 labour force, however we might define it. Where both comparisons point in the same direction, we have grounds for believing the data.

46.   When our results are compared with those of Roger Price, several differences appear. Our occupational classification and his are not identical; many of his totals for participation by industrial categories differ substantially from our own. (See his Table I, p. 165). His portrayal of participation by industry (pp. 164-6) suffers from the fact that he uses absolute numbers of arrests or percentages, rather than rates. But inferences about comparative propensity to revolt must take into account the distribution of trades in the labour force and must exclude workers coming from outside the city.

47.   The description applies to the males charged with involvement in the insurrection, but not to the females. The occupational profile of the tiny group of women who were jailed was markedly different: about a third worked in either the clothing industry or in service jobs. Another large proportion were either merchants or petty traders.

48.   *Moniteur*, 7 and 20 September, 18 October 1848; 11 March 1849.

49.   Chambre de Commerce, pp. 36-7, 48.

50.   Gossez, *Ouvriers*, pp. 181-2.

51.   *Ibid.*, pp. 172-42, 177-8, 203-20.

52.   See especially AHA A 1-125, 'Justice Militaire, 1848'.

53.   Chevalier, *Formation de la population parisienne*, pp. 165, 207, 208, 217, 218, 285.

54.   *Ibid.*, pp. 46, 57, 58. The account of nativity in Paris in 1833 was done by Dr Bertillon, who bases his findings on current death records — an unreliable base for such an estimate, at best. See *Recherches statistiques sur la ville de Paris et le département de la Seine*, M. le comte de Rambuteau, prefect. (Paris, Imprimerie Royale, 1844), V, Table 118.

55.   Honoré de Balzac, *César Birotteau, La Cousine Bette*. See also Chevalier's discussion in *Classes laborieuses*, pp. 220, 238-410.

56.   Rémi Gossez, *'Diversité* des anatagonismes sociaux vers le milieu du XIXe siècle', *Revue économique*, May 1956, pp. 439-57; Pierre Caspard, 'Aspects de la lutte des classes en 1848: le recrutement de la garde nationale mobile', *Revue historique*, 98 (1974), pp. 81-106. We must approach the comparison with Caspard cautiously; the figures he provides for the occupational distribution of the insurgents differ so greatly from our own that we do not entirely trust his figures for the *garde mobile*. Having taken 4,000 names (in an unspecified manner) from the card file of arrestees at the Archives Historiques de l'Armée, for example, Caspard finds 12.4 per cent of the insurgents to be in construction, whereas our proportions are 18.4 per cent. For his 10.9 per cent in wood and furniture, we calculate 6.0 per cent. For Caspard's 6.5 per cent in textiles and clothing, we find 12.4 per cent. Pending further information concerning Caspard's sampling method and his occupational coding, the comparisons which follow remain tentative.

Table 1   Correlations Among Characteristics of *Arrondissements*, Partialed for Total Population

	Migration	Fabricants	Unemployed	Clubs	Workers' Societies	Number Charged	Business	Workers/ Fabricants	Incidents
Net Migration 1841-46	+1.00								
Number of Fabricants 1848	− .66	+1.00							
Number Unemployed 1848	− .46	+ .86	+1.00						
Number of Clubs 1848	+ .30	− .39	− .18	+1.00					
Number of Workers' Societies	− .34	+ .41	− .63	− .16	+1.00				
Number Charged	− .09	+ .38	+ .47	− .43	+ .57	+1.00			
Business Activity 1848	− .51	+ .86	+ .93	− .16	+ .45	+ .18	+1.00		
Workers per Fabricant 1848	− .23	+ .33	+ .70	+ .14	+ .56	+ .02	+ .73	+1.00	
Number of Violent Incidents 1848	+ .61	+ .11	+ .27	+ .20	+ .14	+ .42	+ .13	+ .03	+1.00

Appendix

Table 2 Correlations Among Characteristics of Quarters, Partialed for
Total Population

	Charged	Charged/ 1,000	Rooming Houses	Cholera/ 1,000	Clubs	Workers' Societies
Number charged	+1.00					
Charged/1,000 Population	+ .95	+1.00				
Number of Rooming Houses Jan. 1848	+ .44	+ .54	+1.00			
Cholera Deaths per 1,000, 1849	+ .35	+ .44	+ .42	+1.00		
Number of Clubs	− .18	− .16	− .31	− .32	+1.00	
Number of Workers' Societies	+ .32	+ .24	+ .23	+ .08	− .14	+1.00

RADICALISATION AND REPRESSION: A STUDY OF THE DEMOBILISATION OF THE 'DEMOC-SOCS' DURING THE SECOND FRENCH REPUBLIC

John M. Merriman
Yale University

The *coup d'état* of Louis-Napoleon Bonaparte on 2 December 1851 was not one single event, but the culmination of a long series of blows struck against the radical Republican left. The Second French Republic cannot be explained without an understanding of the repression which demobilised the major part of the democratic-socialist organisation which stood between the would-be eagle and the Empire. Radicalisation, repression, and, in some cases, resistance — this was the story of the Second Republic.

Of the three — radicalisation, repression and resistance — we know considerably more about the first and the third. Several important regional studies, notably Maurice Agulhon's brilliant *La République au village*, Philippe Vigier's study of the Alpine region, and short pieces by Leo Loubère on the Lower Languedoc and Christianne Marcilhacy on the Loiret, have studied the economic and social bases of political radicalisation.[1] The model sketched by Charles Tilly and Lynn Lees in this volume can account for the spread of radicalism in provincial France following the February Revolution of 1848.[2] In fact, Tilly, writing several years ago, was almost prophetic in terms of what historians doing regional studies would find:

> 'My guess is that the Republican, Radical and Socialist organisations, both open and clandestine, spread like vines through the hinterlands of Paris, Toulouse, Béziers, Marseille and Lyon with the great political mobilisation of 1848, that from 1849 on the Napoleonic government was fairly successful at choking or chopping the more visible branches of those organisations, and that the geographic pattern [of resistance] represents the areas in which they and their adepts had survived the thinning out — because they were tough or because they were invisible.'[3]

Indeed, what in Ted W. Margadant's words 'originated in 1848 as an urban ideology of social reform' — 'A genuinely popular government [which] would serve the interests of the poor, not the rich' — also became rural; 'inspired by Montagnard representatives and provincial journalists, Republican militants in central and southern France mobilized a coalition of urban and rural voters around a program of economic reform . . . Henceforth the Democratic and Social Republic was a rural as well as an urban ideal.'[4] These were the *'démoc-socs'*. What they wanted was a government of the people which would be 'social' in the sense that it would be responsive to the needs of the labouring poor. By 1850, the *démoc-soc* organisation was the greatest threat to the government of Louis-Napoleon Bonaparte, as the so-called 'blue' Republicans disappeared and the Monarchists quarrelled and dreamed.

As Tilly suggests, what intervened between the spread of *démoc-soc* commitment and the *coup d'état* was the repression, which has never been adequately studied. Karl Marx understood its role; more recently Howard C. Payne, anticipating the Police State of Louis-Napoleon Bonaparte, described the administrative centralisation of policing during the Second Republic.[5] Both Payne and Marx were right to suggest that the bureaucracy, one of the crucial factors in modern French history, was, from the beginning, a great resource of Louis-Napoleon. It was politicised and hardly neutral. Regardless of the status of the quarrel between Louis-Napoleon and the National Assembly, the bureaucracy was his because he sat at the uppermost desk. The elections of May 1849 provided a sense of urgency for the repression; it was fully organised and institutionalised by November of that year.

Several regional studies have sketched the rough outlines of the repression — the war against the free press and against less regular networks of *démoc-soc* propaganda; attacks against informal and formal associations maintaining collective commitment and organisation for the *démoc-socs* (*cercles* and *chambrées* in the Midi, cafés and workers' associations, and so on); the law against universal suffrage of 31 May 1850; the end of the clubs and the harassment of their more informal successors, electoral organisations; and revocations at every level of officialdom of the disloyal, the wavering and the inefficient.

The repression was national, striking every department in France. Some studies of regional radicalisation have included a discussion of the repression in departments in which there was major resistance against the *coup d'état*. In insurrectionary departments, as Ted W. Margadant demonstrates in the most complete study of the resistance, the repression had failed to demobilise the *démoc-socs*, driving them underground (from electoral politics to conspiracy) into the Montagnard secret societies which spearheaded the resistance.[6] But as a national phenomenon, the repression was a great success; in most departments all but fragments of the radical apparatus had been cut apart by the time of the *coup*; in other departments, particularly in the West, the *démoc-socs* were kept from establishing a foothold.

The specific goals of this national repression varied from department to department, depending on the local strengths of the *démoc-soc* organisation. In Lyon, the target was the intricate network of workers' associations with a history of mobilisation and violence; in Colmar and Nantes, the main object was to eliminate an active and successful radical press; in Jura, to limit contacts with the large colony of political exiles in Switzerland; in the Finistère, to keep the *démoc-soc* emissaries from breaking through the Bretons' physical, cultural and linguistic isolation; in the Ariège, concern with mayors and popular local *démoc-soc* leaders capable of keeping the forest laws alive as a political issue; in the Marne, to prevent the Association Remoise (*'pour la vie à bon marché'*) from becoming a vast network linking cities and towns; and so on. The Ministers of Interior, War and Justice, aided by three separate but closely linked bureaucracies which reached into every commune in France, made it their business to understand the strengths of the *démoc-socs* in every department, and to proceed against them.[7]

Although we have studied the repression in every department, this essay will describe how it worked in two kinds of localities within a specific region. The Limousin radicalised between the February Revolution and the elections of May of 1849; a strong *démoc-soc* organisation spread from Limoges into its hinterland. Yet by December of 1851, this radical apparatus had largely been demobilised, and there was only very limited resistance to the *coup d'état*. We will look closely at the repression in urban and working class Limoges, considered by the administration to be, after Paris and Lyon, the most dangerous city in France; and the radical *arrondissements* of Boussac and Bourganeuf in the Creuse. How did the repression work? How was the *démoc-soc* organisation dismantled by the time of the *coup*? What was it like to live during the first stages of a Police State? If we keep in mind that what will be described was occurring, to varying degrees, everywhere in France, our regional approach should be helpful.

The Repression in Limoges

Limoges, already a grim working class city of about 45,000 in 1848, radicalised early. The February Revolution intensified social conflict in the city; there was a rapid coalescence of bourgeois opposition to the Revolution in the face of radical control of the Prefecture and the mobilisation of the workers, particularly the porcelain workers, who dominated the city's work force. A new and vigorous radical press, an active club — the *Société Populaire* — Municipal Workshops seen as the fulfilment of the 'right to work', and genuine popular enthusiasm for the Republic activated the workers to push for a Republic which would also be 'social'. Three issues divided the city after February: the question of the 'right to work'; popular participation in the National Guard, in that the bourgeois National Guard of the July Monarchy was still officially constituted and armed; and the elections of April 1848 for the National Assembly. The culmination of this social polarisation was the *Affaire de Limoges*, 27 April 1848 in which the bourgeois National Guard was disarmed by the workers, who seized control of the city and forced a new and more radical provisional administration into power. The issues and the violence were essentially the same as in Rouen, where sixteen died on 27-28 April as canons battered the workers' barricades; in both cities, the timing of the violent explosion was even earlier than the days of June in Paris.[8]

Between the *Affaire de Limoges* and the elections of May 1849, radical organisation reflecting a coalition between a small bourgeois elite of socialists and the workers — spread from Limoges into its hinterland and politicised the department of Haute Vienne. *Le Peuple*, Limoges' *démoc-soc* newspaper, editorialised:

'The social question has been posed on the barricades of February; be convinced of this, it will receive a solution . . . We will not have to wait eighteen years for France to be Socialist as it is today Republican . . .'[9]

With this confidence and enthusiasm, the *démoc-socs* brought about a stunning electoral success in May 1849, when all socialist Representatives were elected from Haute Vienne. The *démoc-soc* leadership was successful because they effectively utilised the Republican institutions, gifts of the Revolution — the free press, the right of popular assembly and association, universal suffrage, and new leaders in positions of authority. How, then was Limoges, once controlled by the workers and thoroughly politicised, ultimately demobilised?

When a new Commissioner (in June, Prefect) arrived in Limoges, he appointed a new municipal council and began to move against the *Société Populaire*, which served as a radical caucus before the election of April and channeled the militance of the workers. Commissioner Duché first deprived the *Société* of a place to meet; municipally and privately owned meeting places suddenly became unavailable.[10] The laws against political clubs, passed after the June Days, ensured the dissolution of the *Société Populaire* and made organised political meetings almost impossible. But although disbanded, the *Société*'s leaders, according to the Procureur Général, 'continue[d] to exercise an influence on the rest of Haute Vienne and even beyond the limits of the department'.[11] Another urban symbol of the Revolution, the Municipal Workshops, organised to deal with the economic crisis, also quickly disappeared. First the hours of work were carefully regulated, then the number of workers eligible. By June, only 1,000 workers were left on the rolls, compared to 3,700 in April. The enlarged garrison prevented any disturbances or protests by the workers.[12] The earliest stage of the repression, then, began in the wake of the *Affaire de Limoges* and the June Days.

Even with the loss of their club and the Workshops, Limoges' workers effectively united to elect a Municipal Council half of whose members were socialists, despite the division of the city into electoral districts which gave disproportionate strength to votes in elite districts. The Orléanist paper *L'Ordre* saw the power of the 'men of order' slipping away in the city: 'On April 27, the National Guard was disarmed by a riot; today, the riot has again disarmed the "men of order" by taking away from them the positions that they should have on the Municipal Council.'[13] And although the city voted for Louis-Napoleon in December, there was no contradiction between radical Limoges and such a vote. Raspail and Ledru-Rollin had very little chance, although they received some workers' votes; Cavaignac, the butcher of June, was the enemy, and Louis-Napoleon seemed to be a Republican interested in the fate of the people, and a Bonaparte.[14] In the election of May 1849, Limoges voted overwhelmingly for the *démoc-soc* candidates, Theodore Bac (the most influential leader and defender of *démoc-soc accusés* during the Second Republic), Marcel Dussoubs-Gaston, Coralli, the elder Frichon, Daniel Lamazière, Laclaudure and the utopian socialist Michel de Bourges, who defeated a slate of conservatives by dominating the election in eighteen of Haute Vienne's twenty-seven cantons.[15] The ease of the *démoc-soc* victory was surprising. The Legitimist paper *La Province* expressed the shock of the 'good citizens', at the sweeping socialist victory in a department which had been so conservative the year before ('the socialists have made a call to the *jacquerie*').[16] The repression to date had clearly failed; it had not been carefully coordinated. The election proved this. But in the new Prefect of Haute Vienne, Pierre Paul Edouard de Mentque, the Minister of Interior had at last found the right man for the job.

Commissioners, symbolic of revolutionary times, became Prefects. Commissioner Duché became Prefect Duché in June, and was revoked in August. He was succeeded by Monsieur Titot, a wealthy manufacturer in poor health and planning on retiring soon. His inaugural pronouncement in which he noted that 'democratic institutions contain all of the progress compatible with the existence of family and property', demonstrated to conservatives that he was not going to be, for them, an acceptable Prefect. He viewed the election of Louis-Napoleon as 'anti-democratic' and supported efforts by the porcelain workers to organise producers' cooperatives. Worse still, he wrote that 'the bourgeois party seems to me to be struck with an exaggerated terror; the town was in the power of the workers for fifteen days without any attacks on persons or property.'[17] So it was no surprise when de Mentque, an old professional with nearly two decades of administrative experience during the July Monarchy, arrived to take over a Prefecture which, just a year earlier, had been run by a radical committee of provisional administration.[18] De Mentque met with the approval of the Limoges bourgeoisie, pledging to defend 'the unshakeable maintenance of the sacred principles of family and property'.[19] De Mentque organised and systematised the repression in Limoges, the base of *démoc-soc* organisation in Haute Vienne and the Limousin. First among his priorities was the radical press, which, in the spring of 1849, was changing the nature of politics in the Limousin.

The repression of the press in France began after the June Days, when the 'caution' laws from the Restoration were restored. Political newspapers had to deposit a large sum, usually 1,800 francs, as a 'deposit' — a security deposit — against any future political 'damages'.[20] Limoges' two *démoc-soc* papers, *Le Peuple* and *Le Carillon Républicain*, were both forced out of business. The last issue of *Le Carillon*, which had been originated by the political cartoonist and songwriter Alfred Durin, appeared in black trim and contained an epitaph for its satirical anti-hero, Prefect Duché:

> Ci-gît le fameux Jean-sans-Peur
> Le Chansonnier Carilloneur,
> Ça loi sur le cautionnement,
> L'a fait mourir subitement.[21]

Le Peuple reappeared on 19 October 1848 with a new editor, a former disciple of Pierre Leroux and his 'religion of humanity'. The paper continued to defend the 'democratic and social Republic' and the *accusés* from the *Affaire de Limoges* who went on trial in Poitiers during the spring of 1849. *Le Peuple* suffered confiscations and court convictions but lasted through its major effort, preparation for the May elections. Its editor then joined the political exiles in Switzerland.[22]

In November 1849, there were two more attempts to revive the radical press in Limoges. *Le Carillon Républicain* briefly returned as a monthly, in order to avoid paying caution money. At the same time, other *Le Carillons* were announced in nearby cities, Poitiers, Angoulême and Périgeux, to appear alternately so that, in effect, *Le Carillon* would be a weekly *sans caution*. For their imagination, all four 'editors' were condemned by the Limoges *Cour d'Appel* for 'fraudulent declaration'. Alfred Durin would have to practice his political cartooning in prison. These convictions were announced by the single issue of a paper entitled *Le Gros Bourdin*; the nominal editor of this sheet, a revoked school teacher, was prosecuted and joined his friends in jail.[23]

But, as in most cities in France (particularly Montpellier, Toulouse,

Colmar, Dijon and Nantes), multiple press convictions were not enough
to silence the *démoc-soc* press. *Le Républicain du Centre* first appeared
25 November 1849. The first issue was confiscated because an article
titled 'letter from a sharecropper' was found to be 'offensive'. The
nominal (and therefore legally responsible) editor, a cooper, was prosecuted; the Court declared him 'incapable' of overseeing a publication
and ruled that he could not possibly be the 'serious managing editor'. In
fact, Representative Marcel Dussoubs-Gaston was behind the paper.
When the Prefect closed it down he obtained a list of subscribers in
Haute Vienne; this was valuable information to have because of the role
of the literate in the diffusion of radical propaganda among the illiterate (considerably more than half of the department) in cafés, workshops, market gatherings and homes — anywhere people gathered to
discuss local affairs.24

As an election in March 1850 approached (to replace Daniel-Lama-
zière, convicted by the High Court of Versailles for conspiracy), *Le
Salut du Peuple* appeared to aid the candidacy of the *démoc-soc* candidate, a virtual unknown named Ducoux. His opponent, handpicked in
Paris and aided by Prefect de Mentque, was Louis-Napoleon's personal
secretary, who was a veteran of the Boulogne fiasco. Ducoux won anyway, and *Le Salut du Peuple* disappeared.25

Finally, in November 1851, *Le Travailleur*, newspaper of 'democrats,
socialists, workers, peasants, workers of the land and in industry, living
from our intelligence and the labour of our hands' began with the
financial backing of Haute Vienne's Montagnard Representatives and
with the assistance of public subscriptions sold in the department. The
third issue of *Le Travailleur* announced that it would be the last — de
Mentque threatened to collect some old court costs if the paper continued. Despite numerous attempts, the *démoc-socs* were without a
newspaper in Limoges when the final blow came on 2 December.26

De Mentque was, like his colleagues, also concerned with the 'incessant, mysterious and almost unseizable propaganda' which appeared
in Limoges. Much of this propaganda — brochures, pamphlets, socialist
almanacs or papers such as Joigneaux's remarkably influential *La
Feuille du Village* — was printed in Paris; some of this first originated
with the Solidarite Republicaine, which Theodore Bac and the Creusois
mason Martin Nadaud had helped organise.27 De Mentque and his
colleague in the Creuse believed that the propaganda was coming into
the area with the seasonal migrants returning home each autumn.
However, some of the propaganda was printed in Limoges and was in
violation of the law which required that printers sign and deposit
copies of all their work at the Prefecture; if they failed to comply, they
faced enormous fines (up to 5,000 francs) and loss of licence (*brevet*).
A typical pamphlet was 'Gifts of the Democrats, or the Commissioner

of Police of Limoges', written by a socialist lawyer, which describes, with the scenario of an imaginary banquet, the harassment of workers' associations, electoral meetings and *démoc-soc* leaders by the police.[28] To control *démoc-soc* propaganda, Prefects exchanged information, authorised searches of radicals' homes, and helped coordinate the Gendarmerie's efforts to watch the roads into cities like Limoges and the markets and fairs. De Mentque seems to have been more successful than many of his colleagues in other departments, where copies of Félix Pyat's 'Toast to the Peasants' and *démoc-soc* almanacs were as common as copies of official almanacs and government *affiches*

Démoc-soc propaganda also included 'oral' propaganda, 'developed by reading journals out loud, by seditious speeches . . .'[29] Included in this category were electoral meetings, banquets in honour of radical leaders and Representatives, and even discussion in cafés. The various laws against 'clubs' passed by the frightened National Assembly after the June Days, eventually forbade any kind of meeting which could 'compromise the public peace', which gave the Prefect considerable latitude.[30] The laws meant that anyone could be prosecuted for 'inciting one group of citizens against another group', or, at its logical extension, of 'inciting civil war'. After June 1849, de Mentque interpreted the law to forbid, 'in an absolute manner, clubs or public reunions which deliver themselves to the discussion of public affairs'. These laws were applied to meetings preceding the 1850 election, and to banquets celebrating Republican anniversaries or the arrival of Montagnard Representatives. Soapbox orators on market day could be hauled down for almost anything they said. For example, any reference to Robespierre or to the 'democratic and social Republic' could, by law, be interpreted to 'incite one group of citizens against another' by conjuring up memories of 1793 or of June 1848 (the latter case could also be an 'apology for a criminal deed'). What was said was just as liable to prosecution as what was written.

In the Second Republic, the café became a political institution: it was already a social institution. French Prefects viewed the rapid rise in the number of cafés with alarm, not just because cafés were believed to be the ruin of the working classes, but because they were places where ordinary people gathered to read newspapers or to listen to them being read aloud; the *feuilletons*, serialised stories at the bottom of the first page originally included to bolster regular readership, were now quite often political, and the newspaper's editorial and reporting of the national political news could spark political discussion. Cafés came to be identified by their politics as much as by their ambiance in many regions; as in France today, people frequented the same place for years, without ever venturing into a nearby establishment. They were a major problem for Military Division Commanders and many cafés, particularly in the Paris region, had to be placed off limits. From Limoges, de Mentque reported that 'cabarets and cafés have proven to be veritable clubs'.[31] While preferring to leave cafés open rather than closing them (a *mouchard* or a regular Police Commissioner could come up with all sorts of useful information), de Mentque did shut down the Café des Prolétaires (which was written over the door in bright red) because masons returning from Paris distributed propaganda there.[32] Cafés were now places where both *démoc-socs* and police gathered. The *coup d'état* made superfluous a proposed law which would have formally forbidden reading a newspaper in a 'loud voice' and any 'discourse having a political character'.

Formal associations also were suspect in working class Limoges. New laws tightened control over them, ending the halycon period following the 1848 Revolution when associations were even encouraged. In Limoges, the pamphlet 'Gifts of the Democrats . . .' described the harassment of the 'Fraternal Association of Bakers' Apprentices', which was founded in April 1849 and soon failed as a producers' cooperative. The 'Shoemakers Association' seemed to be in the radical tradition of shoemakers in many areas of France; shoemakers helped organise a public subscription for *Le Travailleur* and were implicated in various attempts to subvert the Limoges garrison. One police search (*visite domicilaire*) uncovered some guns and a moderate supply of ammunition *chez les cordonniers*. One Limoges radical who died in Paris on the barricades after the *coup d'état* was in the capital 'on behalf of the shoemakers'.[33] In August 1851, a number of shoemakers were convicted when the court ruled that their association was a 'secret society' intending 'to fortify and spread socialist ideas of the worst variety'. When the *coup* came, de Mentque was in the process of prosecuting the porcelain workers' association. Even the bourgeois masonic lodge 'The Perfect Union' was vulnerable; it was officially dissolved for discussion of 'dangerous political theories', which was not surprising because many of Limoges' radical elite of utopian socialist lawyers were also masons.[34]

At the same time, de Mentque went after the highly visible and active *démoc-soc* leadership, including the Montagnard Representatives who had become almost folk heroes in Limoges where they were identified with the 'interests of the people'. They linked Paris radicalism and *démoc-soc* organisation in Limoges, and Limoges to its hinterland. The Prefect's task was to isolate this radical elite from the *démoc-soc* rank and file, both by limiting their organisational possibilities and challenging their informal authority with propaganda against them as 'socialists' and 'anarchists'. A strong current of populism pervaded the organisational efforts of the Limoges radicals, a missionary spirit, reflected in the following passage from a letter written in prison by one of the convicted leaders of the *Affaire de Limoges*:

'What you tell us of the Haute Vienne and the progress made by the "social" ideas in the countryside fills us with joy. If Jacques Bonhomme can finally understand the Revolution, it will be three-quarters made; it is he, the mistreated, robbed and beaten, who holds the doors to the Republic. He can open or shut them at his will.'[35]

Thus 'order' was carefully developed as an official ideology, closely identified with the person of Louis-Napoleon Bonaparte and less with the figure of the President of the Republic.[36] The identification of the *démoc-soc* leadership with insurrection, turmoil and anarchy was a persistent theme; strong executive authority was posed as the only alternative to the 'disorder' of the *Affaire de Limoges* and the June Days. The official interpretation maintained that the *démoc-socs* were preparing another insurrection. The discoveries of the *Complot de Lyon* and the *Nouvelle Montagne* in other parts of France helped this theme along. Several committees of 'order' (to be distinguished from the Monarchist 'men of order' who shared the same sentiments but had a different solution in mind) operated in Limoges, similar to the Committee of 10 December so belittled by Marx. One was the Central Committee of General Lugnot, an old imperial soldier. Leon Faucher, no stranger to Bonapartist sentiments, addressed this committee in 1849, and his attack upon the Republic was undisguised.

'Hardly had the Republic been declared in the streets of Paris than the government paved the way for attacks on property by giving gifts to the workers of the barricades . . . Socialism began here, as everywhere, by men who I will call the junior officers of the industrial army . . . above all we must fortify authority and place it above all attack.'[37]

A Central Committee circular in 1851 warned of the coming insurrection by the socialists in 1852: 'The *mot d'ordre* is given, posts are assigned, and each soldier of demagogy waits for the sound of the bell which should blot out even the memories of '93.'[38] The Legitimist paper *La Province* proved to be an invaluable, though often unfriendly ally of the Prefect, attacking universal suffrage in 1850 and picturing each arrest for 'seditious cries' as evidence of a massive plot.[39] A 'fear' peaked among the Limoges bourgeoisie in 1851; in June, a series of fires in the woods near the city sparked rumours that 'anarchists' were prepating to rise.[40]

By 1850, the word democrat was used by the administration in the same way as the words 'anarchist' and 'communist'. The cry 'Long live the democratic and social Republic' was illegal; it could be construed as an apology for the 'crimes' of June. 'Long live the Republic!' was considered to be a seditious cry in official reports, although it could not as yet be prosecuted *per se*; it was an indication of the popular attachment to the Republic.[41] Municipal authorities prevented the celebration of 24 February which *La Province*, helping all of the way, described as 'this forever infamous day . . . the day of insurrection, pillage, and violation of all rights . . . a day of mourning which should be scratched from the official calendar.'[42] In February 1851, a Gendarme reported with obvious satisfaction that he had heard some citizens say that 'they could not understand how people could rejoice in having a Republic' and that 'only the nomad workers' wanted it. In 1850, a number of official reports were already referring to the Prince President. Long before the *coup*, the Republic was already dead as far as the administration was concerned.[43]

The *démoc-soc* leaders were closely watched. A number of influential leaders were jailed or exiled during the Second Republic, some for roles in the *Affaire de Limoges*, others for later political offences. This process of skimming off the top of the radical leadership was common in Second Republic France; as Maurice Agulhon has demonstrated in the Var, this led to a popularisation of leadership and less 'bourgeois patronage'.[44] In Limoges, part of the radical leadership managed to survive, both bourgeois elite and two procelain workers, but their organisational possibilities were severely curtailed. It was difficult for them to meet with their followers in the city, or with contacts in the radical towns of St Yrieix and St Léonard in the department. For example, when Martin Nadaud arrived in the city in 1851, gendarmes were present at each of his gatherings, such as his meeting with twenty-five or thirty 'democrats' in a cafe. Police dispersed a meeting that Michel de Bourges, one of the popular Montagnard stars, planned with 200 to 300 workers in a porcelain factory. The same night, another assembly was broken up; it had been organised by Denis Dussoubs, younger brother of the Representative — he had just been released from prison after serving a two year sentence for his active part in the *Affaire de Limoges*. Police also watched the home of Patapy, a socialist lawyer who was organising a 'Democratic Committee' for the 1852 elections.[45] The police seemed to be everywhere and to know everything, leaving no doubt in anyone's mind both about the danger inherent in maintaining contacts with radicals and the determination of the Prefect and the *Procureur Général* to eliminate *démoc-soc* organisational strength in the city.

While de Mentque worked to weaken the *démoc-soc* organisation and its support among the workers, the Ministry of War increased the strength and reliability of the troops stationed in Limoges. The Army became the ultimate force for repression. Two weeks after the

Affaire, three thousand troops entered the city; never again would Limoges have a garrison which could be neutralised as easily as occurred on 27 April 1848.

The workers first protested the presence of so many troops, an occupying army which, at first, had to be quartered in private homes because of inadequate barrack space.[46] Then they began to subvert the garrison, and apparently had some success in so doing. In early 1850, the Sub-Division Commander in Limoges requested that the Minister of War transfer the troops of the Forty-Sixth line regiment because of their long exposure to the socialism of the Limoges workers. Many of the troops were Parisian, from working class districts; most of these had voted for *démoc-soc* candidates in the elections. An incident on 1 April 1850 confirmed the General's fears. When word reached the barracks that three junior officers had been demoted and that three more were to be sent to Africa (usual penalties for *démoc-soc* political opinions), forty soldiers protested and went into the city to find support among the workers, particularly among a group known as the *'sectionnaires'*. All forty were courtmartialled; penalties ranged from death to being sent to Africa (which could amount to the same thing). An investigation led to the discovery of close contacts between the garrison and the workers, particularly porcelain workers and shoemakers, who apparently were offering the troops 'wine, women and journals', if one report is to be believed. A collection was organised for soldiers who would desert or disobey orders. It was clear that the Forty-Sixth line regiment would have to go, and they did.[47] The units which replaced them drawn from less proletarian environments, proved to be more reliable. The Army became the Army of Louis-Napoleon and not of the Republic. Louis-Napoleon's first plebiscite was to the Army in the first days following the *coup*.

The problem of social control in Limoges was further resolved by the 'Volunteers of Haute Vienne', the elite National Guard of the July Monarchy whom the workers disarmed on 27 April 1848, a day they were not likely to forget. The National Guard, now theoretically open to all active citizens, was officially dissolved and never reconstituted, making Limoges the first of more than 100 towns and cities in France to lose its National Guard for political reasons during the Second Republic.[48] The Volunteers received special permission from the Minister of Interior to continue because of their 'excellent composition', as, 'in Limoges, the bourgeois class, the men of order, are in the proportion of one against three or four workers, more or less corrupted by socialism.[49] The Volunteers, once the workers' *quartiers* had been disarmed, held virtually all of the guns not in the garrison. They drilled regularly, perhaps as often as three times a week, and were trained by junior officers from the garrison. A 'census council' maintained the exclusiveness

of the Volunteers by admitting only those citizens 'presenting true
guarantees for the maintenance of order'. The Volunteers formed a
regular part of policing in Limoges, patrolling the workers' districts; an
undated plan of defence against insurrection shows a carefully coordinated sharing of responsibility with the regular troops. Several brawls
reflected the hostility between workers and Volunteers. There was one
court conviction of a newspaper for attacking the Volunteers — *Le
Peuple* ran a *feuilleton* called 'Note Fallen from the Pocket of a
Volunteer of Haute Vienne'. Until the *coup* two thousand bourgeois
Volunteers were an important part of social control in Limoges; they
symbolised the rapid closing of the ranks by the bourgeoisie after
February 1848.[50]

At the time of the *coup d'état*, the *démoc-socs* in Limoges were
looking forward to the elections of 1852 which they thought they
could again win, despite the loss of 3,700 of 9,000 voters in Limoges
because of the law restricting universal suffrage. Haute Vienne was considered a relatively 'safe' department, as the Minister of Interior
surveyed a map of the departments and pinpointed where trouble could
be expected. The *démoc-soc* network, successful in May of 1849, now
consisted of only a few fragments. They might have been able to make
a strong showing in the elections of 1852, but resistance was another
thing. *Démoc-soc* organisational strength was not able to reorganise
underground in 1851, as happened in at least eighteen departments.
The repression worked in Limoges, and the radical links to the rest of
the Haute Vienne were severely weakened.

The Repression in the Arrondissements of Boussac and Bourganeuf (Creuse)

In the rural Creuse, the repression had a somewhat different focus.
Without a major urban centre, there were fewer possibilities of formal
or informal associations which could maintain collective political commitment to the *démoc-soc* cause; the Creuse was also without the forms
of *sociabilité* found, for example, in the Var — certainly the nature of
its population, as will become clear, would make such forms unlikely.
The Creuse was, and still is, one of France's poorest regions, with only
three tiny pockets of industry, in Aubusson and Felletin (textiles, including the famous tapestries) and Bourganeuf (some porcelain production).
The Creuse was a region of bare subsistence agriculture, divided into
small units (almost 60 per cent of all farms were less than ten hectares,
two thirds of these less than five hectares); some of the land was of
such poor quality that herding was the only way to make ends meet.
The inhabitants were two thirds illiterate, debt ridden, and inadequately clothed; their diet reflected their grim poverty, because most ate

222

only a poor quality of rye bread, chestnuts, potatoes and meat only four or five times a year. The Creuse never could support its population, and, as early as the seventeenth century, seasonal migration played a major role in the local economy and gave the region a distinctive character.[52] Looking at statistics for all communes in the Creuse, one finds that seasonal migration was particularly heavy in certain cantons, reaching as high as 60 per cent of the active male labour force. Most seasonal migrants went to France's largest urban centres, particularly Paris, where they usually worked in the construction industry as masons, tilers, stone cutters and day labourers. The patterns of this migration — where migrants went and what they did there — were set in the past century. For example, two small villages, Lépinas in the canton of Ahun and Rougnat in the canton of Auzances (988 and 2,250 people respectively) provided most of the slaters from the Creuse. The village of Alleyrat (canton of Aubusson) sent all of its seasonal migrants to the North, mostly to Paris but also to Troyes and Auxerre, while the sixty-two workers from nearby St Armand went east to Montluçon or Clermont.[53] Martin Nadaud's fascinating memoirs present an unforgettable and graphic view of the life of the seasonal migrants, who returned to the Creuse each November relatively prosperous, and full of tales of the sights, frivolity and dangers of the capital.[54] Paris and Creuse were very different worlds, but the seasonal migrant was very much part of both.

The new Republic depended on the support of the suddenly enfranchised masses; regions like the backward and rural Limousin, for example, were urged to 'force your brothers of the countryside to accept the glorious heritage of your brothers in Paris: the latter shed their blood, the former gave their sweat.'[55] After the February Revolution, Martin Nadaud, seasonal migrant from the Creuse, met with a commission of masons from their home department, became a *clubiste* and returned home as a delegate of the Club of Clubs and as 'candidate and worker', part of the 'list of candidates proposed by the workers and labourers of the Creuse in Paris'.[56] But Nadaud and the other delegates found the going tough in the Creuse. A few clubs had been formed after the Revolution, but they were far more conservative than their names (the *Société Démocratique of Guéret* and its affiliate in Ahun, etc.) would indicate. Active and very small Republican clubs in Bourganeuf and La Souterraine found considerable opposition from their own *co-citoyens*. In Bourganeuf two clubs competed openly for members; one supported the powerful Legitimist journalist Emile de Girardin, the other was a *Club des ouvriers*, led by a school teacher. Martin Nadaud was one of two delegates from Paris run out of town by the textile workers of Aubusson, who accused him of 'having tried to utter communist ideas' and of opposing the philanthropic intentions of the textile magnate Sallandrouze.[57] Revoked officials from the July Monarchy, led by the ex-Prefect, actively worked for a list of conservatives in the April election. The 45 centime tax was indeed a 'calamity, a general frustration and for the elections an immense mistake' which led to considerable local opposition, including one grave incident in which sixteen peasants were killed in a confrontation with the National Guard of Guéret.[58] The election resulted in a split between conservatives and moderate Republicans. Martin Nadaud did well only in the cantons around his home, near Pontarion. The other radical candidates finished far out of the running.[59]

But by May of 1849, Martin Nadaud and the other *démoc-soc* leaders were known everywhere in the Creuse, and had become identified with the interests of the poor. The repression in the Creuse therefore focused on a specific set of problems; an active Montagnard leadership with strong roots and influence in the department, the link which the seasonal migrants formed to Paris radicalism and organisation, and the allies of the *démoc-soc* elite who had been given official functions in their communes by the Provisional Government after the Revolution.

Radical organisation in the *arrondissement* of Boussac centred on the printing presses of the family of Pierre Leroux, whose influence in the region began when he moved to the town of Boussac in 1844.[60] At the first news of the February Revolution, the founder of the 'religion of humanity' was carried triumphantly on the shoulders of the townspeople to the *mairie* and proclaimed mayor. The Leroux presses and the family influence aided the *démoc-socs* in the 1849 election; an estimated 25,000 copies of Jules Leroux's (Pierre's brother) *profession de foi* were circulating in the Creuse. This proclamation was very effective:

'I am of the people. I am a printing worker, living like the poor, the peasants, the workers, my brothers and comrades . . .I have never stopped fighting . . . against the great (*Gros*), the bourgeoisie, the rich, the powerful . . .'[61]

His 'programme' was attractive in the Creuse; he called for the reimbursement of the 45 centimes tax, the abolition of the salt and *boissons* tax, increased pay for school teachers, free justice, a progressive tax, the proclamation of 'work' as the equal of 'property', and amnesty for those still under arrest from the June Days ('the honourable civil war'), a number which included many Creusois — the Creuse, with the Vosges, had the largest number of arrests in the June Days outside the Paris region. A combined proclamation of Leroux, Nadaud, Gustave Jourdain and three other *démoc-socs*, including a 'Ratier, seasonal migrant', was addressed to the 'true electors, peasants and workers'. These circulars, and tracts like Félix Pyat's 'Toast to the Peasants', originated in Boussac.[62]

The Prefect of the Creuse moved against the Leroux *atelier* shortly before the May election, when he ensured that a Leroux application for funds from the three million francs allotted by the National Assembly for developing industrial associations was turned down: the government was not about to subsidise 'the development of antisocial doctrines'.[63] In July, gendarmes searched the workshops hoping to find hidden guns and ammunition. In October several of the printers were tried for assembling people 'for political instruction of the peasants' and for attacking the concept of 'property' in a public place. Leroux's son-in-law was tried for allegedly trying to persuade people to go to Lyon to aid the June 1849 uprising there. All were acquitted; the Procureur complained that no local jury would convict Leroux's people. But Prefect St Amand was able to close another printing shop directed by the Leroux family, in nearby Chambon. Pierre Leroux's *L'Éclaireur* ended during the same year and he left the Creuse in 1850.[64] In October of that year the Commander of the departmental gendarmerie could report that 'the Leroux family no longer appears to hold the same credit; the peasants appear more disposed to follow the counsel of their landlords'.[65]

In the *arrondissement* of Bourganeuf, Martin Nadaud, from Soubrebost in the canton of Pontarion, was 'the flagbearer of the workers of Creuse' and 'candidate of the Committee of Creusois in Paris . . . member of the working party of the department'.[66] Prefect St Amand had to counter his tremendous influence in the *arrondissement*. One way was to limit Nadaud's contacts with his followers in the towns and cillages of the region, by preventing meetings and banquets, watching the activities of his two lieutenants, lawyer Gustave Jourdain and notary Adrien Rouchon, and having Nadaud followed by gendarmes and police spies. There were searches of the homes of Nadaud's relatives and friends.[67] Because Nadaud's influence was assumed to be greatest among the seasonal migrants, the Prefect tried to turn the peasants against Nadaud by opposing their interests to those of the seasonal migrants. *Le Conciliateur*, founded by a committee of 'order' in 1851 with the supervision and support of the Prefect in order to offer an alternative to *démoc-soc* propaganda, warned the peasants:

'What will be in 1852? . . . When Nadaud will have voted in a project which will consist of covering our soil with construction and phalansteries, with the help of a forced tax on two-thirds of revenues? The masons will be able to pay, but the peasants?'[68]

In these campaigns, agricultural progress was always equated with political order. These appeals to the peasants, most of whom had not, in

225

contrast to the Limoges workers to whom less propaganda was directed, lost their vote, were bound to have some impact in the *arrondissement* of Bourganeuf, whose four cantons had relatively (for the Creuse) low percentages of seasonal migration.

There is some evidence that the propaganda which was aimed at the seasonal migrants themselves was successful. Although the Prefect blamed the seasonal migrants for 'the diffusion of the detestable maxims of socialism' because they returned home each November 'perverted by the evil doctrines which they draw from the large centres of population', there was no correlation between high percentages of *démoc-soc* votes in May 1849 and high percentages of seasonal migration. For example, the canton of Evaux in the *arrondissement* of Aubusson had a percentage of migration of the male labour force (active) which was over 60 per cent in 1846; the canton had the lowest percentage of *démoc-soc* votes in 1849.[69] This could indicate that the administration's identification with 'disorder' and economic crisis was already paying off; in 1848, there had been only limited migration because of the Revolution, which came just before the migrants would leave in a normal year. Workers from outside of Paris were not allowed in the National Workshops after the Revolution, and the construction industry was at a standstill. Mayors granted few passports and the Creuse Representatives had to obtain special permission for the seasonal migrants to leave that department in 1849.[70] But the negative correlation reflected in the statistics from the canton cited may also mean that, in 1849, the large number of seasonal migrants had already left for the North, and therefore did not vote. At any rate, when the number of migrants leaving in the spring of 1851 was estimated at between 30,000 and 40,000, the gendarmerie thought that this fact would help the political situation in the Creuse.[71]

And although seasonal migration undoubtedly provided Creusois radicalism with its leadership and exposure to the 'social question' as posed originally in Paris, other factors were involved in the *arrondissements* of Boussac and Bourganeuf. For example, the canton of Bourganeuf gave 59 per cent of its vote in May 1849 to the *démoc-socs* (and only about 10 per cent of its active male labour force migrated seasonally).[72] The concentration of porcelain workers in the town of Bourganeuf and Nadaud's personal influence were important factors. And there is another factor involved in the radicalisation of these two *arrondissements*, even if we cannot precisely determine the relationship between seasonal migration and radical electoral patterns and continuing radical commitment. This is the number of important communal officials who came to power with the Revolution and who seemed to be winning *démoc-soc* converts in their own communes – this argument also lends itself to an 'organisational' explanation for *démoc-soc* success. The Prefect and his Sub-Prefects, aided by the Prefect's almost unlimited power of revocation (rubber-stamped in Paris), had to root out these dangerous *démoc-soc* influences within each commune, minor dramas of accusations, denunciations, *affiches*, and bitter little rivalries being acted out in thousands of French communes.

The administrative structure of each commune was relatively simple and therefore easy to control, once the Ministers of Interior and Justice, through the Prefects and Sub-Prefects, knew who sat at each desk. The Justice of the Peace, whose authority was cantonal, had considerable formal and informal authority in the communes of his canton; ten out of twenty-four of them were new after the Revolution of 1848.[73] In the commune, the position of the mayor and his deputy (*adjoint* — two in the large towns) became important with the Republic; for the first time in the memory of most people, who was mayor actually mattered, and revocations after the Revolution (of 19 per cent of the department's mayors) sometimes left the *mairies* in the hands of what became disloyal servants, who were usually re-elected in the municipal council elections during the summer of 1848. School teachers also seemed to be 'artisans of disorder' in some departments, including the Creuse. Literate in largely illiterate communities, they became interpreters of elections and law, readers of newspapers and pamphlets, instant political counsels — overnight sages. They could wield considerable political influence, for example in communes where they also might serve as the mayor's secretary (making them, not infrequently, the only person in the *mairie* who could read and write). Electoral organisations of school teachers played a more important role in the May 1849 elections than they had in April 1848.[74] Complaints about the political activities of communal officials, then, frequently reached the desks of the Ministers of Justice and Interior (quite often coming from the Ministry of War).

The disloyalty of ten of the forty-two mayors in the *arrondissement* of Bourganeuf who were new in 1848 became a problem for the Prefect.[75] Communes could be divided into two factions, that of the 'revolutionary' mayor and that of the former mayor — revoked officials were usually understandably bitter and hated the Republic deeply. Having a loyal mayor was essential for the administration (and not only the new mayors were disloyal), much more so than in the days of *censitaire* politics, when only a handful of close friends or close enemies voted. The Prefect depended on the mayors to carry out measures of repression, such as enforcing the law of 31 May 1850 which eliminated universal suffrage (which could put the mayor in an awkward position by possibly cutting into his support within his own commune), checking the spread of *démoc-soc* propaganda, and opposing petitions protesting the end of universal suffrage while later helping distribute

227

petitions in favour of the revision of the constitution to extend the presidency of Louis-Napoleon. The push came from above, and if a mayor was disloyal, or even slow or incompetent, he was removed. For example, the mayors of Augères and Royère were revoked because they were friends of Nadaud; the mayor of Soubrebost, Nadaud's commune, was removed for the same reason. If a municipal council elected the revoked mayor a second time, it could be dissolved and new elections for the municipal council held until the right combination could be found.[76]

Take the case of the commune of Sardent in the canton of Pontarion, which had a population of 2,506 in 1846 and sent 300 masons to Paris each year. The July Monarchy mayor was revoked following the February Revolution, and replaced with a local noted 'red Republican', Monsieur Junien. During June, there were disturbances against the 45 centimes tax; yet Junien, Martin Nadaud's friend, was easily re-elected by the new Municipal Council. Junien enthusiastically worked for Nadaud's election; this enthusiasm was his political undoing, for he was revoked on 29 August 1849. He had read an article 'injurious' to Louis-Napoleon at a communal meeting. Three weeks later, the 'socialist' Municipal Council re-elected Junien as the mayor of Sardent. The Council was therefore dissolved, and in the next election the Prefect was able to get a 'more suitable' composition, despite Nadaud's arrival to work for his friend. But Junien's influence in Sardent continued. When Jules Leroux came to the area, he stayed *chez* Junien; gendarmes searched the house. At the end of 1850, the 'spirit' of disorder persisted in the commune, most noticeably in the National Guard, which had elected a *démoc-soc* Commander and even met occasionally. The Minister of Interior dissolved the National Guard of Sardent and ordered it disarmed. But the new mayor, even with the assistance of the Sub-Prefect, never was able to bring 'order' to Sardent — nor was he apparently very efficient. 'Doubtful' voters remained on the rolls for the 1852 elections, which never transpired.[77]

Similar situations existed in the *arrondissement* of Boussac. In the canton of Jarnages, where the *démoc-socs* won an impressive 73.4 per cent of the 1849 vote, thirteen mayors were revoked for political reasons during 1850 and 1851.[78] Two of these had attended a banquet for Nadaud. When the cashiered mayor of Jarnages ville was re-elected by the Municipal Council, the latter was dissolved. The Justice of the Peace of Jarnages, a post-Revolution appointee and friend of Pierre Leroux, was also sacked. He had participated in a 'club' in Boussac after the Revolution and assisted Jules Leroux in the May 1849 campaign. His replacement was a former Justice of the Peace in La Souterraine, who had been removed from office by the Provisional Government. The latter appealed to the Minister of Justice for another position and, like so many officials revoked in March and April 1848, returned to power eager to do battle with the Republic which had humiliated him. No more loyal ally at the local level could be found for Louis-Napoleon Bonaparte.[79]

Beginning late in 1849, the Prefect turned his attention to the school teachers in both *arrondissements*. Three were dismissed in the *arrondissement* of Bourganeuf (again, Royère and Soubrebost included), and two in that of Boussac.[80] These revocations, combined with warnings from Prefects and the regional committees created by the Falloux law to watch over *instituteurs*, helped impose a voluntary limitation on their political activities. Once suspended or revoked, a school teacher's career was finished unless he could be reinstated; there was little chance of his surviving economically in a department like the Creuse. An upgrading of salaries during the Second Republic probably also lessened the commitment of *instituteurs* to the *démoc-soc* cause.

By 1851, the Creuse was no longer considered to be a politically dangerous department. Socialist activity was limited to minor protests during the year against the obvious ebbing of the Republic. All seemed to occur in Bourganeuf, the only town of any size in either *arrondissement*. There were attempts to organise meetings to protest the proposed revision of the constitution; and demonstrations in favour of the Republic on 24 February, when lights were left burning at night to celebrate the birth of a Republic whose government was systematically repressing its primary and most representative institutions. On one occasion, the National Guard of Bourganeuf refused to present arms, and was dissolved and disarmed. All that remained were occasional 'seditious cries' or scattered placards nailed in the night, like 'Long live the democratic and social Republic . . . Down with the Chouans of Boussac'.[81]

The news of the *coup* caught the Limoges *démoc-socs* by surprise. Hurried meetings were organised and finally a confused attempt on 5 December sent about fifty delegates into the countryside to sound the tocsin and organise a massive march on Limoges. A counter-order was soon given, from the house of the lawyer Patapy, because of the discouraging news from Paris, which included the death of Denis Dussoubs on the barricades in the *quartier Limousin*. Only one column of peasants formed, even though the counter-order was too late to stop the delegates; it passed through the villages of St Paul, St Bonnet, and Linards, where the mayor had been revoked and the National Guard dissolved, before being dispersed by a platoon of twenty-five soldiers. There were two other smaller disturbances in Haute Vienne. There were none in Limoges, where the troops and the bourgeois Volunteers kept order.

In the Creuse, the resistance was equally pathetic. Two hundred peasants marched from two communes to Bourganeuf. They were easily disbanded at the outskirts of the town, crying 'Long live the Republic!' for the last time. One small mobilisation, and that was it.[83]

The final stage of the repression followed the *coup d'état* and finished the task of demobilising the last fragments and links of the *démoc-soc* organisation.[84] The Mixed Commissions, which included the Prefect, Procureur, and chief military Commander of each department, tried virtually every remaining radical leader in Haute Vienne and the Creuse. With the Mixed Commissions the evolution from the repression of participants in movements of protest at the beginning of the Republic to the repression of all ideological opposition was complete; those 'considered dangerous for public security' were also tried, even if they were not involved in resistance to or protest against the *coup*. The penalties they received — dominated by two kinds of 'expulsion' from their departments — were indicative of what had made them so dangerous.[85] They had influence locally and were capable organisers.

The key to the *démoc-soc* success during the Second Republic was their organisation; the repression of that organisation made the *coup* possible, despite the fact that in at least seventeen departments the *démoc-socs* had organised into Montagnard secret societies in 1851. The *coup* itself was just the final act, the death rites of the Republic. What we have described for Limoges and the *arrondissements* of Boussac and Bourganeuf occurred all over France — the usefulness of a regional study should tell us about the national scene. The *coup* was inevitable; it was the repression carried to its logical extreme, the institutionalisation of the State of Siege which had already proven the most successful means of demobilising the *démoc-socs* in the Fifth and Sixth Military Division areas, the Lyon region. In November several more departments were also put under the State of Siege. The *coup* put all of France under the same regime, formalised with the Empire. To understand the repression is to understand the Second Republic and what happened to it.[86] The repression accomplished its task, effectively eliminating the most organised and therefore the most dangerous challengers to the authority of Louis-Napoleon Bonaparte.

Notes

Thanks to Robert Bezucha, Suzanna Barrows and Roger Geiger for comments on an earlier draft.

1.   Maurice Agulhon, *La République au village* (Paris, Plon, 1970); Philippe Vigier, *La Seconde République dans la Région Alpine*, 2 vols (Paris, Presses Universitaires de France, 1963); Leo A. Loubère, 'The Emergence of the Extreme Left in the Lower Languedoc, 1848-51: Social and Economic Factors in Politics',

American Historical Review, 73, 4 (April, 1968), pp. 1019-51; and Christianne Marcilhacy, 'Les caractères de la crise sociale et politique de 1846 à 1852 dans le département du Loiret', *Revue d'histoire moderne et contemporaine*, 6 (jan.-mars 1959), pp. 5-59. There are, of course, many others of varying quality, too numerous to cite here.

2.   Charles Tilly and Lynn Rees, 'The People of June, 1848', in this volume, pp. 170-211.

3.   Charles Tilly, 'How Protest Modernised in France, 1845-1855', in William O. Aydelotte, Allan G. Bogue and Robert William Fogel, eds., *The Dimensions of Quantitative Research in History* (Princeton, Princeton University Press, 1972), p. 235.

4.   Ted W. Margadant, 'The Insurrection of 1851', unpublished manuscript, chapter 8, pp. 2-3.

5.   Karl Marx, *The Eighteenth Brumaire of Louis Napoleon Bonaparte* (New York, International Publishers, 1963), pp. 70-1, 125, etc.; Howard C. Payne, 'Preparation of a *Coup d'État*', in F. J. Cox *et al., Studies in European History in Honor of F. C. Palm* (New York, Bookman Associates, 1966), and *The Police State of Louis Napoleon Bonaparte* (Seattle, University of Washington Press, 1966). The best treatment of the repression is J. Dagnan's essential but largely forgotten *Le Gers sous la Seconde République* (Auch: Imprimerie Brevetée, 1928-9), 2 vols.

6.   Ted W. Margadant, *op. cit.*; and 'The Insurrection of 1851 in Southern France' Two Case Studies [Drôme and Isère]' (unpublished Ph.D. dissertation, Harvard University, 1972).

7.   I am currently writing a general study of the repression, which includes a number of departments as examples; this project began with 'Radicalization and Repression: The Experience of the Limousin, 1848-1851' (unpublished Ph.D. dissertation, University of Michigan, 1972), from which much of the material in this essay has been drawn.

8.   John M. Merriman, 'Social Conflict in France and the Limoges Revolution of April 27, 1848', *Societas — A Review of Social History* IV, 1 (winter, 1974), pp. 21-38.

9.   *Le Peuple*, 31 May 1848.

10.   *Ibid.*, 27 May 1848.

11.   Archives Nationales (hereafter AN), BB[30] 361, dossier 1, piece 63, letter of the Procureur General of Limoges (hereafter, PGL) to the Minister of Justice (MJ), 29 April 1849.

12.   Municipal Council minutes (*Hôtel de ville* de Limoges); *Le Peuple*, 9 May 1848; and Ernest Vincent, 'Les Ateliers Nationaux à Limoges', *Bulletin de la Société Archéologique et Historique du Limousin*, 83 (1951), pp. 336-44. The Municipal Council minutes for 8 December 1848 show that the workshops cost the city 268,189.55 francs up until that date.

13.   *L'Ordre*, 1 August 1848. The *démoc-socs* were frequently described by *L'Ordre* and *La Province* (Orléanist and Legitimist respectively) as 'demagogues', men of 'ambition' and 'envy'. These terms applied to anyone who would try to agitate the masses and undercut the 'natural' leaders of society, whose abilities had provided them with large fortunes; a society in which the 'natural' leaders could not lead was a conservative's working definition of 'anarchism'.

14.   *Le Peuple*, 2 November and 3 December 1848. Voting in Haute Vienne was as follows: Louis Napoleon, 53,522; Cavaignac, 3,566; Ledru-Rollin, 1,737; Raspail, 882; and Lamartine, 114. The cantons of Limoges gave 692 votes to Raspail, 594 to Ledru-Rollin, and 43 to Lamartine.

15.   Marcel Dussoubs-Gaston, a lawyer from St Léonard, was also a utopian socialist with a thick dossier in the Prefecture because of his political activities

during the July Monarchy; Laclaudure helped organise the Société Populaire; Daniel Lamazière became mayor of St Léonard and founded a club there after the Revolution; Coralli began as a moderate Republican, and became radical; and Frichon the elder, with Bac, the most prominent opposition activist during the July Monarchy, Laclaudure and Michel de Bourges, defended the accused from the Affaire de Limoges at Poitiers. The seven *démoc-socs* won easily.

16. *La Province*, 18 May 1849.
17. AN, F^{1b} I, Titot to Minister of Interior (henceforth, Int.), 19 August 1848; also letter of 30 December 1848; Archives Départementales de la Haute Vienne (Limoges, hereafter, ADHV), M 2 (former *côte* number, since changed). The Legitimist paper *L'Avenir National* attacked Titot in its last issue, 26 August 1848.
18. ADHV, M 2. De Mentque's fortune was listed at 11,500 francs.
19. AN, ADXIX^i Haute Vienne 7, Prefect's proclamation of 23 January 1849. I am not using the categorisation 'Limoges bourgeoisie' uncritically: there are problems with such general class analyses, but in Limoges, the 'bourgeoisie' corresponded to an economic and social reality, as well as to a definite mentality.
20. AN, BB^{30} 361, dossier 2, piece 152; Antoine Perrier, 'Un journal Limogeois pendant la Révolution de 1848', *Bulletin de la Société Archéologique et Historique du Limousin*, 96 (1969), pp. 177-87. *Le Peuple* published its last issue in 1848 in late June.
21. *Le Carillon Républicain*, 11 July 1848.
22. ADHV, M 926, Int. to Prefect of Haute Vienne (PHV), 20 October 1849.
23. AN, BB^{18} 1470 C, A 6701, PGL to MJ, 27 November 1849 and 21 March 1850; *Le Carillon Républicain*, 15 November 1849; and AN, BB^{20} 150, 2nd trimester, *Cour d'Assises de la Haute Vienne*. One of the other editors was a defrocked priest from the St Léonard area, an unsuccessful candidate in the 1849 elections.
24. AN, BB^{18} 1470 C, A 6701, by virtue of the law of 11 August 1848, as described in PGL to MJ, 7 January 1850; AN, F^{18} 263, PHV report on the press, 15 September 1850.
25. AN, BB^{18} 1470 C, A 6701, PGL to MJ, 2 and 7 February 1850. Ducoux was the candidate of the Democratic Committee of Haute Vienne, and won by 29,615 votes to 26,651 (AN, C 1335); de Mentque allegedly threatened to cut off a public works project if the workers did not vote for Bataille.
26. AN, BB^{30} 372, piece 178, PGL to MJ, 21 November 1851; *Le Travailleur*, 14, 22 and 28 November 1851. The paper announced that it would appear weekly 'and more often if it can'.
27. AN, BB^{30} 378, dossier 6, piece 2, PGL to MJ, 31 December 1848; BB^{18} 1449, A 3160, PGL to MJ, 13 May 1850; and Archives du Ministère de la Guerre (Vincennes, henceforth AG), F^1 40, report on Solidarité Républicaine, November 1848. The law of 27 July 1848 (especially article 6) was used to control the hawking and peddling of propaganda.
28. AN, BB^{18} 1449, A 3160, PGL to MJ, 26 May 1850; AN, BB^{18} 1470, A 6701, PGL to MJ, 9 January 1850.
29. AN, BB^{18} 1481, A 8169, MJ to Int., 21 November 1851.
30. AN, ADXIX^i Haute Vienne 7, Prefect's proclamation of 15 July 1849.
31. AN, BB^{18} 1481, A 8169, MJ to Int., 21 November 1851.
32. *Le Peuple*, 9 April 1849. The most interesting and complete reports I have seen on the political role of cafés are in Archives Départementales de la Haute Garonne, 4M 70; two cafés were closed in Toulouse and the remainder of the *démoc-soc* establishments closely watched.
33. AN, BB^{18} 1470, A 6701, PGL to MJ, 9 January 1850; AN, BB^{30} 372^B, piece 178, PGL to MJ, 21 May 1850; and Pierre Couxteix, 'L'action ouvrière en Haute Vienne sous la Seconde République', *Bulletin*, 84 (1954), p. 510. A letter

from a shoemaker to a soldier in the Limoges garrison included the following: 'I will tell you also that everything is in the state of agitation . . . the people await any *coup d'état*. Oh! That he finally shows himself! We have waited long enough with impatience! No one moves. I cannot believe it. Poor Republic, you have been beaten enough . . .' This reflects the bravado of at least one shoemaker, prepared to defend the Republic if there was a *coup*; but there is no indication that there was a true secret society in the Limousin or any sort of plan for an uprising in 1852.

34.   The role of the masonic lodges during the Second Republic is unclear; the only real source is a small pamphlet *La Franc Maçonnerie Limousine* by the lodge 'Les artistes réunis' (Limoges, 1949). The dissolved lodge had about sixty members; another in the city had seventy-five. Pierre Leroux was initiated in 'Les artistes réunis' on 4 April 1848 and several *professions de foi* of electoral candidates were read there.

35.   AN, BB[18] 1449, A 3160, a letter dated 8 February 1850.

36.   The popular appeal of the Napoleonic heritage should never be underestimated; even during the July Monarchy the *feuilletons*, or serials, of newspapers often dealt with the Napoleonic era and its glories. There were many veterans of Napoleon's campaigns still alive (noticeably in the gendarmerie, which is important) and Napoleonic bric-à-brac could be found in many homes.

37.   ADHV, M 163, 'Speech of Léon Faucher, made at the reception given him by the Central Committee of Haute Vienne, 20 October 1849'. This speech was printed and distributed.

38.   ADHV, M 163, dated 30 May 1851.

39.   For example, *La Province*, 20 January 1850.

40.   AG, F[1] 45, Commander of the Thirteenth Military Division to the Minister of War, 1 June 1851.

41.   For example, AG, F[1] 38, Commander of the Sub-Division of Haute Vienne to the Commander of the 13th Mil. Div., 20 October 1851. There was earlier considerable correspondence between various Procureurs and the Minister of Justice over whether to add 'social' to 'Long live the Republic' was a crime. It was determined that it was.

42.   *La Province*, 19 February 1849.

43.   AG, F[1] 41 bis, Commander of the 11th Gend. to Minister of War, 25 February 1851.

44.   Maurice Agulhon, *op. cit.*, pp. 479-80.

45.   AG, F[1] 46 bis, Commander of 11th Gend. to Minister of War (MG), 25 August 1851; AG, F[1] 48, reports of Commander of 11th Gend., 3, 4 and 7 October 1851, and report of Commander of 13th Mil. Div. to MG, 6 October 1851; AN, BB[30] 378, dossier 7, piece 17, 4 October 1851.

46.   AG, F[1] 7, Commander of 15th Mil. Div. to MG, 25 May 1848.

47.   AG, F[1] 33, Commander 13th Mil. Div. to MG, 4 and 21 April 1850; AG, F[1] 34, letter of 24 May 1850; AG, F[1] 37, MG to PHV, 14 September 1850; AN, BB[23] 66, register number 6166, PG of Riom to MJ, 1 February 1851; AN, BB[30] 361, dossier 1, piece 123, PGL to MJ, 4 April 1850; AN, BB[30] 378, dossier 6, piece 9, PGL to MJ, 8 May 1850. The soldiers were condemned 31 May 1850 and the condemnation confirmed on 4 June 1850, although at least one of the death sentences was reprieved. A *démoc-soc* lawyer and five workers were also tried and convicted.

48.   AN, F[9] 423, 'Gardes Nationales, dissolutions, suspensions et révocations d'officiers'.

49.   ADHV,Annex, R 196, Mayor of Limoges to PHV, 22 July 1851 and AN, F[9] 733, PHV to Int., 3 June 1849.

50.   *Le Peuple*, 11 February 1849; *L'Ordre*, 9 July 1848; ADHV Annex, R
196, Int. to PHV, 7 June 1849; AN, BB[18] 1470 C, A 6701, PGL to MJ, 16
February 1849; AN, BB[18] 1474A, PGL to MJ, 4 February 1849; and AN, BB[20]
147, 2nd trimester, Haute Vienne.
51.   AN, F[1c] III Haute Vienne, piece 68, PHV to Int., 10 May 1850.
52.   Albert Démangeon, 'La Montagne dans le Limousin', *Annales de Géo-
graphie*, XX (1911), pp. 316-37; Abel Chatelain, 'Les migrations temporaires
françaises au XIXe siècle', *Annales de démographie historique* (1967), pp. 9-28;
A. Corbin, 'Migrations temporaires et société rurale aux XIXe siècle: le cas du
Limousin', *Revue Historique*, 246 (octobre-décembre, 1971), pp. 293-334;
statistics on unit size from *Statistique de la France*, Deuxième Série, XII
(Strasbourg, 1870), p. 6.
53.   Archives Départementales de la Creuse (hereafter ADCr), 6M 250 and 6M
7.
54.   Martin Nadaud, *Les mémoires de Léonard, ancien garçon maçon* (Paris,
Librairie Charles Delagrave, 1912).
55.   *Le Peuple*, 18 March 1848.
56.   Martin Nadaud, *op. cit.*, p. 194; ADCr, 3M 123, *profession de foi* of
Martin Nadaud. He added, as 'candidate and worker', that 'this title which,
hardly a month ago, would have brought a smile of contempt to the lips of the
privileged electors, far from being a motive of exclusion today, should bring
success'.
57.   AN, C 938, dossier 1, piece 260, letter of 10 April (to the President of
the Club of Clubs, Citoyen Longepied), and piece 365, letter of 14 April.
58.   AN, C 938, dossier 3, report of delegate Ratier to Citizen Longepied,
n.d.; Jacques Levron, *Une révolte de contribuables [1848]* (Paris, 1936); AN,
BB[30] 361, dossier 1, pieces 29-49.
59.   AN, C 1325, for exact results; Nadaud finished eleventh.
60.   ADCr, 4M 72, Prefect of the Creuse (hereafter PCr) to Int., 6 May 1847,
3 March and 16 June 1845, Int. to PCr, 28 March 1845; Pierre Félix Thomas,
Pierre Leroux: sa vie, son oeuvre, sa doctrine (Paris, Alcan, 1904), p. 84.
61.   Bibliothèque Nationale, Le[70] 348, '*profession de foi*' of Jules Leroux.
62.   ADCr, 3M 124, and *ibid.*
63.   AN, F[12] 4618, 'General state of workers' associations'; ADCr, 4M 72,
Minister of Agriculture and Commerce to PCr, 9 April 1849 and 5 March 1850.
64.   AG, F[1] 17, five days report, 1-5 July 1849; AN, BB[20] 147, Creuse, 2nd
and 4th trimesters; AN, BB[30] 378, dossier 6, piece 4, PGL to MJ, 8 February
1850; and ADCr, 4M 72, Pierre Leroux to PCr, 31 August 1849 and PCr to
Min. of Ag. and Commerce, 5 March 1850.
65.   AG, F[1] 38, Commander of Gendarmerie of Boussac to MG, 8 October
1850.
66.   Bibliothèque Nationale, Le[70] 278, '*profession de foi*' of Martin Nadaud.
67.   ADCr, 1m 157, Sub-Prefect of Aubusson to PCr, 1 December 1849; AG,
F[1] 46 bis, Commander of Gend. Creuse to MG, 29 August 1851; AG, F[1] 49,
Commander 11th Gend. to MG, 26 October 1851; AG, F[1] 41 bis, Commander
of Gend. of Bourganeuf to MG, 28 February 1851.
68.   *Le Conciliateur*, 23 October 1851; the paper also announced the formation
of a 'committee of order' like that in Limoges.
69.   Compiled from ADCr, 6M 250 and Jacques Bouillon, 'Les élections
législatives du 13 mai, 1849 en Limousin', *Bulletin*, 84 (1954), pp. 467-96.
70.   AN, ADXIX[i] Creuse 7, February 1849.
71.   AG, F[1] 44, Commander of Gend. of Guéret to MG, 5 May 1851.
72.   See n. 69.
73.   ADHV Annex, 3U 50 *trois*.

74.   See, for example, Alfred Cobban, 'The Influence of the Clergy and the "instituteurs primaires" in the French Constituent Assembly of April 1848', *English Historical Review*, 57, 227 (July, 1942), pp. 334-44; AN, F[17] 9313, 'Rapport sur la situation de l'instruction primaire en 1849'; AN, BB[18] 1484, A 8556; and J. Dagnan, *Le Gers sous la Seconde République*, I, pp. 299-306.

75.   ADCr, 1M 147 and 3M 184.

76.   ADCr, 3M 184 and AN, F[1c] III Creuse 5, PCr to Int., 31 October 1850.

77.   ADCr, 6M 250 and 6M 7 (census), 3M 215 to 258 (Sardent), 255, PCr to Int., 17 July 1849; AG, F[1] 8, Commander of Gend. Creuse to MG, 14 June 1848, AG, F[1] 46 bis, Commander 11th Gend. to MG, 26 August 1851; AG, F[1] 49, Commander 11th Gend. to MG, 1 September 1851; AG, F[1] 39, Commander of Gend. of Bourganeuf to MG, 3 November 1850 and Int. to MG, 18 November 1850.

78.   ADCr, 1M 165 and 3M 185; AG, F[1] 9, MG to Int., 30 June 1849.

79.   AN, BB[8] Parrot, Justice of the Peace of Boussac (personal dossier).

80.   AN, ADXIX[i] 7 Creuse, 10 September 1849; see n. 74.

81.   AN, BB[20] 150, Creuse, 2nd trimester, 1850; AG, F[1] 41 bis, Commander of Gend. Bourganeuf to MG, 28 February 1851 and 4 August 1851; and BB[30] 361, dossier 1, piece 89, MG to MJ, 14 December 1849.

82.   John M. Merriman, 'Radicalization and Repression: The Experience of the Limousin, 1848-51', pp. 190-8, drawn principally from AN, BB[30] 397; AG, F[1] 51; AN, BB[30] 396; AN, BB[30] 401; and AG, F[1] 52-3. See also August Pillou, *Le Coup d'état du 2 décembre, 1851 en Limousin* (Limoges, 1968). Eugène Ténot, *La Province en décembre, 1851* (Paris, 1868) ignores the resistance in the Limousin; Howard C. Payne, *The Police State of Louis Napoleon Bonaparte*, erroneously indicates that there are no reports available from the Creuse and Corrèze (p. 36).

83.   Merriman, 'Radicalization and Repression', pp. 198-9; account is drawn from AN, BB[30] 396, piece 440, and BB[30] 401.

84.   *Le Travailleur* was formally banned; two cafés in Limoges were closed down and four workers' associations dissolved; four Justices of the Peace in Haute Vienne and one in the Creuse were revoked, along with an unknown number of mayors (forty-five in neighbouring Corrèze). See Merriman, 'Radicalization and Repression', pp. 202-4.

85.   *Ibid.*, pp. 205-11; sources, AG, B 266 and 276, and AN, BB[30] 401, piece 583. One hundred and thirty-two people were tried by the Mixed Commission for Haute Vienne and seventy-three in the Creuse; a total of five were sent to Cayenne, thirty-five to Algeria, and seventy-six expelled from France or from their department (all from Haute Vienne).

86.   Ted W. Margadant, 'The Insurrection of 1851', chapter 7, n. 44 estimates the strength of the Montagnard secret societies by communes in the following departments: Basses Alpes, Hautes Alpes, Ardèche, Bouches-du-Rhone, Drôme, Gard, Hérault, Pyrénées Orientales, Var, Vaucluse, Allier, Cher, Nièvre, Yonne, Gers, Lot-et-Garonne and Tarn.

MASKS OF REVOLUTION: A STUDY OF POPULAR CULTURE DURING THE SECOND FRENCH REPUBLIC

Robert J. Bezucha
Northwestern University

The legally authorised holiday of the Second Republic was the anniversary of its proclamation on 4 May 1848. The February days were commemorated with prayers not parades, as public officials throughout France attended requiem masses for the souls of those who had died on both sides of the barricades. Gathered in an auberge in the village of Châteldon (Puy-de-Dôme) in 1851, a group of citizens decided 'qu'il faudrait fêter l'anniversaire du 24 février 1848'. Their initial plan, to plant an (by then) illegal Liberty Tree in the public square was abandoned when they were seen by a neighbour in the forest. Then someone had another idea. As the Procureur General of Riom later wrote:[1]

'As the Mass ended, inoffensive groups gathered on the square. But soon one saw ten or twelve young men . . . leading a young man named Rivet, who was costumed *en Paillasse*, that is to say, dressed in white from head to foot, as they promenaded through the streets of Châteldon. Chambriard, Goutard, Planche, and Maziour wore red cravats which fell to their knees. Chambriard had a rope around Rivet's neck; Planche held him by the cravat with an agricultural tool called a *pigot*; his hands were rudely tied behind his back. In this condition Rivet was dragged to a well where they threatened to drop him in. Then, arriving on the public square, they pretended to hit him with brooms and sticks; and finally they brought him before an oven into which they appeared disposed to throw him. The gendarme adds that five of these persons feigned to torture Rivet.'

Planting a Liberty Tree seems to us a comprehensible way to celebrate the anniversary of the February days because it involves a recognisable political symbol, but the meaning of the parody of drowning, assault and burning is obscure. This is the case because, as Clifford Geertz observes, 'meaning varies according to the pattern of life by which it is informed' and the mimeodrama at Châteldon took place within a 'universe of symbolic action' with which we are unfamiliar.[2] In order for us to understand how the participants associated such behaviour with the idea of a fête we must use the Procureur's letter as an anthropologist might interpret a field note prepared by a distant colleague. The incident becomes more intelligible, I believe, with the additional fact that 24 February 1851 fell during the Lent Carnival (*Carême-Carnaval*) cycle at a time when village youths were preparing their traditional Mardi Gras and Ash Wednesday masquerades. The spectators understood the meaning of the parody because they and the actors shared the same patterns of life. Our task is to learn enough about them to understand it also.

In his impressive study of the Var during the first half of the nineteenth century Maurice Agulhon has traced a double evolution in village society: from traditional to progressive in political life and from *folklore* to modernity in daily life. These phenomena were parallel but did not move at the same velocity, so that when villagers sought to express an advanced political idea it was often within the context of a local folkloresque event.[3] Such 'marriages of politics and *folklore*', as Agulhon has called them elsewhere,[4] are the subject of this essay. Applying French ethnographical studies of the *Carême-Carnaval* cycle to the reports of the Procureurs Generaux (BB[30]) in the Archives Nationales, I shall examine a number of incidents officially classified as *affaires politiques* that occurred on Mardi Gras and Ash Wednesday during the Second Republic. The Procureurs' accounts are unusually rich in detail, and I have intentionally quoted them at length so that readers can look for levels of 'meaning' that I may have omitted or missed altogether.

Carnival was traditionally a time when the residents of a community stretched the limits of tolerated behaviour and local authorities were always concerned to make clear what would and would not be allowed. An *Ordonnance concernant les masques pendant le carnaval* from Toulouse in 1833 tells us about the kind of trouble expected in an ordinary year:[5]

'Each individual who appears masked or disguised in the streets . . . can carry neither a stick nor a weapon of any kind. It is forbidden to take a disguise analogous to any cult or which would be of a nature to trouble public order or cause a scandal. It is forbidden for any masked person, either on foot or on horseback, to be in the streets . . . after sundown . . . No one, under the pretext of masking, is permitted any sort of insult or provocation . . . toward another person, or to throw ashes or bran or any other object which could be injurious . . . It is equally forbidden to provoke or insult persons, who are masked, costumed, or disguised.'

Where the news of the February Days in Paris had already rubbed the nerves of villagers raw, the high jinks of carnival could take a serious turn. In March 1848, the Procureur General of Montpellier reported an incident near Narbonne:[6]

'There exists in Fleury, as in almost all other communes, two parties which cannot be distinguished by political nuance; these are rivalries of family and locality. Since the last revolution nothing has changed in the administration and M. le maire has continued to govern. Although his adversaries had witnessed a desire that a provisional commission be constituted at Fleury as elsewhere, they had not taken any hostile action to achieve it. Around eight o'clock on Tuesday evening, at the end of the libations of Carnival day, when spirits were heated, a crowd composed of around 150 or 200 persons gathered under the windows of the mairie and raised tumultuous cries against the authorities. M. le maire was in the mairie along with ten members of the National Guard and several of his friends. When members of the crowd invaded the staircase on their way to debate with him, the mayor became alarmed and ordered the National Guard to oppose this manifestation.'

The crowd withdrew, shouting 'A bas le maire! Nous ne voulons pas le maire!', and the eventual result was the establishment of a 'mixed commission', as the Procureur put it, 'divided with half in each of the local parties'. At Fleury, in other words, the local revolution in 1848 was carried out behind the masks of carnival.

Where municipal upheavals brought village radicals to power, the celebration of carnival the next year might become a theatrical extension of revolutionary politics. In Paulham (Hérault) in 1849, a majority of the municipal council was composed of agricultural day labourers and, according to the Procureur General, the town drummer was sent to accompany the *Société des Montagnards* on its nocturnal forays to harass the local 'men of order'. For the carnival parade that year the adjoint mayor donned a red burnous, arranged its hood to resemble a Phrygian bonnet, and hung a medallion set with a portrait of Barbès around his neck. Carrying a trident in his hand (Paulham was near the seacoast) he marched about, proclaiming, 'Je vais à la peche aux blancs' and 'Je porte Dieu sur ma poitrine'. When a citizen watching the procession refused to kiss the medallion, he was struck on the head with a bottle wielded by a member of the municipal council costumed in his son's red choir robe. In this case the masquerade did not represent the customary chance to mock established institutions such as the Church, to enjoy a *monde à l'envers* for a single day; rather, for the 'men of order' in Paulham the Second Republic itself was the world turned upside down.[7]

And where the notables were still strong, the carnival of 1849 was an opportunity for *le peuple* to deliver a thinly veiled message. In Narbonne, for example:[8]

'A troupe of maskers, carrying a mannequin dressed like the light cavalry of the National Guard, threw it into the river from the heights of a bridge after first pretending to decapitate it. No one could doubt the meaning of this act; its authors wanted to show publicly the hatred they have for a light cavalry company of the National Guard formed from the elite of Narbonne's society.'

It was incidents such as these that made mayors so apprehensive about the approach of carnival once the systematic repression had begun. Some learned, however, that it was dangerous to tamper with customary behaviour. On Mardi Gras (5 March) 1851, the mayor of the commune of Brou (Eure et Loir) reacted to a rumour that 'a rather large number of individuals proposed to take advantage of the liberty of carnival to make an anarchistic demonstration' by cancelling the next day's procession. That evening, a masked and costumed crowd gathered in the town square 'where they burned a mannequin representing Mardi Gras'. Attached to the dummy were symbols of the land surveyor's trade (the mayor's profession), copies of the conservative *Le Journal de Chartres*, and two small white flags. When the mayor and the local gendarmes arrived on the scene, the crowd began to chant 'Vive la République! A bas les aristos! A bas les blancs! A bas le maire!' In spite of the fact that the Prefect supported the mayor's decision, a majority of Brou's municipal council subsequently resigned to demonstrate a loss of confidence in his judgement.[9]

If we cannot either verify or disprove the rumours, the evidence suggests that this *affaire politique* was not the result of some seditious plot and was caused by the last minute cancellation of a popular local event. Masks and costumes had already been made or taken out of the family trunk and the young people of Brou had prepared a mannequin as they had each year for as long as anyone could remember. Rather than waste their effort, the villagers put these traditional materials to use, adding a statement about the mayor by means of other objects readily at hand — a compass and plumb line, some newspapers, and a piece of white cloth. Official fear had politicised the fête.

The year before, the mayor of Pézénas (Hérault) had refused to authorise any parades after Ash Wednesday. Nevertheless, on the evening of Friday, 15 February 1850, a masked band 'preceded by an individual carrying an emblematic mannequin representing Carnival and destined to be drowned' danced through the streets singing 'democratic and burlesque songs'. One person was stabbed and the police were beaten when they attempted to make arrests.[10] Were the local 'Reds' behind this incident? It seems unlikely, since attempts by village youths to extend carnival celebrations into the Lenten period were a familiar form of collective deviant behaviour in rural France.[11]

A similar collision between *folklore* and political repression occurred

239

in the same region in February 1851. 'The custom exists in the country-side of this department,' wrote the Procureur General of Montpellier, 'to give a *charivari* to widows or widowers who have married a second time.' The authorities ordinarily 'shut their eyes' (or their ears) to such carousing, but the mayor of one commune decided to ban them as a threat to public order. Accordingly, when he and the local gendarmes tried to break up a *charivari*, they were assaulted by the young farm-hands who were beating on pots and pans and shouting sexual remarks under a villager's window.[12]

The Prefects and Procureurs almost always spoke of prosecution for such *affaires politiques*, but where we know the results of actual trials, it appears that acquittal was common. The representatives of the Paris government — educated men observing the activities of rural citizens — were either ignorant of or chose to forget that 'public outcry' (*vindicte publique*) was an established part of the ritual of carnival. They sounded horrified that these imagined, innocent festivals were being polluted by 'politics'. For example, when a group of men dressed in red lead a group of men dressed in white in a procession, the Procureur General of Riom said they had transformed 'the common, inoffensive travesties of Mardi Gras into a menacing, bloodthirsty parade'.[13]

For all the talk of 'the indignant alarm of honest folks',[14] the residents of the towns and villages themselves proved to be more tolerant. 'Although composed in the great majority of men of order,' wrote the Procureur General of Montpellier in explaining an acquittal, 'the jury chose to see in the events only the character of a carnival scene.'[15] With regard to another, he lamented: 'The Court considered it only a masquerade excused by the follies of the last days of carnival.'[16] As rough and frightening as these burlesques often were, they were generally accepted by villagers who knew in their bones what the ethnographer Arnold Van Gennep has to remind us: that carnival was characterised by 'the temporary suspension of the rules of normal collective life . . . One profits from this period of traditional license to mock the constraints of the State and the Government to which the collectivity submits in normal times . . .'[17] When political repression depended upon the cooperation of the rural community, in other words, it ran foul of custom.

The nature of the incidents discussed to this point has allowed us to remain as spectators and to consider them principally as problems for harried officials. We have seen enough, however, to recognise the same three elements that Edward Thompson has found in the behaviour of eighteenth century English crowds: a tradition of anonymous protest, the use of theatrical symbolism, and a capacity for swift, direct action.[18] Let us keep them in mind as we now join the fête. Our attempt to interpret the 'meaning' of the five case studies which follow will be made within the context of regional carnival customs and the political evolution of the Second Republic.

1.   The first is from Uzès (Gard) in 1849:[19]

'February 21 was Ash Wednesday. On this day in the Midi of France, the young people belonging to the popular class [*la classe du peuple*] are accustomed to hold a burlesque divertissement whose theme is the burial of Carnival. They cover or blacken their faces, don bizarre costumes, arm themselves with kitchen bellows, and go through the streets of the town, one after the other, each trying to use the bellows on the person in front of him. At the head of the procession, they carry a mannequin called *Carimantran* (*carême entrant* [the arrival of Lent]), which they dance around at each stop and end by throwing into the water.

This year its authors, since they belong to the Legitimist party, have not neglected to give the festivities a significance which was insulting to the Republic. In place of a bellows each of them carried a broom, and at a given signal they all began to sweep, raising a cloud of dust, while at the same time singing a song called "The Song of the Sweeps".

But what gave the parody an extremely clear meaning was another, smaller group of persons preceding the sweepers and who, by the various emblems they wore, obviously represented the Republic. One of them rode a wretched nag and held a dirty tricoloured flag which from time to time he let trail on the ground behind him.

From time to time the sweepers would draw close to this flag bearer, pretending to hit him with their brooms and to force him to descend and give his place to another. In addition, five or six persons on foot and wearing clothing of various colours, in contrast to the completely white costumes of the sweepers, marched in front of them with an issue of the journal *La Réforme* displayed on their chests. Thus, it seemed that the white troupe was sweeping away the tricolored flag and those gathered around it.'

This *danse des soufflets* (or *bouffets*) resembled the Ash Wednesday snake dances such as the *danse de la chemise* and the *danse du feu aux fesses* of other southern French towns. Probably a parody of the religious processions of the *pénitents*, in each of them youths dressed in women's petticoats or nightshirts amused the spectators by attempting to catch the person in front of him, whether to set his skirts on fire or to squirt him with ashes.[20] What made the carnival in Uzès in 1849 an event of historical significance was the trouble caused by the conscious alteration of an established ritual; the ethnographers Daniel Fabre and Jacques Lacroix refer to this process as 'the mechanism of

241

improvisation' in the celebration of a fête.[21]

From the Camisard wars of the seventeenth century to the White Terror of the Restoration, the Gard department had been the scene of recurrent religious conflict. The Protestant elite of Uzès had gained control of the town's administration and National Guard as a result of the Revolution of 1830. The fall of their co-religionist, Guizot, in 1848 handed power locally to their old enemies, the poor Catholic majority. Although the new officials professed allegiance to the Second Republic, the Protestants feared that a third restoration of the Bourbons was in the wings. For this reason, many of them became supporters of the 'democratic and social Republic' as a means of opposing a government they distrusted.

Religion, politics, and social structure were inextricably entwined in Uzès. In fact, the Procureur first reported the carnival trouble in 1849 with the news that persons from 'the Republican café' had assaulted 'a farandole composed of Catholics' with billiard cues.[22] In retaliation the following day, there was rioting in which bands of Catholic youths attacked the homes and business places of local Protestants.

The Revolution of 1848 everywhere opened cleavages along lines of pre-existing strain and in this case the result was a popular demonstration by the Right against an elite on the Left. The costumes of the sweepers were customary, but the colour white also symbolised the legitimist, Catholic party. Their dance was a familiar one, but by substituting their brooms for bellows and adding a tricoloured flag and a few copies of La Réforme, the theme of the parody was no longer the burial of Carnival, rather the burial of the Republic. Fuelled by social and religious rivalries, the mechanism of improvisation was capable of setting violence in motion.

2.   The second case occurred on Ash Wednesday 1849 in the Puy-de-Dôme:[23]

'On the 21st of this month a masquerade thusly composed appeared on the main square of Issoire: an individual wearing bourgeois clothing, his face covered with a mask of white material and holding a cattle pike in his hand, pretended to be a herdsman driving cattle. Behind him were two persons joined together by a yoke and dressed like workers, their faces covered by masks of red material. Following them came a cart pulled by a horse and containing five or six persons supporting a straw dummy which in this part of the country is called Guillaume. The allegory was highly transparent: the bourgeois aristocracy was forcing the people [emphasis in the original text] under the yoke of its power.

At the same time in another part of town, another group of

242

maskers was going about in a cart; one person wore a red bonnet and carried a wooden staff which he jabbed into the side of a straw dummy which was wearing a white bonnet. This last masquerade was the opposite, or rather the complement, of the first allegory: it was *the people* in turn taking its vengeance by the destruction of the aristocratic bourgeoisie.

Finally, elsewhere in the town, a band of young peasants went about shaking their fists, singing, and shouting "A bas les blancs!" '

According to Van Gennep, the organisation of the carnival procession fell by custom each year to adolescent males (first to the traditional age cohort called *la jeunesse* and later to military conscripts).[24] We should not assume, however, that a Mardi Gras or Ash Wednesday parade was a single event. The example of Issoire illustrates that in a large enough place, even in a large village, there were multiple events where competition between individuals, neighbourhoods, social groups, or trades was common.[25] Although we cannot be certain here whether the simultaneous scenes were intentionally related, they clearly shared a vision of society. The principal difference between them was that the mannequin, *Guillaume*, was only a witness to the action in the first allegory, while in the second he was at the centre of the drama. No longer a symbolic representation of Carnival, he personified the masker's enemy, the so-termed bourgeois aristocracy.[26]

Four days after the Ash Wednesday parade, on Sunday, 25 February, the police commissioner of Issoire heard the noise of a crowd in the streets, rushed to his window, and observed a remarkable cortège. In a horse drawn cart decorated with red cloth, green garlands and the motto *Honneur au travail*, rode a costumed figure representing Liberty, her (his, for Liberty was played by a man) hands on the shoulders of The Worker and The Farmer. Behind Liberty stood her children, Genius and Instruction; next to her were two men, one with a large open book and the other with a sign reading *La République fera la tour du monde*. The cart was lead by a villager dressed as a Roman herald and followed by the figure of Time.

An honour guard of ten persons preceded the cart and behind it came five persons in chains: one was dressed as a priest or a jesuit, a second in white, a third in black, and the final two as nobles wearing signs marked *Privilège* in their hats. Completing the procession was a crowd of perhaps one hundred and fifty men, marching arm in arm and singing *La Marseillaise* and *La Chant du départ*. As they passed the home of a retired subprefect, a peasant was heard to shout 'Vive le sang!'

The police succeeded in identifying twenty-four persons: four farmers, three bakers, two inn keepers, two children, a *marchand*, a

243

wood merchant, a locksmith, a weaver, a painter, a brewer, a joiner, a butcher, a carter, a cobbler, a plasterer and a jeweller. Every known member of this typical pre-industrial crowd was a resident of Issoire.[27]

Readers who are familiar with the recent work of Mona Ozouf on *fêtes révolutionnaires*, the official pageants staged in the 1790s,[28] will be impressed by their similarity, albeit on a much larger scale, to this symbolic presentation of the triumph of the Revolution of 1848. In Issoire, however, the cortège was not only unofficial but also took the local authorities by surprise. Where, then, did the people get the idea? The procession was certainly not a spontaneous event; in the absence of any evidence, we can speculate that it was planned by a local *chambrée* or Republican club to celebrate the first anniversary of the revolution. Nevertheless, its form likely owed much less to an attempt to reproduce some *image d'Épinal* of 1794 purchased from a peddler than to Issoire's carnival tradition of allegorical drama. This *fête révolutionnaire* was an Ash Wednesday parade without masks.[29] As Maurice Agulhon has noted about the Var during the Second Republic, 'Popular expression was more often channeled by *folklore* than by history.'[30]

Five months later, the Minister of Justice had news of yet more trouble in the same town:[31]

> 'From time immemorial, the inhabitants of Issoire have lighted fires in the streets on Saint John's and Saint Peter's days. Dances begin and go on well into the night. This year the authorities gave permission for dancing until eleven o'clock on Saint Peter's night. This hour having passed, the police went into each neighbourhood and invited the celebrants (*bruyans*) to go home. The latter did not respond to these repeated injunctions . . . and the gendarmes had to draw their swords in order to dissolve the groups, which had become menacing . . .'

As the Procureur's report intimates, Saint John's fires (*les feux de la Saint-Jean*) and Saint Peter's fires were a characteristic feature of a summer fête whose popularity rivalled those of Christmas and Carnival Lent in the traditional calendar.[32] But consider their timing in 1849. Saint John's day (24 June) and Saint Peter's day (1 July) fell shortly after the passage on 19 June of a repressive law which gave the government the right to close all clubs and cancel any public meeting. Probably concerned with the potential for protest presented by nocturnal dancing and bonfires, officials in Issoire placed a curfew on the Saint Peter's night activities. The townspeople in turn were angered by the sudden imposition of boundaries on an event which by custom was limited only by human endurance. The result: a brief challenge to authority, an *affaire politique*.

Ash Wednesday, the first anniversary of the Revolution of 1848, Saint Peter's night: the case of Issoire in 1849 underscores the complex interplay of popular *mentalité* and political expression in provincial France.

3.   The third case comes from the Bas-Rhin department:[33]

'About nine o'clock on the morning of 20 February [1849], the day of Mardi Gras, 15 or 20 youths from the commune of Labrogue lifted a sort of guillotine which they had built into a cart, and, after passing through the streets of Labrogue with this horrible machine, set off toward the communes of Schirmeck and Barembach. All were disguised, most wore masks, and some were armed with flails, hatchets and sticks. One of them, wearing a red belt and smeared with a colored substance imitating blood, was supposed to be an executioner. This ghastly procession stopped from time to time in front of the homes of the most notable residents, where the executioner dispatched a mannequin said to represent Louis Philippe, all the time crying "We'll do the same to those who aren't content".'

While on the route to Schirmeck the actors in this 'ignoble and detestable comedy', as the Procureur called it, were heard to shout 'long live Robespierre! Long live the guillotine! The big shots [*les messieurs*] cry "Long live Cavaignac" We cry long live the guillotine.' They also proclaimed their intention to execute the curé, his sister, and the forest inspector.

Our search for the meaning of this incident will surely fail if we automatically invoke that slippery concept, the French Revolutionary Tradition. The young men of Labrogue did not learn about the Terror from reading Michelet. Perhaps, like a scene out of Balzac's *A Country Doctor*, some of them had listened to a grandfather's tales of the revolutionary army or had heard about Robespierre from a local bourgeois, Maurice Agulhon's model for the diffusion of political radicalism into the countryside.[34] Nevertheless, I suspect that they were less intent on restoring the Year Two than on demonstrating a popular notion of justice.

During the July Monarchy, even the most advanced democrats had argued that the Terror was the result of special circumstances and would not be a part of a future Republic.[35] One of the first actions taken by the Provisional Government in February 1848 was the abolition of the death penalty for political crimes. Nonetheless, the guillotine had been appropriated as a symbol of popular justice and the authorities were highly sensitive to rumours about it. When a hemp cutter from the Drôme was overheard to say 'The executioner's trade is a trade like any other', this remark was passed up the bureaucratic chain all the way to Paris.[36] Lists said to bear the names of local persons marked for execution were reported in a café in the village of

Saintes (Vienne). Then someone looked into a joiner's workshop and thought he saw a guillotine capable of cutting off twenty heads at a single blow. When the police arrived, however, they found only a model for a bridge pile cutter intended for display at an industrial exhibition.[37]

Returning to the incident in Labrogue, perhaps the most familiar of all Mardi Gras and Ash Wednesday rituals was for masked youths to place a mannequin representing Carnival in a cart, take it through the town, hold a mock public trial, and then execute it by means of burning, drowning or decapitation for 'crimes' against the community. Even the use of imitation blood was not unknown.[38] The maskers of Labrogue did not carry the pikes of the *sans culottes*, rather the kinds of ordinary tools which local officials constantly tried to ban from parades. Finally, for young men from one village to transport their carnival parody to a neighbouring one might be seen as an example of the violent territorial rivalries which characterised rural adolescence. Only a month later, for example, the lads from the commune of Seix (Haute Garonne) who became eligible for military service in 1849 took the opportunity of the drawing of lots (*le tirage*) in Oust, the *chef lieu* of the canton, to march with flag and drum through the streets of the rival town. Their honour threatened, the conscripts of Oust climbed through the window of an inn to steal the drum. Explaining the fighting which followed, the Procureur wrote: 'The germs of disorder have divided the two communes for a long time.'[39]

The maskers of Labrogue were also exercising what Nicole Belmont calls 'the right of personal and collective insult' of the carnival season.[40] In this case the targets were certain wealthy residents, the forest inspector, the curé, and his sister. The church was often the object of ridicule by maskers and the latter two targets may also have been the recipients of an equally common expression of sexual derision. With regard to the former two, the inspector enforced the hated Forest Code of 1827 which forbade gleaning and grazing in woods most often the property of local notables.[41] If carnival pictured the world turned upside down, here it meant the disappearance of government intervention and the restoration of common lands.

The carnival incidents in Uzès and Issoire were not lacking in threat, insult, or social statement, but these were delivered through the veiled medium of allegory. In Labrogue, on the other hand, there was a concreteness to the action which commands our attention. The mannequin was not *Carimantran* watching the sweepers or *Guillaume* posing as the bourgeois aristocracy, it represented a specific person and its customary execution was by the uncustomary method of the guillotine. The fate of 'Louis Philippe' was less the traditional end of carnival than a prediction of what lay in store 'for those who aren't content'. If the local notables (*les messieurs*) who had voted for Cavaignac in the recent Presidential election failed to accept the victory of Louis Napoleon, they would be summoned before the court of popular justice.

4.   The fourth case occurred on Ash Wednesday 1850 in the Deux Sèvres:[42]

> 'I have the honor of informing you that a seditious manifestation took place on the occasion of carnival in the *bourg* of Mauzé . . . known as an ardent foyer of communism. Under the pretext of burying carnival, a long procession passed two times through the *bourg*: a certain Pascal Geay, an apprentice joiner, aged 19 years, coiffed in a red bonnet, wearing a white robe and a red belt around his body, his right wrist held by a chain which fell to his feet, and holding a tricolored flag, thus represented Liberty enchained. He was carried by eight or ten men on a litter decorated with laurel.
>
> The cortège was composed of two carts filled with masked men carrying illuminated lanterns and a large number of persons bearing farm instruments. Dancing the carmagnole, this crowd went through the *bourg* singing a political song whose refrain went *"aux prochaines elections – il faut, compagnon* [sic]*, nommer des montagnards"*.'

Carnival returned each winter as part of the cycle of seasonal fêtes, while the political life of the Second Republic moved on a different course. Kings fell and rich men trembled in Labrogue one year, Liberty herself was in chains in Mauzé the next. This comparison of symbols causes us to question the interpretation offered by the adjoint mayor of Mauzé that 'No one could mistake the meaning of this masquerade; all men of order went home saying "Voila! It's '93 come back to life".'[43]

The mechanism of improvisation, I suspect, was operating on two levels when a beardless youth dressed as a woman was borne through the streets of Mauzé. First, the maskers were probably transposing a custom that in regions where a mannequin of Carnival was not a traditional part of the procession, an adolescent male might portray 'the wife of Carnival'.[44] Second, they did not choose to have Liberty appear in triumph, rather she was shown to be in danger. The 'meaning of this masquerade', to repeat the adjoint mayor's phrase, was not intended to be the return of the Terror but the premonition of a new Thermidor.

The future of the Second Republic looked different on Mardi Gras 1850 than it had on the same day in 1849. The repression which began after the legislative elections in May 1849 had taken its toll: the clubs were closed, cafés and the press were closely watched, and the men in power in Paris spoke only of Order. For the residents of a poor wine producing region like Mauzé, the most serious blow was perhaps the recent restoration of the tax on beverages which the Constituent Assembly had abolished on its last day of existence. The villagers knew, moreover, that in less than a month, elections would be held to replace twenty-one deputies of the extreme Left who had been stripped of their seats for participating in a street demonstration the previous June.[45] In order to discover these facts at work in the minds of the masqueraders, we need only listen to their song.

It was called *Le Chant des Vignerons* ('The Song of the Wine-growers') and was written by Claude Durand, who had been the mayor at Mauzé for a brief time after the Revolution of 1848. Seeking to capitalise on the established popularity of the songs of Pierre Dupont (*Le Chant des ouvriers, Le Chant des paysans*, etc.),[46] Durand had had copies printed in a shop in Châtellerault.[47] With this specific case in mind, the Minister of the Interior expressed a strong opinion about political verse in general:[48]

'These songs, published for the most part under the inspiration of the socialist party, have the purpose of stirring the hatred of the poorer classes against the rich and society itself. Their popularity makes them highly dangerous. These productions, whether with regard to form or composition, are so mediocre as to seem to condemn them to distain or indifference. Because they are addressed to scarcely enlightened minds and an impassioned public, however, they produce an unfortunate effect on the masses.

In general, they appear in a format of printed leaflets or small collections sold at a low price . . .'

Responding to the Minister's complaint that he had authorised a tax stamp for the publication of *Le Chant des Vignerons*, the Procureur of Châtellerault explained:[49]

'Certainly I could impede the circulation of printed material. But how would I impose silence on the 500 workers who will serenade me with song the next day? They know it all by heart! If I am going to ban the publication of songs, I'll have to forbid singing.'

Bureacratic measures of repression were ineffective in the face of a rural popular culture in which thought was principally expressed by the spoken (or sung) rather than the written word. Not only a vehicle for conserving the collective wisdom of the community, the oral tradition was also a means of introducing new (political) ideas.[50]

Now that we know how *Le Chant Les Vignerons* made its way into the streets of Mauzé, let us look at the text:[51]

Good villagers vote for the Mountain,
It's the hope of poor winegrowers;
For with it, good countryfolk,
Will disappear the beverage tax.
   Good, good winegrowers,
   At the next election
   You must, *campagnard*,
   Name the men of the Mountain.
[Second verse omitted]
Poor worker, you construct for the master
Fine homes, sumptuous palaces;
You also build prisons for yourself,
For you know the rich never go there.
   Good, good winegrower . . .
Listen no longer to the aristocracy
Which converts your cares into coin;
When you've had enough, usury and tyranny
In a single day will all disappear.
   Good, good winegrower . . .
When the election is democratic,
All the taxes of poor workers
Will be, in our fine Republic,
Better placed on the biggest landowners.
   Good, good winegrower . . .
It's you, poor one, who fights the wars,
You forge the chains of mankind.
Sometimes you shoot down your brother,
Who, alas, has risen out of hunger.
   Good, good winegrower . . .
[Seventh verse omitted]
In the hamlets agricultural banks
Will be opened for you, good peasant:
You'll also have free schools —
And money at two percent.
   Good, good winegrowers . . .

Here was the programme of 'the democratic and social Republic', a
picture of a future free of exploitation calculated to appeal to village
artisans, smallholders and fieldhands gathered in Mauzé for the fête.
The Republic is in danger! Vote for the Mountain and Liberty will
cast off her chains!

5.   The final case comes from Albi (Tarn) in 1851:[52]

'On Ash Wednesday, a cart pulled by a bay-brown horse left the courtyard of the veterinarian Brette next door to the café of Jean-Jean. These two individuals are known for the exhaltation of their Republican opinions. This chariot carried six masked persons, arranged three to each side of the wagon. They were dressed in white and some of them had a small chain around their necks . . . All six had the date 1852 written in large red numbers on their backs. A seventh individual disguised with a false beard and a false nose led the cart. While passing two persons, several of the maskers cried in a significant, yet somewhat timid manner, "A bas la réaction". Word has circulated that one of the maskers carried a hatchet and that the chariot made a tour of and even stopped on the square used for executions . . .'

The Procureur noted that this 'political charade' had disappeared from the streets as rapidly as it had appeared. He also added that none of the twenty-eight witnesses interviewed either could or would identify the participants.

Examples illustrate and suggest, but do not prove anything. Yet, from Uzès to Albi, I think we can see some significant differences in the five case studies of carnival incidents which found their way into the judicial archives. In Uzès, Issoire and Labrogue in 1849, the common people of the community were shown triumphant. In Albi in 1851, they were the victims of a renewed reaction looking toward a turning point that never arrived: the elections for the Assembly and the President of the Republic scheduled for 1852. The political history of the Second Republic was being played on the stage of the popular theatre of carnival.

In 1851, there were no open threats or songs boldly sung, only a few cries significant for their timidity. In 1851, there was no festive parade, no crowd surging behind the cart, rather a hasty tour and a quick retreat before the police could react. In 1851, the parody had not been organised by the town's youths, instead it was the work of two men whose occupations speak volumes about the way radical political ideas were circulated in the provinces. The citizens who witnessed it offered the actors protection from the authorities but did not join them in the streets. In 1851, there was neither a mannequin nor a human representation of an allegorical figure. Without the presence of Carnival or his surrogate, the men in the cart might have been on their way to a real execution. In 1851, finally, the masks seem less a part of a traditional ritual by which men drop the masks of deference they ordinarily wear, than a way to make a public statement and avoid detection: these are two different kinds of anonymity. It was a marriage of *folklore* and the politics of repression.

Let us return to the village of Châteldon and the *affaire politique* of 24 February 1851 where we began this essay. As I read the Procureur's description, the mimeodrama had five elements: (1) a band of youths (2) in red and white costumes (3) paraded through the streets; (4) not only did they stage a mock trial (the 'torture' of Rivet) but they also (5) twice simulated the execution of their pretended victim. From what we have learned, its meaning is no longer obscure: it was a *jugement carnavalesque*, the verdict of the 'democratic and social Republic' (the Reds) against the 'party of Order' (the Whites) rendered in the symbolic court of carnival.

'*Folklore*', as Maurice Agulhon reminds us, 'was . . . perhaps more alive in the middle of the 19th century than it has ever been in . . . [France's] history.'[53] Two concepts of fête co-existed in the minds of those who decided 'qu'il faudrait fêter l'anniversaire du 24 février 1848'. Because the political repression (their fear of the consequences of having been seen selecting a Liberty Tree) had foreclosed the possibility of staging a modern, if illicit celebration, Rivet and his friends turned to the other form of fête they knew. They donned the masks of revolution and entered the world of *folklore'*

Notes

The research upon which this essay is based was made possible by a grant from the National Endowment for the Humanities. I want to thank Michael R. Marrus, James J. Sheehan and Susan L. Woodward for their advice and comments.

1. AN BB[30] 391: Procureur General Riom to Minister of Justice, 1 March 1851.
2. *The Interpretation of Cultures* (New York, Basic Books, 1973), pp. 14 and 24.
3. *La République au village* (Paris, Plon, 1970), pp. 265-6. The term *folklore* has been italicised throughout this essay to remind readers that I am using it in the French sense, that is, the nexus of traditional customs, beliefs and practices. For a further discussion of the term, see: Nicole Belmont, *Arnold Van Gennep, le créateur de l'ethnographie française* (Paris, Petite Bibliothèque Payot, 1974).
4. *1848 ou l'apprentissage de la République, 1848-1852* (Paris, Éditions du Seuil, 1973), p. 109.
5. Archives Départementales Hte. Garonne, HM 207. I am grateful to Ron Aminzade for sending me a copy of this document. An abridged version dating from the Restoration is quoted by Daniel Fabre and Jacques Lacroix, *La Vie quotidienne des paysans du Languedoc au XIXe siècle* (Paris, Hachette Littérature, 1973), p. 439.
6. AN BB[30] 362: Procureur General Montpellier to Minister of Justice, 10 March 1848.
7. *Ibid.*, n.d. and 6 March 1849. See also the suggestive article by Jacques Cochin, 'Mondes à l'envers, mondes à l'endroit', *Arts et traditions populaires*, 17 (1969), pp. 233-57.
8. AN BB[30] 362: Procureur General Montpellier to Minister of Justice, 27 February 1849.

251

9.   AN BB³⁰ 392A: Procureur General Paris to Minister of Justice, 17 and 18 March, 1 April 1851.
10.   AN BB³⁰ 362: Procureur General Montpellier to Minister of Justice, 19 February 1850.
11.   Gerard Bouchard, *Le village immobile: Sennely-en-Sologne au XVIIIe siècle* (Paris, Plon, 1972), p. 293.
12.   AN BB³⁰ 392A: Procureur General Montpellier to Minister of Justice, 25 February 1851. For a discussion of charivari as a form of popular protest, see: E. P. Thompson, '*Rough Music*: Le Charivari anglais', *Annales, E.S.C.* (1972), pp. 285-312.
13.   AN BB³⁰ 365: Procureur General Riom to Minister of Justice, 23 February 1849.
14.   *Ibid.*
15.   AN BB³⁰ 362: Procureur General Montpellier to Minister of Justice, 27 June 1849.
16.   AN BB³⁰ 392A: Procureur General Montpellier to Minister of Justice, 12 June 1851.
17.   Arnold Van Gennep, *Manuel de folklore française contemporaine* (7 vols.; Paris, Picard, 1938-1958), 1 III, pp. 981-2.
18.   E. P. Thompson, 'Patrician Society, Plebian Culture', *The Journal of Social History*, vol. 7, no. 4 (summer 1974), pp. 400-03.
19.   AN BB³⁰ 363: Procureur General Nîmes to Minister of Justice, 1 April 1849.
20.   Van Gennep, *Manuel de folklore française contemporaine*, 1 III, pp. 1059-60; Nicole Belmont, *Mythes et croyances dans l'ancienne France* (Paris, Flammarion, 1973), p. 77.
21.   Fabre and Lacroix, *La Vie quotidienne des paysans du Languedoc*, p. 436.
22.   AN BB³⁰ 363: Procureur General Nîmes to Minister of Justice, 22 February 1849.
23.   AN BB³⁰ 365: Procureur General Riom to Minister of Justice, 26 February 1849. The article by E. Dagnan, 'La Réaction conservatrice dans l'Ouest', *La Révolution de 1849* (1909), p. 221, simply reports the action without commenting on its *folkloresque* dimensions.
24.   Van Gennep, *Manuel de folklore française contemporaine*, 1 I, pp. 196-213 and 1, III, p. 973.
25.   Fabre and Lacroix, *La Vie quotidienne des paysans du Langeudoc*, p. 437.
26.   'Bourgeois aristocracy' was a popular term to describe wealthy notables. For an example of its use during the French Revolution, see: Albert Soboul, *The Sans-Culottes*, tr. Remy Inglis Hall (New York, Doubleday Anchor Books, 1972), p. 6.
27.   AN BB³⁰ 365: Procureur General Riom to Minister of Justice, 1 March 1849 (covering letter) and *Procès verbal* by the Police Commissioner of Issoire, 25 February 1849 (copy).
28.   'La Fête sous la Révolution française', *Faire de l'histoire, t. 3: nouveaux objects*, ed. J. Le Goff and P. Nora (3 vols.; Paris, Gallimard, 1974), pp. 256-77.
29.   It also illustrates Clifford Geertz's (*The Interpretation of Cultures*, p. 360) contention: 'Human thought is consummately social: social in its origins, social in its function, social in its forms, social in its application.'
30.   Agulhon, *La République au village*, pp. 416-7.
31.   AN BB³⁰ 365: Procureur General Riom to Minister of Justice, 16 July 1849.
32.   For a discussion of the *cycle de Saint-Jean*, see: Belmont, *Mythes et croyances dans l'ancienne France*, pp. 97-106.
33.   AN BB³⁰ 362: Procureur General Nancy to Minister of Justice, 4 March

1849.
34. Agulhon, *La République au village*, p. 279.
35. For example: *Nouveau catéchisme républicain, par un prolètaire* (Lyon, 1833).
36. AN BB[30] 360: Procureur Geberal Grenoble to Minister of Justice, 1 March 1850.
37. AN BB[30] 362: Procureur General Poitiers to Minister of Justice, 1 August 1849.
38. Van Gennep, *Manuel du folklore française contemporaine* 1 III, p. 980.
39. AN BB[30] 365: Procureur General Toulouse to Minister of Justice, 6 March 1849.
40. Belmont, *Mythes et croyances dans l'ancienne France*, p. 75.
41. For a discussion of opposition to the Forest Code, see: Agulhon, *La République au village*, pp. 44, 84.
42. AN BB[30] 364: Procureur General Poitiers to Minister of Justice, 15 February 1850.
43. The leaders of Mauzé's radical Republican faction were arrested and later acquitted by a jury. Several of them were deported after 2 December 1851 and one person ended his days with Étienne Cabet in Navoo, Illinois (R. Germond, 'La Mascarade séditieuse de Mauzé en 1850', *Bulletin de la Société historique et scientifique de Deux-Sèvres*, 11, 1961, pp. 551-5).
44. Van Gennep, *Manuel du folklore française contemporaine*, 1 III, p. 936; André Varanac, *Civilisation traditionnelle et genres de vie* (Paris, Rivière, 1948), p. 105.
45. For a discussion of the period of *l'ordre conservateur*, see: Agulhon, *1848 ou l'apprentissage de la République*, pp. 140-9.
46. *Ibid.*, p. 109.
47. AN BB[30] 364: Procureur General Poitiers to Minister of Justice, 4 April 1850.
48. AN BB[30] 364: Minister of the Interior to Minister of Justice, 9 April 1850.
49. AN BB[30] 364: Procureur General of Châtellerault to Procureur General Poitiers, 2 April 1850.
50. For a discussion of the role of *la parole* in the formation of the worker movement, see: Michelle Perrot, *Les Ouvriers en grève, 1871-1890* (2 vols.; Paris and La Haye, Mouton, 1974), II, pp. 607-10.
51. AN BB[30] 364: Text copied on stationery of the Procureur General Poitiers, 4 April 1850.
52. AN BB[30] 366: Procureur General Toulouse to Minister of Justice, 28 March 1851.
53. Agulhon, *1848 ou l'apprentissage de la République*, p. 108.

MODERNISATION AND INSURGENCY IN DECEMBER 1851: A CASE STUDY OF THE DRÔME

Ted Margadant

Modernisation and protest are interrelated themes of special interest to historians of rural France during the Second Republic. Were the collective protests which swept the countryside from 1848-51 hostile outbursts of impoverished peasants against capitalism, communal reactions against the centralising activities of the state, or revolutionary movements on behalf of new political ideals? These questions focus attention on three distinct aspects of the modernisation process: economic development, state centralisation, and political mobilisation. An economic approach to rural protest searches for structural changes or cyclical trends in market relationships which undermined living standards and exacerbated social tensions in the countryside. In this view, the driving force behind collective violence was misery. An approach which emphasises the process of state centralisation looks instead for changes in the structure and functions of bureaucratic authority which stimulated conflict between local communities and the state. From this perspective, the outbreak of such conflicts depended less on the extent of rural poverty than on popular perceptions of the effectiveness and legitimacy of state power. As for an approach centred on the process of political mobilisation, it investigates societal and governmental changes which facilitated popular participation in competitive struggles for power, such as electoral campaigns. According to this line of reasoning, communications networks, ideological orientations and organisational aptitudes were more important than poverty or repression in precipitating large scale protest during the Second Republic.

Charles Tilly has recently formulated a typology of collective violence which discriminates between the social impact of these several processes of modernisation. He argues that pre-industrial social groups in small towns and rural communities were losing wealth and power in mid-nineteenth century France. Victimised by market expansion and state centralisation, they lashed out against their fate in 'reactionary' protests which remained localised, or 'communal', in form. By contrast, the economic and political changes of the period were creating new opportunities for workers in the cities. Instead of resisting centralisation, they demanded a larger share of power in the emergent nation-

254

state. As they entered the electoral process, they utilised specialised associations such as trade unions and political parties as instruments of pressure on the government. Their protest became 'associational' in form and 'modern' in content. These divergent sociopolitical trends among rural and urban populations explain why the Second Republic witnessed both a last, desperate surge of reactionary violence in the countryside and a rising tide of modern strikes, demonstrations and rebellions in the cities.[1]

Such a typology provides guidance for analysing urban and rural protest in 1848, but it seems less appropriate to the provincial setting of insurgency in December 1851. Historians are generally familiar with the image of revolutionary cities and reactionary villages in the early months of the Republic. While skilled artisans in Paris, Limoges, Marseille, Lyon and other cities organised demonstrations to support their demands for 'socialistic' policies, peasants in many villages rioted to escape from the power of tax collectors or forest guards. Yet by December 1851 a curious shift had taken place in the social geography of left wing Republican protest. Now most of the larger cities were calm, while armed uprisings in the name of a 'Democratic and Social Republic' broke out in nearly 800 small towns, bourgs and villages of southern and central France. Instead of retreating from the state, these Republican insurgents tried to conquer it. They proclaimed revolutionary commissions in over one hundred communes, marched on eleven prefectures, and clashed violently with troops or gendarmes in sixteen departments. Furthermore, all the major uprisings in 1851 were organised by secret 'Montagnard' societies which linked urban and rural militants together in regional networks of leadership. These societies comprised a Republican underground which mobilised a supposedly 'reactionary' social base in defence of an ostensibly 'modern' political ideal.[2]

If the insurrection is difficult to classify in Tilly's terminology, this suggests that processes of economic, administrative and political change may have been operating in different directions along the tradition/modernity axis. For example, the pace of political mobilisation may have been accelerating in the countryside although markets for agricultural produce were declining. Over the long run, such a combination of increasing rural participation in politics and decreasing involvement in markets is improbable. The commercialisation of agriculture is an important aspect of the broader societal process of urbanisation which facilitates political organisation among farmers. Yet in the short run, agrarian depression and peasant radicalisation may have been strongly correlated, as several historians of the Second Republic have recently argued.[3] Similarly, state centralisation may have been growing at the expense of political democracy instead of in harmony with it. Here again the long run integration of a competitive electoral system with a centralised bureaucracy in modern France needs to be distinguished from short run conflicts between the rights of participants and the authority of bureaucrats. In the case of the Second Republic, national and regional historians have shown that from 1849-51 agents of the state tried systematically to destroy the movement for electoral democracy which Republicans had launched in 1848.[4] Administrative repression may have been counterproductive in some areas of the nation, stimulating conspiracy and revolt instead of reducing opposition to the government.

In so far as market trends generated massive discontent with the socioeconomic order, the insurrection of 1851 can be described as a revolt against the notables; to the extent that administrative repression heightened political tensions, it can be analysed as a revolt against the state; and in the degree that conspiratorial organisations tried to seize and exercise power, it can be interpreted as an abortive revolutionary movement. Although these several perspectives are not mutually exclusive, I would like to review some evidence that political tensions and conspiratorial leadership were more important than economic grievances in determining the localisation, form and objectives of the revolt. To present detailed information within the scope of an article, I will base my remarks on one rebel zone of southeastern France, the department of the Drôme. This department, which Philippe Vigier has included in his recent history of the 'Alpine region' during the Second Republic, is bordered to the west by the Rhône river valley, to the east by the Alps, to the north by the region of Lyon, and to the south by Provence. The insurrection in the Drôme was extensive and violent: nearly 5,000 rebels from around 60 communes fought against regular troops of the army on 6-7 December. These clashes, which resulted in several dozen casualties, took place on the outskirts of two towns, Crest and Montélimar, both located in the west-central section of the department (the central Drôme). Although several hundred men from the small town of Dieulefit joined one of three columns which fought at Crest, most of the rebels came from market bourgs, villages, hamlets and farmsteads in the region. Among the twenty-seven communes of the central Drôme which mustered over 100 rebels, all but one (Dieulefit) had a majority of their adult male labour force employed in agriculture. In this region of the nation, armed resistance to the *coup d'état* was predominantly a rural phenomenon.[5]

What was the economic fate of rural communities in the central Drôme during the Second Republic? There are several ways of looking at this problem, depending on whether structural changes or short term fluctuations in the rural economy are emphasised. Structurally, peasants may have been suffering from some combination of overpopulation, agricultural innovation and industrial competition. Alternatively, demographic growth may have been mild, technical changes in agriculture beneficial, and industrial competition non-existent, but the rural populations may still have been reduced to misery by a temporary crisis in the market place. These four distinct approaches to rural poverty, which can be characterised as Malthusian, Marxian, Schumpeterian and Labroussian, all exist in the literature on French peasant protest. From the perspective of the central Drôme, the first two are largely inappropriate, the third is suggestive, and the fourth is directly applicable to the study of economic distress in the countryside.

Ironically, it was Karl Marx who first developed a Malthusian analysis of French rural history in the generation preceding the Revolution of 1848. According to Marx, the bulk of the smallholding peasants were caught in a vicious circle of population growth, land hunger, diminishing productivity and endebtedness: 'In the measure that the population and, with it, the division of the land increases, does the instrument of production, the soil, become dearer and its fertility decrease, does agriculture decline and the peasant become loaded with debt.'[6] Through their enslavement to capital, the smallholding peasants were being ruined. This Malthusian model presupposes a closed economy of subsistence producers, without cash crops, craft production for export, social constraints in the birth rate or geographical mobility. It is doubtful whether any rural communities of the Drôme fulfilled all these conditions in isolation. Most of them participated in an export-oriented economy to some degree, and they adjusted population to resources via the age at marriage, birth control, or migration. In the mountainous cantons of the eastern Drôme, where market opportunities were very restricted, the population actually declined between 1831-46, largely due to emigration. In the plains and foothills of the central Drôme, just as to the north, more and more peasants were planting mulberry trees and producing raw silk for the lucrative silkspinning industry of the region. Vigier cites statistics to show that the value of the silk harvest in the Drôme increased from 2.8 million francs in 1811 to 6 million francs in 1834 and around 15 million francs a year in the 1840s.[7] During these same years, grain farmers of the northern and central Drôme were carrying out an 'economic revolution' of their own. By planting the fallow fields with fodder crops, they succeeded in growing wheat on soils which had previously been suitable only for rye, and they increased their grain output by 50 per cent or more.[8] Yet throughout the cash crop zone which rebelled in 1851, the population had increased by only 7 per cent during the July Monarchy.[9] Far from outstripping the resource base of the peasantry, population growth lagged considerably behind the expanding output of silk, wheat and livestock.

According to Albert Soboul, most peasants suffered nonetheless from these agricultural improvements because they lost the security of the 'traditional village community'. Soboul applies the Marxian theory of social change in the English agricultural revolution to nineteenth century France. He argues that proponents of the new techniques of production had to strip the rural poor of their traditional rights of usage over common lands and open fields. This issue of enclosures polarised rural society in southern France during the July Monarchy. Threatened with proletarianisation, the smallholders who joined the insurrection of 1851 had been fighting a long battle against agrarian capitalism: 'There is an astonishing continuity of peasant reactions, always similar, in 1851 and 1848, as in 1789 and 1830: the traditional peasantry was defending the old collective rights which guaranteed its existence against the innovations of the new agriculture.'[10] As Vigier has shown, this theory completely misconstrues the pattern of social change in regions of southeastern France such as the central Drôme. Raw silk and fodder crops were introduced into pre-existing field systems without any enclosure movement, and they increased demand for peasant labour. The result of higher agricultural productivity and rising peasant incomes was a brisk market in land, and property became more widely distributed among small owners. Indeed, Vigier finds some evidence that large properties were being subdivided into small plots through speculative land sales at high interest rates. The basic trend in the private land market was the inverse of that described by Soboul.[11]

What about the issue of collective rights of usage to common lands? Public protest did erupt over forest lands in one district of the eastern Drôme − la-Chapelle-en-Vercors − but this peasant anger was directed against state forest guards, not private landlords. Such conflicts between rural communities and the state seem to have discouraged peasant support for the Republic: the Vercors voted solidly conservative in 1849 and remained calm in 1851.[12] As for disputes over collective rights of usage to private forests, Agulhon has shown that this issue had a radicalising effect in Provence, but comparable tensions rarely influenced political alignments in the central Drôme.[13] Even at the village of Saou, where disputes over private forests were at the basis of factional hatreds, the largest forest owner patronised the Republicans instead of the Legitimists. His business manager sent personal orders for the lumbermen in the forest to mobilise on 6 December.[14] Only at Mirmande did an enclosure of common lands have a direct impact on protest in 1851. According to the leader of the insurrection in this commune. the conservative assistant mayor was extremely unpopular: 'I had accused him of being a crook at the occasion of the irregular sale of communal woods', and during the revolt 'everyone at Mirmande, where he has many enemies, was shouting at him and threatening him'.[15] None of the other rebels or witnesses confirmed this testimony, but the issue of common lands may have influenced popular motivation in this one instance.

Tilly has recently developed a third line of reasoning to explain rural poverty and protest during the Second Republic. He argues that while the first phase of the industrial revolution brought large numbers of peasants into craft production for export, by the 1840s urban factories were threatening these rural artisans with ruin. In this Schumpeterian perspective on the costs of technological obsolescence, industrial progress in the cities brought economic collapse in the countryside: 'As forging, spinning and weaving concentrated in industrial cities, a vast number of artisans remained, workless, in the old towns and the deindustrialising countryside.'[16] This phenomenon of deindustrialisation helps explain the heavy participation of rural artisans in the insurrection of 1851:[17]

'The provincial disturbances of 1848 through 1851 brought out not only the dying peasantry, but also large numbers of people — semirural semi-industrial workers whom the deindustrialization of the countryside was driving into oblivion . . . More so than we have realized, the midcentury provincial disturbances recorded the final outraged cries of whole classes whom the growth of a centralized capitalistic, industrial nation-state was stripping of political identity and means of existence.'

Tilly's theory identifies a significant component of social change in some rural communities of the central Drôme. Wool textile production had been dispersed in many bourgs and villages around Crest and Dieulefit during the eighteenth century, but by 1851 it was mainly concentrated in these two towns.[18] Only one market bourg, the cantonal seat of Bourdeaux, still had a few small *fabricants*, but their technology was 'outmoded' due to a 'lack of capital', and the output, 'formerly 1,200-1,500 pieces of wool cloth per year', had shrunk to 200-300 pieces by 1848.[19] It is doubtful, however, whether this industrial decline spelled ruin for many families in the region. Social geographers who have studied the problem link the breakdown of the putting-out system for wool production to the rise of the silk industry and the growth of agricultural productivity.[20] It was not that wool abandoned peasants; they abandoned wool. By the early years of the July Monarchy very few rural inhabitants were trying to enter the wool industry, as the draft lists of twenty-year old men indicate: in 1829-31 only 1.3 per cent (15/1,150) of those residing in bourgs and villages of the region described themselves as weavers, carders or wool workers, as compared with 7.9 per cent (15/199) of those residing at Crest and Dieulefit; in 1839-41 these figures had become 1.0 per cent (11/1150) vs. 14.9 per cent (33/222) and in 1849-51 they had diverged still further to 0.6 per cent (7/1222) vs. 15.9 per cent (38/252).[21] The census lists for the year 1851 show negligible numbers of wool workers in rural communities of the region.[22] Even at Bourdeaux, this gradual disappearance of the wool industry was more than counterbalanced by the establishment of two silkspinning factories and by the growth of other trades: while the adult male labour force employed in wool textiles fell from fifty-four to twenty-three between 1806-51, that employed in other crafts and commerce rose from fifty-seven to eighty-nine and that employed in agriculture barely changed at all (from 228 to 230).[23] By the mid-nineteenth century the rural economy of the central Drôme no longer depended on the putting-out system. Its fortunes were henceforth linked to urban demand for raw silk and other agricultural commodities.

If peasants were benefiting from expanding markets, so they would suffer from contracting markets. This is the main idea behind a 'Labroussian' explanation of radicalisation and insurgency in the Drôme. Although Labrousse's own model of economic crises in pre-industrial France links high agricultural prices to rural distress, several of his students have inverted it to argue that low prices undermined rural living standards during the Second Republic. For Labrousse most peasants had too little land for subsistence in early nineteenth century France, so they had to purchase food in the market place. Harvest shortages and high grain prices would reduce their purchasing power, causing a depression in the textile industry. Such a crisis in agriculture and textiles occurred in 1846-7, provoking widespread food riots in export-oriented areas of the north and centre. But what if peasants had to produce cash-crops for the market in order to reimburse loans, pay taxes and purchase craft goods? Under these circumstances, low agricultural prices would reduce their profits and increase the burden of their debts and taxes. Small owners who had contracted mortgages to purchase their land would face expropriation. Furthermore, such a conjecture of low prices and profits would reduce the supply of capital for agricultural improvements, construction projects or consumer purchases. The result would be a crisis in the labour market for agricultural workers and local craftsmen.[24]

Vigier is the foremost advocate of this conjunctural interpretation of rural poverty and discontent during the Second Republic. In his study of the Alpine region, he argues that an agrarian depression, caused by low grain prices and dwindling silk revenues, drove many owner-farmers into bankruptcy, especially in the Drôme. From 1849-51 there was 'an astonishing increase in the number of forcible expropriations', and with each new foreclosure, hatred of money lenders increased. 'Innumerable endebted landowners reached the point of hating their creditors, and, more generally, of hating the bourgeois exploiters of the countryside.'

Citing examples of expropriated owner-farmers who led the insurrection, he infers that *endebted landowners*, men who had been recently expropriated or who were threatened with expropriations, were *very numerous among the soldiers and leaders of the insurrection*. Montagnard propaganda, with its themes of cheap credit and fiscal justice, reached especially receptive audiences in villages of the central Drôme. The 'miserable situation' and 'great difficulties' of the 'very numerous' medium and small landowners in the cantons of Dieufelit and Marsanne (near Montélimar) explain in large part their support for the secret societies and the revolt. Social anatagonisms were even more directly linked to political extremism in the two cantons of Crest, where urban usurers had been exploiting the peasants ruthlessly. 'Out of hatred for the usurers of Crest', the endebted small and medium landowners of nearby villages voted left wing in 1849, joined the Montagnard socities, and marched on Crest in 1851. Their armed offensive against the town resembled an archaic pattern of anti-urban revolt:

'The peasants from the cantons of Bourdeaux, Dieulefit, Crest-nord and Crest-sud, pouring out of their mountains and their plateaux 5,000-6,000 strong on December 5, 1851 [actually 3,000 strong on December 7], in order to occupy the town of Crest, makes us think of those mountaineers of the Atlas, of Calabria or of Albania descending to pillage or at least to teach a lesson to the wealthy bourgeois of the towns in the plains who traditionally exploit them.'

Vigier alludes to other factors which aided the Montagnard cause, such as Protestantism and patronage, but his major explanation of conspiracy and revolt is economic: misery and social hatred motivated the endebted and expropriated owner-farmers who comprised the mass base of rebellion in the Drôme.[25]

To test the validity of this interpretation, it is useful to distinguish between the economic conditions which existed in rebel communities during the Second Republic; the social base of participation in the revolt; and the conscious motives or latent antagonisms expressed by those who marched in arms. In all three respects, the evidence which I have gathered from the central Drôme indicates that social conflict between debtors and creditors played a minor role in radical politics. The economic difficulties of the period certainly influenced the social base of recruitment and the goals of the Montagnards; but they do not explain why the rural populations of the central Drôme took arms in December 1851.

The political crisis of 1848 provoked a sharp decline in commerce throughout the silk producing zone of the Drôme, and agricultural incomes remained depressed for the duration of the Republic. Vigier has proved this for the department as a whole, and cantonal enquiries, notarial registers, census returns and draft lists confirm the depressed state of the rural economy in the central Drôme.[26] The cantonal commissions established in 1848 to investigate agricultural and industrial conditions reported from Bourdeaux, Crest, Dieulefit, Loriol and Montélimar that commerce was stagnant and agriculture suffering. As the commission from Montélimar wrote, 'The extent of prosperity in the canton depends on the price of silk cocoons. This year, when the cocoons have little value, there exists a general malaise.'[27] Although silk prices rose again from 1849-51, silkworm diseases reduced the size of the crop, and profits dwindled accordingly. For example, the municipal council at one village near Crest (Grane) wrote just one week before the revolt: 'At this moment, because of bad weather, the absence of silkworms for the past several years, and the disaster of the hailstorm which struck a large part of the commune this year, the landowners find themselves in such an embarassed position that they can't employ the workers.'[28] Lower profits implied continuing shortages of capital, and the loan market declined as a consequence. On the basis of notarial registers for the two cantons of Crest, I have estimated that loan transactions fell by one third in number and one quarter in value between 1844-7 and 1848-51. Similarly, property transactions fell by one third in number, as measured by sales entered in the same registers.[29] Demographic trends were also reversed. The four cantons most heavily engaged in the revolt (Bourdeaux, Crest-sud, Dieulefit, Marsanne) had increased their population by 2.7 per cent from 1836-41 and by 2.1 per cent from 1841-6, but they had zero population growth from 1846-51.[30] Because of the commercial recession, young peasants may have had more difficulty entering a trade. In earlier decades artisans and shopkeepers, who were generally more dependent on commercial exchange than their farming neighbours, had comprised around one quarter of the military draft class in this region; from 1849-51 their share fell to only 18 per cent in five sample cantons.[31] All these measures of socioeconomic change are concordant: market conditions deteriorated in the central Drôme during the Second Republic.

Despite the tight money market, systematic data on expropriations and land sales show that relatively few families were actually ruined. Vigier infers that because the annual rate of expropriations doubled between 1840-7 and 1848-51, it reached catastrophic levels.[32] Yet if the rate is expressed in per capita terms, it becomes much less impressive: 1 per 2,000 before 1848 and 1 per 1,000 thereafter. More concretely, around 100 out of the 7,000 households in the cantons of Crest-nord, Crest-sud and Bourdeaux suffered expropriation during the Second Republic.[33] To this number should be added the property owners who sold land under duress in order to reimburse their creditors. Such disguised expropriations increased somewhat after the

February Revolution, and they probably involved two or three times as many households as did court imposed sales.[34] In combination, these two patterns of debt redemption harmed less than 5 per cent of the families in the rebel zone around Crest. Furthermore, some compulsory sales of property benefited more families than they injured. The victims of expropriation tended to resemble bankrupt businessmen pursued by multiple creditors rather than marginal peasants ruined by implacable usurers. In a sample of over 100 expropriations in the *arrondissment* of Die (including Crest and Bourdeaux), 48 per cent involved over five creditors and 79 per cent involved more than one creditor. Indeed, 28 per cent of these debtors were merchants or artisans rather than 'proprietors' or cultivators.[35] It was these bankrupt tradesmen, not peasants, who sometimes played a conspicuous role in the insurrection of 1851. Thus, nine tenths of the 154 individuals whom I have located in the registers of expropriation for the central Drôme escaped arrest (in a region with 815 prosecutions), but the nineteen expropriated men who were prosecuted included nine Montagnard leaders – two of them *négociants*, three innkeepers, two professional men and only two owner-farmers.[36]

If the recession did not create a mass base of expropriated peasants, did it nonetheless foster class conflict between peasant debtors and urban creditors, as Vigier has argued with respect to Crest and its rural hinterland? Some evidence concerning this problem of urban financial domination of the countryside can be derived from the notarial registers of property sales, promissory notes and personal loans made in the cantons of Crest-nord and Crest-sud. I have drawn random samples of 10 per cent of the sales (344 cases) and 20 per cent of the loans (522 cases) registered in these cantons from 1844 through 1851. A rough measure of peasant subordination to urban capitalists can be obtained by analysing the places of residence of the persons involved in these financial transactions. With respect to the land market, urban control would be substantial if townsmen frequently sold land to villagers at inflated prices before 1848, and if they purchased land at depreciated values thereafter. Yet from 1844-7 the seller resided at Crest in only ten of the 184 cases involving a rural buyer; and from 1841-51 the buyer was from Crest in only eight of the 105 cases where the seller was from a rural commune. Nine tenths of the buyers *and* sellers in rural property transactions were themselves inhabitants of bourgs and villages. With respect to loans, the role of Crest was more appreciable but still far from dominant: moneylenders in the town made 21 per cent of the 439 loans to rural debtors within the sample, while rural creditors made 72 per cent of these loans and residents of other towns accounted for the remaining 7 per cent. The urban share of the rural loan market was probably no greater around Crest than it was around Dieulefit, whose townsmen and rural populations joined the rebellion together in 1851.[37]

More detailed analysis of creditors and debtors within particular villages indicates that loan capital was dispersed throughout the countryside in obscure networks of kinship, patronage and commercial exchange. If we examine those cases involving a debtor from Grane, Puy-St-Martin, Roynac, Saou and Soyons (five rebel communes in the canton of Crest-sud), we find that 125 separate people made the 139 loans in the sample. Four fifths of these creditors resided in the countryside, half of them (forty-eight cases) in the same commune as their debtor, and the other half (forty-eight cases) in another bourg or village of the central Drôme. In many cases rural creditors had the same occupational status as those to whom they loaned money: 62 per cent of them were listed in the notarial registers as 'proprietors', and so were 64 per cent of their debtors. Most of their loans were for relatively small sums of money: 88 per cent involved less than 1,000 francs. It was to obtain larger amounts of capital that villagers occasionally contracted loans from townsmen. Half the loans to these five villages which did involve over 1,000 francs originated at Crest or other towns. The urban lenders in the sample, who were usually merchants or professional men, probably required more surety for their funds than the bulk of the peasantry could provide. It is likely that poor access to urban capital rather than its burdensome terms or baleful consequences was the main problem for endebted farm families in the central Drôme. When they needed funds — less often to buy more land than to repay old debts, to finance commercial transactions, or to settle dowries and estates — they usually had to rely on wealthier friends, neighbours or kinsmen in the countryside. In such a fragmented, secretive and personalised loan market, the exploitative relationship between creditors and debtors was often veiled by ties of patronage. It is noteworthy that a few Republican patrons in the central Drôme were also moneylenders: Oscar Vernet, the left wing mayor of Bourdeaux, made nineteen small loans *sous seing privé* to peasants and artisans in 1848-9; Mme Sabatier, a longstanding opponent of the government at Mirmande, financed the leaders of the Montagnard party in that village with 250,000 francs worth of loans; and Defaysse-Soubeyran, a banker at Dieulefit, used his financial influence over the countryside to further the Montagnard cause.[38] Generally speaking, however, creditors and debtors do not seem to have been linked in any systematic manner to political extremism. Thus, among the 116 debtors and 48 creditors in the above sample, equally small proportions were prosecuted after the *coup d'état*: eleven (7 per cent) of the debtors and three (6 per cent) of the creditors. Yet a total of 161 individuals from these five communes were prosecuted for their role in the rebellion.

Just as neither expropriations nor debts were closely related to the mass base of militancy, so peasant landowners were not in the forefront of resistance to the *coup*. If we examine the occupational background and household status of men who were denounced to the authorities as active and willing participants in the revolt, we find that craftsmen, shopkeepers, dependent sons of owner-farmers, and agricultural labourers were more frequently compromised than their landowning neighbours and parents. This can be shown by comparing the percentile distribution of conspicuous participants drawn from these several social categories with the percentile distribution of all adult males from these same categories. The ratio of these percentages measures the extent to which each social group was over-represented (greater than 1.0) or under-represented (less than 1.0) in the rebel ranks.[39] Table 1 presents the summary results for twelve representative communes in the central Drôme, classified into artisanal centres (over 15 per cent of the male labour force employed in crafts and commerce) and primary villages. We can see that artisans and shopkeepers were the most heavily compromised social group in both types of rural communes, followed by the sons of owner-farmers and agricultural labourers. Owner-farmers who headed households (and who presumably controlled the land) comprised only 23 per cent of the 423 voluntary rebels traced in the census lists of these communes. The lukewarm political temper of landowning peasants is also suggested by the age and marital distribution of the 134 cultivators in the central Drôme who admitted belonging to Montagnard societies: 80 per cent of them were under forty years old and 49 per cent were unmarried.[40] Direct evidence of property holdings at the important communes of Bourdeaux and Grane (which mobilised nearly 1,000 insurgents between them in 1851) confirms that men who were compromised in the revolt tended to be landless: over two thirds of the militant farmers and nearly two thirds of the militant artisans from these communes did not own any taxable property, and less than one fifth owned land with a taxable income of over 50 francs a year.[41] Although the mass mobilisations at Bourdeaux, Grane and other rebel communes in the region did include owner-farmers, the middle aged men often escaped arrest by claiming that they had been forced to march. In the eyes of the government, the subversives in rural society were younger men, the future heirs of property rather than its present owners.

Turning from the economic circumstances and social background of the rebels to their professed objectives, it is important to distinguish between the conspiratorial and insurrectionary phases of opposition to the government. The leaders of the underground movement for a Democratic and Social Republic in the Drôme definitely appealed to the economic aspirations and social resentments of the rural poor.

Table 1   Voluntary Participants in the Insurrection, by Occupation and Type of Rural Commune

	Day labourers	Owner farmers (household heads)	Owner farmers (dependent relatives)	Other farmers	Artisans shopkeepers	Others (landlords, professional men, employees)	Total
I Artisanal Centres (15-30 per cent of male labour force are artisans and shopkeepers)							
Number of Participants	40	50	37	23	103	28	281
Per cent of Participants	14	18	13	8	37	10	
Per cent of Population	12	28	13	15	20	12	
Ratio of Participation	1.2	0.6	1.0	0.5	1.8	0.8	
II Primary Villages (under 15 per cent artisans and shopkeepers)							
Number of Participants	9	45	46	14	16	2	132
Per cent of Participants	7	34	35	11	12	2	
Per cent of Population	6	44	26	13	8	4	
Ratio of Participation	1.2	0.8	1.4	0.8	1.5	0.5	

Sources: Dossiers of prisoners and witnesses in A.D. Drôme, M1353-1371, and A.D. Rhône, Archives du tribunal militaire de Lyon; nominative census lists in 1851 for the artisanal centres of Beaufort, Bourdeaux, Lachamp (3 hamlets), Mirmande, Puy-St-Martin, St Gervais and Sauzet; and for the primary villages of Autichamp, La-Roche-sur-Grane, Roynac, Soyons and Suze.

Some Montagnards admitted this to magistrates in their interrogations and testimonies after the revolt. Tax reform rather than cheap credit was the dominant theme of this economic propaganda. As one leader from Grane reportedly told some initiates:[42]

'Citizens, there exists a society which you do not know about yet; this society has for its aim to change the government, to lower taxes, to equalize better the public charges in such a manner that a small window does not pay as much as a large one, to reduce the large government salaries, in a word, to improve the condition of the people.'

Fiscal equality was a traditional concern of rural populations in the Drôme, and it had helped ensure their favourable response to the French Revolution of 1789. Now once again, peasants and artisans with low incomes hoped to shift the tax burden from the poor to the rich. Tax reform or reductions in government salaries were the economic goals most frequently recalled by confessed Montagnards in their interrogations and testimonies, followed by vague improvements in the condition of the people (19) and free education (5). Only one Montagnard in the central Drôme alluded to cheap credit as a motive for joining the underground.

During the revolt, however, traces of economic propaganda seem to have been very rare. Out of some 2,000 interrogations and testimonies from participants and witnesses in the rebel communes, there are only a handful of references to economic motives for insurgency. A band told one middle aged owner-farmer that the window tax was unjust and primary schools should be free; a sharecropper argued with another landowning farmer that because his taxes would be reduced in half, he should be pleased instead of reluctant to march; and an artisan told an agricultural labourer that 'they were working for the labourers who would receive 2,50 francs per day in the future (instead of 1,50)'.[43] By comparison with these faint echoes of earlier economic promises, dozens of insurgents and witnesses reported hearing that rebels wanted to defend the Republic and secure the release of political prisoners. Hundreds more said that they were following orders, imitating their neighbours, trying to help the nearest town, responding to rumours of a general uprising, attempting to restore 'good order', or marching under the threat of force. Where collective hostility did erupt in December, it was directed against individuals who had revealed their anti-Republican loyalties and repressive zeal before the uprising. Gendarmes, *mouchards* (stool pigeons) and whites (Monarchists) were targets of peasant hatred in precisely those communes where political conflict had been most intense before the *coup*. Once the economic aspirations of younger peasants and artisans had been projected into the Montagnard cause, specifically political loyalties and resentments acquired a momentum of their own. It is this political momentum which explains the most salient features of the revolt in the central Drôme — conspiratorial preparations among bands of villagers, appeals to the broader community for support, punishment of government collaborators, and coordinated marches on the towns.

The secret societies of the Montagnards were the most obvious political force behind the insurrection. Indeed, contemporary administrators were convinced that conspiratorial leaders were solely responsible for resistance to the *coup*. With their false promises and diabolical initiation rites, these 'anarchists' and 'demagogues' had seduced or intimidated the ignorant populations of the countryside. Having planned in advance to overthrow the government, they demanded action in December 1851, but many of their initiates took arms only to flee at the earliest possible moment. This administrative view of manipulative leaders and passive recruits, however inconsistent with an economic interpretation of angry rebels, shares the presupposition that peasants lacked any political motives for action. To evade arrest, some Montagnard initiates did claim afterward that they had been recruited on the false premise that the society was a mutual benefit association. Although Vigier stresses the role of Montagnard leaders in organising the revolt, he accepts such testimony at face value in order to minimise the political content of the insurrection. 'Many neophytes, at the moment of their affiliation, believed firmly that they were only entering a mutual benefit society, and they were astonished, frightened, even terrified to find themselves confronted with a political commitment in their oaths.' Despite their loss of innocence, such recruits 'quickly lost interest in the society and waited for the first opportunity to leave it and even to betray it'. They were equally ignorant, befuddled and poorly motivated when their leaders issued a call to arms after the *coup d'état*: 'Most of the peasants, even the artisans, who marched on Digne [prefecture of the Basses-Alpes] or Crest knew nothing about the Constitution, indeed, they knew nothing about politics at all.' The Montagnard programme and political organisation was 'deficient', and many members were reluctant rebels: 'Many suspects from the Drôme confessed that they had obeyed the orders given by their leaders to take arms because they were members of the secret society in their commune and had to remain faithful to their oath. Very often, however, they had almost no desire to do so.'[44]

This version of events infers from the aftermath of the revolt — military collapse and demoralisation — that the insurgents often lacked political motivation *before* the *coup d'état*. Yet throughout the central Drôme Montagnards had inherited an active and successful Republican electoral movement; their conspiratorial preparations had increased the regional orientation and local militancy of the rural populations; and their struggle against administrative repression had earned them the sympathies of entire communities. These overlapping dimensions of collective action — deliberate, organised support for the Republic, and spontaneous, diffuse hostility toward the state — comprise the political dynamics of insurgency in the central Drôme.

The first Montagnard societies in the Drôme were imported from the neighbouring department of the Vaucluse, where Carbonari rituals, already present during the July Monarchy, were revived for electoral purposes in the winter of 1848-9.[45] Provençal political culture, with its factional disputes, bourgeois social clubs (*Cercles*) and popular forms of sociability (religious brotherhoods and the secular derivatives, known as *chambrées* or *sociétés*), proved receptive to clandestine propaganda.[46] Nonetheless, historical tradition generally favoured the Legitimists in the plains of the Vaucluse and the southern Drôme. The anti-Legitimist families in this region, embittered by memories of the White Terror but intimidated by their royalist enemies, might conspire in the dark but they lost the elections in May 1849. By contrast, opponents of the 'Whites' (Legitimists) in the central Drôme campaigned openly for Republican candidates at that time, and very few of them joined the underground until the following year. The rural populations to the north of Montélimar and Dieulefit, whether Protestant or Catholic, shared more positive memories of the French revolution than their counterparts to the south; influential landowners, merchants and professional men encouraged their interest in Republican politics; and urban militants arranged for them to attend electoral rallies in the towns. The well organised Republican campaign in this area resulted in a landslide victory for the departmental list of Republican candidates, which notables from Montélimar, Dieulefit, Crest, Bourdeaux and Sauzet (canton of Marsanne) had helped to choose. Public propaganda, not conspiratorial intrigue, sparked popular involvement in the Republican cause throughout the central Drôme.[47]

The shift from electioneering to clandestine preparations for revolt occurred in a context of administrative repression and legal disenfranchisement. To begin with, the government revived authoritarian controls over political activity. Just as earlier regimes had suppressed Republican associations as threats to public order, so now the ministers of Louis Napoleon set about to destroy the Republican electoral movement. Political clubs were abolished, front organisations (*cercles* and mutual benefit societies) dissolved, electoral rallies banned, and newspapers prosecuted. Nowhere was repression more severe than in the Drôme, where the state of siege was imposed for electoral purposes in July 1849 and retained until 1852. In addition to prohibiting all written propaganda, public meetings and 'unauthorised' (i.e. Republican)

269

associations, the military authorities used troop columns to disarm and intimidate the rural populations, especially in the central Drôme. Even the most trivial displays of Republican sentiments — songs, slogans and emblems — were outlawed, cafés with Republican clienteles were closed down, and offenders were sentenced to heavy prison terms by military tribunals. Meanwhile, the royalists in the national assembly passed a new electoral law in May 1850 which effectively disenfranchised one third of the voters. Harassed by the government and threatened with a substantial reduction in their electoral base of support, some Republican leaders in the central Drôme became involved in the so-called 'Plot of Lyon'. This attempt to create an interdepartmental network of Montagnard societies for the armed defence of the Republic brought a dramatic increase in the pace of conspiratorial recruitment around Crest, Dieulefit and Montélimar. Radiating outward from the towns with the assistance of some notables in the bourgs and large villages (a revoked tax collector at Bourdeaux, a landlord at Mirmande), Montagnard societies were implanted in many rural communities of the central Drôme during the year 1850. By the eve of the *coup*, they existed throughout the region, as Vigier has shown.[48]

These Montagnard societies transformed the political situation in four respects. For one thing, their ceremonial activities, welfare functions and secret meetings provided ordinary inhabitants of the countryside with leadership opportunities. As long as public electoral committees had controlled the Republican movement, leadership roles had been largely restricted to landlords, professional men and merchants, aided by some craftsmen and shopkeepers in the towns and bourgs. Now the peasants themselves began exercising political responsibilities as Montagnard initiators, presidents, vice-presidents, treasurers, 'centurions' and 'decurions'. Of the 125 such leaders whom I have identified in rural communes of the central Drôme, fifty-one were cultivators, forty-five were artisans or shopkeepers, and only twenty-seven were landlords, professional men or merchants.[49] In addition to broadening the social base of leadership, the Montagnard societies strengthened the political solidarity of rank-and-file members. Youth groups and café clienteles had already been politicised to some extent during the electoral campaigns, but now these forms of popular sociability were explicitly integrated with a political organisation. Montagnards frequented the same cafés, they attended the same dances and festivities, and they shared the same political convictions. Especially in the rural communities, the young men, or *la jeunesse*, joined the Montagnard societies *en masse*; not to belong was tantamount to declaring oneself an antisocial being. As one nineteen year old stonemason from a village near Montélimar testified, 'For a long time I noticed that the young men of Sauzet seemed to despise me, and then I found out that it was because I didn't belong to their secret society; since everyone else was a member, my position was not tenable, so I decided to join.'[50] Thirdly, Montagnard organisational links between towns, bourgs and adjacent villages fostered a regional consciousness of political solidarity. The men of each commune looked toward nearby market centres for political leadership, and they identified with their comrades elsewhere in the region. Through the prevailing network of markets and fairs, Montagnards entered a regional brotherhood with a national orientation. For example, the assistant mayor at Crest observed in May 1850 that 'known demagogues from Grane, Saillans, Puy-St-Martin and Bourdeaux come sometimes to meet with their *frères et amis* at Crest'; and the police commissioner reported after the town festival in September 1851 that 'the democrats from the surrounding communes were there in force, shaking hands with their *frères et amis*'.[51] Finally, members of the underground were committed to extreme measures in defence of the Republic. Although some of them may have agreed only to vote for Republican candidates, more commonly they swore to take arms at the command of their leaders. Some even promised to 'abandon' their families — fathers and mothers or wives and children — if ordered to march.[52] Threats of death impressed upon them the solemnity of their engagement and the absolute necessity for secrecy. Whether at the polls or in the streets, they would reveal their accumulated strength only at the moment of combat for a 'Democratic and Social Republic'.

Subversion provoked further repression, which in turn stimulated more opposition to the government. This cycle of repression and resistance was especially characteristic of the central Drôme, whose population (24 per cent of the departmental total) experienced half the political prosecutions and three fifths of the military and police operations reported in the department in 1850-1. During the eleven months preceding the *coup d'état*, twenty five of the thirty military raids and seventeen of the nineteen prosecutions for conspiracy and related offences took place in the central Drôme.[53] Several villages near Montélimar were first visited by troops in July 1849, following denunciations by local Whites.[54] Much more extensive operations were launched in August 1850, after the prefect learned the names of some high ranking Montagnards from a secret informer.[55] Troops marched from Valence to Crest, where they were sent to Bourdeaux, Dieulefit and Marsanne in support of house searches against a few dozen suspected leaders.[56] When gendarmes from Loriol tried to make a political arrest in the commune of Mirmande as a part of this repressive campaign, a crowd rescued the prisoner and two days later (4 September) Montagnards at the nearby village of Cliousclat mobilised in arms to protect another political leader. These 'revolts' precipitated a massive influx of troops, but most of the thirty men who had been compromised took flight.[57] The troops were withdrawn to their garrison at Valence, and gendarmes patrolled the forested region between Mirmande, Grane and Marsanne for months thereafter, searching fruitlessly for the suspects. They finally stumbled across an armed band of peasants near Grane on 17 June 1851, but two of them were wounded and the fugitives escaped.[58] Outraged by this defiance of military authority, the commander of the state of siege flooded the region with troops, who arbitrarily searched hundreds of houses without success.[59] Eleven soldiers stationed at Grane were even compromised along with twelve civilians in an alleged plot to rebel immediately.[60] While most of the civilians fled arrest, the government nervously withdrew all the troops at the end of the month.

Instead of dismantling the Montagnard societies, these troop deployments created martyrs to the Republican cause and antagonised entire populations. The government's political intelligence was too poor for effective use of its military forces. Not a single initiate in the central Drome made a full confession before the *coup* (only a handful admitted anything), only four rural mayors reported any signs of conspiracy (none conclusive), and only four or five anonymous informers supplied the names of any leaders.[61] The only reliable agents of centralised authority were the military commander, the subprefect, the public prosecutor, the gendarmes, and the police commissioner at Montélimar; the gendarmes, the police commissioner and the municipal authorities at Crest; and the gendarmes at Loriol. Isolated from the rural populations, these few officials ended up treating everyone in the countryside as suspects. They managed to jail or put to flight only eleven Montagnard leaders in the seven cantons, but they prosecuted at least seventy men from sixteen communes in the region, and they raided the homes of hundreds more.[62] The procureur general at Grenoble, who had praised the state of siege in July 1850 for inspiring fear in the Montagnards, recognised in September 1851 that indiscriminate repression had radicalised the populations:[63]

'Subordinate officials do not always behave with moderation and justice in their investigations and police raids. Men who were harmless or undecided, men restrained by wise instinct or healthy opinions, find themselves treated as if they were dangerous and guilty. In their irritation they abandon caution and enter the general current [of opposition to the government].'

The military dragnet in the cantons of Crest-sud, Loriol and Marsanne had merely driven the populations into the arms of Montagnard activists. According to the procureur general, the region had been 'entirely lost to the cause of order' and 'just about all the inhabitants share the most extreme opinions'.[64]

272

Against this background of conspiracy, repression and massive opposition to the government, insurgency in December 1851 typically involved secret preparations among Montagnard militants, followed by public appeals for community support. The preliminary phase of armed revolt was everywhere the same: Montagnard emissaries conveyed orders from the towns and market bourgs to the villages, and local militants alerted each other secretly. Although regional planning was poor, leaders at Crest, Bourdeaux, Dieulefit and Montélimar all received word from Valence, the departmental capital, that a general revolt was scheduled for 6-7 December. The purpose of this uprising was to seize the prefecture at Valence, with the more distant goal of marching all the way to Paris in defence of the Republic. Urban leaders within the central Drôme drew up specific plans of action on 5-6 December: villagers near Crest were supposed to reach town at noontime of 6 December; those near Montélimar were assigned a rendezvous just east of town at 6.00 p.m.; and those near Dieulefit were expected in town at 10.00 p.m. Despite some delay and confusion, the columns of peasants which marched on Crest from the northeast (valley of the Gervanne) and the southwest (Grane) on the afternoon of the 6th, those which reached St Marcel (near Montélimar) shortly after midnight, and those which entered Dieulefit at about the same time were all responding to these plans. So were the rebels from the canton of Bourdeaux, whose leaders coordinated their action with townsmen at Dieulefit. Sweeping northward, the contingents from Bourdeaux and Dieulefit, aided by all the villages en route, numbered nearly 3,000 men from thirty-three communes when they approached the town of Crest on the afternoon of 7 December. Even the rebellions of Mirmande and Cliousclat, which did not begin until the early morning hours of 8 December, followed this same pattern of urban-rural communications among Montagnard leaders: two men from Loriol had arrived during the night with written orders to march on the town.[65]

It was local Montagnard initiative which assured the success of these regional mobilisations. To begin with, leaders of Montagnard societies assumed responsibility for organising the rural mobilisations throughout the central Drôme. Their precise role can be ascertained in thirty-two bourgs and villages of the region, and it can be inferred from the pattern of events in nearly all the communes. Montagnard leaders sought additional information, alerted neighbouring villages, held surreptitious meetings, instigated public demonstrations, gave public speeches and led their compatriots to the prearranged points of assembly near the towns. Even where all the rebels denied any prior knowledge of Montagnard societies, bands of militants had spread the alert in advance of the revolt. Commonly they had urged everyone to go with their weapons to the village square as soon as they heard the church bells ring. Preliminary alerts and secret meetings took place in at least forty-five rebel communes. Furthermore, local bands rather than outsiders generally triggered the public phase of the mobilisations. In defiance of the law (though sometimes with tacit approval of municipal authorities), they obtained the church keys and rang the tocsin, or they demonstrated in the village streets to the sound of the drum. Such public displays of power were especially characteristic of communes where the Montagnards enjoyed majority support. Thus, the tocsin rang in twenty-seven of the thirty-five communes where a majority of the men mobilised ('majoritarian communes'), as compared with fourteen of the thirty-nine communes where only a minority of the men turned out to march ('minoritarian communes')' Finally, Montagnard bands recruited manpower by force. Again, compulsory recruitment occurred more often in majoritarian communes (19/35 cases) than in minoritarian communes (8/39 cases). If Montagnards demanded that everyone march, it was not only because their leaders issued orders to that effect. Rank-and-file participants were often the first to insist that everyone share the risks of combat, including those who had opposed the Republicans in earlier months. Where such a spirit of 'communal unanimism' existed, all the men of the locality formed a column under military command, and they marched to the accompaniment of a drummer and a flag bearer. At least twenty communes exhibited this transformation of Montagnard crowds into military columns, inspired by earlier traditions of National Guard units and village solidarity.[66]

Especially in the majoritarian communes, the issue of repression imparted momentum to the revolt. This can be seen with respect to the precipitation of public mobilisations, the forcible recruitment or disarmament of opponents, and the legitimation of armed demonstrations against the government. At Grane, for example, the Montagnard leaders were still awaiting new orders from Crest, where the tocsin had failed to ring as scheduled at noontime on the 6th, when gunfire erupted a mile west of the village: bands of peasants, including political fugitives, were under attack by the gendarmes from Loriol! The tocsin rang, the gendarmes fled, and the peasants swarmed into the village, led by the fugitives. In an impassioned mood, they celebrated their liberation from oppression, seized several of their political enemies, including two priests, and marched, 500 strong, toward Crest. In the words of the mayor's secretary, a leader of the movement, they were marching 'to conquer our rights and our prisoners'.[67] A similar pattern of events occured at Mirmande two days later, when a band of conspirators took public action only after a patrol of conservative national guardsmen had arrested one of their men. Storming into the town hall, they rescued the prisoner, rang the tocsin, and began a massive mobilisation, aided again by fugitives. Here, too, their leaders called for the release of

274

political prisoners.[68] Indeed, all the major mobilisations in the central Drôme expressed tensions derived from political prosecutions before the *coup* or preventive arrests thereafter. Such tensions were increased by rumours that fighting had already begun in the towns of Crest and Montélimar or elsewhere in France. At Beaufort and Montclar (Crest-nord), Puy-St-Martin and Roynac (Crest-sud), Bourdeaux and Dieulefit, Marsanne and St Gervais, the call to arms was a call to defend those in jail, those in flight, or those in open rebellion against the heavy hand of a suspicious and authoritarian state.[69]

As political demonstrations of Montagnard strength within the countryside, these insurrections were a temporary success. Once the rebels collided with troops, however, the military weakness of their position became self-evident. Although they heavily outnumbered the troops who were defending Montélimar and Crest, their military organisation was deficient in every respect. They had no command structure to link the various communes together, their prior military experience was usually limited to marching in formation, and they had few rifles and very little ammunition. Furthermore, many insurgents expected the army to fraternise with them or to retreat in the face of their superior numbers. When the troops guarding Crest and Montélimar opened fire, the columns from Grane and those from the canton of Marsanne both disintegrated. Only the men from Bourdeaux, who marched as a National Guard unit, fought at all effectively, and even they abandoned the struggle after skirmishing with the soldiers at Crest for a few hours. As a result of the swift collapse of rebel forces, relatively few men were killed or injured in the region: around ten rebels and three soldiers died, and around thirty rebels and six soldiers were wounded.[70] The demoralisation of the rebels became complete once the government launched an extensive military and judicial operation to restore order. Over 1,100 men in the central Drôme were prosecuted by the 'mixed commission' established at Valence to regulate the purge. This massive repression succeeded where the sporadic repression before the *coup d'état* had failed. From all the villages came professions of loyalty and pleas for mercy. Erstwhile militants foreswore all interest in politics and promised 'full and entire submission' to the government.[71] With the police state of Louis Napoleon finally in control of the rural populations, the political crisis of the Second Republic was over.[72]

In sum, resistance to the *coup d'état* in the Drôme was a political protest movement under military guise rather than either a social revolt or a revolutionary war. As an outcome of both conspiratorial organisation and communal hostility to the state, it combined 'modern' and 'reactionary' dimensions of protest in an unusual manner. The Republican ideals and electoral aspirations of the Montagnards helped shape the political future of peasants in the Drôme, but their myth of 'the people in arms' had been shattered once and for all. The failure of insurgency in 1851 marked the definitive separation of Republican electoral politics from the reactionary tradition of violent peasant protest. Henceforth, when rural voters wanted to oppose the state, they would leave their pitchforks and their hunting rifles at home.

Notes

1. Charles Tilly, 'The Changing Place of Collective Violence', in Melvin Richter, ed., *Essays in Theory and History: An Approach to the Social Sciences* (Cambridge, Mass., 1970), pp. 139-64; and Tilly, 'How Protest Modernized in France, 1845-1855', in W. Aydelotte, *et al., The Dimensions of Quantitative Research in History* (Princeton, N.J., 1972), pp. 192-255.

2. The only detailed narrative of provincial resistance to the *coup d'état* was written over one hundred years ago by Eugène Ténot, *La Province en décembre 1851. Étude historique sur le coup d'état* (Paris, 1865). Recent analyses using national statistics and monographic literature include the above articles by Tilly; Roger Price, *The French Second Republic, a Social History* (London, 1972), pp. 283-326; and Maurice Agulhon, *1848 ou l'apprentissage de la République, 1848-1852* (Paris, 1973), pp. 174-97. The best monographs on particular regions are by Agulhon, *La République au village* [on the Var] (Paris, 1970), and Philippe Vigier, *La Seconde République dans la région alpine* [on the Basses-Alpes, the Hautes-Alpes, the Drôme, the Isère, and the Vaucluse] (2 vols., Paris, 1963). I am currently writing a book on the insurrection.

3. Including Vigier; Price; and Claude Levy, 'Notes sur les fondements sociaux de l'insurrection de décembre 1851 en province', *Information historique*, XVI, no. 4 (1954), pp. 142-5.

4. Howard C. Payne, 'Preparation of a Coup d'État: Administrative Centralization and Police Powers in France, 1849-1851', in *Studies in Modern European History in Honor of Franklin Charles Palm*, ed., Frederich J. Cox, *et al.* (N.Y., 1956); Vigier, II, pp. 170-306; and Jean Dagnan, *Le Gers sous la Seconde République*, vol. I (Auch, 1928).

5. These quantitative estimates are based on an exhaustive study of the interrogations of suspects, the testimony of witnesses, and the reports of officials in the cantons of Bourdeaux, Crest-nord, Crest-sud, Dieulefit, Loriol, Marsanne and Montélimar, the region which I define as the 'central Drôme', *Archives départementales de la Drôme* (henceforth A.D. Drôme), M1348-1371; *Archives du Tribunal militaire de Lyon* (A.T.M.L.), dossier 5, 'Insurrection de décembre 1851', A.D. Rhône; Archives nationales (A.N.), BB^{30} 395-396, 400*.

6. Karl Marx, 'The Class Struggles in France 1848-1850', in Marx and Engels, *Selected Works*, I (Moscow, 1962), p. 216. See also Marx, 'The Eighteenth Brumaire of Louis Bonaparte', in *Selected Works*, pp. 336-8. For a recent critique of Marx's analysis, see Price, *The Second Republic*, pp. 20-6.

7. Vigier, *La Région alpine*, I, p. 31. See also Pierre Léon, *La Naissance de la grande industrie en Dauphiné et Provence* (Paris, 1927), pp. 349-59, 456; and Raoul Blanchard, *Les Alpes occidentales*, vol. IV, *Les Préalpes françaises du sud* (Grenoble, 1945), pp. 358-60.

8. Faucher, *Plaines*, pp. 456-81; and Blanchard, *Les Préalpes*, pp. 358-60.

9. Between 1831-46, the population of the cantons of Crest-sud, Bourdeaux, Dieulefit and Marsanne (central Drôme) increased by 7 per cent; and that of Bourg-de-Péage, Le Grand Serre, Romans and St Vallier (northern Drôme) increased by 8 per cent. Population tables in A.D. Drôme.

10. Albert Soboul, 'Les troubles agraires de 1848', in *Paysans, sans-culottes et*

Jacobins (Paris, 1966), pp. 349-50.
11.   Vigier, *La Région alpine*, I, pp. 23-72; and Vigier, *Essai sur la répartition de la propriété foncière dans la région alpine et son évolution des origines du cadastre à la fin du Second Empire* (Paris, 1959).
12.   Vigier, *La Région alpine*, I, pp. 205-6; II, p. 211 (map of the electoral results in May 1849).
13.   Agulhon, *La République au village*, pp. 42-92. 361-75.
14.   Adolphe Crémieux, a Parisian lawyer and minister of justice in the provisional Republican government, who bought part of the forest of Saou in 1850. A.D. Drôme, 2C 25 Canton of Crest, public civil acts, sales entry, 9 October 1850. On the rebel role of his business manager Jean Louis Culty, see A.D. Drôme, M1359, dossier Culty. For the historical background of factional conflicts over forests at Saou, see A.D. Drôme, 13M, municipal elections, dossier of Saou; and the forthcoming doctoral dissertation of Richard Malby (Balliol College, Oxford) on the French revolutionary epoch in the Drôme.
15.   Int. Pierre Delaine, baker at Mirmande, A.T.M.L., dossier 5.
16.   Tilly, 'The Changing Place of Collective Violence', p. 155.
17.   *Ibid.*, pp. 160-2.
18.   Faucher, *Plaines*, pp. 429-36; Blanchard, *Les Préalpes*, pp. 409-13; Léon, *La grande industrie*, II.
19.   'Enquête sur le travail de 1848', cantonal commission of Bourdeaux, A.N., C951, Drôme.
20.   Faucher, *Plaines*, pp. 359-62; Blanchard, *Les Préalpes*, p. 413.
21.   'Listes du tirage au sort', cantons of Crest-nord, Crest-sud, Bourdeaux, Dieulefit and Marsanne, 1829, 1830, 1831, 1839, 1940, 1841, 1849, 1850, 1851, A.D. Drôme, series R.
22.   'Listes nominatives', arranged alphabetically by commune, census of 1851, A.D. Drôme, 35M.
23.   Census list of adult males, 1806; census list of all households, 1851, both in the communal archives at Bourdeaux.
24.   For an analysis of these two types of economic crisis in mid-nineteenth century France, see the departmental monographs published by Ernest Labrousse, ed., *Aspects de la crise et de la dépression de l'économie française au milieu du XIXe siècle, 1846-1851* (La Roche-sur-Yon, 1956).
25.   Vigier, *La Région alpine*, II, pp. 34, 62, 63, 408, 411, 163-4.
26.   See Vigier's detailed analysis of the rural economy and society in the Alpine region during the Second Republic, *ibid.*, I, pp. 260-82; II, pp. 10-165.
27.   A.N. C951, Drôme.
28.   'Register du conseil municipal de Grane', 30 November 1851, communal archive of Grane.
29.   Calculations based on a random sample of 20 per cent of the notarised loans ('billets à ordre' and 'obligations') and 10 per cent of the notarised property sales registered in the cantons of Crest-nord and Crest-sud from 1844-51, A.D. Drôme, 2C 25.
30.   The population of these four cantons was 37,045 in 1846 and 37,048 in 1851, A.D. Drôme, population tables.
31.   From 1829-31, 24 per cent of the draft class cited in n. 21 were employed in crafts and commerce (329/1395), from 1839-41, the figure was 23 per cent (336/1471), and from 1849-51 it fell to 17 per cent (270/1559).
32.   Chart in Vigier, *La région alpine*, I, p. 269; discussion in vol. II, pp. 32-5.
33.   Calculations based on the registers of expropriations (one third sample) for the *arrondissment* of Die, Feb. 1848 to Sept. 1852 (six out of nine registers are extant, listing sixty-nine expropriations in the cantons of Crest-nord, Crest-sud and Bourdeaux), A.D. Drôme, unclassified *Procès-verbaux de saisie.*

34. Calculations based on the 10 per cent sample of notarised sales cited in n. 29. From 1844-7, 21/208 cases (10 per cent) involved a cash transfer from the buyer to a creditor of the seller; such sales comprised 28/136 (21 per cent) of the sample from 1848-51.

35. Calculations based on the ten extant registers of expropriations out of the fourteen which originally existed for the *arrondissement* of Die, April 1844-September 1852.

36. These 154 expropriations took place in rebel communes in the *arrondissements* of Die and Montélimar; thirteen of the eighteen registers from February 1848 through September 1852 are extant. All the names have been compared with the judicial records of prosecutions after the *coup d'état*, cited in n. 5.

37. On the basis of incomplete notarial registers for the canton of Dieulefit (January 1847-end of 1848), I calculate that 25 per cent of the loans to rural debtors were made by residents of the town.

38. Entries in the register of *actes sous seing privé*, canton of Bourdeaux, A.D. Drôme, 2C 268; Int. Mme Sabatier and comment of the gendarmes, A.D. Drôme, M1370; judicial comment on Defaysse-Soubeyran in his dossier, A.D. Drôme, M1360.

39. This statistical measure is derived from William H. Sewell's analysis of the social base of Republican militancy in Marseille during the Second Republic, 'La classe ouvrière de Marseille sous la Seconde République', *Le Mouvement social*, 76 (July-September 1971), p. 50.

40. Calculations based on the *état civil* of suspects and witnesses who confessed after the *coup d'état*, sources cited in n. 5.

41. Tax rolls for the four direct taxes, 1846-51, communal archives of Bourdeaux; *Cadastre*, communal archives of Grane; dossiers of suspects from these communes, sources cited in n. 5.

42. Tem. Ant. Grontier, owner-farmer/day labourer at La-Roche-sur-Grane, reporting the speech of Faure, cadet, a cult, at Grane, dossier La Roche, A.D. Drôme, M1355.

43. Tem. A. Rouin, 45, landowner, dossier La-Roche-sur-Grane; Tem. L. Eymery, 57, landowner, dossier Roynac; tem. Colombor, day labourer, dossier Montclar, A.D. Drôme, M1354-1355.

44. Vigier, *La Région alpine*, II, pp. 265, 330, 336, 325.

45. *Ibid.*, I, pp. 309-11; II, pp. 183, 190-1. A Carbonari conspiracy was discovered in the plains of the Vaucluse in 1841; see the 'Acte d'accusation', Procureur general (P.G.) of Aix, 15 September 1841, A.N. BB[18] 1472.

46. See Agulhon's fundamental analysis of political culture in the Var, *La République au village*, especially pp. 149-284.

47. Vigier notes these contrasting political traditions in *La Région alpine*, II, pp. 403-4; for his discussion of the electoral campaign of May 1849 in the Drôme, see vol. II, pp. 195-6, 198-203, 206-7, 216-9. I have analysed this campaign in my doctoral dissertation, 'The Insurrection of 1851 in Southern France: Two Case Studies' (Harvard University, 1972), pp. 32-50.

48. For a discussion of repression and conspiracy in southeastern France from 1849-51, see Vigier, II, pp. 222-304; for an analysis of the central Drôme, see Margadant, 'Two Case Studies', pp. 75-223 *passim.*

49. Tabulation based on the evidence of the judicial investigation after the *coup d'état*, cited in n. 5.

50. Tem. J. Jarrian, dossier Sauzet, A.D. Drôme, M1355.

51. Letter from the *adjoint* of Crest, 11 May 1850; and letter from the police commissioner at Crest, 1 October 1851, A.D. Drôme, M1672.

52. Out of 127 confessed Montagnards in the central Drôme who described features of their oath to magistrates after the *coup d'état*, twenty-one referred to

voting, twenty-nine to marching in arms, and fifteen to abandoning their closest relatives. Sources cited in n. 5.

53.   Calculations based on judicial, administrative and military reports in 1850-51, supplemented by a published list of persons convicted by the military tribunal at Lyon for offences during this period before 2 December 1851. A.N. BB[18] 1485[A], BB[30] 378, 319-394; Military Archives at Vincennes, F[1] 46, general correspondence; A.D. Drôme, M1345-1347; L. Goudier, ed., *Livre d'Or des victimes du coup d'état de 1851 . . . Drome* (Valence, 1883).

54.   See the report of lieutenant Houdeville, commander of the state of siege at Montélimar, undated (early August 1849), A.D. Drôme, M1344.

55.   Letter from the prefect to P.G. Grenoble, 31 May 1851, A.N. BB[30] 391.

56.   Letters from P.G. Grenoble to General Castellane, 18 and 20 July 1850, A.N. BB[30] 391; reports from General Lapène to the prefect, 2 and 3 August 1850, A.D. Drôme, M1345.

57.   On these events at Mirmande and Cliousclat, see A.T.M.L., 'Sociétés secrètes de la Drôme', and A.N. BB[18] 1474[A], BB[30] 360.

58.   Letters from P.G. Grenoble to the Minister of Justice, 10 June and 23 September 1851, A.N. BB[30] 393.

59.   'Exposé des mesures militaires prises dans le courant de juin 1851 pour purger des bandes armées les cantons de Loriol, Marsanne and Crest-sud, June 8, 1851, Valence', in Archives militaires de Vincennes, F[1] 46, 'Correspondence générale', July 1851.

60.   This 'Complot de Grane' resulted in a courtmartial at Lyon, briefly described in *La Gazette des Tribunaux*, 6 June 1852.

61.   Administrative correspondence cited in n. 53.

62.   *Ibid.*

63.   Letter from P.G. Grenoble to the Minister of Justice, 19 September 1851, A.N. BB[30] 378.

64.   *Ibid.*

65.   For a detailed analysis of these Montagnard plans, based on the interrogations of militants, see Margadant, 'Two Case Studies', pp. 309-16, and 316-411 *passim.*

66.   These tabulations of mobilisation patterns are based on the descriptive evidence provided by hundreds of participants, cited in n. 5. See Margadant, 'Two Case Studies', pp. 299-308. Concerning the spirit of 'communal unanimism', see Agulhon's interesting discussion in *La République au village*, pp. 362-7, 451-455.

67.   Int. Pr. Gilles, cult., A.D. Drôme M1362. For a reconstruction of these events at Grane, based on scattered archival sources, see Margadant, 'Two Case Studies', pp. 351-60.

68.   *Ibid.*, pp. 400-11.

69.   *Ibid.*, pp. 316-410, *passim.*

70.   *Ibid.*, pp. 450-75. The 'body count' provided by authorities at Crest was greatly exaggerated (over 100 supposedly killed), as Ténot learned when he visited the region in the 1860s, *La Province*, p. 205. The names of five dead insurgents are inscribed on a granite monument in the cemetary of Crest, and thirteen wounded rebels who fought at Crest are mentioned in the subsequent judicial investigation.

71.   Letter from Louis Cherfils, owner-farmer and rebel leader from Mirabel, 3 March 1852, in dossier Cherfils, A.D. Drôme, M1359.

72.   For a detailed analysis of the restoration of government authority in the central Drôme, see Margadant, 'Two Case Studies', pp. 476-535 *passim.*

THE PREFECTS AND POLITICAL REPRESSION: FEBRUARY 1848 TO DECEMBER 1851

Howard Machin

The repressive activities of the prefects did not begin on the 24 February 1848, nor did they end when the Empire was established on 2 December 1852. It was during the Second Republic, however, and in particular in the period after the *coup d'état* of 2 December 1851, that prefectoral repressive brutality attained its zenith; the almost fanatical persecution of all those who protested against the *coup d'état*, and the seemingly pitiless witch hunt of republicans during the early months of 1852 won for the prefects the undying hatred of their victims. In some respects, however, these authoritarian activities after the *coup d'état* were simply a logical conclusion to the development of prefectoral repressive duties which had been an almost continuous process during the entire period before December 1851, starting from February 1848. The administrative purge by the *commissaires* of Ledru-Rollin, the press censorship restrictions on public meetings under Cavaignac, the gradually increasing attack on all republican demonstrations, organisations and propaganda under the Prince-President and his conservative ministers, all prepared the way and provided the means for what was to follow the *coup d'état*.[1]

An examination of the developing role of the prefects in the repressive machinery in the departments before 2 December 1851 reveals a number of interesting features of this repressive system and is especially enlightening about the role of the prefectoral corps in French provincial life. This study, however, is centred upon only three basic questions. First, to what ends and by what means was the political repression in the provinces extended? This question inevitably requires some analysis of the effectiveness and consistency of the repressive apparatus. The other two questions both directly concern the work of the prefects. What exactly did the prefects do and how important was their influence in determining the extent of the repression? And finally, to what extent was the repressive role of the prefects concomitant with their other administrative and political duties and with their own views of their functions and careers?

The study of these questions reveals both the inadequacies of the repressive machinery and the fundamental importance of local circumstances and personal factors in determining the nature and the extent of repression. In the period before December 1851, the scope of provincial political repression was undoubtedly vastly expanded and its efficiency greatly improved, but a totally coherent, consistent and effective repressive system was never achieved. The enormous variety of local situations and of personal administrative ideals and political interpretations meant that the extent of the repression differed from one department to the next and from month to month. Far from depending on a totally unified and loyal prefectoral corps, Louis-Napoleon had to work with an administration which was divided and dislocated by differing political views, administrative circumstances and local pressures.

The Development of the Repressive System in the Provinces

As the political situation in Paris and the provinces evolved, so successive governments made increasingly numerous demands to their prefects for repressive action. By November 1851, the Government, like many of the conservative notables who supported it in the provinces, had developed a 'siege mentality' − a sad reflection of the transformation of attitudes since the days of utopian optimism in February 1848. Between these two dates, four stages of the extension of the repressive machine may be identified, corresponding to four political phases. A study of the development from stage to stage reveals the significance of specific political events, more general economic and social changes, and the growing attitudes of fear and hatred in explaining some of the measures adopted.

The first stage of development, the last days of February and first weeks of March, was a period of political jubilation and great social harmony. One slogan of the new regime was 'liberty', and hence little repression could be justified, but, in any case, the July Monarchy had few friends left to mourn its passing, so there was almost no-one to repress. Universal suffrage and freedoms of the press and of association were soon established. Two minor types of repression were needed, however, and both involved the prefects. The first was to purge the administration, and the second, to maintain public order. A purge of administrative personnel was inevitable in the light of the universal belief that the activities of the administration − and in particular those of the local administration under the prefects − determined the result of elections. Prefectoral electoral interventions during the Restoration and July Monarchies had become notorious, and the continued success of governmental candidates was generally ascribed to the prefects' 'machine'. The removal of the local administrators appointed by Louis-Philippe was thus inevitable.[2]

What was unusual about the 1848 prefectoral purge was that it was total and that even the official titles of the monarchy were discarded. In previous purges in 1814, 1815 and 1830 handfuls of prefects had survived, and indeed one prefect had not been touched by any of them. In 1848, however, all the prefects of the July Monarchy were sacked, and the men appointed to replace them were given the title of *commissaire*.[3] In practice, the transfer of power to the commissaires took place in some chaos, partly because the Government delayed some appointments, and partly because in thirty departments prefects were *de facto* replaced at once by self-appointed *commissions provisoires* of local republicans. In some cases the Provisional Government later legitimised the existing situation by officially naming the leader of the commission as the commissaire. To further the confusion, three men were appointed as *commissaires generaux* with prefectoral responsibilities for several departments, whilst in certain other departments two or three commissaires were appointed to share prefectoral duties. A total of 110 men were thus involved in the first 'prefectoral' appointments of the Republic.[4]

The new commissaires were themselves responsible for purging the lower ranks of the local administration. It was assumed that they would make many dismissals, but no precise instructions were given from Paris. As a result, the extent of this first administrative purge varied greatly from one place to the next; almost all sub-prefects were soon replaced by *sous-commissaires*, but the numbers of mayors, justices of the peace and other civil servants who lost their jobs depended largely on the wishes of the local commissaire. By this purge the Second Republic created its first victims of repression: men who lost their posts, incomes and social position because of the advent of the new regime.[5]

The second kind of repression in this first period was concerned with maintaining public order. The new commissaires and their subordinates had to contain Luddite attacks on textile machinery and railways in the northeast and Normandy, the pillage of Louis-Philippe's chateau at Neuilly and that of the Rothschilds at Suresnes, antisemitic outbursts in Alsace, the plunder and destruction of convents in Lyon and Bourg, and the pillage of state forests in many departments. These disturbances illustrated the unreadiness of the commissaires and caused some alarm amongst the property owning classes.[6]

The second phase of the development of repression, from mid-March to early May 1848, was the period of the ascendancy of Ledru-Rollin and of the elections to the Constituent Assembly. The economic depression continued, the taxes were increased, the *atéliers nationaux* were set up, the working day was limited by law, the Commission at the Luxembourg began its work, the *garde nationale mobile* was created, the elite companies of the National Guard were disbanded and

Cabet, Raspail and Blanqui began to spread socialist ideas in the political clubs. The euphoric social harmony started to evaporate as the possibilities of large scale economic and social change became apparent and the upper classes increasingly worried. The frequent demonstrations in Paris, and the postponement of the elections after that of 17 March, can have done little to calm anxious provincial notables.[7]

In the departments the administrative purge was renewed and extended, and the first real political violence had to be quelled. The political predominance of Ledru-Rollin in late March enabled him to launch a new wave of appointments of commissaires, including twenty-one new commissaires généraux with responsibility for several departments. By early April, twenty-four commissaires généraux held supervisory powers over the commissaires in sixty of the eighty-five departments. Furthermore, where the existing commissaires were of known moderate views, new radical commissaires were sent to share their duties and powers. In this way, whilst few of the original commissaires were dismissed, many lost much of their influence and some resigned. Most of the original commissaires had been moderate middle class republicans. As a result of the mid-March changes, however, three quarters of the departments were subject to some radical influence, either from a new departmental commissaire or from a commissaire general. Consequently, a new series of purges at the lower levels of local administration took place, producing further numbers of resentful provincial notables. The blatant electioneering of many of the new commissaires, frequently in support of their own candidatures, and the ministerial circular of 8 April did little to enhance the popularity of these men outside radical republican circles.[8]

Reactions to the results of the April elections led to a very different kind of repression. In several provincial towns, police intervention was needed to stop brawls between rival political groups. In Limoges workers refused to accept the election results, invaded the prefecture and took over the departmental administration for two weeks; only when troops arrived did they disperse. And in Rouen, the elections led to the first political bloodshed of the Republic; workers supporting Deschamps, the radical commissaire beaten in the election by the moderate republican procureur general Sénard, demonstrated in protest, were violently dispersed by the middle class National Guard, and began to construct barricades. The procureur called in the army and two days later the revolt was crushed, with thirty dead and seventy wounded.[9] Clearly, the political harmony of February had by now disappeared. The elected Representatives to the Constituent Assembly, at their first meeting on 4 May, faced an awesome task of governing a country marked by bitter divisions and growing tensions.

The next phase in the evolution of repression in the provinces was the period from May to December 1848, the seven months of moderate republican dominance, of the Executive Commission and then the Government of General Cavaignac. It was a period which began with the removal of the Provisional Government, was marked by the bloodbath of the June Days, the take-over by Cavaignac, the restoration of public order in Paris and in the provinces warmly supported by the 'party of order' in the Assembly, and which ended with the election of Louis-Napoleon to the presidency. The fear of Representatives from the provinces of the Paris mob after the 15 May and the June Days, and the desperate anxiety of all conservative notables at the challenge to the existing economic order by the continuation of the crisis, the projected nationalisation of the railways, and the widespread refusal to pay taxes, explain their keen support for new repressive measures, and, indeed, for Louis-Napoleon in the December presidential election. For the moderate republicans who initiated and implemented the repression, the disorders and destruction by the 'reds' not only threatened the rule of law, but also the very existence of the Republic.[10]

The June Days in Paris were undoubtedly the most important repressive action during this period, and indeed during the entire existence of the Second Republic: they resulted in over 2,000 deaths and 15,000 arrests. The details of this repression, directed by Cavaignac himself, are outside the scope of this study. There were also, however, violent demonstrations in several provincial towns, notably Lyon and Marseille at the time of the June Days in Paris. In Marseille, despite the efforts of the Prefect Ollivier, bloodshed was needed before order was restored. Troubles in Lyon, especially in the Croix-Rousse district, continued into July despite the military interventions called for by the procureur general. Rumours of socialist plots for the assassination of General Cavaignac, which circulated in Paris in summer and autumn did little to silence demands for continued or increased repression.[11] It was a sad irony of the situation that moderate republicans, acting to preserve the Republic, should have to carry out the first large scale repression of the Republic against the radical republicans, and that this repression should have the full support of those most opposed to the Republic.

As a consequence of the June Days, minor political demonstrations were viewed by the authorities as challenges to public order. It was thus in no way surprising that protests against the infamous '45 centimes', extremely numerous throughout France in the summer of 1848, were dealt with speedily and rigorously. The five hundred anti-tax demonstrators at Guéret in the Creuse, for example, who marched through the town armed with scythes, sticks and hay forks threatening to hang anyone who paid his taxes on the town's *arbre de liberté*, were swiftly dispersed by local firemen and National Guards called out by the prefect. In many departments of the Midi, especially those where radical republicans were numerous and active, minor incidents in any way related to politics brought swift police action. Sometimes the police forces intervened simply to remove left wing symbols; a typical example was the cutting down of red flags attached by over-zealous radicals to local *arbres de liberté*.[12] Paradoxically, in the weeks after the June Days, when there was very little trouble in Paris, tax protests and symbolic socialist outbursts were frequent occurrences in the provinces, and in consequence both the anxieties of provincial notables and the repressive duties of the prefects grew considerably.

In reaction to the June Days, a number of political liberties which had been granted in February, were abolished or severely restricted. The first repressive restriction to reappear was press censorship. Under the state of siege powers, eleven newspapers were seized and their editors arrested on 25 June. In August, new press laws brought back stamp duties and cautionary deposits as under the July Monarchy (although smaller sums were required). By September, the Minister of the Interior was writing to his colleague at Justice to ask for more effective use of these laws against a number of provincial newspapers.

The government also initiated legislation restricting political liberties in two other areas. Seditious libel — 'inciting hatred or contempt for the republican government' — was made illegal, and strict limits were placed on the activities and organisation of political clubs. It should be noted, however, that these laws did not bring an immediate end to all left wing republican agitation; newspapers and clubs still continued to operate, and a new campaign of banquets was even tolerated. Repressive laws had reappeared, but they were applied in a moderate and legalistic way.[13]

Moderation was also shown in the changes of administrative personnel of the Cavaignac government. Many new appointments were necessary to replace those elected to the Constituent Assembly or compromised by radical election campaigns. The situation was also complicated by the decision to restore the title of prefect and to return to the system of one prefect to each department. Given these constraints, all three Ministers of the Interior, Recurt, Sénard and Dufaure, were far less rigorous than might have been expected. Some Orléanists were reappointed as prefects, but several committed republicans were retained, although some, such as Ollivier, the commissaire at Marseille since February, were demoted. By November, the majority of the corps was formed of moderate republicans. Demands from conservative leaders for the dismissal of certain radical prefects (notably that of the Prefect at Toulouse who had the audacity to attend a left wing banquet) were strongly resisted.[14]

Successive Ministers of the Interior also replaced the *sous-commis-*

saires by sub-prefects. Many former sub-prefects of the July Monarchy found new posts, but equally large numbers of those appointed since February were retained so that there was great political diversity amongst the sub-prefects. At lower levels of the administration, the election of municipal councils by universal suffrage, and the election of mayors by these councils (in communes of under 6,000 inhabitants), meant that over two thirds of the mayors were much freer from prefectoral interference than in the past.[15]

The concern for legality and fairness which characterised many activities of the Cavaignac government did surprisingly little to endear it to much of the population. For radical republicans Cavaignac was hated as the butcher of June, the *'prince du sang'*, for Orléanists and conservatives, he was distrusted as a republican and disliked as inadequately tough. The defeat of Cavaignac by Louis-Napoleon in the December election was in no way unexpected. It also heralded the start of a final and different phase of repressive development.[16]

The period of the presidency of Louis-Napoleon was the final phase of the growth of repressive activities before the *coup d'état*. During this time, the politically dominant 'Party of Order' was constantly preoccupied by its own internal divisions and by the threat of the 'red peril'. Despite the large numbers of republican leaders dead, in prison or in exile, and the ever increasing repression, many of the party of order had a curious tendency to consider electoral victories as defeats and minor disturbances as ominous of an imminent political cataclysm. The electoral success of the party of order in 1849 produced little rejoicing; for it seemed that the 'reds', far from being entirely crushed, had replaced the moderates as the most numerous republicans in the Assembly, and had spread their influence into rural areas. The fact that the 'Montagne' had peasant voters in the Allier, Var, Cher, Dordogne and Lot-et-Garonne caused great concern. If 'socialist propaganda' could win hearts in these departments, why not all over France? The results of the 1850 by-elections were equally alarming, as the Montagne retained many of the seats contested. The restriction of universal suffrage by the law of May 1850 soon followed, but by no means allayed all fears.

News of the *complôt de Lyon* in October 1850, later claims by Maupas about a similar plot in Toulouse, repeated warnings of rapidly approaching doom by prefects and porcureurs, pamphlets such as Rómieu's famous 'Le Spêctre rouge de 1852', the very limited extent of the economic revival, and the growing optimism of the Montagne for electoral victory in 1852, all fed the neurotic anxiety of the party of order. Fear of the destruction of a social order, grotesque interpretations of left wing ideas in terms of murder, pillage, rape and arson, and a failure to understand the relatively weak position of the 'democratic socialists', explain much of the keen support of many prefects and local notables for increased political repression.[17]

Large scale military action was needed only once during this period. The demonstration led by Ledru-Rollin in Paris on 13 June 1849 was dispersed by the army with very little trouble. In several provincial towns, such as Grenoble, Valence, Strasbourg, Perpignan and Toulouse, the prefects easily quelled similar but much smaller non-violent protest demonstrations. In Lyon, however, on 15 June, a violent battle took place between workers and the army; this resulted in over 200 deaths and 1,200 arrests. This was the last military defeat of the left wing republicans in the streets before the *coup d'état*; it brought about the death, exile or imprisonment of several more republican leaders, but also clearly demonstrated the futility of such revolutionary attempts and the necessity of adapting and organising to achieve victory by means of the ballot box.[18]

During the rest of this period, many of the repressive actions at the local level were concerned with preventing the republicans from organising for this purpose. First, the provisions of the clubs law of Cavaignac were fully exploited, even to permit the dissolution of *La Solidarité républicaine* by Faucher in January 1849. After June 1849, new measures were taken to provide what amounted to a prohibition on all political clubs. From this time, republicans tended to group in illegal secret societies, to congregate within other associations which were tolerated (notably the mutual aid societies), or simply to meet informally in certain cafés and bars. In response, repressive action was taken against all of these. The prefects were instructed to search out and destroy all secret societies, to treat all voluntary associations with deep distrust, and to disperse public meetings of any kind. As for cafés and bars where republicans were reputed to meet, the prefects were authorised to close these down.[19]

The destruction of channels of communication between republicans was another major goal of the repressors. Hence, the press laws of 1848 were reinforced in 1849 and made even stricter in July 1850. Many prefects instigated attacks on republican newspapers by frequent prosecutions for minor offences so that fines could be imposed at magistrates' courts. Fining into silence in this way was just as effective and involved far less risk of failure than major prosecutions before juries at assize courts.[20]

Individuals who carried republican propaganda or messages were also persecuted. Every movement of Representatives of the Montagne outside Paris was scrutinised by prefectoral agents. Mayors of known republican sympathies were also subject to police surveillance, and in some districts the police even spied on country doctors whose political views were suspect. Tinkers and peddlers were widely assumed to be republican messengers, and some prefects suspended their licences, banned them from selling certain goods and ordered frequent searches of their sale goods.[21]

For some conservatives the sight alone of republican symbols was an intolerable demonstration that a republican movement still existed and hoped for victory in 1852. To some prefects even the continued growth of the 1848 crop of *arbres de liberté* was an anathema, and pretexts were found to justify their felling. Singing of republican songs and wearing any red clothes were both regarded as subversive activities and so banned by certain prefects.[22]

All these policies were inevitably accompanied by a continuous political purge. In early 1849, Faucher made sweeping changes of prefectoral personnel. He dismissed notorious republicans (such as Avril of the Calvados and Ollivier of the Haute-Marne) and appointed men from the party of order (mostly Orleanists with some administrative experience). The return of Dufaure to the Interior in June 1849 led to few changes, but Ferdinand Barrot, Baroche, Vaisse and Thorigny all made numerous dismissals, appointments and promotions. The last changes took place in November 1851, and not all the prefects had arrived at their new prefectures by the time of the *coup d'état*.[23]

The prefects themselves continued the purge of the lower ranks of the administration. Whilst they still only appointed the mayors of communes of over 6,000 people, the prefects could always suspend or even dismiss elected mayors of smaller communes, if they did not perform their functions satisfactorily. Of perhaps greater importance, however, were the powers delegated to the prefects by the new education laws to dismiss unsatisfactory primary school teachers. Almost at once these powers were widely employed. Finally, the prefects could sack for unsatisfactory conduct most of the other minor civil servants in their departments for whose appointment they were formally responsible.[24]

The role of the prefects

The prefects were directly involved in provincial repression in two ways: they organised and supervised the work of all police agents, and they were responsible for taking most major decisions on the basis of the information provided by these subordinates. They received information and instructions from the Ministry of the Interior and had the responsibility of ensuring that the local administrative machine operated effectively to carry them out; and, in general, they wielded the formal powers for taking initiatives at the departmental level.

In their organisational capacity the prefects ordered regular reports on the political situation from the sub-prefects, police commissioners, and gendarmerie commanders. Normally, such reports were presented each fortnight, but when there was any disturbance of public order the prefect would ask for detailed information to be provided more frequently. In response to specific demands from Paris the prefects ordered special investigations to be carried out: this was, for example, the general rule in January 1849 after Faucher had decreed the dissolution of *La Solidarité républicaine*.[25] As the antirepublican hunt intensified, so prefectoral organisation initiatives were multiplied. In some departments, for example, lists were compiled of all who had taken part in 'the events' of 1848 and their subsequent political activities. Many prefects asked either their sub-prefects or police commissioners for detailed accounts of the political sentiments and activities of all mayors and assistant mayors, all village school teachers and even, in certain departments, of all priests! Some prefects demanded to be informed not only of factual information but also of rumours and suspicions, however ill-founded.[26]

In addition to these reports from the sub-prefectures and police forces, information was also requested from other administrative services less directly under prefectoral supervision. The press laws, for example, obliged prefects and procureurs to work together and to pool their knowledge. Some *ingénieurs* were consulted about the staff of the *ponts et chaussées*, and many *inspecteurs d'académie* and *recteurs* received a request for details of the politics of lycée or university teachers. In certain departments, the prefects asked the more reliable Representatives of the 'party of order' for their views and information of the political situation, and occasionally, for specific questions, mayors were asked for details concerning their communes.[27]

On the basis of this information from all these sources, the prefects had to make decisions of three types. First, as part of their global responsibility for public order and using their powers of *police générale*, they had to make such by-laws (*arrêtés*) as they deemed necessary. Typical of prefectoral rulings of this kind was that of Aubiers, Prefect of the Basses-Alpes in 1850, which banned all public meetings, dinners and gatherings on the grounds that they might lead to disturbances of the peace. Another interesting example was the May 1850 *arrêté* by Neveux, Prefect of the Gironde which prohibited tinkers and travelling salesman from selling newspapers. An overenthusiastic prefect like Charnailles, in the Allier, interpreted his power of *police générale* so liberally as to justify a ban on the wearing of red ties or belts! A more frequent, and more easily justifiable ruling was that which ordered the cutting down of all 'arbres de liberté qui menacent la voie publique'.[28]

A second group of powers wielded by the prefects were those specifically delegated by legislation. Hence, for example, it was for the prefect to decide on the dissolution of clubs, and later of any association or society judged 'political', on the evidence from the police commissioners or gendarmerie. In this context, in departments such as the Var where the republicans were very active the Prefect found himself repeatedly prohibiting organisations grouping the same people which reformed under a new name after each successive ban. Some prefects used these powers somewhat excessively; the Prefect of the Pyrénées-Orientales ordered the disbanding of a *société de bienfaisance* at Prades which had existed for over seventy years; the Prefect of the Aisne not only closed down the masonic lodge at Château-Thierry but even ordered a constant spying on the acitivities of a choir formed at Laon.[29] Under the press laws, the prefects could order the seizure of local newspapers and even the search of the offices of these newspapers. As the authorisers of permits for cafés and bars the prefects could and did order the closing down of establishments where republicans congregated; in a department of some republican ardour like the Pyrénées-Orientales many café and bar owners lost their livelihoods by prefectoral decisions of this kind.[30]

Most of the political purging of the administration by the prefects was authorised by similar specific legislative provisions which granted appointive and dismissive powers to the prefects. Curiously, the dramatic purges by the more radical commissaires of Ledru-Rollin were not authorised in this way and had only had the authority of the 'unlimited powers' circular. Prefectoral sackings of village school teachers in 1850, however, were directly authorised by the new law, and the prefects were able to dismiss or suspend republican mayors and their assistants under their *tutelle* powers.[31] It was by direct prefectoral decisions of this kind that many individuals lost jobs and status at the local level.

The other type of prefectoral decision was that of making specific recommendations for repressive action to other authorities. In this way, prefects advised *recteurs* about the undesirability of republican lycée teachers, or informed the procureurs of unreliable magistrates. In some matters the prefects made specific recommendations to the government. The disbanding of politically untrustworthy National Guard brigades was decided by the government, but almost always on the advice of the prefect. In a similar way, the prefects could recommend the dissolution of politically unreliable municipal councils and the holding of new elections, although the formal decision was made by a decree of the President of the Republic.[32] Whilst prefectoral recommendations were not always respected, the prefects were expected to give advice of this kind.

With so many responsibilities and powers the prefects appear to have played a dominant role in provincial political repression. There were, however, several significant checks on prefectoral influence.

The Limits of Prefectoral Influence

1. Information

To a large extent, effective prefectoral repressive action was dependent upon the prefects being fully informed. Despite their own efforts to organise efficient investigations, many prefects did not obtain information of sufficient detail or sufficient accuracy. The limited numbers of the police forces available, the abilities and political sympathies of the sub-prefects, police commissioners and officers of the gendarmerie, and the local contacts and friendships of many police agents at all levels were serious constraints upon the organisation of efficient systems of political spying.

The inadequate numbers and limited abilities of the municipal police agents was a constant complaint of both prefects and procureurs généraux throughout the Second Republic. In many departments there were too few police commissioners and other municipal police officers were very limited in number, so that the prefects were mainly dependent on the gendarmerie. The total number of gendarmes was only 18,000 in December 1848 and did not increase significantly until 1852. Both gendarmes and municipal police were preoccupied with 'normal' police duties and detailed political investigations were an additional duty which sometimes overburdened them.[33]

A second facet of this problem of prefectoral reliance on information provided by their subordinates was the inability of the prefects to change collaborators they disliked or thought incompetent. Sub-prefects and prefectoral councillors could only be dismissed by governmental decree and prefects were frequently disappointed that their requests were ignored. Disagreements between prefects and sub-prefects were not as rare as might be expected, and prefectoral views did not always triumph. Many sub-prefects had powerful patrons in Paris whose support could be calculated to outweigh any prefectoral complaints to the Minister of the Interior. In the Dordogne, for example, the Prefect Sainte-Croix was in frequent dispute with Calvimont, Sub-Prefect of Bergerac; and despite prefectoral complaints Calvimont kept his job due to the support of Magne, then Secretary of State for Finances.[34] Nor had the prefects any greater freedom of manoeuvre with the officers of the gendarmerie, as the latter remained part of the Army under the supervision of the Minister of War, and prefects' requests for personnel changes could only be indirectly expressed via the Interior.

Even the police commissioners were not under complete prefectoral control: for their municipal and rural police duties they were answerable to the mayors, and for judiciary police functions they took instructions from the procureurs. Appointed by the Minister of the Interior, in practice they relied upon good working relations with the mayors. The *sergents de ville*, and *gardes champêtres* who were the local police personnel of the commissioners were appointed by and responsible to the mayors. In practice, therefore, the prefects were reliant on the cooperation of the mayors in the repression; an uncooperative or politically hostile mayor might prove a real obstacle to effective repression. If the prefect could not find a suitable alternative mayor, either from within an existing municipal council or by getting the government to bring about a new municipal election, there was very little that could be done. As Haussmann himself discovered in the Var, republican mayors could effectively sabotage prefectoral efforts to obtain complete political information.[35]

It should also be noted that exhortations from the prefects for greater zeal did not always produce the results intended. Indeed, an over enthusiastic *conseiller de préfecture* such as Jules Astier in the Manche might become more of an embarassment than an asset even to an ardent antirepublican like Tanlay. The simple request for fortnightly political reports from the police commissioners was perhaps to some extent counterproductive. The need to report something, to show some repressive zeal could result in reports which 'ne contiennent le plus souvent que les racontars, des niaiseries, parfois de pures inventions'.[36]

2. Dependence on other administrators

Before becoming Prefect of the Basses-Alpes in 1850, Aubiers wrote a succinct account of the difficulties of prefects with other officials:

> 'Les rapports du préfet avec les principales autorités du département forment une des plus grandes difficultés de sa position: à côté du pouvoir administratif il y a le pouvour *militaire*, le pouvoir *ecclésiastique*, le pouvoir *judiciaire* avec lesquels il faut trouver un moyen de vivre en bonne intelligence ... Le préfet est le *primus inter pares*, ce qui est un premier tort qu'il n'est pas dans son pouvoir d'éviter. Mais si à ce premier tort il en ajoute un second, celui de faire sentir son autorité il est rare que sa mésintelligence n'éclate pas aussitôt ...'

A second edition of this book in 1852 contained no modification of these views in the light of his own experience.[37]

Clearly disagreements could, and did, arise. The experience of the commissions mixtes in 1852 was to illustrate the difficulties of getting generals, prefects and procureurs to cooperate together. Even a strong prefect such as Bret in the Loire might be criticised to the government by a fanatic like General Castellane. The views of the procureurs generaux varied considerably: whilst the one at Aix-en-Provence criticised the Prefect of the Var for 'des scruples de légalité', his colleague at Caen was reproaching the Prefect of the Calvados for his excessive zeal against tinkers and peddlers.[38] Furthermore, when court action was necessary, the prefects were completely dependent on the agreement of the procureurs or their *substituts*. In other areas, too, the prefects could only propose repressive actions. Hence they made suggestions to the *recteurs* about the purging of lycée teachers, but these were not always acceptable; in some cases, at least, the *recteur* investigated complaints about his staff with greater care than that shown by the prefect. In this context, prefectoral influence in deciding dismissals of primary school teachers was less than is suggested by the statutory position: the need to consult the *comité supérieur* of the *académie* on all dismissals, and the suggestions of suitable cases for dismissal by other administrators (like the procureurs or their *substituts*) effectively limited prefectoral freedom of action.[39]

3. The Government

Whilst successive governments gave their prefects ever increasing encouragement in carrying out repressive tasks, the prefects had relatively little freedom of manoeuvre to take initiatives of their own. In the first place, the government could only allow the prefects to act within the letter of the law, and there were many complaints that the law was too strict. Prefectoral actions might be challenged in the *Conseil de préfecture* or even at the *Conseil d'Etat*, and complaints of illegality could be made directly to the Minister of the Interior. The prefects also depended on the government for support in cases of disagreements with other administrators or conflicts with municipal councils and mayors. Weak or unfounded prefectoral demands were doomed to failure, particularly given the inevitable tendency of most ministers to sympathise with the views of the civil servants of their own Ministries. Finally, prefectoral initiatives could only be expected if the prefects were left to carry out their repressive duties undisturbed. This was far from the case. Paris, like a suspicious lover, was ever eager to discover what its provincial partners were doing. The prefectures were swamped with circulars giving advice or requesting information and personal letters to inform the prefect of ministerial approval or disapproval for particular actions were all too frequent. In short, the activities and attitudes of the government did little to encourage prefectoral initiatives.[40]

4. Universal suffrage

The advent of universal suffrage by providing representatives, municipal and general councillors with democratic legitimacy undermined the position of the prefects and ultimately was to bring about a considerable reduction of prefectoral influence and prestige. At the parliamentary level, leading members of the 'party of order' realised that they could demand to be consulted about appointments to their own departments. The prefects in turn soon learned that the approval of Representatives who supported the government from their departments was essential to their own position. The dislike of a leading Orléanist or the hostility of a prominent Bonapartist could bring a premature end to a promising prefectoral career. Even Representatives of the Montagne could rely on a degree of prefectoral deference to their position; they might be constantly watched, but they were rarely interfered with.

The election of the general councils also created new difficulties for the prefects. In many departments both prominent conservatives and republicans were at once elected to these bodies thus giving them considerable political weight. The prefect sometimes found himself in the uncomfortable position of·being cross-pressured by a majority of parliamentary Representatives of one political shade and a general council of a very different colour. Giraud-Teulon, for example, in the Hautes-Alpes was opposed by most of the general council but had the enthusiastic support of the influential Representative Allier.[41]

Practical difficulties of a different kind were produced by the election of municipal councils by universal suffrage and by the election of the mayors by these councils in communes of under 6,000 people. A prefect might remove a republican mayor, but if the council then elected another republican, the prefect had either to accept this result or to ask the government to dissolve the council. In this latter case, new elections were held, but if these produced the same majority in the council there was very little the prefect could do.

5. Local circumstances

During the Second Republic, the conservative parties were dominant in many departments. In the west, northwest, north, northeast and east, with the exceptions of the Bas-Rhin, Nord and Seine-Inférieure, the republicans were relatively weak in organisation and few in numbers. In these areas the repressive duties of the prefects were clearly much less onerous than elsewhere. Sometimes a determined prefect, such as Tanlay in the Manche, might attempt to root out reds where virtually none existed, but the usual result was only to stir up unnecessary trouble.[42]

In many areas of the Midi, Massif central, Rhône valley and Provence, the republicans were both numerous and well-organised. In the 1849 elections the lists of the Montagne had won absolute majorities in sixteen of these departments and over 40 per cent of the vote in another seventeen. Particularly troublesome departments included the Basses-Alpes, the Var, Herault, Aude, Pyrénées-Orientales, Ariège, Gers, Lot-et-Garonne, Dordogne, Corrèze, Haute-Vienne, Cher, Nièvre, Allier, Ain, Jura and Saône-et-Loire in addition to the departments which contained the large industrial towns. These were the areas where repression was most wanted by the government, but also where it was most difficult for the prefects to carry it out. It is conceivable that by constantly providing republican martyrs, the prefects may have assisted the continued mobilisation of those they sought to demobilise.[43]

There were also other kinds of local problems for the prefects. Frontier departments had their own special troubles: the Jura and Ain were invaded with republican propaganda and aid from Geneva, whilst the departments of the Pyrenees were occasionally disturbed by the arrival of groups of Spanish political refugees. In Corsica there were frequent crimes of violence, attributable more to clan feuds than to republican agitation. The Ariège, too, had a tradition of local anarchy, but there it was tempered by strong republicanism. Clearly, none of these conditions facilitated prefectoral tasks.[44]

6. *Other prefectoral duties*

It is clearly impossible to understand the repressive role of the prefects without some consideration of their other duties. In addition to their repressive tasks, the prefects also had important electoral and purely administrative functions, and it was almost inevitable that some 'role conflict' should result from these differing demands.

Not only were the prefects expected to repress the 'reds', but they were also called upon to create electoral support for the party of order. In practice, two things were required: first, that they should rally in support of the President all local conservative notables, whether Bonapartist, Orléanist, Legitimist, or even moderate republican; and secondly, that they should gain the sympathies of the lower classes for the government. These 'positive' political functions could only be successfully performed if the prefects were liked and trusted. If, however, excessive 'negative' action, or repression, upset the susceptibilities of notables or caused widespread ill-will amongst workers or peasants, prefectoral efforts at increasing support for the government were doomed to fail. In reality, prefects tended to concentrate on one political function or the other; thus, Chapuys de Montville in the Isère sought above all to create a united part of order with widespread popular support, while Ferlay, in the Drôme, was much more concerned with simply silencing the 'reds'.[45]

Both types of political functions had little in common with the purely administrative duties of the prefects. Since the first Empire, successive governments had defined a large number of precise administrative tasks for the prefects to perform. As a result of this development, the prefects had less time for political tasks, and in some contexts administrative efficiency was impaired by political action. Once again, individual prefects differed greatly in the importance they attached to these functions.[46]

7. Prefectoral stability

Since the creation of the prefectoral system, effective action by the prefects has depended on their possessing a high degree of familiarity with the problems and people of their departments. As this could only be attained by staying in the same department for a number of years, the prefect who was only appointed for a few weeks or months could not hope for great success in any of his activities, whether political or purely administrative. The establishment of good working relations with subordinates, but also with the general and local procureur, was absolutely vital for successful repressive action, but very difficult to achieve in the space of a few weeks. During the Second Republic, however, the constant administrative purge meant that there was very little prefectoral stability. The Ariège, for example, had no fewer than three commissaires and six prefects — and one month when the prefecture was run by a *conseiller de prefecture* — during the period from February 1848 to December 1851. During this same time, there were eight departments where the occupant of the prefecture changed eight times, and another thirteen with seven changes. It should perhaps be noted that the greatest instability occurred in 1848 and 1849, and that some of the prefects appointed in 1849 — such as Foy in the Ardennes, Suleau in the Bouches-du-Rhône, Fluchaire in the Aveyron, Ferlay in the Drôme and Brian in the Charante-Inférieure — were still in the same posts when the Empire was established. Nonetheless, the general picture is one of great prefectoral instability, and the usual result was reduced effectiveness. If the purges had produced a politically homogeneous prefectoral corps they might have been worth this sacrifice; this however, was not the case.[47]

8. Prefectoral attitudes

The view that 'the prefects were a near solid phalanx in December 1851' is not completely accurate, as was demonstrated by a recent study of prefectoral reaction at the time of the *coup d'état*. Throughout the life of the Second Republic, the prefects were extremely heterogeneous in their political views and administrative origins, and even at the end of the Republic the numerous changes of personnel made by successive governments of the Prince-President had not produced a unified and consistently loyal prefectoral corps, let alone a Bonapartist one. As late as March 1851 Louis-Napoleon himself expressed his distrust of many prefects and his wish for further changes: '. . . Lorsque j'apprends de sources certaines que les dépositaires de mon autorité dans les provinces, non seulement n'emploient pas leur influence dans un sens qui peut m'être favorable mais qu'ils sont tout le contraire, alors je crois qu'il est dans mon droit comme dans mon devoir de retirer ma confiance.'[48]

Subsequent changes had not produced the desired effect by December 1851. At that time, of the eighty-six prefects the firm Bonapartists numbered only nine, and only sixteen others could be considered as true converts to the cause of Louis-Napoleon. The prefectoral corps included fifty-two men who had begun their administrative careers under the July Monarchy, and another fourteen who had first been appointed by the Provisional Government or by Cavaignac. Immediately after the *coup d'état*, eight prefects resigned in protest, another six were dismissed as being politically unreliable and a number of others were listed as unsatisfactory.[49] It is in no way surprising that throughout the Second Republic there was never a consensus amongst the prefects about the goals or desirability of severe repression, when there was never a consensus about which group within the party of order should dominate or indeed, about which side would triumph in the conflict between the President and the Assembly.

It should be noted that political beliefs are by no means the only determinant of prefectoral actions. If political objectives were predominant for many of the commissaires and for some of the later prefects, there were undoubtedly some men who entered the prefectoral corps with a sense of public service, and yet others who were primarily careerists. The notion of public service appears to have inspired moderate, conciliatory and 'administrative' prefects, such as Dausse, Brissot-Thivars, Bret and Delmas, whereas the tortuous tactics of Neveux in the Gironde and Haussmann in the Var both indicate some real concern with career prospects. Only rare fanatics like Maupas really believed in the antirepublican witch hunt.[50]

Concluding Observations

Whilst the exact contribution of the prefects to the political repression in the provinces is almost impossible to calculate, it is clear that the prefects did not bear sole responsibility for all repressive activities. In practice, prefects were obliged to work in close cooperation with the procureurs généraux, and were constantly dependent upon the sub-prefects, police commissioners and gendarmerie. In real crises, moreover, the army took over full control of all repressive actions. Any idea that the prefects were omnipotent overlords of all repression in the provinces is thus clearly inaccurate.

The notion that the prefects as representatives of the government in the departments attempted to impose a common set of standards all over France is equally misleading. The political problems faced by the prefects varied considerably from one department to the next, so that the extent of political repression also inevitably varied greatly. Furthermore, the prefects did not all approach their tasks with the same enthusiasm, nor indeed with the same goals. In any one department, the extent of the political repression would depend on the political situation, the size and skill of police forces, the attitudes of the procureur, the general, and any Representatives dominant in the party of order, and finally, the views and dynamism of the prefect. The number and the force of these variable factors meant that national standards of political repression were clearly an impossibility.

It should also be noted that political repression in the provinces, whilst attaining its primary objective of maintaining the regime under Louis-Napoleon, was not a total success. Certainly, the repressive activities of the commissaires of the Provisional Government and of the prefects of General Cavaignac were totally inadequate to preserve the existence of either of these governments – although this was not the aim of the early repression. Paradoxically, the activities of the commissaires and Cavaignac prefects provided the conservatives with repressive methods which could be imitated and expanded, but also, by the administrative purges and toleration of threats to the existing social and economic order, scared many moderates into supporting an increasingly rigorous repression of all republicans. But even under Louis-Napoleon the repressive machine was never totally effective; the widespread resistance to the *coup d'état* and the subsequent mass condemnations by military tribunals and *commissions mixtes* revealed that significant pockets of unrepressed republicanism still existed at the time of the *coup*.

In the light of this study, a number of observations may be made about the workings of the prefectoral system in mid-nineteenth century France. First, it is clear that the prefectoral political machine was not adequate either for obtaining information or for creating 'public opinion': the number and frequency of reports was in no way indicative of the competence, impartiality or detailed knowledge of their authors, and the police forces were simply not up to the task imposed. It is equally evident that the theoretical control of the prefects over all administrative activities of the state in their departments was in practice neither all-embracing nor always effective: the procureurs, for example, in some cases checked prefectoral excesses, and in others encouraged the prefects to greater efforts. Finally, this study illustrates the ironical situation in which the prefects, widely resented and attacked as the agents of brutal centralisation, were dependent, in reality, on the people and politics of the departments they were supposed to dominate. Many prefects of the Second Republic, staying for brief periods of weeks or months in departments which they did not know, depending for support and promotion on patrons in Paris with friends amongst the departmental notables, had no real choice but that of accepting the advice – and hence the influence – of these local elites. The 'colonisation' of the prefectoral corps by those whom the prefects theoretically 'colonised' was by no means an innovation of the Third Republic.

Notes

1. There are few studies of the work of the prefects during the nineteenth century. In English there is only one book, N. Richardson, *The French Prefectoral Corps 1814-1830* (Cambridge, 1966), and a long historical chapter in Brian Chapman, *The Prefects and Provincial France* (London, 1955). In French, there is scarcely more: Pierre Henry, *Histoire des Préfets* (Paris, 1950); J. Regnier, *Les Préfets du Consulat et de l'Empire* (Paris, 1907); J. Savant, *Les Préfets de Napoléon* (Paris, 1958); J. Siwek-Pouydesseau, *Le corps préfectoral sous la Troisième et la Quatrième République* (Paris, 1969). The most comprehensive study in either language is also the most recent: B. Le Clère et V. Wright, *Les préfets du Second Empire* (Paris, 1973), of which pp. 19-32 are specially relevant to this study. On the repression after the *coup d'état*, see H. C. Payne, *The Police State of Louis Napoleon Bonaparte* (Seattle, 1966), pp. 34-72; V. Wright, 'Le corps préfectoral et le coup d'état du 2 décembre 1851', *Revue administrative* (1960), and the essay by the same author in this collection.

2. See N. Richardson *op. cit.*, p. 2. On prefectoral electoral interventions during the July Monarchy, S. Kent, *Electoral procedure under Louis-Philippe* (Yale, 1937).

3. For comparisons with earlier and later purges see Pierre Henry, *op. cit.*; On the appointments and backgrounds of the commissaires, P. Haury, 'Les commissaires de Ledru-Rollin en 1848', *La Révolution française* (1909) pp. 438-74.

4. See: P. Vigier, *La Seconde République* (Paris, 1966), p. 25; P. Vigier, *La Seconde République dans la région alpine* (Paris, 1963), vol. 1, pp. 186 (Isère), 188 (Vaucluse), 190-91 (Hautes-Alpes), 191-2 (Basses-Alpes), 193-4 (Drôme); C. Seignobos, *La Révolution de 1848 – Le Second Empire* (vol. 6 in E. Lavisse (ed.), *Histoire de la France contemporaine* (Paris, 1921)), pp. 18-19; Pierre Henry, *op. cit.*, pp. 155-7; P. Haury, *op. cit.*, pp. 443-50; Paul Muller, *La Révolution de 1848 en Alsace* (Paris, 1912), pp. 52-3 (Bas-Rhin); A. Charles, *La Révolution de 1848 et la Seconde République à Bordeaux et dans le département de la Gironde* (Bordeaux, 1945), p. 98; L. de Tricaud, *Histoire du département de L'Ain du 24 février au 20 décembre 1848* (Bourg, 1872), pp. 19-46; Octave Beuve, *La République de 1848 à Troyes* (Troyes, 1911), p. 5; J. Godechot (ed.), *La Révolution de 1848 à Toulouse et dans la Haute-Garonne* (Toulouse, 1949), pp. 139-45.

5. On the purges of the lower ranks of the administration see P. Vigier, *La Seconde République, op. cit.*, p. 25; A. Charles, *op. cit.*, pp. 106-11 (Gironde); J. Godechot, *op. cit.*, pp. 226-8 (Haute-Garonne); in the Ain Guigue de Champvans, the commissaire, had received orders from his friend Lamartine to sack nobody and to reassure all, see L. de Tricaud, *op. cit.*, p. 47.

6. C. Seignobos, *op. cit.*, pp. 19-20; L. de Tricaud, *op. cit.*, pp. 22-7, 38-41.

7. C. Seignobos, *op. cit.*, p. 67; P. Vigier, *La Seconde République, op. cit.*, pp. 26-7; Maurice Agulhon, *1848 ou l'apprentissage à la République* (Paris, 1973), pp. 20-40.

8. L. de Tricaud, *op. cit.*, pp. 101-11; in the Ain, the two new commissaires were so unpopular that a delegation of local republicans went to Paris and obtained their dismissal by Ledru-Rollin, but the original commissaire Guigue de Champvans was so well liked that he was elected to the Constituent Assembly in April. On the new commissaires, see P. Haury, *op. cit.*, pp. 455-72; on their

electoral efforts, P. Vigier, *La Seconde République, op. cit.*, pp. 30-32; on their purges, P. Vigier, *La Seconde République dans la région alpine, op. cit.*, vol. 1, pp. 207-8, 209-11, 215-6; J. Godechot, *op. cit.*, pp. 159-64; G. Rougeron (*et al.*), *La Révolution de 1848 à Moulins et dans le département de l'Allier* (Moulins, 1950), pp. 15-17.

9.   Maurice Agulhon, *op. cit.*, pp. 56-7; P. Vigier, *La Seconde République, op. cit.*, p. 35; C. Seignobos, *op. cit.*, pp. 80-1; F. A. de Luna, *The French Republic under Cavaignac 1848* (Princeton, 1969), pp. 182-3; see also the commissaire's report on A.N. F 1 b I 157[15].

10.   Maurice Agulhon, *op. cit.*, pp. 66-7; Roger Price, *The French Second Republic – a social history* (London, 1972), p. 32.

11.   F. Dutacq, *Histoire politique de Lyon pendant le révolution de 1848* (Paris, 1910), pp. 412-50; F. A. de Luna, *op. cit.*, pp. 201-2; Roger Price, *op. cit.*, pp. 190-1.

12.   C. Seignobos, *op. cit.*, pp. 110-12.

13.   F. A. de Luna, *op. cit.*, pp. 203-8; Irene Collins, *The Government and the newspaper press in France 1814-1881* (Oxford, 1959), pp. 105-17.

14.   J. Godechot, *op. cit.*, pp. 365-6; F. A. de Luna, *op. cit.*, p. 328.

15.   F. A. de Luna, *op. cit.*, pp. 231-4; Maurice Agulhon, *op. cit.*, pp. 77-8.

16.   A Dansette, *Louis Napoléon à la conquête du pouvoir* (Paris, 1966), pp. 236-55; Maurice Agulhon, *op. cit.*, pp. 82-7.

17.   G. Genique, *L'Eléction de l'Assemblie législative en 1849* (Paris, 1921); C. Seignobos, *op. cit.*, pp. 134-6, 150-2. On the *complôt de Lyon*, P. Vigier, *La Seconde République dans la région alpine, op. cit.*, vol. 2, pp. 286-93; F. Dutacq, 'Notes et documents sur le complôt de Lyon', *La Révolution de 1848*, vol. 24, pp. 345-57. A typical example of the reports of these times is that of the procureur general at Besançon dated 26 April 1851: '. . . les anarchistes triomphent et proclament comme infaillible leur victoire en 1852 . . . les hommes d'ordre, faibles et découragés, ne doutent pas de leur defaits . . .', in A.N. BB[30] 373; Maurice Agulhon, *op. cit.*, pp. 97-113.

18.   See Georges Renard, *La Deuxième République 1848-1851* (Paris, 1919), pp. 152-3; P. Muller, *op. cit.*, pp. 54-65; J. Godechot, *op. cit.*, pp. 367-8; *Rapport spécial ai préfet 14 juin 1849*, in A.D. Pyrénées-Orientales, III M[1] 71.

19.   G. Rocal, *1848 en Dordogne* (Paris, 1933), pp. 34-5; G. Génique, *op. cit.*, pp. 20-1; C. Seignobos, *op. cit.*, pp. 139-40.

20.   Irene Collins, *op. cit.*, pp. 110-7; A. Charles, *op. cit.*, pp. 223, 263-5; J. Godechot, *op. cit.*, pp. 372-3; G. Rougeron, *op. cit.*, pp. 36-7, 75-7.

21.   C. Seignobos, *op. cit.*, pp. 155-6.

22.   Consequently those who sang republican songs around an *arbre de liberté* decorated with a *bonnet rouge* at Prades (Pyrénées-Orientales) were severely repressed; *Rapport au préfet, le 20 mars 1849*, in A.D. Pyrénées-Orientales IIIM[1] 71.

23.   V. Wright, 'Le corps préfectoral . . .', *op. cit.*

24'   A. Charles, *op. cit.*, pp. 268-9, 303; J. Godechot, *op. cit.*, p. 372; G. Rougeron, *op. cit.*, pp. 53-64; see also *Rapport du procureur général à Besançon au Garde des Sceaux, le 1 février 1850*, in A.N. BB[30] 373.

25.   See the letters and reports from the sub-prefects in A. D. Aude 5M 32; see also A. Charles, *op. cit.*, pp. 222-3.

26.   See, for example, the police reports in A.D. Pyrénées-Orientales III M[1] 71, and the political registers in A.D. Tarn IV M[2] 38, and in A.D. Lot 6 M 10; see also, E. Dagnan, 'La réaction conservatrice dans la Gers', *La Révolution de 1848*, vol. 9, p. 116.

27.   *Idem.*, pp. 116-7.

28.   A. Charles, *op. cit.*, pp. 223, 263; R. Moliner, *Essai sur les mentalités populaires en Roussillon* (Mémoire, Montpellier, 1974), pp. 24-8; J. Cornillon, *Le Bourbonnais en décembre 1851* (Paris, 1903), pp. 26-30.

29.   H. Aragon, *La vie civile et militaire de Perpignan sous le général de Castellane 1830-1852* (Perpignan, 1926), pp. 330-4; G. Rocal, *op. cit.*, p. 86; A. Charles, *op. cit.*, p. 266; J. Cornillon, *op. cit.*, p. 372; G. Rougeron, *op. cit.*, pp. 53, 73-81.

30.   See the police reports in A.D. Pyrénées-Orientales III M^1 73, notably that dated 19 February 1851 about the café belonging to Joseph Canal: '. . . cette buvette était le réfuge de tout ce qu'il y a à Perpignan de plus mauvais tant sous le rapport moral que sous le rapport politique . . . il se tient . . . un espèce de club où sont développées les théories socialistes les plus effrenées; . . . on y discute les questions les plus subversives . . .'. See also J. Cornillon, *op. cit.*, pp. 40-6.

31.   G. Rocal, *op. cit.*, pp. 36-9; see also the lists of mayors dismissed: A.D. Aude II M 221, 222, 274; A.D. Pyrénées-Orientales III M^1 72; A.D. Tarn II M^7 59.

32.   See for example the letters Ministre de l'Intérieur-Préfet de la Corrèze, dated 14 March 1851 and 23 June 1851 in A.N. F 1 b I 156^{39}; and the letter Ministre de l'Instruction publique au Ministre de l'Intérieur, le 29 août 1849 in A.N. F 1 b I 155^9.

33.   R. Marlin, *L'Epuration politique dans le Doubs* (Dôle, 1958), p. 3; H. C. Payne, 'Preparation of a *coup d'état* — administrative centralisation and police powers in France 1849-1851', F. J. Cox (ed.), *Studies in Modern European History in honor of F. C. Palm* (New York, 1966), pp. 177-81.

34.   G. Rocal, *op. cit.*, pp. 32-3; G. E. Haussmann, *Mémoires* (Paris, 1890), vol. 1, pp. 321-2.

35.   G. E. Haussmann, *op. cit.*, pp. 324-6; C. Seignobos, *op. cit.*, p. 157; P. Vigier, *La Seconde République dans la région alpine, op. cit.*, p. 233.

36.   E. Dagnan, *op. cit.*, pp. 119-27; L. Deries, *Un apprenti sous-préfet sous la Deuxième République* (St Lo, 1923).

37.   V. des Aubiers, *Manuel des préfets et sous-préfets* (Paris, 1852), p. 30.

38.   See the correspondence in Bret's dossier, A.N. F1 bI 156^{44} and the reports of the procureurs généraux at Aix, dated 13 July 1850, and Caen, dated 1 January 1850 in A.N. BB^{30} 370 and BB^{30} 375.

39.   L. Deriès, 'L'Affaire du régent de rhétorique Canivet', *La Révolution de 1848*, vol. 10, pp. 267-76; also the reports of the procureurs généraux at Aix (14 February 1850) and Amiens (5 April 1850) in A.N. BB^{30} 370 and BB^{30} 371.

40.   For example, the detailed instructions about clubs in A.D. Cantal 37 M 1; the correspondence in 1850 in A.D. Lot 6 M 9; A.D. Pyrénées-Orientales III M^1 72; and A.D. Aude II M 273.

41.   See A. Charles, *op. cit.*, pp. 167, 330-3; P. Vigier, *La Seconde République dans la région alpine, op. cit.*, vol. 2, p; 230.

42.   L. Deriès, 'Un apprenti . . .', *op. cit.*, pp. 20-2.

43.   See for example the police reports in A.D. Aude 5M 31-32; also P. Vigier, *La Seconde République, op. cit.*, p. 30; Maupas, *Mémoires sur le Second Empire* (Paris, 1884), vol. 1, pp. 179-84.

44.   For examples: the reports of the procureurs généraux at Besançon (30 November 1849 and 17 January 1850), Bastia (7 May 1850) in A.N. BB^{30} 373; and police reports in A.D. Pyrénées-Orientales III M^1 71.

45.   C. Seignobos, *op. cit.*, pp. 67, 146, 195; P. Vigier, *La Seconde République dans la région alpine, op. cit.*, vol. 2, pp. 231-2; lettre, préfet de l'Ariège au Ministre de l'Intérieur, le 18 mai 1849, in Bauguel's dossier, A.N. F 1 b I 156^9.

46.   See B. Le Clère and V. Wright, *op. cit.*; also the notes on Brissot-Thivars, 26 March 1850 in his dossier, A.N. F 1 b I 156^{46}; and the letter

of complaint against Aubert in his dossier A.N. F 1 b I 155[9].

47.　In July 1848 Bauguel, prefect of the Ariège complained of this problem: 'la difficulté qui résultera pour moi dans cette tache de l'affaiblissement moral de l'autorité par suite des changements multiples de ses dépositaires', lettre au Ministre de l'Intérieur, le 19 juillet 1848, in A.N. F 1 b I 156[9]; V. Wright, 'Les préfets démissionnaires en décembre 1851', *Revue administrative*, février 1968, pp. 19-24.

48.　Quoted in B. Le Clère and V. Wright, *op. cit.*; see also F. Maupas, *op. cit.*, vol. 1, pp. 97-8.

49.　V. Wright, 'Le corps préfectoral . . .', *op. cit.*, pp. 153-7.

50.　A..Bremond, *Histoire du coup d'état dans le département de la Haute Garonne* (Toulouse, 1870), pp. 25-6; A. Charles, *op. cit.*, p. 220; G. E. Haussmann, *op. cit.*, vol. 1, pp. 325-65; H. C. Payne, 'The Preparation of . . .', *op. cit.*, pp. 185-9; lettre, préfet du Finistère au Ministre de l'Intérieur, le 22 décembre 1848 in Brissot-Thivars' dossier in A.N. F 1 b I 156[46].

THE COUP D'ÉTAT OF DECEMBER 1851: REPRESSION AND THE LIMITS TO REPRESSION

Vincent Wright
London School of Economics

From 2 December 1851, the date of the *coup d'état* of Louis-Napoleon, until 27 March 1852, France lived under a regime of extraordinary police powers.[1] The period of repression did not begin on 2 December, for the *coup d'état* represents the culmination of nearly four years of intense antirepublican activity. Nor did political repression end on 27 March 1852. In April and May of that year, war councils were still passing vicious sentences on Republicans involved in active resistance to the *coup d'état*. Moreover, from December 1851 to March 1852 many of the traditional police powers were reinforced and new ones were granted, which were to be used with great effectiveness against the Republican opposition during the Empire.[2]

The four months in question are extremely revealing not only about the procedures, the means and the consequences of repression — they also illuminate several important aspects of the functioning of the politico-administrative system in mid-nineteenth century France. Two main conclusions emerge from any study of that period. First, that the repression was more far-reaching and appalling than the official figures might suggest, for accompanying the official repression was widespread, insidious and unrecorded unofficial repression. The true extent and nature of the repression is studied in the second section of the essay: it follows a brief outline of the chronology of repression.

The second main conclusion to emerge from this study is that the repression, however terrible, could have been far worse — section III of this essay is devoted to analysing the constraints upon repression. It will be shown that these constraints were of a personal, professional, political and social nature. Yet whilst they acted to limit the extent and full impact of repression they could never efface the bitter memories formed during that period: the consequences of the *coup d'état* of December 1851 and the repression which followed were still being felt a generation later.

I The Chronology of Repression

The four months of extraordinary police powers represent, in many senses, a curious period. Throughout, there was an underlying uncertainty which reflected the conflicting sentiments of the principal actors involved in repression: the taste for vengeance on the part of many traditional minor notables who had seen their local positions progressively usurped by the 'agents of disorder'; at the other extreme, the reticence of Louis-Napoleon himself and the hesitations of some of his liberal advisors; and between the frightened right wing notables and the tormented Prince-President and his Paris advisors were the local agents of repression — the prefects, the procureurs and the generals — who were divided over the strategy and the tactics to be employed.

Orders were given only to be countermanded a few days later, and instructions were issued only to have their substance altered by later circulars. Periods of vicious repression were punctuated by moments of uneasy leniency. Nevertheless, it is possible to discern four distinct phases during this period. Essentially, the first period was one of intense and indiscriminate repressive activity, the second was one of growing uncertainty, the third was characterised by an attempt to rationalise the entire process of repression, and the final phase was marked by a policy of reducing the extent and minimising the impact of the repression.

The first phase covers the month of December 1851. It opens with the pre-emptive strikes made against those leaders of the Republican opposition who were likely to cause trouble. In Paris, the over zealous Maupas, Prefect of Police since 26 October 1851, ordered the arrest of Royalist and Republican Deputies, anti-Bonapartist generals and left wing agitators. In the departmental *chefs-lieux* many leading left wingers were immediately rounded up by the prefectoral authorities to prevent them from organising resistance to the *coup d'état*. During the rest of the month, other Republicans were arrested, accused of resisting the *coup d'état* or of being over-active in spreading anti-Bonapartist propaganda during the plebiscite. It was during this month, too, that men accused of minor political offences were tried by the courts: shouting a Republican slogan could earn a man a month in prison. Finally, it was during December that the *conseils de guerre*, established on 19 December to deal with the mass insurrectionary movements of parts of the centre and the south, began to dole out their harsh sentences. They functioned in the thirty-two departments which, since the beginning of December, had been placed under official state of siege.

The second phase of repression covers the month of January, a month characterised by embarassed and frightened indecision. The success of the *coup d'état*, the triumph of the December plebiscite, the remarkable state of peace which prevailed, all indicated that there was little to fear from the left. Yet memories — and fears — were too recent to be wiped out by one month of social and political peace, and the

reports of the prefects and the procureurs during this period are replete
with neurotic warnings to Paris not to relax vigilance: for certain elements of the right, the price of order was eternal repression. During this
second phase, attempts were made by Paris to impose some form of cooperation between its provincial agents in order to solve the massive
problems created by the arrest of thousands of political prisoners.
There was certainly no question of allowing the ordinary courts of justice to try these men: many magistrates were politically suspect, and
trials could be dangerous, since they might be used as forums of propaganda. Furthermore, Paris was increasingly aware of the need to put an
end to the many conflicts which were arising between the prefects, the
procureurs and the generals. Circulars of 11 and 18 January laid down
the guidelines of cooperation, but were singularly unsuccessful in putting an end to the disputes between the departmental authorities. The
problem was compounded by customary bureacratic inertia, and at the
end of January the prisons were still overcrowded with political suspects. Moreover, it was rapidly becoming clear that within the eighty-
six departments different patterns of repression were emerging: in
some, the authorities were harsh whilst in others they were very lenient.
It was an unsatisfactory situation, and it gave rise to constant bitter
complaints. At the end of January, Persigny, who had just become the
Minister of the Interior, ordered the departmental authorities to release
all those prisoners who had been merely led astray by the 'socialist'
leaders. However, before the order could be executed, new instructions
were received by the local authorities. Maupas, the head of the newly
created Ministry of Police, ordered, by a circular of 3 February 1852,
the setting up in each department of a *commission mixte*.

With the circular of 3 February opens the third phase of this period
of extraordinary police powers: it was a phase of rationalising the
procedures of repression. The embarassed vacillation of the previous
month was brought to an end. The commission mixte in each department comprised the Prefect, the departmental Procureur (or State Prosecutor) and the general commanding the department.[3] The basic purpose of the commissions mixtes was to ensure cooperation between the
prefectoral, judicial and military authorities. Their task was to speed up
the process of dealing with the thousands of political prisoners who had
been arrested since December 1851, by suggesting common measures
against anyone who was politically suspect: they were instructed to act
against not only those actively involved in resistance to the *coup
d'état* but also against those 'pernicious elements' considered to be
dangerous to society. They had the right to make the following recommendations for those whom they tried:

(1)   For those accused of murder or attempted murder, a court

martial.

(2) For the especially culpable who also had a previous police record, transportation to the penal colony of Cayenne.

(3) For those judged particularly dangerous, transportation to a penal colony in Algeria (a penalty known as 'Algeria plus').

(4) Transportation to a town in Algeria where the prisoner would be surveilled but not imprisoned (a penalty known as 'Algeria minus').

(5) Permanent expulsion from France.

(6) Temporary exile to a country of own choosing.

(7) Forced residence and surveillance in a French town which was to be decided by the authorities (a penalty known, perhaps misleadingly, as 'internment'): the *interné* had to report twice a month to the local mayor or police and needed prefectoral permission to leave the town.

(8) To be left in the hands of the local police for further investigation.

(9) To be sent to a detention centre — a penalty reserved for young offenders.

(10) To be surveilled by agents of the Ministry of Police in a residence of own choosing. In practice, the *surveillé* had to report to the local police station once a month.

(11) To be released.

(12) To be left in the hands of the civil courts for further investigation.

The powers given to the commissions mixtes were wide ranging and ill defined, and problems of interpetation were soon raised by a number of scrupulous magistrates. But the government was insistent that the powers of the commissions should be interpreted in as repressive a manner as possible. The government's reply to the apprehensive procureur général of Metz is revealing in this respect:

'La circulaire n'est qu'énonciatrice et non limitative en ce qui concerne les inculpés judiciaires; mais tous les individus qui, par leurs actes, leurs discours, leurs menées, ont, même antérieurement au 2 décembre, préparé les populations au désordre, au mépris du principe d'autorité ... et à la haine et à l'envie contre les classes riches, pourront être l'objet de l'examen et d'une décision du tribunal mixte, qui est investi à cet égard d'un pouvoir discrétionnaire. Ceux qui ne se sont pas montrés après le 2 décembre ont pu avoir la satisfaction de voir cependant que leurs efforts antérieurs n'avaient pas été stériles. Leur responsabilité est grande par le passé et le gouvernement doit se préoccuper de l'avenir. Il ne peut du reste y avoir de difficultés à considérer dès à présent comme inculpés les individus qui ont été arrêtés administrativement, puisque MM. les préfets étaient investis de pouvoirs analogues à ceux de l'autorité judiciaire, et il est certain que de nouvelles inculpations pourront encore être faites par l'autorité administrative.'[4]

Similarly, when the commission mixte of the Vendée expressed its regret at being unable to recommend measures against doctor Clemenceau (the father of the future Prime Minister) and Gallois, a Republican journalist, on the grounds that they had played no part in the resistance to the *coup d'état* and had remained 'politically quiet' ever since, it was informed that it could do so,

> 'car si on ne leur impute aucun fait matériel de participation aux événements postérieurs au 2 décembrre, ils peuvent certainement être considérés comme ayant, par leur funeste propagande, poussé les populations à l'insurrection. Cela suffit pour que le tribunal mixte, investi d'un pouvoir discrétionnaire, puisse proposer à leur égard des measures de sûreté générale.'[5]

The commissions deliberated throughout the month of February, and made recommendations to Maupas on more than 26,000 Republicans.

The fourth and final phase in the period of extraordinary police powers begins with the attempt by the government to attenuate the rigour of the decisions of the commissions mixtes. Indeed, the Prince-President intervened as early as 9 March when a Committee of Political Pardons was created 'dans le but de donner son avis sur les mesures de clemence qui seraient sollicitées en faveur des insurgés à l'égard desquels les commissions mixtes auraient statué'. The Committee had its first meeting on 15 March, and within days made many recommendations for clemency.[6] Louis-Napoleon also sent three men — Canrobert and Espinasse who were two of his aides-de-camp, and Quentin-Bauchart, a liberal minded Councillor of State — into the provinces with the duty of examining the decisions of the commissions mixtes with a view to recommending measures of clemency.[7]

The regime of extraordinary police powers was brought to an end by a decree of 27 March 1852. The state of siege (which had been decreed in certain departments in early December) was now raised, and the commissions mixtes were abolished. Henceforth, all political arrests and prosecutions would be conducted by the normal judicial authorities. Two days later, 29 March 1852, Louis-Napoleon announced at the official opening of the parliamentary session that 'the dictatorship confided in me by the people' had come to an end.[8] Thus ended the final phase of a period of extraordinary police powers which had lasted only four months but which was durably to mark the mind of the following generation.

II. The Extent and Nature of the Repression

Assessing the extent of the repression during this period raises at least three very complex problems. First, it is extremely difficult to arrive at an exact figure for the number of men arrested and imprisoned during this period. Second, apart from the official repression, recorded in the macabre registers established by the prefects, the procureurs and the army officers, there was an unofficial oppression which affected a great many people. Third, even if a quantitative estimate of the extent of the repression were possible, it would give no real indication of the intensity of that repression.

There seems to be general agreement about some of the statistics of repression. The total number of people killed during the December resistance in Paris was 380.[9] The three decrees of 9 January 1852 resulted in the transportation of five members of the Legislative Assembly, the expulsion of sixty-six (including Hugo and Raspail) and the temporary exile of eighteen others (including Thiers, Changarnier and Lamoricière). There is also general agreements about the repressive measures taken by the commissions mixtes: A total of 26,885 men were tried by these commissions:[10]

(1)	Sent for trial by a Council of War	247
(2)	Sent to Cayenne	239
(3)	Sent to a penal colony in Algeria	4,549
(4)	Sent to Algeria but to residence of choice	5,032
(5)	Expelled from France	980
(6)	Temporarily exiled	640
(7)	Forced residence determined by the authorities	2,827
(8)	Left in the hands of the police	645
(9)	Sent to a detention centre	29
(10)	Surveillance by the Ministry of Police in the residence of their own choice	5,194
(11)	Release	5,857
(12)	Left in the hands of the civil courts	645

It has been too frequently assumed that the number of men tried by the commissions mixtes represents the total affected by the repression. But this is clearly not so. Whilst rejecting the grossly inflated figures of some republican propagandists,[11] it must be recognised that the figures now normally quoted represent a serious underestimate. In truth, it is virtually impossible to calculate the total number of men arrested during the four months of exceptional police powers, since many were arrested, placed in preventative detention, and were released without any further action being taken against them — either by the courts or the commissions mixtes. In the department of the Rhône, for example, 840 men were arrested but 'only' 472 were tried by the commission mixte.[12] In the Maine-et-Loire, of the sixty-two arrested and imprisoned during this period thirty-two were tried by the commission mixte,[13] and in the Loir-et-Cher, the commission mixte examined the cases of only fifty-two of the 137 men who had been arrested in the department.[14] Such examples could be multiplied.[15]

Other men do not appear to be tabulated in the 26,884 tried by the commissions. These would include the 480 leading Paris left wingers who had been immediately rounded up by Maupas (the Prefect of Police) and had been sent to Algeria by early January — at least three weeks before the first meetings of the commissions. They would also include those men who were killed or summarily shot in skirmishes with the military authorities,[16] those who were injured whilst trying to escape the marauding activities of the military mobile columns which scoured the countryside of certain departments, and many of those such as the Reclus brothers who fled abroad to escape arrest.[17] There is also no place in the official statistics for men such as Angot, an inoffensive Republican tax collector, who committed suicide whilst awaiting arrest,[18] or Frison, a lawyer, who hanged himself with his own neck tie, or Denoize, an ex-Deputy, who attempted to blow himself up but succeeded only in horribly mutilating himself.[19]

The full extent of the repression must be judged not only by those physically affected. Many were to suffer in other ways. There was a host of civil servants whose 'only' punishment was dismissal: Parent, the Secretary General of the town hall at Clamecy for the previous twenty-seven years; Huet, a first class naval surgeon from Brest; de Jouenne d'Esgrigny d'Herville, a *garde des fôrets* in the Vienne,[20] Similarly, whilst 261 primary and fifty-four secondary school teachers were tried by the commissions, many more were quite simply dismissed. Other teachers followed the example of Jules Simon who resigned his post, being unable to swear the required oath of allegiance to the new regime.[21] Countless other men were to suffer economically as the result of the repression. Thus, whilst the official statistics do indicate that 168 *officiers ministeriels* were tried by the commissions mixtes, they do not reveal that their lucrative practices were often quite simply confiscated. Nor do they indicate that several men belonging to this professional category and who were not tried by a commission mixte were put under very strong pressure to sell their practices at scandalously low prices.[22] Similarly, whilst the names of 325 doctors appear on the lists of the commissions, many more were to suffer. Particularly revealing in this respect were the cases of Girault and Piedallu, doctors in the Loir-et-Cher, whose practices (worth 10,000 fr.

a year) were ruined after December 1851 because they were compromised by their republicanism.[23] Similarly, whilst ninety journalists are included in the official figure of repression, many more were affected, since they lost their jobs in the general onslaught against the press.

The repressive measures taken against the press varied greatly according to the local authorities: the most affected department was the Haute-Garonne where eight of the nine local newspapers were suppressed, The action taken against the press by certain departmental authorities (now armed with full powers by the early decree of Morny) betrayed an appetite for vengeance fed by three years of frustration: owners, editors and journalists were arrested, presses were seized or smashed, and offices were closed (often after being ransacked).[24] A decree of 31 December 1851 removed all future press offences from the jurisdiction of the Courts of Assizes where, during the July Monarchy and the Second Republic, juries had all too frequently acquitted the accused demagogues. Henceforth, all press cases would be tried by the local tribunals where it was hoped the magistrates would be more compliant in condoning the repressive measures of the prefectoral authorities. The government suspected, not without some justification, that juries were unlikely to comply with the new arbitrariness: in mid-January for example, in a totally unpublicised case, Gastineau, editor of the *Ami du Peuple du Gers et des Hautes-Pyrénées* which had been seized before the *coup d'état*, was acquitted by a jury in the Gers. The case was all the more remarkable since the Gers was a department under martial law, Gastineau was in prison for his resistance to the *coup*, and the *Ami du Peuple* had been suppressed in the early days of December.[25] It was the last newspaper case until the new press laws of 1868 to be tried by a jury. The law of February 1852 regularised the situation created by the decree of 31 December, and even extended government control of the press.

The list of purely economic victims of the repression seems endless: Gallois, owner of the left wing newspaper *Le Démocrate Vendéen* whose presses, worth 100,000 francs were smashed by the police;[26] Touzet, the owner of the bookshop which sold republican newspapers and pamphlets;[27] Lemonnier, a tailor from Mortain (Manche) who, after his house had been searched by the police, was ostracised by his erstwhile customers, and as a result was economically ruined and died in poverty.[28] David, a wealthy merchant from Nantes whose 'belle et lucrative position' was completely destroyed: his customers deserted him for fear of being compromised by any contact — even commercial — with this notorious republican.[29] Another typical case was Scelles, an *expert-géomètre* of Marigny (Manche) who was also ruined as the result of the repression but who does not appear in the register of the departmental commission mixte:

310

'Au coup d'état, la gendarmerie pénétra la nuit dans son domicile pour y faire une perquisition, puis pour l'arrêter et le transferer à la prison de Saint-Lô. Après avoir subi une interrogation, il resta enfermé pendant 13 ou 15 jours, puis fut remis en liberté. Cette arrestation éloigna sa clientèle, composée de gens de la campagne alors en grande majorité entièrement hostiles à la République.'[30]

Finally, mention should be made of those many men whose *débit de tabac, débit de vin* and cafés were quite simply closed by prefectoral order during this period. As a result of the decree of 29 December 1851, the prefects' powers in this domain were made more wide-ranging. Some were to exercise these powers very extensively: for instance Tonnet, Prefect of the Calvados, was to close 700 cafés and *cabarets* in six years.[31]

The third type of repression after the *coup d'état* was purely political. The purge of the town halls which had continued unabated during the previous three and a half years was now completed. To the mayors who resigned (they included those of such relatively important towns as Cahors, Niort, Compiègne and Villeneuve-sur-Lot) must be added the many who were summarily dismissed, and their councils dissolved or suspended. This aspect of the repression (which was completely unpublicised because there was no opposition press) has never been fully studied, although there is reason to believe that the purge was fairly extensive.[32] In such a way, hundreds of locally elected officials, often representing the local Republican elite, were suddenly deprived of office and political status. Although they appear on no official register of the commissions mixtes, they must nonetheless be counted amongst the victims of the *coup*.

The official figures not only underestimate the extent of the repression, they also reveal little of the real nature and intensity of that repression. It is easy to conjure up the horrors of transportation and imprisonment in the grim penal colonies of Cayenne and Lambessa (Algeria). The frustrations and privations of exile are equally easy to envisage, as are the appalling conditions in prisons which were designed for many fewer inmates.[33] In those prisons, the bitter cold, the damp, the darkness, the vermin and the filth combined with ill-treatment to render life unbearable. When Alphonse Bon, a minor official of Le Puy and father of fifteen children, was sent to the local prison he was 'bien portant . . . et encore jeune' but he 'en sortit courbé et vieilli, et ses cheveux entièrement blanchis'. His story is typical of many others.[34]

There are other aspects of the repression which immediately spring to mind. Many men were not only given heavy sentences but also lost their means of livelihood. Even for many who were given relatively light sentences the full consequences could be terrible and lasting. The cases of Solvain and Roux perfectly illustrate this point. Solvain was a building contractor of Le Puy who employed fifty men and who enjoyed 'une aisance qui eut amené la richesse et qui lui promettait d'envisager tranquillement l'avenir'. After he was sentenced to be placed under police surveillance by the commission mixte of the Haute-Loire, he lost everything – his fortune, his health, his social standing.[35] Roux, a hotel owner of Agen, owned a personal fortune assessed at 50,000 francs, but he, too, was completely ruined after his sentence to police surveillance by the departmental commission mixte.[36]

The frightful personal suffering of many of the victims of the *coup d'état* was not the figment of overexcited Republican imaginations. The repression is a catalogue of deep and lasting suffering, a series of appalling personal dramas:[37] Vazeilles, a hard working and respected primary school teacher of Le Puy who could find no work after his dismissal and was driven 'to drink and moral depravity'; Claverie who went blind as the result of an illness contracted in exile in Algeria and who died at the age of 32; Ducros who went completely deaf as the result of his imprisonment; Segalon who was treated as a common criminal and took years before he could find an employer who would give him work.[38] To the suffering of the men who were affected by the repression must be added the personal and economic misery of many of their families. Some of these families slowly disintegrated under the pressures of economic privation and social ostracism.[39]

The *coup d'état* is a tale not only of suffering but also of mass humiliation inflicted upon the victims by vindictive minor officials and soldiers. The official figures do nothing to evoke the traumatic memories of men who were hunted like wild animals by mobile military units which, aided by Royalist *milices civiques*, scoured the villages and countryside of certain departments of the south and the centre.[40] Republicans were rounded up and roped together like beasts in those infamous 'chasses aux rouges'. Others were paraded through the streets like common criminals. The mayors of Billy and Pousseaux in the Nièvre were led by a rope around the neck through the streets of their own villages[41] whilst Vazeilles, a mild mannered primary school teacher of Le Puy, was dragged from in front of his class in similar fashion.[42]

Mass humiliation and personal grievance was compounded by a sense of acute political frustration. It was not only that the apocalyptic vision of 1852 was now shattered: so, too, were a thousand more personal dreams of these little men – *les petits* – who, as Vigier and Agulhon have so convincingly demonstrated, began to emerge as local political leaders during the Second Republic.

The repression was, therefore, more wide ranging and terrible than the oft-quoted figures suggest. It is only by understanding its full extent and intensity that the deep seated and enduring bitterness of the Republicans be fully appreciated.

III. The Constraints upon Repression

Amongst the most interesting — and certainly the least studied — aspects of the repression following the *coup d'état* are the nature and extent of the constraints upon that repression. These limitations were defined, for personal or political reasons, by the provincial agents of repression themselves, or they emerged as the consequences of the divisions of opinion between those agents. Other limitations resulted from the resistance of certain sections of the local population or they were imposed by the Prince-President and certain of his advisors.

By examining the outlook and opinions of the government's agents in the provinces, by analysing the work of the commissions mixtes, and by studying the reactions of Louis-Napoleon and many of his prominent supporters, it is possible to discern, however imprecisely, the political and social limitations which were imposed upon repression in a country at a period in which it had all the appearances, and many of the attributes, of a police state.

(a)   The provincial agents of repression

The three main provincial agents of repression were the prefectoral administration, the army and the magistrature. The prefectoral administration was under the direct control of Morny, the cynical, decisive and cool headed Minister of the Interior, who replaced his bewildered predecessor on the morning of the *coup d'état*. Morny was the principal instigator and coordinator of repression until his resignation on 22 January and replacement by the faithful Persigny. His replacement was taken as an occasion to review the policy of concentrating and strengthening all police powers in the hands of the Minister of the Interior, since a new Ministry of General Police was created to centralise prefectoral police action. It was headed by Maupas, the ex-Prefect of Police, who like all essentially weak men, excelled in gratuitous severity and specialised in over-reacting to most situations. Under his control were placed not only the prefectoral administrators but also the newly created police inspectors. These inspectors were given ill-defined and wide ranging powers which duplicated many of those exercised by the prefects. The latter were, not unnaturally, resentful of this new state of affairs[43] and, secretly encouraged by Persigny, the only Minister they recognised, showed a singular lack of enthusiasm in cooperating with the new police inspectors. Conflict was in the very nature of things, and it was not slow in breaking out between Persigny and his prefects on the one hand and Maupas and his inspectors on the other. The conflict was not resolved until the abolition of the Ministry of General Police in June 1853.[44]

The second main instrument of repression was the army which, since 16 October 1851, had been under the control of Leroy de Saint-Arnaud, the brutal, self-seeking, insensitive and thoroughly obnoxious Minister of War. Placed under his direct control, was the army and also the gendarmerie. The role of the army was especially important in those thirty-two departments placed under martial law: on 5 December, the Allier and the Saône-et-Loire were placed under official state of siege and these departments were quickly followed by the Basses-Alpes on 9 December and the Lot, the Lot-et-Garonne, the Gers and the Var on the following day. In the thirty-two departments under state of siege, the army assumed full powers, and from 19 December 1851 there functioned in these departments military commissions comprising three high-ranking officers. Those appearing before the commissions were classified according to three types of recommendation: release, transportation or further trial by courts martial. On the whole, these commissions acted with the dispatch and sensitivity to be expected from a military tribunal, and on 19 January the Minister of War had to warn (perhaps unwillingly) the commissions to be more moderate in their decisions. The military commissions were replaced by fewer military councils, established on 18 January. On the same day, to the disgust of men such as General de Castellane, the powers of the civil authorities were reinforced in the departments under martial law.[45] Conflicts between the military and the civil authorities soon broke out.[46]

The third group of agents of repression was the judiciary, headed first by Rouher and then, from 22 January, by Abbatucci. Two types of magistrate were involved in the repression — the *magistrature assise* and the *magistrature debout*. The former — the irremovable magistrates of the bench — were responsible for trying those who were brought before the courts, accused of precisely motivated civil offences. The latter — the state prosecutors — led by the twenty-seven procureurs généraux and comprising an army of subordinate *procureurs de la République*, were responsible not only for initiating legal proceedings against those whom they considered culpable but also for collaborating with the other authorities in ordering arrests and issuing search warrants. They were also responsible for the legal prosecution of the accused. In a sense, they were the political arm of the judiciary: indeed, one of their traditional functions was to inform Paris of the state of political opinion within their departments.

Later Republican propagandists saw only a unanimity of views amongst the army officers, the prefects and the magistrates, supported in their repressive zeal by their subordinates (and all aided and

314

spiritually abetted by the church . . .): 'toute l'armée administrative suivit docilement l'impulsion partie du ministère de l'intérieur et prêta son concours au coup d'état.'[47] But propagandists inevitably indulge in caricature. Naturally, the 'administrative army' generally welcomed the *coup d'état*. But enthusiasm was by no means universal.

Amongst the high-ranking army officers there was very widespread acceptance of the new regime[48] but Cavaignac, Le Flô, Bedeau, Changarnier, Lamoricière and Charras were not the only ones to manifest their hostility.[49] The prefectoral administration, contrary to the commonly accepted assumption, was also far from unanimous in welcoming the *coup*. Eight of the eighty-six prefects resigned in protest against it,[50] and other prefects were clearly less than enthusiastic in their support of the new regime. The Prefect of the Finistère was the most extreme in his hostility, since he posted an anti-*coup d'état* proclamation in the main town of the department and also got the *Conseil Général* to vote an official protest against the *coup d'état*.[51] Amongst the prefects' subordinates there were also elements of resistance: in the Nord the sub-prefect of Hazebrouck had to be dismissed because of his hostility, and two *conseillers de préfecture* handed in their resignations; in the Maine-et-Loire, the sub-prefect of Semur resigned; in the Lot, the *secrétaire-général* and one of the *conseillers de préfecture* resigned; in the Haute-Vienne one of the most respected *conseillers de préfecture* resigned; in the Dordogne, the officials of the prefecture gave a very cool reception to the news of the *coup d'état*.[52]

Most of the opposition of officials towards the *coup d'état* came from the magistrature. Certainly, parts of the *magistrature assise*, imbued with Orléanist sympathies, were clearly highly critical, and whilst the great majority of judges rallied to the new regime, there were a number of revealing exceptions. Thus the magistrates at Douai (one of the most important courts in the country) showed their dislike of the new situation by imposing ludicrously light sentences on Republicans involved in anti-*coup d'état* demonstrations. The Tribunal of the town also declared illegal the seizure of the newspaper *Le Libéral* by the Prefect.[53] In similar fashion, the Tribunal of Bayonne condemned the sub-prefect's seizing on 4 December of the Republican newspaper *L'Eclaireur* as illegal.[54] One of the most distinguished judges of the Toulouse Court of Appeal showed his sentiments by refusing to preside over one of the electoral bureaux of the town during the plebiscite of 19 December.[55] At Rodez, the President of the Tribunal was considered to be so violently opposed towards the new political order that he was arrested, and later exiled by the commission mixte of the department.[56] At Périgueux, Larroque de Mons, President of the Civil Tribunal, openly declared in the early days of December that the Prefect was an outlaw, and only the threat of being imprisoned managed to silence him.[57] The Prefect of the Deux-Sèvres had to warn the Government that the enthusiasm of the local magistrates for the new regime was less than lukewarm, and that the vice-president of the Tribunal of Niort (the *chef-lieu* of the department) could speak of nothing but illegality and the need for resistance.[58] In the Gironde, two judges, Ballot des Minières (father of a future Bishop of Poitiers) of Bordeaux and Cellerieu of Lesparre were dismissed because of their obstructive opposition to the new regime.[59]

Even certain *magistrats debout* — the politically sensitive public prosecutors — very early displayed their political antagonism towards the new situation. At Angoulême, Marrot, the deputy procureur, resigned in unpublicised silence.[60] In the department of the Nord, two procureurs were less than cooperative with the political authorities: the procureur at Cambrai refused to seize the *Echo de Cambrai* which had accused the Prince-President of high treason, and the procureur at Avesnes actually protested against the *coup d'état* at a public meeting (he was arrested and later tried by the commission mixte of the department).[61]

(b)   Divisions of opinion amongst the agents of repression

The month of December was punctuated by resignations and dismissals of politically hostile or unreliable army officers and members of the prefectoral corps and the magistrature. Yet this political purge did not ensure unanimity of views amongst officials on the policy of repression to be pursued. Naturally, there was general agreement that some form of repression was required, indeed essential, since the persistence of the political, economic and social agitation of the preceding few years was considered intolerable. Moreover, having narrowly escaped 'the judgement of 1852' the forces of conservative France were now apparently in a position to ensure the indefinite postponement of that judgement. The 'red spectre' was the theme of many a report emanating from the prefectures and *parquets* between 1849 and 1851, and it seemed to materialise in the insurrectionary resistance to the *coup d'état* shown in certain French provinces. In February and March 1852, in spite of the state of total peace which reigned in France, nervous fear outweighed grateful relief in the minds of most government officials. However, whilst the principal agents of repression may have issued from the same social milieux and have shared similar political views their long official training had inculcated somewhat different professional prejudices and reactions: all generals were professional soldiers, many of whom had enjoyed military experience only in Algeria; all the procureurs had started life as practising lawyers and many had some experience on the bench before taking up their posts; of the eighty-six prefects of 1 February 1852 only four had no previous prefectoral experience before taking up their posts and forty-three had had at least ten years such experience. On the whole, during this period the generals' view of a repressive measure was governed solely by its immediate efficacy and physical practicability, whilst the prefects prudently calculated its political cost, and the procureurs frequently questioned its legality. In short, the soldier was interested in the logistically possible, the prefect in the politically expedient, and the magistrate in the legally prescribed.

During the period of extraordinary police powers the generals were to prove the most brutal. There were, of course, exceptions. Certain officers belonging to the three man military commissions which functioned between 19 December 1851 and 17 January 1852 were very moderate: this was certainly the case in the Isère and in the Eure-et-Loire where the prefect was highly critical of their leniency.[62] Certainly, their leniency contrasted with the harshness of other military tribunals, notably those of the Gers and the Drôme: the latter, on 30 December 1851, sentenced a *garde champêtre* to twenty years hard labour for having given shelter to two Republicans who were on the run.[63] Mention should be made, too, of General Chadeysson who was in charge of the Basses-Alpes and who was replaced after refusing to execute unnecessarily harsh orders.[64] Such cases were, however, rare: the officers on the whole followed the very tough line laid down by their Minister. The most typical examples were Generals Rostolan, Eynard and Castellane. Rostolan was later denounced by the Prefect of the Hérault as having acted, under the influence of his legitimist friends, with almost blind brutality.[65] Eynard, a blustering, boorish man of limited political intelligence, pursued the Republicans of the Allier with a viciousness which bordered on fanaticism: amongst his first acts were two decrees ordering the confiscation of the property of leading Republicans and a warning that anyone suspected of carrying arms would be summarily executed. The bilious and self-opinionated General de Castellane displayed as much (and possibly more) aggression in fighting the left wingers of Lyons as in combatting the external enemies of France. He was to have many later dishonourable emulators.

The prefects of 2 December 1851 inherited an impressive array of police powers, many of which had been elaborated in the preceding three years. To the traditional prefectoral powers were added three new ones of a wide ranging nature. The first of these new powers was outlined in a decree of 8 December. It gave prefects great administrative discretion in dealing with suspected members of secret societies. First, it enabled them to transport to an overseas penal colony anyone 'recognised guilty' of belonging to a secret society. In fact, anyone who had previously been found guilty of such a crime was now in danger of being re-arrested and transported without further judicial process. Second, the 8 December decree gave a prefect the right to transport any ex-member of a secret society who had failed to comply with the residence qualifications imposed by the police after previous sentence. Finally, the administration was empowered to establish the residence of any ex-secret society member even though he had completed all the stipulations of the previous sentence. In none of these three cases did the man involved have any right to judicial appeal. Morny also insisted that his prefects interpret the decree in as wide a manner as required. He insisted that the decree could be used to embrace those who were merely suspected of membership of a secret society, and evidence of a judicial nature was not required.[66] Although severely restricted as a result of pressure from the Minister of Justice the powers contained in the 8 December decree remained a powerful and totally arbitrary instrument: it was, wrote Granier de Cassagnac, an effective means of defending society against 'the army of vice and crime'.[67]

The second new police power accorded the prefects enabled them more effectively to deal with the opposition press, whilst the third, contained in the decree of 29 December 1851, gave the prefects the right to close all bars and cabarets many of which were suspected as 'foyers of revolution'. The decree was welcomed by the prefects as a means of combatting 'les funestes inspirations' which appeared to flow with as great a profusion as the drink which was sold in these establishments.[68]

The general impression of the period of exceptional police powers is one of savage repression, with prefects outbidding one another in dismissing mayors, dissolving local councils and national guards,[69] sacking left wing officials, closing down newspapers and imprisoning journalists, relentlessly pursuing innocent Republicans. Certainly, Morny in his early despatches and circulars urged his prefects to use to the full all their powers. Yet, prefects varied enormously in how they exercised their very considerable police powers and in the general policies they pursued. Nowhere was this more marked than in the policies adopted towards the departmental press.[70]

Throughout the period of exceptional police powers, some prefects such as Pougeard-Dulimbert in the Pyrénées-Orientales and Sivry in the Meurthe acted with indiscriminate vindictiveness.[71] Others, however, such as Durckheim of the Haut-Rhin, Gauja in the Loire-Infèrieure, Cambacerès in the Basses-Pyrénées, Calvimont in the Dordogne and Chapuys de Montlaville in the Isere proved themselves to be reasonably moderate and humane men.[72] In the Vaucluse, the prefect, Costa de Bastelica, earned himself the reputation of being much too lenient with the Reds[73] and was taken to task for such leniency by the local magistrates.[74] The prefect of the Corrèze, Baron Michel, was reminded very pointedly by his mother that his father, an imperial general, had been a political prisoner during the Restoration Monarchy: Michel had to intervene on several occasions against a hard-line procureur. The prefectoral authorities often acted unofficially in an humanitarian manner: there were numerous small examples of certain prefects and sub-prefects intervening to attenuate the repressive zeal of subordinates and collaborators. Some, for example, warned their *administrés* of possible persecution, thus enabling them to flee the area or even the country.[76]

With one or two notable exceptions, the procureurs were to display the greatest reluctance in exercising full and untrammelled police powers:[77] the months of December and January are marked by small yet revealing conflicts between the judicial authorities on the one hand and the military and prefectoral authorities on the other. In mid-December, a bitter dispute broke out between the procureur at Brive (backed by his superior, the procureur general at Limoges) and the sub-prefect of the town (backed by his superior, the prefect of the Corrèze): the magistrates felt that once a man had been imprisoned he should be left completely in the hands of the judicial authorities who alone would decide what measures to take. The Minister of Justice agreed with this point of view, but his colleague at the Interior backed his prefectoral subordinates in claiming jurisdiction over the prisoners. The government eventually decided to back the prefectoral authorities.[78] At much the same time, there was another dispute between Rouher at Justice and Morny at the Interior over the interpretation of the decree of 8 December on secret societies. Rouher, an ex-lawyer, alarmed by the totally arbitrary nature of the decree, successfully intervened to limit its full impact. He insisted that mere suspicion of the offence was insufficient, and underlined the fact that the decree was to have no retroactive effect.[79] There were other examples of the magistrates clashing with the military and prefectoral authorities. At Nîmes, for example, the procureur general refused to deliver certain files to the army, and also declined to issue arrest warrants against men whose guilt was based on not the slightest shred of evidence.[80] His colleague, the procureur general at Rouen, refused a prefectoral request to arrest a prominent Republican journalist,[81] whilst another colleague, the procureur general at Agen was in constant conflict with the military authorities of the department of the Lot-et-Garonne.[82] The procureur general at Rennes had several disputes with the local prefect over the release of men whom he considered to be perfectly innocent.[83] In the Basses-Alpes, the local magistrates made no attempt to hide their anxiety about the excessive severity of the army which had succeeded in creating an atmosphere of terror in the department.[84]

Conflicts between the agents of repression emerged most clearly within the commissions mixtes. Unfortunately, nothing is known of the debates within the commissions over individual cases: that the register of the commissions gives no clues is scarcely surprising, since the members

319

were asked by the government to submit unanimous recommendations. Yet such unanimity almost certainly masks differences of opinion in reaching those final recommendations. It certainly reveals nothing of the scruples of some of the magistrates: the procureur general of Aix who declared his unease at sitting in judgement on men whose arrests were based merely on 'slanderous denunciations';[85] the procureur general of Bordeaux who attempted to moderate the rigour of his two collaborators;[86] the procureurs généraux of Metz, Montpellier, Tours and Rouen who expressed some distaste at sentencing men whose sole crime was to be a socialist leader or to be resolutely hostile to the government;[87] the procureur general at Lyons who wondered whether it was really possible to take measures against Republicans whose release had been ordered by the Prefect who had considered them to be perfectly harmless.[88]

The hostility of parts of the magistrature to the *coup d'état* and the moderating influence of other parts during the following repression have never been fully documented. The magistrates themselves preferred to pull a discreet veil over a period in which so many had been compromised, and those who played any part in a commission mixte (even as an advocate of clemency) preferred to forget the entire episode. The leaders of the regime were clearly intent on not advertising the reticence of certain magistrates when faced with repressive measures. For the Republicans, all was black and white: in the manichean universe, any participation in the repression constituted a mortal sin not to be expunged by a few faint soul-searchings.

(c) The work of the commissions mixtes

It must be remembered that the commission mixtes, the object of so much Republican hatred, were not merely blind instruments of repression. Some certainly gave that impression — notably those of the Meurthe, the Pyrénées-Orientales, the Cher, the Gers, the Basses-Alpes and the Jura. Others, however, showed surprising moderation, and provoked the anger of part of the right which demanded sterner measures: Espinasse, in his report to the Emperor, criticised many commissions on the grounds that they had sinned by excess of indulgence. Commissions mixtes such as those in the Finistère and the Ille-et-Vilaine took measures against no-one, even though the main towns (especially Rennes and Brest) had been troubled by left wing activists since 1848. In fifteen departments fewer than five men were even tried by the commissions. Some of the commissions of the highly troubled departments of the Midi decided not to pursue many of those poor and ignorant peasants who took part in the insurrectionary movement of protest[89] whilst in the Haute-Vienne, a left wing stronghold, most of the peasants of Linards who had been involved in an armed clash with the police were also left in peace.[90] The commission mixte of the Gironde — generally considered to be tough — was sent 500 cases to consider by the zealous Inspector General of Police, but decided to examine 'only' eighty-six of them.[91] In the Gard, a department with a long history of left wing agitation, the commission displayed a generosity which was later recognised by the Republicans themselves.[92]

The commission mixte of the Loir-et-Cher even expressed grave doubts about its role and eventually sat under duress,[93] and the example of the commission mixte of the Morbihan is equally startling in this respect. When it met on 21 February it recommended penalties against no-one. This was considered to be an act of pusillanimity by Maupas, the new Minister of Police, who immediately ordered a new meeting of the commission to look again at the cases of the department's leading left wingers. The procureur of Vannes told the Minister of Justice that the peace of the department had at no stage been troubled: while a few men had been arrested in December they had been released in January, and it was no longer possible to take any measures against them:

> 'il est de mon devoir de ne pas vous laisser ignorer que ces mesures quelles qu'elles soient seront trop tardives pour être favorablement accueillies ici. Elles auront, je le crains bien, pour résultat non de rassurer, mais d'inquiéter les esprits. On comprend difficilement que, dans l'intérêt de la paix publique, il puisse être actuellement utile d'expulser du territoire ou d'éloigner de leur residence des hommes qui n'ont pas paru assez dangereux pour être constitués ou maintenues en état d'arrestation, immédiatement après les événements du 2 décembre et contre lesquels en l'absence de faits précis et certains, on n'a pas pu diriger, alors, de poursuites judiciaires.'

Rouher replied on 10 March that the commission had wide discretionary powers: 'tous les individus qui par leurs menées antérieurs au 2 décembre ont préparé les populations au désordre peuvent être l'objet de l'examen at d'une decision de la commission.' On the insistence of Paris, the commission mixte met again, 1 April, and passed sentence on twenty-eight men.[94]

For the Republicans, the commissions mixtes were simply instruments of terror and oppression. And their view seem confirmed by the judgement of men such as Granier de Cassagnac and Espinasse who regarded the commissions as a means of scourging France of those inveterate troublemakers who were intent on destroying society, abolishing the family, undermining religion and sharing out property. Yet, for the government, the commissions were really created as an effective and quick means of putting an end to a month of wavering and conflict which had characterised the work of its provincial officials. Contemporary apologists of the commissions point out that France was in an exceptional situation and that, compared with the summary justice meted out by Cavaignac's military tribunals after the June days, the commissions mixtes were a model of humanitarianism and judicial propriety.[95] For Haussmann, then prefect of Bordeaux, the commissions had the basic task of moderating the zeal of local subordinates who wanted a far greater purge.[96]

It is, in truth, very difficult to generalise about the work of the commissions mixtes; their recommendations varied enormously, and appeared to depend on several factors. First, the nature of the decisions depended, to some extent, on the personality and temperament of the members who composed the commissions.[97] Second, the commissions met at different times: the first (that of the Côtes-du-Nord) met on 5 February, the last (that of the Morbihan) on 1 April. During that eight week period, opinion was moving in favour of clemency, as it became apparent that the regime was solidly established: the results of legislative elections which took place during the period were an eloquent affirmation of the popularity of the new regime and confirmed the results of the plebiscite of 10 December. Third, as has already been made clear, many commissions mixtes were unclear about the exact nature of their powers.[98] There was also some confusion over the procedures to be adopted: for example, before making their recommendations, certain commissions such as those of the Pyrénées-Orientales, the Basses-Pyrénées and the Hautes-Alpes interrogated the accused, whilst others merely consulted a file established by administrative subordinates. Fourth, in spite of explicit assurances and constant proddings from Paris, several commissions tried only those actually involved in active resistance to the *coup d'état*.[99] Most other commissions, however, widened their net to embrace as many left wing agitators as possible. This was certainly true in Paris. It was also true in the departments of the Rhône and the Loir-et-Cher where very little resistance had been shown to the *coup d'état* and where public order had not been threatened at any point.[100] In certain parts of the alpine region, the repression took on the aspect of a gigantic settling of old scores political, local and personal.[101] This settling of local and personal scores characterised some of the decisions of other commissions.[102]

A fifth factor which clearly determined the recommendations of the commissions was, of course, the extent of the resistance to the *coup d'état*: hence the savage sentences meted out in the Var, the Hérault, the Basses-Alpes, the Drôme, the Nièvre and the Yonne. Certain commissions were also obviously influenced by the general history of political turbulence (or lack of it) in the department: this would explain the severity of the commissions of Paris and Lyons where resistance to the *coup d'état* was minimal, and it would also explain the moderation of

commissions such as those in Britanny and that of the Basses-Pyrénées.[103]

Finally, the departmental commissions were clearly pursuing
different ends. Some were intent on liquidating the leadership of the
Republican Party whatever the social standing of the men involved.
This was certainly the case in the Morbihan where the commission
reserved its severest recommendations for four lawyers (two of whom
were described as wealthy), a rich doctor, two prosperous landowners
and Cresson, 'un négociant d'une position de fortune très aisée'.[104] In
the Gironde, the commission decided to spare the *vulgum pecus* (Haussmann's own expression) and strike at the leaders of the opposition.
These leaders included the nephew of comte Lemercier (Senator of the
Empire), several rich landowners (including the son-in-law of General
Favereau) and three notoriously hostile Orléanists (one of whom had
been *Directeur des colonies* during the July Monarchy).[105] In most
other departments, the Royalists were left untouched, and in some
departments even prominent and potentially active Republican leaders
were left free.[106] Some commissions were clearly intent on a social
purge: men who had no political antecedents were given savage sentences. In the Pyrénées-Orientales, the decisions of the commission
were dictated partially by a desire to clean the department of *la pègre*
— the socially obnoxious,[107] — and in the Doubs, the commission acted
with great severity against 'les dévoyés, les déclassés, les tarés et les
ratés', inevitable actors in every revolutionary movement.[108] The attitude of the commission mixte of the Meurthe is particularly revealing
in this respect. It sentenced Antoine Quesne of Nancy to Cayenne
although he took no part at all in the resistance shown by the Republicans of the town to the *coup d'état*: 'mais sa situation précaire, ses
déplorables antécedents, sa mauvaise nature qui le porterait à continuer
partout son genre de vie, ont déterminé la décision prise.' It was also
particularly harsh with Michel Chaudron whose taste for the bottle was
more pronounced than his taste for politics. He took no part in the
resistance to the *coup*, yet in a bar at Nancy on 28 December he shouted 'A bas Napoléon! Vive la guillotine! Vive le sang! Vive la tête de
Napoléon a la guillotine!' All this whilst drawing his index finger
across his neck in theatrical fashion. These drunken imprecations earned
their author a sentence of exile to Algeria.[109] Most commissions were
influenced by both social and political considerations. Fairly typical, in
this respect, were the recommendations of the commission mixte of the
Basses-Pyrénées. This commission did not hesitate to punish Delissalde,
a merchant whose fortune was evaluated at 100,000 francs, Minvielle, a
notary worth 125,000 francs, Bergerot, a wealthy landowner, and
Sempé who 'appartient à une famille qui compte dans son sein des
hommes considérés et très dévoués à la cause de l'ordre'. It was also

very moderate in its treatment of those whom it considered merely to have been led astray. But it was vicious in its policy towards those whose personal character left something to be desired. Like many other commissions mixtes, it took the opportunity of ridding the department of troublesome elements: Barrère, the capable yet drunken and immoral worker; Dindaburu, an equally drunken and ferociously anticlerical Basque notary; Claverie whose past misdemeanours had included the rape of the daughter of the mayor of his home town.[110]

(d)   Other constraints upon repression

In the weeks during and immediately following the period of emergency powers a network of protection was woven which limited, to some extent, the full impact of the horror of arbitrary repression.

In some departments, this protection was provided by the local populations: in the Pyrénées-Orientales they attempted to resist the arrest of leading Republicans;[111] in parts of the Gers and the Drôme, they gave refuge to fugitive Republicans in spite of the appalling sentences passed against those found guilty of such a 'crime';[112] in parts of the Creuse, they refused to collaborate with the police in their search for incriminating evidence against the Republicans;[113] in many departments, led by mayors and deputy mayors, they organised petitions for the release or pardon of the accused.[114]

The network of protection was also constructed by some prominent supporters of the new regime. The Prince-President himself was involved at a number of stages and in several ways. He was easily persuaded by George Sand to order the release of several important Republicans. He also acted directly to procure the release of men such as Frédéric Degeorge (a man who had opened his newspaper during the July Monarchy to him when in exile) and Capo de Feullide, a Republican journalist and old personal friend.[115] The most significant interventions of the Prince-President took place in March 1852 when he set up the Committee of Political Pardons,[116] and when he sent three commissaires into the provinces to review the recommendations of the commissions mixtes. General Espinasse who was sent to the departments of the southwest recommended only 300 pardons or commutations and General Conrobert, who visited the departments of the centre, only 727. But Quentin-Bauchart recommended a generous 3,441 pardons and commutations, and was warmly congratulated for his leniency by the Prince-President: 'vous seul avez compris ma pensée.'[117]

On 25 March — while certain commissions mixtes were still deliberating — a circular was sent to the departmental authorities ordering them temporarily to halt all transporations to Algeria. As a result of this measure and of the pardons which were rapidly granted, 3,430 men who were sentenced to Algeria never saw that country. Louis-Napoleon was also to show clemency towards the fifty-nine men who were condemned to death by courts martial, since fifty-four of those men were pardoned.

Amongst the many other prominent men who intervened on behalf of the condemned Republicans were Prince Napoleon Bonaparte, Enfantin (the ex-Saint-Simonian), and Randon, Governor General of Algeria.[118] But it was at the local level that the most effective pressure was exerted in favour of the condemned men. The church may have welcomed the *coup d'état* as an occasion for settling with the ungodly, but many members of the clergy retained a humanitarian concern even for the Republicans of their flocks. The Bishop of Nevers strongly protested about the treatment of some of the poorer Republicans who enjoyed no effective family or political protection,[119] whilst the Bishop of Nantes intervened successfully to ensure the safety of René Waldeck-Rousseau, father of the future French Prime Minister.[120] Many local notables also attempted to protect their relatives, friends, neighbours or administrative subordinates[121] exerting pressure on prefects or sub-prefects, or even writing to Paris.[122]

The motives of those who intervened were mixed: some men were undoubtedly inspired by personal friendships, family obligations or simple humanitarianism; some liberal supporters of the new regime remembered the battles they had conducted in cooperation with the Republicans against the July Monarchy, or they saw in their interventions in favour of the condemned men a means of salving their political conscience; some discovered in such interventions a way of proving their status with the new authorities, and others considered them a relatively cheap means of courting favour with the local populations many of whom were alarmed by the totally unjustifiable repression; some, scenting the hesitations and scruples of the Prince-President, played a purely opportunistic game and adopted generosity as a method of currying his favour; finally, there were those such as the Mayor of Angers who warned that severe repression was politically inopportune.[123]

Whatever the motives, it is clear that the authorities were assailed by 'des plaintes des personnes éminément respectables . . . des étonnements et des récriminations sans fin'.[124] And this constant pressure must have been a factor in encouraging a policy of leniency. Pardons and commutations were quickly accorded: the national holiday of 15 August 1852, the proclamation of the Empire in December 1852, the marriage of the Emperor on 4 February 1853 were all occasions for demonstrating the regime's policy of leniency.[125] By the end of September 1853 — eighteen months after the creation of the commissions mixtes — the position was the following:[126]

		Decision of Commissions	Position 30 Sept. 1853
(1)	Trial by a Council of War	247	244
(2)	Cayenne	239	198
(3)	Penal Colony in Algeria	4,549	1,718
(4)	Free residence in Algeria	5,032	1,288
(5)	Expelled from France	980	368
(6)	Temporarily exiled	640	299
(7)	Forced residence in France	2,827	1,199
(8)	Left in the hands of the police	645	611
(9)	Detention centre	29	6
(10)	Surveillance by the Ministry of Police	5,194	7,676
(11)	Released	5,857	12,632
(12)	Left in hands of civil courts	645	645

By mid-1859, of the 9,581 who had been condemned to exile in Algeria by the commissions mixtes, 1,200 still remained,[127] but of that number many had refused to ask for a pardon on the grounds that such a request was technically an admission of guilt. All traces of official repression were wiped out by the general amnesty of 16 August 1859, a measure promulgated to celebrate the victory of French arms during the War of Italian Independence.

The system of protection had the undoubted effect of attentuating the rigour of the measures taken against the Republicans. But the way in which the system operated in practice had another, less desirable, consequence: it accentuated the arbitrary nature of the repression, since the system worked in favour of some but not all of the condemned Republicans.[128] Moreover, the pattern of indulgence seemed to be as haphazard as that of the initial repression, and bitter complaints about the situation soon flowed into Paris.

Concluding Remarks

The *coup d'état* of 2 December 1851 was technically a success, accepted and welcomed by the army, the church, the administration, financial and business circles and the provincial notables. It was also quickly 'consecrated' by the brilliant success of the December 1851 plebiscite. Yet, in many respects, it was a failure. Politically, it separated Louis-Napoleon from the left, and left him as the effective head of the Party of Order, the right wing coalition with which he had little temperamental or political sympathy. Morally, the *coup d'état* stamped the regime with the indelible stigma of illegality and unconstitutionality. Intellectually, too, it was a failure: henceforth, the regime was to be deprived of the support of the intellectual elites of the nation.

Le régime du deux décembre was not only a description but an insult employed by enemies of the Second Empire, and it was all the more telling since it touched a sensitive chord in the Emperor who never shed his guilt over the origins of his own regime. Curiously, the attitudes of many Republicans towards the resistance shown in December was ambiguous. Yet that attitude is understandable. In the first place, the resistance was a complete failure, and in most parts of France totally non-existent: hardly the stuff with which to create myths. Second, the ambiguous reticence of many future Republicans springs from the nature of the resistance itself. It was, notes Maurice Agulhon, 'un mouvement insurrectionnel destiné à défendre la constitution, elle était en somme légaliste par sa finalité et révolutionnaire par sa méthode'.[129] The extreme left wing Republicans were to denounce the legalistic ends of the insurrection, the moderate Republicans were to harbour grave doubts about the revolutionary means employed.

For the Republicans, the real significance of the *coup d'état* lies less in the event itself or in the resistance offered but in the repression which followed. Widespread, enduring and intense persecution engendered a bitter hatred which could unite all sections of the Republican party. They had suffered whilst the conservatives had applauded, unanimously encouraged — apparently at least — by the church, the army and the administration. It is revealing that one of the first acts of the Republican Government of National Defence, formed in September 1870, was to carry out a total purge of the prefectoral administration and to decree the dismissal of all those magistrates who had belonged to the commissions mixtes in 1852. Furthermore, the poisoned relations between the Republican authorities and the army during the war of 1870-71 may be partly explained by the terrible memories formed twenty years previously. The church was also to suffer for its complicity in the repression of 1851-2 as soon as the Republicans took over complete control of the Third Republic.

It has been argued that the repression following the *coup d'état* was not as bloody as that which accompanied the first Revolution.[130] It has also been pointed out that in December 1851, 380 people were killed, a figure which compares favourably with the 800 killed or injured at the time of the funeral of General Lamarque in June 1832, with the 300 killed and 800 injured at the time of the insurrection of June 1834, or with the 4,600 killed during the June Days of 1848.[131] Apologists also underline the clemency shown by the authorities after the initial period of repression. And, as has been emphasised in this essay, whilst the repression was terrible it could have been far worse. Personal, professional, political and social constraints combined to limit its extent and impact: the new regime was not a totalitarian system, but an embryonic police state riddled with conflicts, imbued with doubts and plagued by hesitations.

Why, therefore, was the impact of the repression so deep and durable? First, it must be remembered that the *coup* represented the culmination of a three year process of systematic repression and purge. Second, as already made clear, the repression following the *coup* was far greater and more enduring than the official figures suggest. Third, the measures of leniency often served to heighten the impression of the extraordinarily arbitrary nature of the repression. Finally, the *coup d'état* was not only the culmination of a period of repression, but also the starting point of another such period. Moreover, after December 1851, there was no '1852' on the immediate horizon: the millenium receded, and the persecuted were deprived even of the consolation provided by hope. Deprivation, humiliation and frustration were the ideal ingredients of that bitter hatred which emerges so clearly from Hugo's *L'Histoire d'un crime*.[132] It was a hatred which renders comprehensible the bigotry, the narrow mindedness and the intolerance of the Republicans of the early Third Republic.

Notes

1.   The literature on the *coup d'état* is very considerable and the events in the *départements* mainly affected have been studied in great detail (a notable exception is the Nièvre). The works of Eugène Ténot (*Paris en décembre 1851* and *La Province en décembre 1851: Etude historique sur le coup d'état*), written towards the end of the Second Empire, remain indispensable. On the historiography of the *coup d'état*, see Maurice Agulhon, 'La résistance au coup d'état en province: esquisse d'historiographie', *Revue d'histoire moderne et contemporaine*, vol. XXI, January-March 1974. For brief but good accounts of the events of the *coup*, see Maurice Agulhon, *1848 ou l'apprentissage de la République*, Paris, 1973, pp. 165-205; Adrien Dansette, *Louis Napoleon à la conquête du pouvoir*, Paris, 1961, pp. 343-83; Roger Price, *The French Second Republic: A Social History*, London 1972, pp. 183-326; on the motives behind the insurrectionary movements in parts of the centre and south of France, see Roger Price, *op. cit.*, pp. 296-301 and 307-13, and the very perceptive analyses of Maurice Agulhon, *La République au Village*, Paris, 1970, pp. 418-83. Phil. Vigier, *La Seconde République dans la région alpine*, Paris 1963, vol. II, pp. 319-37, and Claude Lévy, 'Notes sur les fondements sociaux de l'insurrection de décembre 1851 en province', *Information Historique*, no. 4, pp. 142-4.
2.   Howard C. Payne, (*The Police State of Louis Napoleon Bonaparte 1851-1860*, Seattle 1966, pp. 34-72) provides one of the best general accounts of the repression following the *coup*.
3.   For a general account of the work of the commissions see Ch. Seignobos, 'Les opérations des commissions mixtes en 1852', *La Révolution de 1848*, May-June 1909, pp. 59-67.
4.   Letter from the Minister of justice to the procureur general of Metz, 11 February 1852, A.N. BB[30] 398.
5.   L. Morauzeau, *Annuaire de la Société d'Emulation de la Vendée*, Année 1960, Luçon 1960, p. 90.
6.   For details, see A.N. BB[30] 462.

7. See below, p. 320.

8. Howard Payne, *op. cit.*, p. 70.

9. The figure reached by Adrien Dansette after careful sifting of the evidence: see his *Louis Napoléon à la conquête du pouvoir, op. cit.*, pp. 356-7.

10. Figures from A.N. BB[30] 424, summarised by Maurice Agulhon, *1848 . . ., op. cit.*, pp. 235-7.

11. B. Gastineau, (*Les transportés de décembre 1851*, Paris 1869, p. 13),suggests that 150,000 men were arrested and 50,000 of those men were transported, exiled or interned. Hopplyte Magen claimed that 26,000 men were arrested in Paris and over 100,000 in the provinces (*Histoire de la terreur bonapartiste*, Paris 1872, p. 170).

12. G. Vergez-Tricom, 'Les événements de décembre 1851 à Lyon', *La Révolution de 1848*, 1920-21, p. 243.

13. Abbé Courant, 'L'Anjou et le coup d'état du 2 décembre 1851', *Anjou Historique*, 1953, pp. 40-1.

14. George Dupeux, *Aspects de l'histoire sociale et politique du Loir-et-Cher 1848-1914*, Paris 1962, p. 373.

15. In the Saône-et-Loire, the departmental commission tried 391 of the 467 people who had been arrested, in the Haute-Vienne 104 of the 239, in the Marne 77 of the 200, in the Ille-et-Vilaine none of the 18.

16. Ph. Vigier, *op. cit.*, vol. II, p. 313 and Maurice Agulhon, *La République . . ., op. cit.*, p. 448.

17. Although the official figures do include many who fled or who were in hiding.

18. The source — the Bonapartist newspaper *La Patrie*, 20 December 1851 — is impeccable.

19. Ph. Vigier, *op. cit.*, vol. II, p. 352.

20. Dossiers in A.N. F[15] 4016 Nièvre (for Parent), F[15] 3908 Finistère (for Huet) and F[15] 4111 Vienne (for de Jouenne).

21. On the dismissal of school teachers, see Paul Gerbod, *La condition universitaire en France*, Paris 1965, pp. 296-8; A.N. F[17] 11554-11557 (Condamnations des instituteurs primaires); A.N. F[17] 11581-11611 (Mesures disciplinaires contre instituteurs).

22. See, for example, the cases of Levallois in A.N. F[15] 4053 (Manche) and Gambon in A.N. F[15] 3968 A (Nièvre).

23. Dossiers of Girault and Piedallu, in A.N. F[15] 4044 (Loir-et-Cher).

24. For a general account of actions against the press, see Irene Collins, *The Government and the newspaper press in France 1814-1881*, London 1959, pp. 114-5; H. Payne, *op. cit.*, pp. 48-56.

25. B. Gastineau, *op. cit.*, pp. 7-8.

26. Dossier Gallois, A.N. F[15] 4111 (Vendée).

27. Dossier Touzet, A.N. F[15] 4053 (Manche).

28. Dossier Lemonnier, A.N. F[15] 4053 (Manche).

29. Dossier David, A.N. F[15] 4053 (Loire-Inférieure).

30. Dossier Scelles, A.N. F[15] 4053 (Manche).

31. B. LeClère and V. Wright, *Les préfets du Second Empire*, Paris 1973, pp. 122-3.

32. J. Décembre and A. Alonnier, (*Histoire des conseils de guerre de 1852*, Paris 1869, pp. 320 and 332-3) claim that thirty-two mayors in the Bas-Rhin were dismissed, and in the Haute-Saône, 'a large number' of mayors were dismissed and their councils dissolved. In the Basses-Pyrénées, about thirty mayors were dismissed by mid-January 1852: see *Mémorial des Pyrénées*, 10, 13 January 1852. In the Basses-Alpes, thirty-three mayors and forty deputy mayors were replaced between 15 and 27 December 1851: see Ph. Vigier, *op. cit.*, vol. I, p. 342.

33.   Schoelcher, Durrieu and Magen all give eloquent, if somewhat embroidered, accounts of the sufferings endured by the victims of the *coup d'état*. See also the article by Boysset in *Le Progrés de Saône-et-Loire*, 1 June 1880; Georges Rougeron, 'La terreur bonapartiste dans le département de l'Allier', *Révolution de 1848*, September-October 1937, pp. 161-9; A. Charles, *La Révolution de 1848 et la Seconde République dans le département de la Gironde*, 1951, pp. 344-5. René Boudard, 'La répression policière en Creuse au lendemain du coup d'état de 1851', *M. Soc. Sci. Nat. Archeol. Creuse*, vol. 31, p. 432. A. Papon, *La République et le coup d'état dans le département de l'Eure*, Paris 1869, p. 91.

34.   Dossier Bon in A.N. F^{15} 4044 (Haute-Loire). Many other dossiers in the same series recount the same fate.

35.   Dossier Solvain, A.N. F^{15} 4044 (Haute-Loire).

36.   Dossier Roux, A.N. F^{15} 4045 (Lot-et-Garonne).

37.   We have many personal accounts of those sufferings in A.N. F^{15}. Amongst the most revealing of other accounts, see Gallois, 'Carnet d'un proscrit', *Revue Retrospective*, vol. 92, pp. 47-71; E. Jambert, 'Souvenirs du 2 décembre 1851', *Bull. Soc. Basses-Alpes*, 1905, vol. 12, pp. 9-22; A. Saint-Ferréol, *Les proscrits français en Belgique*, Brussels 1870; Charles Delescluze, *De Paris à Cayenne*, Paris 1869; J. Robert, *Le Coup d'état du 2 décembre et mon histoire de proscrit*, Paris 1884; Théodore Labourieu, *Mémoires d'un déporté*, Paris 1881; Colonel Mouton, *La transportation en Afrique*, Paris 1870; Léon Goupy, *Le coup d'état dans la Mayenne*, Paris 1871; Ribeyrolles, *Les bagnes d'Afrique*, Brussels 1853; Paul Perceveau, 'La très véridique histoire de Jules Charlet, opposant au coup d'état de 1851', *Bugey*, 1954, pp. 69-82; R. Esparseil, 'Marcou, proscrit du 2 décembre 1851', *M. Soc. Arts et Sciences de Carcassonne*. 1954, vol. 9, pp. 181-6; Léonce Boniface, 'Un proscrit varois de décembre 1851 dans le comté de Nice: le docteur César Provençal (1814-1868)', *Provence historique*, 1953, vol. 3, pp. 126-30.

38.   Dossiers in A.N. F^{15} 4044 (Haute-Loire), F^{15} 4216 (Basses-Pyrénées) and F^{15} 4135 (Nièvre).

39.   G. Thuillier and V. Wright, 'Pour l'histoire du coup d'état: une source à exploiter', to appear in *Mouvement Social*.

40.   Maurice Agulhon, *La République . . ., op. cit.*, p. 442, and Ph. Vigier, *op. cit.*, vol. II, pp. 315, 338-40.

41.   E. Ténot, *La Province en décembre 1851: Etude historique sur le coup d'Etat*, Paris 1868, p. 46. Ténot confirms the details given by an apologist of the *coup d'état*: see Ph. Mayer, *Histoire du 2 décembre 1851*, Paris 1869, p. 231.

42.   Dossier of Vazeilles in A.N. F^{15} 4044 (Haute-Loire).

43.   Baron Georges Eugène Haussmann, *Mémoires*, Paris 1890, vol. I, pp. 513-14.

44.   There is an excellent account of the Ministry of General Police in Howard Payne, *op. cit.*, pp. 73-103. See also B. LeClère and V. Wright, *op. cit.*, pp. 102-4.

45.   *Journal du maréchal de Castellane*, Paris 1895, vol. IV, p. 355.

46.   H. Payne, *op. cit.*, p. 38. See also below p. 316.

47.   E. Ténot, *op. cit.*, p. 4.

48.   Pierre Chalmin, *L'Officier français de 1815 à 1870*, Paris 1957, pp. 264-8.

49.   The general commanding the Gironde was hostile (see A. Charles, *op. cit.*, p. 341), as were several officers in the Nord (see Max Bruchet, *op. cit.*, pp. 97-8).

50.   Of the Ain, the Aisne, the Finistère, the Loir-et-Cher, the Haute-Loire, the Hautes-Pyrénées, the Somme and the Tarn-et-Garonne.

51.   V. Wright, 'Le corps préfectoral et le coup d'état du 2 décembre 1851', *Revue Administrative*, January-February, 1968, no. 121, pp. 19-24 and March-April, 1968, no. 122, pp. 153-60.

52.   See Max Bruchet, *op. cit.*, pp. 99-100; J. Décembre and A. Alonnier, *op. cit.*, p. 76; G. Rocal, *1848 en Dordogne*, Perigueux, 1934, vol. II, p. 205; P. T.

Chéron de Villiers, *Chapitre inédit de l'histoire du coup d'état: Limoges en 1851*, Paris 1869, p. 24.

53. Max Bruchet, *op. cit.*, pp. 95-6.

54. Correspondence in A.N. BB^{30} 395 and Letter from Prefect to Sub-prefect of Bayonne, A. Dépt. Basses-Pyrénées M^1 2.

55. Alphonse Brémond, *Histoire du coup d'état dans le département de la Haute-Garonne*, Toulouse 1871, pp. 54-5.

56. A. Correch, *La Cour d'Appel de Pau*, Tarbes 1920, pp. 365-6. See also his personal dossier A.N. BB^6 II 152 (Paul Fabre).

57. G. Rocal, *op. cit.*, p. 205.

58. Report of the Prefect, quoted in I. Tchernoff, *Le Parti républicain au coup d'état et sous le Second Empire*, Paris 1906, p. 50.

59. Baron Haussmann, *op. cit.*, vol. I, pp. 519-20.

60. A. Robert and Cougny, *Dictionnaire des parlementaires français*; Notice on Marrot.

61. Max Bruchet, *op. cit.*, pp. 95-6.

62. H. Payne, *op. cit.*, p. 63.

63. It was reported in most of the newspapers of the time, which suggests that the severity of the sentence was designed to dissuade others from giving shelter to Republicans.

64. J. Décembre and A. Alonnier, *op. cit.*, pp. 23-4.

65. Report of the Prefect of the Hérault, dated 7 September 1852, quoted in I. Tchernoff, *op. cit.*, p. 79.

66. H. Payne, *op. cit.*, pp. 41-2.

67. Quoted in: H. Guillemin, *Le coup du 2 décembre*, Paris 1951, p. 415.

68. Letters of the prefects of the Seine-Inférieure, the Saône-et-Loire, the Nord, the Dordogne and the Bouches-du-Rhône, March to May 1852, A.N. F^{1a} 11.

69. For details, see A.N. F^{1a} 131^{10}.

·70. H. Payne, *op. cit.*, pp. 48-56 gives a good account of these differences.

71. Horace Chauvet, *Histoire du Parti républicain dans les Pyrénées-Orientales 1830-1877*, Perpignan 1909, p. 107 (on Pougeard-Dulimbert) and M. Ravold, *Les transportés de la Meurthe en 1852*, Paris 1872 (on Sivry).

72. Paul Muller, 'Autour du coup d'état dans le Haut-Rhin', *La Révolution de 1848*, September-October 1909, pp. 105-6, and by the same author, *La Révolution de 1848 en Alsace*, Paris 1912, p. 148 (on Durckheim); dossier David, A.N. F^{15} 4053 (Manche) (on Gauja); A.N. F^{1b} I 157(4) correspondence of 1851 and 1852 (on Cambacerès); G. Rocal, *op. cit.*, p. 214 (on Calvimont), and Ph. Vigier, *op. cit.*, vol I, pp. 356-7 (on Chapuys de Montlaville).

73. Dossier of Costa de Bastelica, A.N. F^{1b} I 157(32).

74. M. Glockner, *Le parti républicain à Avignon au coup d'état et sous le Second Empire*, Diplôme d'histoire, Aix-en-Provence, 1964, p. 44.

75. Capitaine Breillout, 'La Révolution de 1848 en Corrèze', *La Révolution de 1848*, July-August 1922, p. 184.

76. c.f., for example, the cases of Breillet of Saint-Jean-du-Corail in the Manche (A.N. F^{15} 4053) who went into hiding in the Orne, and of the famous Reclus brothers who, after a warning from the sub-prefect of Orthez, left for England. (Elisée Reclus, *Correspondance*, Paris 1911, vol. I, pp. 43-4.)

77. The most notable exceptions were the procureurs at Apt and Digne who used their powers to establish their own local power base. See Ph. Vigier, *op. cit.*, vol. I, pp. 353-4.

78. Long correspondence in A.N. BB^{30} 397.

79. H. Payne, *op. cit.*, p. 42. Correspondence in A.N. BB^{30} 403.

80. H. Payne, *op. cit.*, p. 63.

81. M. Bruchet, *op. cit.*, pp. 95-6.
82. Correspondence of the prefect of the Lot-et-Garonne and the procureur general of Agen in A.N. BB^{30} 397.
83. I. Tchernoff, *op. cit.*, p. 71.
84. Ph. Vigier, *op. cit.*, vol. I, p. 339.
85. H. Payne, *op. cit.*, p. 65.
86. A. Charles, *op. cit.*, pp. 344-5.
87. Correspondence in A.N. BB^{30} 398.
88. *Ibid.*
89. Maurice Agulhon, *op. cit.*, p. 195. In the Basses-Alpes, where more than 15,000 people took part in the resistance (Ph. Vigier, *op. cit.*, vol. I, p. 327) 'only' 1,669 were tried by the commission mixte.
90. P. T. Chéron de Villiers, *op. cit.*, p. 19.
91. Baron Haussmann, *op. cit.*, vol. I, p. 518.
92. J. Décembre and A. Alonnier, *op. cit.*, p. 117.
93. Charles Seignebos, *op. cit.*, p. 64.
94. For details, see Correspondence, A.N. BB^{30} 402.
95. P. T. Chéron de Villiers, *op. cit.*, pp. 33-4.
96. Baron Haussmann, *op. cit.*, vol. I, p. 518.
97. See Phil. Vigier's excellent analysis of the work of the commissions in the alpine region (vol. I, pp. 356-9).
98. See also letter of the procureur of Vannes, 22 February 1852, and that of the procureur of Saint-Brieuc, 9 February 1852, A.N. BB^{30} 402.
99. For example, those of the Nord and the Basses-Pyrénées. See Max Bruchet, *op. cit.*, pp. 103-4; and BB^{30} 402 (dossier 2).
100. G. Vergez-Tricom, *op. cit.*, p. 243 (on the Rhône) and G. Dupeux, *op. cit.*, p. 373 (on the Loir-et-Cher).
101. Philippe Vigier, *op. cit.*, vol. II, pp. 354 and 359.
102. It was the case in the Loir-et-Cher (see dossiers Dubus and Mitteau in A.N. F^{15} 4044 (Loir-et-Cher)) and in the Pyrénées-Orientales (see extensive correspondence in Arch. Dépt. Pyrénées-Orientales III M^1 91).
103. Letter of the procureur of Saint-Brieuc, 9 February 1852, A.N. BB^{30} 402, and the letter of the procureur general of Pau, 19 November 1852, A.N. BB^{22} 130.
104. Correspondence in A.N. BB^{30} 402 (Morbihan).
105. Baron Haussmann, *op. cit.*, vol. I, pp. 519-21.
106. André Armengaud, *Les populations de l'Est-Aquitaine au début de l'époque contemporaine*, Paris 1961, p. 392; report from the procureur general of Pau, 4 May 1852, A.N. BB^{30} 412 and report from the procureur general of Douai, 16 January 1852, A.N. BB^{30} 396.
107. Reports and correspondence in Arch. Dept. Pyrénées-Orientales, III M^1 81.
108. Roger Marlin, *L'épuration politique dans le Doubs à la suite du coup d'état du 2 décembre 1851*, Dole 1958, pp. 28-9.
109. Report of the commission mixte of the Meurthe, A.N. BB^{30} 401.
110. Report of the commission mixte of the Basses-Pyrénées, A.N. BB^{30} 396.
111. Horace Chauvet, *op. cit.*, p. 107.
112. See especially *Le Mémorial des Pyrénées*, 21 December 1851.
113. See particularly the letter from the procureur general of Limoges to the Minister of Justice, 31 December 1851, A.N. BB^{30} 397.
114. Correspondence concerning the Creuse in A.N. BB^{30} 466, See also Victor Schoelcher, *op. cit.*, pp. 54-6, and H. Druard, *Une page de l'histoire du deux décembre 1851: le coup d'état dans l'Ain*, Bourg 1885, p. 29.
115. See Communiqué du Ministère de la Guerre, 9 November 1853, A.N. BB^{22} 172 A-C, P 2195.

116. See above, p. 307.
117. On these missions, see Pierre Quentin-Bauchart, *Etudes et Souvenirs sur la deuxième République et le Second Empire*, Paris, 1901, pp. 450-70; *Souvenirs du général Espinasse* (only a few copies were published and then privately circulated, M. Adrien Dansette kindly allowed me to consult his copy); P. Quentin-Bauchart, 'Après le coup d'état', *Carnet*, 1901, vol. IX, pp. 41-52.
118. Details: A.N. BB^{22} 130. See also Guy Frambourg, *Le docteur Guépin* (1805-1873), Nantes 1964, pp. 271-3 and Maurice Agulhon, *1848 . . ., op. cit.*, pp. 203-4.
119. Letter to the Minister of the Interior, 13 February 1852, A.N. BB^{30} 462.
120. Pierre Sorlin, *Waldeck-Rousseau*, Paris 1966, p. 54.
121. See for example, the undated letter of the *recteur* at Perpignan in favour of eight primary school teachers. Arch. Dept. Pyr.-Orient. III M^1 97.
122. There are many such examples in A.N. BB^{22} 130.
123. Letter from the Mayor to the Prefect of the Maine-et-Loire, 15 January 1852, quoted in Abbé Courant, *op. cit.*, pp. 41-2: 'je ne terminerai pas, Monsieur le préfet, sans vous dire en toute franchise que je suis convaincu que des mesures rigoureuses non justifiées par des faits produraient un effet contraire à celui que le gouvernement espère et amèneraient infailliblement un sentiment de réaction fâcheuse.'
124. Baron Haussmann, *op. cit.*, vol. I, p. 518.
125. Details in A.N. BB^{30} 403 and 'Etat des individus qui après décembre ont été l'objet de mesures pénales'. Report from the Minister of Police to the Emperor, undated, but the figures quoted relate to 27 January 1853. See *Papiers et Correspondance de la famille impériale*, Paris 1870, vol. I, pp. 216-7.
126. Figures quoted in Maurice Agulhon, *1848 . . ., op. cit.*, p. 236.
127. Details in A.N. BB^{30} 448.
128. Roger Marlin, *op. cit.*, p. 23.
129. Maurice Agulhon, *1848 . . ., op. cit.*, pp. 178-9.
130. Roger Marlin, *op. cit.*, p. 26.
131. Adrien Dansette, *op. cit.*, p. 357.
132. For other examples of the deep-seated nature of that hatred, see Pierre Sorlin, *op. cit.*, p. 54; Alphonse Brémond, *op. cit.*, p. 180.